Awakening to Radical Islamist Evil

The Hamas War against Israel and the Jews

Touro University Press Books

Series Editors
Michael A. Shmidman, PhD (Touro University, New York)
Simcha Fishbane, PhD (Touro University, New York)

Awakening to Radical Islamist Evil

The Hamas War against Israel and the Jews

Monty Noam Penkower

NEW YORK
2025

Library of Congress Control Number: 2024948276

ISBN 9798887197715 (hardback)
ISBN 9798887197777 (paperback)
ISBN 9798887197722 (adobe pdf)
ISBN 9798887197739 (epub)

Copyright © Touro University Press, 2024
Published by Touro University Press and Academic Studies Press.
Typeset, printed, and distributed by Academic Studies Press.

Touro University Press
Michael A. Shmidman and Simcha Fishbane, Editors
3 Times Square, Room 654,
New York, NY 10036, USA
press@touro.edu

Book design by Kryon Publishing Services
Cover design by Ivan Grave
Typeset, printed, and distributed by Academic Studies Press
1007 Chestnut St.
Newton, MA 02464, USA
press@academicstudiespress.com
www.academicstudiespress.com

To the Israel Defense Forces

The Lord will give strength to His people;
The Lord will bless His people with peace.
—Psalms 29:11

Contents

_____

Preface	ix
1. The Slaughter Begins	1
2. Boots on the Ground in Gaza	27
3. The War Grinds On	49
4. . . . and On	77
5. Ring in the New Year	110
6. From Khan Younis to Rafah	142
7. Resolution Awaits	179
Conclusion	219
Appendices	239
Index	255

Preface

Ofir Leibstein, the fifty-year-old mayor of the Sha'ar HaNegev regional council's 6,000 people living in ten kibbutzim and one communal farm, had an extraordinary dream. A long-time resident of Kfar Aza in the northern Negev, three kilometers from the Gaza Strip, he was sure that most Palestinian Arabs in Gaza wanted what Israelis did: peace, well-paid jobs, care for their families. He set out to provide them. It was hard to deal directly with Palestinians since the border was almost entirely sealed. However, in partnership with the city of Sderot, which lay less than one kilometer from the border fence, he planned a development called Arazim Industrial Zone around the Erez Crossing. This could draw up to 10,000 Gazans to work in Israel every day. He actually allocated land from his council for this project. There would also be a training hub for Palestinians, educational programs, and a medical center, with solar panels to provide renewable energy and a project to bring fresh water for the people of Gaza.

Leibstein's most popular idea, though, was to leverage flowers. In 2007 he and his wife Vered founded the *Darom Adom* ("Red South") festival to celebrate the anemones which, for a few weeks in early spring, spread scarlet through the woods and fields. Inspired by his election in 2018 to a ten-year term as mayor of the council, he had already incorporated the poorly treated Bedouin into his anemone festival and was chairman of a museum where their culture was celebrated. Perhaps Palestinians could become involved in Sha'ar HaNegev in the same way, once the two sides had learned to respect each other.

Pipes were installed by Leibstein all along the Strip for water, but Iran's terrorist proxy Hamas organization uprooted them to launch rockets against Israel. In 2018, youths in Gaza tied incendiary devices to kites and balloons and sent them floating across, where he watched with horror as trees, crops, and gardens exploded in flames. In May 2021 Hamas rockets fell on Sha'ar HaNegev for eleven straight days. Even though everyone in Kfar Aza had steel-and-concrete safe rooms in their homes, in 2022 Leibstein sent the mothers and children away to the north. A study had found that most of the local children had post-traumatic stress. Yet he insisted that those scary times were rare. That was just life on the edge: five percent hell, but ninety-five percent paradise. His main Facebook picture showed a view of lush, rolling, improbably green hills dotted with trees.

The brochure for Leibstein's Israel-Gaza Economic Development Unit spoke of allowing about 10,000 workers to come out of Gaza every day and earn dignified salaries. Alongside industry, a medical facility would be established in the park, as well as a branch of an international-level university. "We aim to improve the infrastructure in Gaza, namely sewage, water, and electricity," the pamphlet went on, and to enable "high-level training for Gazan farmers to optimize agricultural resources" including "a training program for Gazan high-tech engineers and entrepreneurs based around the Sha'ar HaNegev incubator and nearby Sapir College in the northwestern Negev desert."

One of Leibstein's last Facebook posts was about him meeting Israeli youth from the region. "They ask questions, take interest, and show that the future of the Negev Gate is important to them," he wrote. "With young people like this, the future looks optimistic and promising." He also strove every day to close the gaps between those in the core of the country—like Tel Aviv, Jerusalem, the Gush Dan area. He made a profound impact on the Habonim Dror Socialist-Zionist youth movement as its national chairperson. Working with contacts in Cape Town, Jewish National Fund Australia, and San Diego (a sister city with Sha'ar HaNegev), he would be recalled as "always smiling, always positive, with a unique and infectious laugh."

In his last post on Facebook, Leibstein wrote this: "Simchat Torah is a celebration of finishing reading the book of the Torah and continuing reading it again from Genesis. The end indicates the beginning, marks the journey we went through, and gives us a moment to say thanks for being, and to be filled with hope for what's coming. Together, we'll continue to do good for the future of the Negev Gate [the literal translation of the name Sha'ar HaNegev]. Shabbat Shalom and happy holidays, Ofir."

In mid-September 2023, Liebstein had met at the Gaza border to discuss such basics as water, sewage, and energy. But the factories of Arazim were not yet built when, early in the morning on October 7, swarms of Hamas terrorists broke through the border fence. They had been preceded by a barrage of missiles that turned the sky overhead a chalky white. The residents of Kfar Aza had already been warned by text not to go outside, but Leibstein, a member of its local security team, disobeyed his own order. Answering fire with fire, he rushed out to defend both his kibbutz and his dreams, including those lovely anemones that dyed the dry ground red.

About seventy Hamas terrorists breached the Kfar Aza fence that morning. Sixty-three residents were killed in a short time. In the initial hours of the massacre, victims were beheaded, dismembered, and burned alive. Corpses were found with their hands tied. In an exchange of fire with the invaders, Leibstein would be the first of the blameless human beings to die at Hamas's brutal hands across southern Israel on what would soon be called "Black Sabbath." His mother-in-law, eighty-one-year-old Bilha Epstein, and nephew, twenty-two-year-old Netta Epstein, who threw himself on a grenade to save his girlfriend, would be murdered there. The body of Leibstein's nineteen-year-old son, Nitzan, would be found twelve days later. Nineteen innocents from the bucolic kibbutz were kidnapped, to be taken as hostages to Gaza, joining 236 others from the surrounding communities. Nine hundred managed to escape, having waited more than thirty hours before the military rescued them from safe rooms on October 8. All were then evacuated to hotels, the government footing the bills for their meals.

It took two and a half days for the Israel Defense Forces (IDF), the paratroopers of Unit 71 leading the assault and joined by the Duvdevan (17) Unit of the Commando Brigade, to regain full control of the area. The foreign press was first invited on October 10 and then a month later to witness the inhumane crimes, much as the Allies had done after they defeated Adolf Hitler's armies in World War II and liberated the Holocaust death and concentration camps. Rows of once tidy streets lined with palm trees and banana plants were shrouded by the smell of death and disfigured by the wreckage of war. Nearly half the houses sustained varying degrees of destruction—bullet holes everywhere, some homes entirely blackened out, their walls pockmarked with holes made from grenade fragments. Others were left with gaping holes in their exterior walls from Rocket-Propelled Grenade (RPG) impacts. One house had the sentence "human remains on the couch" written in black paint on the outer wall. DNA samples were needed on occasion to identify victims. In one bedroom, a family of five—parents, two children, and a grandmother—was found "standing in a circle, hugging each other, locked arms." Volunteers from ZAKA, an organization that specializes in search and rescue for bodies, were tasked with detangling the family. Only the birds made noise, along with the humming of an Elbit Hermes 450 drone overhead, the kind used for surveillance and airstrikes. Life claimed no presence here in what was left of a once lush communal farm called Kfar Aza.[1]

In a note which the IDF presented on CBS, found on the body of a Hamas terrorist, were found these words: "Know that this enemy of yours is a disease that has no cure, other than beheading and extracting the hearts and livers. Go attack them!" The operatives of what Hamas termed "the Al-Aqsa Flood" carried out their orders everywhere, methodically with fury and glee, while filming the atrocities. One excitedly called his parents on the phone of an Israeli woman he had just murdered in Kibbutz Mifalsim; "Dad! Dad! I killed ten Jews! With my own hands... Are you proud of me? Be proud of me!" The father uttered unending recitations of *"Allahu akbar!"* ("God is Most Great!") while the mother got on the phone and told her son to come home.[2] Rape and mutilation often preceded murder. Families were killed whole. Babies were a priority.

More than 1,200 victims met a grisly death in the systematic slaughter, including at least 364 youth who were gunned down at a Nova music festival billed as "a journey of unity and love" in a field near Re'im. Kibbutzim Kfar Aza, Be'eri, Nahal Oz, Nir Oz, Alumim, Re'im, Kisufim, Ein HaShlosha, and Sufa; cities Ofakim, Sderot, and Netivot; *moshavim* (agricultural villages) nearby, which, taken together, constituted what Israel called *Otef Aza* ("the Gaza Envelope" within seven kilometers of the Gaza Strip)—their names will forever go down in the history of world terrorism and genocide.

Since the beginning of Hamas's war against Israel on October 7, 2023, the deadliest assault in one day on the Jewish people since the *Shoah*, I have been writing a daily account of its local, regional, and international ramifications. Fully aware that, unlike my scholarly endeavors over the last five decades, access to primary archival documentation will most likely await the long passage of time, I have sought a chronological approach based on a wide-ranging use of articles, books, media reportage, and internet sources in offering what *Washington Post* publisher and later co-owner Philip L. Graham famously called journalism: "a rough first draft of history."

With the end of the war still shrouded in uncertainty, I decided to halt the narrative on day 177 of the armed conflict, just shy of six months since the savage Hamas attack on Israel erupted. Chapters one and two examine the major developments of October 2023, leading up to the IDF invasion of the Gaza Strip. Chapters three and four review significant events in the months of November and December, with chapters five, six, and seven examining those for January through March 2024. A conclusion, although tentative, offers perspectives which I consider warranted at that point in time.

An appendix of five sections, enhancing the text, begins with Moshe Dayan's poignant and prescient eulogy in April 1956 on the murder of a young Nahal Oz resident by Palestinians and my own letter of acceptance upon being awarded a 2023 Bernard Lewis Book Award for the volume *After the Holocaust*. These are followed by the letters to their families of three IDF soldiers who subsequently died in the fighting (before going into battle, soldiers write a letter home in case they are killed in action), and by Israeli President Yitzhak (Isaac) Herzog's address marking the first one hundred days of the war. Finally, eight "poems of our time" by Israelis present an IDF reservist's message to his daughter; biblical references evoking safe rooms, the Israeli hostages in Gaza, and the names of the dead; a mother's prayer for her captive son; and eulogies in memory of twenty-six-year-old Sgt. Maj. General (res.) Yakir Hexter, twenty-five-year-old Sgt. First Class (res.) Maoz Fenigstein, and twenty-two-year-old Staff Sgt. Maoz Morell, who paid the ultimate price in Gaza. The seventh poem, conscious of a war whose first day of genocidal, uncompromising bloodbath was unprovoked and unprecedented in Israeli history, hails the pervasive unity brought forth in the Jewish world that may serve as a new expression of the traditional notion of *tikun* (repair), atoning for the biblical Joseph's fate at the hands of his jealous brothers. The last, raising fundamental questions, movingly captures the uncertainties of war.

My late, dear parents, Rabbi Murry S. and Lillian Stavisky Penkower, imbued me with the dream of Zion and the miracle of *Medinat Yisrael* reborn. Their voices guide me still. I shared a blessed marriage of almost forty-seven years with my beloved Yael. Fond memories of this Jerusalemite's warmth, beauty, and intelligence do not fade with the passage of time. Cherished Phyllis has restored the fullness of joy in my life. Making the heart sing again, she is a daily wonder. Our children and grandchildren, and my siblings and their spouses, have always been supportive of my scholarly pursuits. I trust that our great-grandchildren will one day come to appreciate what has been a very demanding endeavor. I have tried throughout to keep in mind the warning of California's isolationist Senator Hiram W. Johnson in 1917 as the United States embarked on World War I: "The first casualty when war comes is truth," an astute observation attributed to the Greek playwright Aeschylus, often described as the father of tragedy. Professor Emeritus Michael Popkin, a long-time colleague at Touro College and admired friend, once again read the text for clarity and purpose. Thanks are also due to the collaborative effort, as in the past, of Touro University Press and Academic Studies Press in bringing the manuscript to ultimate publication.

Awakening to Radical Islamist Evil: The Hamas War against Israel and the Jews is dedicated to the members of the Israel Defense Forces (*Tzahal*, in the Hebrew acronym), who ensure the security and destiny of the national home of the Jewish people, history's ultimate survivors. My fervent prayers at this moment are threefold. First, that those within its ranks who fell in battle will not have died in vain, that the hostages still captive in Gaza return safely to their families, and that the remarkable unity exhibited by world Jewry and its supporters during the war will continue to flourish—recalling the denouement of the Purim story, when a genocide of Jews in the ancient Persian empire was thwarted and for whom there "was light and joy, gladness and honor" (Esther 8:16). Second, that the combatants of radical Islamist evil be vanquished, and their present champions come to understand its grave, existential menace for world civilization's embrace of free inquiry and toleration. Third, that peace will one day reign between the State of Israel and all its Arab neighbors. May tranquility's countenance shine across this troubled region, with the citizens of the biblical Promised Land, whose national anthem is the *Hatikva* ("The Hope"), contributing their share to forging a better tomorrow.

Jerusalem
Purim 5784

Endnotes

1. Times of Israel, Oct. 25, 2023, and Nov. 7, 2023; *Telegraph*, Oct. 7, 2023; *South African Jewish Report*, Oct. 12, 2023; *Economist*, Oct. 19, 2023; FDD, Mar. 21, 2024; *Guardian*, Oct. 11, 2023; Isabel Kershner, "Ravaged Israeli Border Community Ponders: What's Next?," *New York Times*, Dec. 11, 2023; Seth J. Frantzman, "Looking into Kfar Aza, Five Months After the October 7 Massacre—Analysis," *Jerusalem Post*, Mar. 20, 2024. Lt. Col. (res.) Meir Karmi was one of the first to grasp the magnitude of the disaster on October 7 and rushed to bring his 71st Reserve Paratrooper Battalion into action without waiting for approval or orders. Thanks to his quick thinking, the soldiers under his command were able to arrive relatively early in Kfar Aza, long before the other forces—and, fighting ferociously, to save entire families from the massacre. Israel National News, Apr. 1, 2024. The fullest account of one such kibbutz, Alumim, is Bruce Maddy-Weitzman, "Black Sabbath," Tablet, Mar. 21, 2024.
2. Israel National News, Oct. 25, 2023; The State of Israel's Official Twitter Account, managed by the @IsraelMFA's Digital Diplomacy team, https://twitter.com/Israel, Oct. 24, 2023; also quoted by Ruth Wisse, speech at Jewish Leadership Conference, New York City, Oct. 29, 2023. A kibbutz, usually agricultural, is organized under collectivist principles. The name "Mefalsim" means "those who clear a path." That kibbutz, founded in 1949 by Jews from Argentina and Uruguay, was named after the immigrants from Latin America who cleared the path for others to come on *aliya* ("ascent" in Hebrew, meaning moving to live in Israel).

CHAPTER 1

The Slaughter Begins

October 7, 2023—a date that would alter the State of Israel forever. Some 3,800 terrorists from the Hamas group's elite forces, launching a methodically planned stealth attack at 6:29 that Saturday morning, the joyous holiday of Simchat Torah, invaded southern Israel. They were joined, according to the Israeli army's Gaza Division, by 2,200 "terrorists and looters from Gaza" and another 1,000 other terrorists assisting within the Gaza Strip by firing rockets and helping the forces that crossed into Israeli territory. After the initial firing of thousands of rockets from sites in Gaza less than four kilometers away and multiple drones attacking observation cameras and guard posts with explosive charges, this heavily armed force used bulldozers, tractors, rocket-propelled grenades (RPGs), and explosives to breach 119 points in the Israeli high-tech forty-mile barrier fence separating Gaza from the Jewish State and proceeded to merciless, calculated, mass murder. Within minutes, a flammable toxic gas suffocated fifteen female surveillance operators (*tatzpaniyot*) and three sergeants of the Israel Defense Forces (IDF) in the operations room of the army's Nahal Oz command center, less than one kilometer from the Gaza border. Eleven IDF bases were attacked simultaneously.

At these sites, and especially the Gaza Command Center in Camp Re'im, Hamas teams systematically dismantled communication, observation, and surveillance equipment with the intention of disrupting the IDF's command-and-control capabilities. Hamas's strategic and tactical unprecedented surprise effectively blinded the IDF, impairing its capacity to respond swiftly and efficiently, and sowing widespread civil, military, and political disorder. With crucial input from Gazans employed in Israeli homes they had scouted and mapped for the purpose, gunmen also took over twenty-two villages, held on to portions of those villages from twelve to forty-eight hours, and stormed the Sderot police station after killing some thirty civilians and police officers there.

They killed more than 1,200 Israelis—many shot at point-blank range, including 318 in military service and 59 police, entire families, and at least 364 youth at a Nova music festival in the desert. "Drunk with hatred and evil," wrote the leading Israeli novelist David Grossman, "they chased them and shot them with the glee of hunters, as if they were figures on some computer game."[1]

The merciless, grisly slaughter included the decapitating and burning of bodies, victims' hands tied behind backs—babies, women, the infirm and the elderly, some Holocaust survivors. The sadistic explosion of violence also involved the gang-raping of young girls—even on lifeless bodies, with family and friends often forced to watch, and taking 253 hostages, many with serious medical conditions, to Gaza, including thirty children ranging from infancy to age eighteen. Hamas operatives mutilated female soldiers' faces, breasts, and genitals. They murdered parents and children in each other's presence. One young woman learned that her grandmother had been slaughtered because a terrorist took her grandmother's cell phone, filmed her murder, and then uploaded the video to the grandmother's own Facebook page, ensuring her family would see it. At least eighteen people killed in this landscape sown with death and devastation were Bedouin, who comprise some four percent of the population, from villages scattered around the Negev and Rahat, the biggest city in an impoverished, predominantly Bedouin area of southern Israel. Ten days later, the number of injured brought to Israeli hospitals had passed 4,200, with 344 hospitalized and 82 in serious condition.[2]

On October 7, 2023, the blackest day in the history of the State of Israel, more Jews fell victim to the enemy's carnage—perhaps too soft a word—than on any other day since the Holocaust. The magnitude of the tragedy and the sheer savagery carried out by Hamas, this annihilationist fury set loose operating under the leadership of Nukhba, its elite Special Forces Unit, made this monstrous onslaught markedly different. The number of those killed on that Sabbath day in what Israelis called *Otef Aza* (the Gaza Envelope), murdered simply because they were Jews, far surpassed the number of the Israelis who were killed in the 1956 Sinai Campaign (231), the 1967 Six Day War (776), the 1982–1985 First Lebanon War (654), and the 2006 Second Lebanon War (164). The 2,656 Israelis who died during the three-week Yom Kippur War in October 1973 were all soldiers who had fought in sparsely populated areas. Only the 1948 War of Independence, when almost 2,000 civilians were among the 6,400 Israelis dead, saw more civilians killed in total than those butchered in the Hamas methodical assault that Saturday.[3]

Genocide, the term so unarguable a synonym for evil. Visiting the morgues at the Shura military base near Ramle and the Sammy Ofer Fortified Underground Emergency Hospital in Haifa, that one word continually came to the mind of Dr. Qanta A. Ahmed, a devout British-American Muslim and a senior fellow at the Independent Women's Forum. "No matter how it emerges, the monster is easy to recognize." Not an emotional frenzy of killing with rabid emotion like the pogroms suffered by Jewish communities in the past, this was a premeditated, systematically executed operation. "More different, more barbaric" than any of the scenes she had witnessed of Islamist *jihad*[4] attacks in Pakistan and Iraq, the Hamas genocide, Ahmed wrote in the *Wall Street Journal* on November 10, was "corrupted with cosmic enmity for the Jewish people, global Jewry, and the Jewish state." She concluded thus: "The world has been silent in the face of Jewish genocide before. When we now say never again, we must mean it." Jamal Waraqi, an Arab Muslim with the ZAKA volunteers who worked round-the-clock identifying and burying body remains in the slaughtered communities, providing a last honor to those from whom it was so violently taken, told Israeli TV's Channel 12 three days later: "What happened there is not related to Islam or any religion. It's related to cannibals, cruelty, and unbridled hatred, not religion." Hamas had booby-trapped many of the bodies to kill anyone attending to them, and workers had to be evacuated. A shaken first respondent at Kfar Aza captured the ghastly scenes there and elsewhere: "The depravity is haunting."[5]

The spiritual leader of Hamas, an outgrowth of the Muslim Brotherhood founded in Egypt by the Sunni Islamic scholar Hassan al-Banna in 1928, was a Gazan sheikh named Ahmed Yassin. In the years after the 1967 Six-Day War, this blind, wheelchair-bound cleric had established a range of social service organizations in Gaza. He stressed *da'wa*, the call towards God as expressed in the Qur'an, the central religious text of Islam. Yet, as a way of keeping militants within the fold and of keeping pace with the Palestine Liberation Organization (created in 1964 with its stated "complementary goals" of Arab unity and the liberation of Palestine) as a force of resistance, Yassin sanctioned the import of arms and the formation of nascent armed groups.[6] In December 1987, when the first Palestinian *intifada* ("uprising" or "shaking off") against Israel began, in Gaza's Jabaliya refugee camp, Hamas, an Arabic acronym for *Harakat al-Muqawama al-Islamiya* (the Islamic Resistance Movement), was born. Four years later, Hamas established its military wing, the Izz ad-Din al-Qassam Brigades, in memory of a sheikh who, regarded as the most venerable figure of Palestinian *jihad* against the Zionist settlement, was killed in 1935 by British mandatory forces. By the early 1990s, Hamas was mounting attacks against Israelis, to which Prime Minister Yitzḥak Rabin responded (unsuccessfully) by trying to banish four hundred Hamas activists to Lebanon.

In initiating what it dubbed *Tufan Al-Aqsa* (Operation Al-Aqsa Flood), coming one day after the fiftieth anniversary of the commencement of the Yom Kippur War, Hamas appealed to "the resistance fighters of the West Bank" (the biblical Judea and Samaria), as well as to "Arab and Islamic nations," to join in the war against Israel, which it accused of "illegally occupying" Palestinian Arab land. Backed by the Islamic Republic of Iran, the theocratic despotism whose radical Shi'ite eschatology remains an anomaly to the Western mind, and which had regularly threatened Israel with nuclear extinction, Hamas attributed the onslaught to the long-standing tensions between Israel and Palestinians, especially the fight over the Al-Aqsa Mosque compound in Jerusalem.[7] Iran had also been behind the bombings by its terrorist proxy in Lebanon, Hezbollah, of the Israeli Embassy in Buenos Aires on March 17, 1992, which killed 29 people and wounded 242 others, and of the Jewish community center there on July 18, 1994, killing 85 people and wounding over 300.[8]

The deadliest attack in Israel's history, a killing rampage live-streamed for the world media by Hamas fighters who linked disciplined planning with barbarism and brutality, was directly connected to Iran. Hamas had been funded, armed, and trained by the Iranian Revolutionary Guard Corps (IRGC) since the early 1990s. That included the provision of the Kornet anti-tank missile and the long-range Iranian Fajr and Syrian M-202 missile systems. Hamas opened an office in Tehran during the same decade. Despite these longstanding ties, the Palestinian Arab terror group had a rocky relationship with the Islamic Republic of Iran in recent years. In 2012, Iran cut off funding to Hamas after it refused to support the dictatorial Ba'athist regime of Bashar al-Assad in the Syrian Civil War (2011–2017). That war had resulted in the deaths, including by chemical weapons, of tens of thousands of pro-democracy militia fighters, recalling the slaughter in February 1982 of 30,000–40,000 civilians in Hama, and nearly 4,000 Palestinians in refugee camps.

Iran resumed financial assistance to Hamas in 2017. "Relations with Iran are excellent, and Iran is the largest supporter of the Izz ad-Din al-Qassam Brigades with money and arms," declared Yahya Sinwar, who had taken over the Hamas leadership in Gaza from Ismail Haniyeh in February 2017, at the time. In 2020, the US State Department reported that Iran had provided more than $100 million annually to Hamas and Palestinian Islamic Jihad (PIJ), a smaller militant group in Gaza created in 1981 as an offshoot of the Muslim Brotherhood. A CBS News report on October 26, 2023, indicated that while the unemployment rate in Gaza was forty-seven percent and more than eighty percent of its population was living in poverty according to the UN, Hamas's annual military budget ranged from $100 million to $350 million, with a combined income from different sources of up to $450 million per year. In 2022, Hamas leader Haniyeh told Al-Jazeera, the news network of Hamas-financial sponsor Qatar, which did the most to disseminate images of the destruction in Gaza caused by the Israeli air strikes after the October 7 assault and hewed closely to Hamas's vocabulary of "resistance fighters" battling against an "occupation army," that Iran had paid $70 million to the group to support its defense plan.[9]

Sinwar, born into a Khan Yunis family that had been forced out of the Palestinian town of Majdal, now Ashkelon, in the wake of Israel's 1948 War for Independence, was well known to the Israeli military command. His BA degree in Arabic Studies at the Islamic University of Gaza, co-founded in 1978 by Sheikh Ahmed Yassin, had brought him close to Hamas's spiritual guide. Rising quickly in the Hamas ranks as chief of an internal security unit known as Al-Majid, he was arrested in 1982 and 1985 for what Israel termed subversive activities. Upon his second release, he earned himself the nickname of "Butcher of Khan Younis" for killing Palestinian collaborators with Israel and others suspected of violating Islamic morality laws, viewing his efforts as a religious duty. Having first been convicted in 1988 for the murder of two Israelis and four Palestinians suspected of collaborating with Israel, Sinwar spent twenty-two years in an Israeli prison in Beersheba as inmate no. 7333335 from 1989 until his release in 2011. There, then Police Commissioner Orit Adato told *Times of Israel* on May 11, 2017, brain surgery in the nearby Soroka Hospital saved his life. Sinwar had been convicted on multiple murder counts by an Israeli court and sentenced to five life sentences, which he was supposed to serve until his death. However, he was freed with more than 1,000 Palestinian prisoners in a 2011 swap for the Israeli soldier Gilad Shalit, which Prime Minister Binyamin Netanyahu had personally pushed for.[10]

"No doubt this is a nationalistic moment par excellence, one of the big strategic monuments in the history of our cause," Sinwar crowed publicly when freed. Privately, however, he told Yuval Bitton, then head of intelligence at the prison, he had urged Hamas leaders in exile to reject the deal because all the Palestinians in Israeli jails, including those with Jewish blood on their hands, had to be released. He was overruled by the more pragmatic Saleh al-Arouri, the founding commander of its military wing, the Izz ad-Din al-Qassam Brigades. A two-state solution was impossible, he told Bitton, "because this is the land of Muslims." Hours after his release from prison, a defiant Sinwar told Hamas's Al-Aqsa TV that "we shall spare no efforts to liberate the rest of our brothers and sisters." Soon he became head of Hamas's military wing. In the Gaza elections of 2017, the fifty-five-year-old militant effectively abolished its civilian branch, thereby creating authoritarian rule, then set out to build relationships with Egypt and other Arab states. Israel tried to kill Sinwar with an air strike in May 2021. Ten days later, he declared that if the world did not take action to stop Israel, "there will be a religious war in the region."[11] Two years and five months later, he would launch that *jihad*. Its aim, according to documents found on captured Hamas attackers, was not only to focus on killing civilians and seeking hostages, but to seize the Gaza corridor and open a pathway to Tel Aviv.

Israel has accused Sinwar, alongside Mohammed Deif, the commander of Hamas's Izz ad-Din al-Qassam Brigades, of coordinating the brutal October 7 attacks. The Israeli military declared that it was searching for him along with other targeted senior Hamas officials in the Palestinian coastal enclave. Israeli officials believed that he was likely hiding in the labyrinth of tunnels—Sinwar boasted of 311 miles in length, some thirty meters deep—used by Hamas members in Gaza, A week after the Hamas invasion, an Israeli military spokesman, Lt. Col. Richard Hecht, called Sinwar a "dead man walking."[12]

Hamas strongly opposed the 1993 Oslo Accords, whereby Israel had assented to the creation of the Palestine Authority (PA) and the latter assuming governance in the West Bank and Gaza Strip over a five-year period. It gained popularity over the years through providing social services such as clinics and schools to the people of Gaza. Having defeated the Fatah-controlled PA[13] in the Palestinian Legislative Council elections over Gaza on January 25, 2006, the Palestine Authority under President Mahmoud Abbas in de jure control of that territory ever since Israel's unilateral withdrawal from Gaza in the summer of 2005, Hamas overpowered the PA armed forces in June 2007. It proceeded to execute 350 prisoners, banish hundreds of others, and impose authoritarian rule. Hamas then used Iranian support to launch several wars against Israel, including in 2008, 2009, 2014, and 2021.

These were a far cry from Hamas's killing of IDF soldiers Avi Sasportas and Ilan Saadon in February and May 1989, its first victims, and publicly claiming its initial suicide bombings against Israelis a few years later. The first, on April 13, 1994, killed five people in Hadera; the second, on February 25, 1996, near Jerusalem's Central Bus Station, killed seventeen civilians and nine soldiers. Over the course of the next decade, Hamas would mount a total of seventy suicide bombings against Israel, killing 483 Israelis. The Shin Bet, Israel's Intelligence Security Agency (ISA), would assassinate Hamas's chief bomb maker, Yahyah Ayyash, the man responsible for the death of more than one hundred Israelis, on January 5, 1996.

Hamas also benefited from Iranian know-how to help build its extensive network of tunnels throughout the Gaza Strip and underneath the Israel-Gaza border in order to conceal weapons and kidnap Israeli civilians. It continued to develop itself militarily, such as launching a commando navy unit that became operational in recent years. Hamas also continued to hold the bodies of two Israeli soldiers who were killed and then brought into Gaza in 2014, Hadar

Goldin and Oron Shaul, and two civilians, Avera Mengistu and Hisham al-Sayed, who had crossed the border in 2014 and 2015, respectively.[14]

According to a report on October 8, 2023, in the *Wall Street Journal*, corroborated a week later in the *New York Times*, Iran's IRGC helped Hamas plan the previous day's attack on Israel, determined its actual timing, and approved it in a meeting in Beirut the prior week. It appears no coincidence that Esmail Qaani, the head of the IRGC-Quds Force, was in Beirut days before the attack, and then traveled there again the day after it was executed. The premeditated strike was intended to hit Israel while that country appeared distracted by internal political divisions. It was also aimed at disrupting accelerating US-brokered talks to normalize relations between Saudi Arabia and Israel that Iran saw as threatening, according to senior Hamas and Hezbollah members. Israel's building on peace treaties with Egypt (1979) and Jordan (1994) while expanding its ties with Gulf Arab states could create a chain of American allies linking three crucial choke points of global trade—the Suez Canal, the Strait of Hormuz, and the Bab-el-Mandeb strait connecting the Red Sea to the Arabian Sea, according to Hussein Ibish, senior resident scholar at the Arab Gulf States Institute in Washington. "That's very bad news for Iran," Ibish observed. "If they could do this, the strategic map changes dramatically to Iran's detriment."[15]

The bloody, unprovoked invasion caught Israel's vaunted military and intelligence services by total surprise. In the judgment of Miri Eisin, a former senior intelligence officer in the Israel Defense Forces (IDF), the Hamas operation was the result of at least two years of planning, a period that included two conflicts between the IDF and the PIJ. At the time, Hamas was criticized for standing on the sidelines as PIJ leaders were eliminated by Israeli air strikes. In 2018, when Sinwar pushed the strategy of mixing nonviolent border protests with low-grade violent attacks on IDF guards, Israeli intelligence viewed him as willing to use less-daring tactics to achieve geopolitical goals—all without risking too much. Each time Israel fought Palestinian Islamic Jihad, and Hamas stayed out of the fighting, Israeli intelligence concluded that Sinwar was extremely deterred from taking the risk of angering the IDF too much. Unusual Hamas activity along the Gaza border at the end of September 2023 resulted in boosted troop presence as the IDF braced for a Yom Kippur attack. When violence along the border wound down, the Israeli army thought it had deterred Sinwar. Consequently, a defenseless Gaza border greeted Hamas on October 7, completely shattering that paradigm.

It was part of a vast con, said Eisin, "to lull Israel into complacency," while Hamas had gathered intelligence and quietly built up its capabilities. The invaders' apparent knowledge of Israeli border towns could have been gleaned in part from the thousands of Gazans who crossed the Israeli border daily to work, Eisin said, earning wages in the same communities that were later overrun; some of the Hamas fighters carried data files on the territories and settlements which they raided. In a rare all-staff memorandum made public two days after the incursion, Ronen Bar, the director of Israel's Shin Bet, took responsibility for the failure to foresee the assault: "The responsibility is mine," Bar wrote. "Despite a series of actions we carried out, unfortunately... we were unable to establish sufficient deterrence so as to thwart the attack."[16]

Underlying this complacency lay a flawed multi-year plan for the Israeli military, formulated in 2013 by the then IDF chief of staff, Lt. Gen. Benny Gantz. Called *teuza* ("prowess" or "fearlessness"), it shifted priorities away from the ground forces in favor of air force and cyber capabilities, intelligence, special operations forces, and stand-off precision fire. This came atop a cut of twenty-five percent in the ground forces budget between 2002 and 2006. Gantz did not think that the IDF would need to fight conventional army forces in the foreseeable future, nor have to conduct large-scale ground maneuvers in enemy territory. His predecessors and successors were "all party to this grand conceptual error to one degree or another." "Obviously," concludes David M. Weinberg of Jerusalem's Misgav Institute for National Security and Zionist Strategy, they were "dead wrong." Responding at the time to Gantz's plan, Eitan Shamir and Eado Hecht of the BESA Center warned that "neglect of the IDF's ground forces poses a risk to Israel's security. There are real battles ahead against well-entrenched Hamas and Hezbollah armies." Back then, however, no one was listening.[17]

Hamas's charter (1988) calls for the "obliteration" of Israel, *jihad* as the path, and "raising the banner of Allah over every inch" of the country, a commitment shared in the 1985 manifesto of Hezbollah. Although never elected to lead the country, Hezbollah effectively paralyzed the parliament and ignored the Lebanese army.[18] In 2017, a new document declared that Hamas's fight was with Zionism, not with the Jewish people as such, but it unhesitatingly reaffirmed its ultimate ambition of eliminating the "Zionist entity."[19] Yet, despite a few reports which Israeli intelligence had received on the night of October 6 of an impending Hamas campaign, the devastating attack and accompanying atrocities on this massive scale were not foreseen. The suspicion was of a minor rocket round or a minor border penetration, such as had occurred many times before. In addition, over the last two years, the border had been relatively quiet. There was significant growth in trade between Gaza and Israel; thousands of Gazan workers crossed into Israel every day and earned money to take home, and there were increasing international investments in Gaza.

Avigdor Liberman, Yisrael Beyteinu leader and opponent of the unilateral withdrawal from Gaza in 2005, warning in 2016 that Hamas was building up terror capabilities, had called for a more aggressive Israeli policy against the extremist group. Netanyahu and the military establishment rejected his position in favor of focusing on threats in the north, including increased Iranian entrenchment in Syria. When the right-wing coalition cabinet chose a cease-fire after a two-day period in November 2018 of 400 Hamas rockets at Israel and enabled the transfer of Qatari $10 million in cash to Hamas, Liberman resigned as defense minister. In the last days of September 2023, visiting the Gaza border with Eshkol Regional Council head Gadi Yarkoni, he wondered why there were no soldiers around just when Hamas carried out real violence, along with some firing, at the border fence. Despite their video of that dangerous situation, Netanyahu and the IDF repeated that Hamas was deterred and had no interest in escalation.[20]

In both March and July of 2023, Brig. General Amit Saar, heading the research division at IDF intelligence, had written to Netanyahu warning that Hamas, Hezbollah, and Iran recognized that Israel was "in a blistering, unprecedented crisis threatening its cohesion" and saw an opportunity "to create the perfect storm." According to *Haaretz*, Saar concluded that the enemy saw Israel's chaos and vulnerability as "the practical fulfillment of their basic world view—Israel is a foreign implant, a weak, divided society that will ultimately disappear." And had not Sinwar in a speech in December 2022 made little secret of his ultimate intentions? He then publicly warned Israel: "We will come to you, God willing, in a roaring flood, with endless rockets, we will come to you in an endless flood of soldiers, we will come to you with millions of our people, like the repeating tide."[21]

An investigation by the BBC would later report that the IDF female lookouts on the Gaza border noticed highly suspicious behavior on the border for several months before the Hamas invasion, but their reports and concerns were often ignored, told that their job was only to watch. They saw terrorists practicing every day what the raid would look like, including how to take over a model tank, how to destroy weapons on the fence, how to coordinate taking over Israeli armed forces, how to kill and to kidnap. They saw people detonating bombs on the wall between Gaza and Israel to test its strength in the weeks leading up to October 7. They later recalled seeing vehicles filled with elite Nukhba fighters, men taking photographs of the border fence, farmers moving closer and closer to the border. These lookouts were told that their messages were being passed on, probably to IDF intelligence, but they never received an answer about what they had reported and conveyed.[22]

A subsequent investigation also revealed that IDF intel saw Hamas using several dozen Israeli SIM cards in Gaza the night before October 7. The fact that so many Hamas members were switching to these cards could have been strong evidence of a potential invasion. Despite this evidence, the overall view at the time of IDF intelligence and other army officials was that Hamas would not dare to try such an invasion. This was because Israel's technology would give prior warning and any invaders would be killed by overwhelming Israeli air power and reinforcement forces which would arrive in time to stop an invasion, as well as the assumption that the IDF counterattack after such an attempted invasion would be devastating.[23]

In hindsight, some Israeli commentators reminded their readers that the Second Intifada (September 28, 2000–February 8, 2005), whose bloodiest month, March 2002, with 130 Israelis killed led to Operation Defensive Shield in successfully ending the terrorist bombings, had broken out after the last Israeli army units withdrew from Lebanon on May 4, 2000.[24] Over 1,000 Israelis had been killed and approximately 3,000 Palestinian Arabs in the Second Intifada. On June 25, 2006, one year after Israel departed from Gaza, Hamas entered Israel through a 400-meter tunnel dug during an Egyptian-mediated cease-fire, killed two soldiers and abducted nineteen-year-old corporal Gilad Shalit, then observed Israel's ponderous, passive response. An emboldened Hezbollah, Hamas's terrorist rival, killed ten IDF soldiers in an ambush and took two of the bodies for ransom. The month-long Second Lebanon War between Israel and the Hezbollah resulted. Although the IDF killed as much as a quarter of all of Hezbollah's forces and destroyed a large part of its infrastructure, Hezbollah nevertheless continued to rocket Israeli cities. Vilified in the media for acting disproportionately, and increasingly pressured by the international community, Israel was compelled to accept a UN cease-fire. Hezbollah was allowed to rearm.

In 2011, in exchange for Shalit's release, 1,027 Palestinian prison inmates were deported, most to Gaza. Hamas's network in the so-called West Bank, under the PA's jurisdiction, would then be operated by these former security prisoners. Deadly attacks on Israeli citizens followed, most notably the killing of three Jewish teenagers in June 2014, among the triggers of the war in Gaza one month later.[25] The Hamas attack of October 7, 2023, now showed that organization to be an existential threat to Israel, not a small one to be contained. It had to be seen as an outpost in the Islamist war on Western civilization.

The IDF's underestimation of Hamas, viewing it as static, satisfied with short-term incentives, and deterred for not engaging into multiple rounds of conflict between Israel and the PIJ, was coupled with the Israeli prime minister's focus on two other fronts. Netanyahu, while championing himself as

"Mr. Security," concentrated on broadening the breakthrough Abraham Accords between Israel and the United Arab Emirates (UAE) and Bahrain on September 15, 2020,[26] with Saudi Arabia and additional Arab nations as a counter to Iran and its militant proxies. Domestically, he had pressed for curbing the power of the unabashedly liberal Israeli Supreme Court, maintaining that reform was necessary because the judiciary had too much control over public policy, and a better balance was needed between democratically elected Knesset (parliament) legislators and the judiciary. The issue, polarizing the Jewish citizenry for many months, further convinced Israel's enemies of the country's growing weakness and loss of united resolve.

Netanyahu also cultivated Hamas as a strategic partner with which Jerusalem held indirect negotiations via Cairo, to be purchased with millions in cash from the wealthy gas-producing Gulf country of small Qatar, delivered in suitcases through Israeli border crossings. (United Nations [UN] agencies had spent nearly $4.5 billion in Gaza from 2014 to 2020.) The strategy was designed at the expense of PA president Abbas and Palestinian statehood. Thus was Hamas included in discussions about increasing the number of work permits that Israel granted to Gazan workers, which kept money flowing into the Gaza Strip. The policy aimed to provide food for families and the ability to purchase basic products. The number of permits, reaching up to 3.000 toward the end of Netanyahu's fifth government in 2021, soared to nearly 20,000 since he returned to power in January 2023.[27]

Israel's "Pearl Harbor" of October 7, 2023, recalling the surprise Japanese aerial attack of 353 planes against the US Pacific naval base of Battleship Row in Hawaii that killed 2,335 military personnel and 68 civilians on December 7, 1941, which President Franklin D. Roosevelt deemed "a date which will live in infamy,"[28] signaled an unprecedented military campaign far more traumatic on the country's population than any number of American "9/11"s. As horrific as the Al-Qaeda operation of four coordinated Islamist suicide terrorist attacks was on the morning of September 11, 2001, against the United States,[29] the October 7 attack on Israel, which concentrated on civilians, killed a far greater proportion of that country's much smaller population. The outcome was the equivalent of the United States, having experienced over 40,000 dead, rather than the 2,977 terrible losses that had been sustained in the attacks of 9/11.[30] On September 11, it was planes; on October 7, it was thousands of rockets, fighters, motorized paragliders, explosive drones, motorcycles, and pickup trucks, with the express order to slay civilians as much as possible. What Hamas unleashed, in Amotz Asa-El's phrase—"modern warfare's first mass deployment of terrorists" bent on systematic massacre, was extraordinary.[31]

Besides Israel's intelligence debacle with which the nightmare began, the IDF's slow response raised serious questions and distrust across the country about the political/military upper echelons. Where was the air force, supposed to react quickly, and why were not tanks sent directly to the border without delay? Why were not IDF commandos dispatched to the border to stop the terrorists from bringing hostages to Gaza? Why did it take a day or two for the army just to secure the area? Why did no agents embedded with Hamas in Gaza give warning of a planned attack? Many local forces and individuals fought heroically, and many soldiers and police died, in that period of several deadly hours, but it was not enough to prevent colossal disaster. The unthinkable had happened.

Shocked into the realization that Israel faced a genocidal regime on its southern border, the IDF command immediately announced that this war, forced on Israel, had to be faced without compromise. "The IDF is responsible for the safety of the country and its citizens, and on Saturday, near Gaza, we didn't succeed," said Chief of Staff Herzi Halevi on October 12. He went on to commit to improve it in the future and "return the security" to Israel. In the words of his predecessor, Aviv Kohavi, the army had decided to "eradicate" Hamas.[32] Yitzhak Herzog, Israel's president, went further, calling the attack part of "the axis of evil," rooted in a radical Shi'ite *jihad* against Western ideals, that had to be defeated fully for the sake of the region as well. "I have ordered a complete siege on the Gaza Strip," declared Defense Minister Yoav Galant on October 9: "We are fighting animals, and we are acting accordingly."[33] Yet how to do this against a terrorist infrastructure embedded in a civilian population, in hospitals, playgrounds, and schools, with Gaza housing 2.2 million Palestinian Arabs in a 141-square-mile enclave, and the hostages' fate uncertain?

General David Petraeus (Retired), who commanded US forces in Afghanistan and Iraq, warned Israel: "Destroy Hamas or they will return." In a CBS News interview on October 16, he stated frankly that he could hardly imagine "a more challenging task" for the Israeli military, which would have to clear Hamas tunnels and every room in Gaza from planted explosives. Civilian losses were inevitable, and Israeli soldiers would die as well. A former director of the CIA, Petraeus could not understand why both US and Israeli intelligence had missed the planned attack. Its dramatic assault reflected a major improvement in Hamas's operational security, and was "very creative." At the end of the war, Israel could not ignore the power vacuum created in Gaza. What its future plans were for that eventuality, Petraeus concluded, was also of paramount importance.[34]

The IDF air force, aided greatly by its use of unmanned Hermes 460 Zik drones, began to hammer Hamas's command posts and rocket launching pads in Gaza, and to strike successfully at a number of its leading military officials. 300,000 army reservists were called up to strengthen the 150,000 in IDF service. Most were sent southwards, with a good number to the north against a possible Hezbollah attack. By October 12, Israel had dropped 6,000 bombs on the densely populated territory, equivalent to the total number of airstrikes on that area during the entire Gaza-Israel conflict of fifty days in 2014.[35] Israel advised civilians in northern Gaza by leaflets and media to leave their homes immediately for their safety and head south, suggesting that a ground invasion was imminent. Several thousand did, but Hamas, continuing to dispatch rockets into Israel, called on Gazans not to leave. Hamas also blocked roads to the south and even fired on some seeking haven, saying that "displacement and exile are not for us." While Egypt refused entry into the Sinai, Hamas declared that it was ready "for all options, including a war and an escalation at all levels."[36]

It seemed clear on Thursday, October 12, that the ground invasion of Gaza would start either on that Friday, the evacuation deadline for northern Gaza to expire at midday, or on Saturday. Yet another week passed with commentators searching for reasons which seemed to have caused a delay. A growing concern of the military was that Hezbollah was waiting for when most IDF ground forces were committed to Gaza in order to open a full front against the IDF in the north. Perhaps additional time was required to examine Hezbollah's intentions, as well as to further reinforce the northern forces in case the worst would come to pass. There was also a deepening recognition in the army and at the political level that the IDF had not done anything like this in decades, and that rushing into Gaza unprepared to satisfy the wider population's thirst for retribution could be a large mistake, as had occurred in the 2006 Second Lebanon War.

The Gaza reality presented additional concerns. Planning a tactical surprise against Hamas in a ground invasion was a separate factor to consider. US pressure to avoid civilian casualties in Gaza (which Hamas claimed already reached a couple thousand dead and many more wounded) also had to be taken into account. As did the world's response, domestic concerns about the Israeli hostages, and giving more time for Gazans to evacuate. Finally, a clear plan as to Gaza's future after the IDF would topple Hamas's rule had to be agreed upon at the top levels of the Israeli command.[37]

Confronting the Lebanon front brought to Israeli minds grim memories of two lethal attacks in that area by the Popular Front for the Liberation of Palestine in 1974. On April 11, three of its members had crossed the border into Kiryat Shmona. Eighteen people were killed, eight of them children, and sixteen civilians were wounded. As Israeli soldiers entered the building, the three invaders blew themselves up. One month later, on May 25 in Ma'alot, some 115 Israelis, including children and teenagers, were held for two days by three members of that terrorist organization. On the second day, the captives were liberated by elite IDF commandos. This ended in the murder of twenty-five hostages (including twenty-two children) and six other civilians. Five days later, addressing the Knesset, Prime Minister Golda Meir concluded her remarks thus: "These attacks underline Israel's true solidarity, which transcends differences and contradictions. Terrorism will not weaken our spirit. We must be fully prepared if we are to succeed in preventing terrorist activity and in overcoming it."[38]

Five decades later, Hezbollah, long declared a terrorist body (as was Hamas) by the United States and many other nations, presented a far deadlier threat to Israel. This Iran proxy currently had 150,000 rockets at the ready, a number as much as ten times that of Hamas, and with more disastrous precision missiles which the IDF was less able to intercept. Missile attacks from Lebanon began not long after the Hamas invasion in the south, which drew the IDF to retaliate with tank and artillery fire, as well as air strikes.

One of the most violent days of the current war took place on October 17, with a Hezbollah anti-tank missile attack targeting Metula. The intense, rising tension in the air could be felt by visiting reporters, who continued to hear gunfire and large booms in the air. It seemed that more people in the area and across the nation were starting to think that perhaps Hezbollah was readying itself for a larger and more deadly conflict. To prevent civilian casualties, Israel evacuated twenty-eight villages and towns within approximately five kilometers from Lebanon. The IDF also deployed a strong proportion of its available forces in defensive positions along the Lebanese border.[39]

In the narrative world arena, Hamas scored a victory with its version about the bombing on October 18 of the Al-Ahli Anglican Hospital in central Gaza. According to the Hamas-run health ministry, Israeli air strikes on that building caused the death of almost five hundred civilians. IDF chief spokesman Rear Adm. Daniel Hagari countered with aerial footage showing clearly that an errant rocket from the Palestinian Islamic Jihad had caused the damage, further proven by the IDF's supplying a recorded conversation to that effect between two Hamas operatives. Iran and other Arab countries quickly accepted Hamas's claim, although US President Joseph Biden, on a brief visit of support that same day to Israel, cited American intelligence to confirm Israel's charge.

Subsequent evidence revealed that the projectile had hit a parking lot and not the hospital, and that it likely killed between ten and fifty people. Yet the BBC, CNN, the *New York Times*, and other prestige outlets lost no time in disseminating via lockstep coverage the Hamas assertion—offered without proof—which was eagerly believed by countless Westerners. Those three major media outlets later admitted the veracity of Israel's charge, but the damage had been done. "The war," in Yossi Klein Halevi's phrase, "has found its symbol." And Gazans continued to bury their dead, who had become tragic pawns in an international game of influence.[40]

While denying involvement in the Hamas attack of October 7, Iran warned Israel against targeting its allies in Lebanon, adding that it is "probable" that a new front would open against Israel if it continued "war crimes" in Gaza. Soon thereafter, Iranian Foreign Minister Hossein Amir Abdollahian met in Qatar with former Hamas head Haniyeh. Iran also called on Iraqi Shi'ites to join in the "holy" war against Israel on the northern front. Seeking what the mullahs of Tehran term *wahdat al-saha'at* ("a unity of the arenas") to gather under its leadership all Islamic forces arrayed against Israel, Amir Abdollahian announced on October 16 that the "Axis of Resistance" might carry out "preemptive measures" against Israel within "a matter of hours."[41]

To many in the West and those Arab rulers who had signed the pioneering Abraham Accords, there was no cause for complacency. Tehran, operating under the banner of the "Axis of Resistance," posed an alarming and significant threat to the Middle East and to global security. Joined to its race to achieve nuclear capability were its nested rings and intricate, organized layers of transnational terrorist networks. The range of Iran's missiles, over 2,000 kilometers, was sufficient to terrorize the entire region.

Hamas's urging fellow Palestinian Arabs in what they termed the West Bank to join in its war with Israel caught some traction. On October 19, the IDF announced that its troops had arrested 524 wanted Palestinians across that area, including more than 330 affiliated with Hamas, since the war began. Over the past day, sixty-three Hamas members were arrested, the military added. It also confirmed that troops demolished the home of a Hamas terrorist who had killed a soldier in the West Bank in July during an overnight operation in the village of Qibya. In recent days, several clashes broke out between IDF soldiers and Palestinians in the West Bank, where support for Hamas had risen considerably, together with several attempted Palestinian terror attacks. According to the PA health ministry, at least sixty-nine West Bank Palestinians had been killed by Israeli forces and settlers since October 7.[42]

Quickly responding to the surprise Hamas assault, PA President Abbas had stressed the Palestinian people's right "to defend themselves against the terrorism of settlers and the occupation forces." According to the official *Wafa* news agency, he also gave directions to provide all that was necessary "to bolster the resilience and steadfastness of the Palestinian people in facing the crimes committed by the Israeli occupation and settler gangs." Blaming the victim of barbaric onslaught was consistent with his charge one month earlier that Adolf Hitler had ordered the mass murder of Jews in World War II because of their "social role" as moneylenders, rather than out of animosity to the Jewish people, leading the German ambassador to Israel, Steffen Seibert, to remark: "The Palestinians deserve to hear the historical truth from their leader, not such distortions." Abbas's Foreign Ministry also released a statement blaming the Jewish State for Hamas terrorism: "Israel's disavowal of the signed agreements and noncompliance with international legitimacy resolutions led to the destruction of the peace process and the absence of a solution to the Palestinian issue after 75 years of suffering and displacement."[43]

In fact, no Palestinian leader since the State of Israel's rebirth, beginning with Yasser Arafat and continuing to this day with Mahmoud Abbas (now serving the nineteenth year of what was in fact his election to a four-year term as PA president), had shown any serious interest in reaching a peace agreement with Israel. Already in November 1947, the Palestinian Arab leadership under Nazi collaborator Haj Amin al-Husseini, the former Grand Mufti of Jerusalem, had rejected the UN General Assembly's majority vote to partition British mandatory Palestine into a Jewish state and an Arab state. (Ten years earlier, it had turned down the British Peel Commission's partition proposal of seventy-five percent of Palestine to an Arab state.) In 2000, PA president Arafat rejected Israeli Prime Minister Ehud Barak's offer at the Camp David Summit, which had US President Bill Clinton's strong support, of an independent Palestine state comprising ninety-five percent of the West Bank (an area slightly smaller than the US state of Delaware), the Gaza Strip, and a divided Jerusalem into recognized Arab and Jewish areas. Months later, the Second Palestinian Intifada erupted. In 2008, Abbas rejected Prime Minister Ehud Olmert's even more generous offer of statehood to cover about ninety-five percent of the West Bank, along with a link to the Gaza Strip, and placing Jerusalem's Old City entirely under international control.[44]

This should not be surprising, as the Palestinian Authority, to use the phrase of Yossi Kuperwasser, is guilty of "incentivizing terrorism." Its education system, a European Union (EU) report revealed in June 2021, regularly published school textbooks replete with antisemitism and incitement to violence, glorifying terrorism while demonizing Israel and Jews. One year later, despite EU pledges to work with the Authority to revise these textbooks, terrorists were still hailed as heroic resistance fighters and Zionism was deemed racism. Further, videos of kindergarten children acting out the killing of Israelis and youngsters expressing the hope to become *shaheeden* ("martyrs") in the struggle against the "occupier" Israel, are proudly displayed. Even more blatantly, the PA's official "pay for slay" program, Kuperwasser recently documented for the Jerusalem Center for Public Affairs, rewards $300 million annually to imprisoned and released terrorists, in addition to the families of "martyrs."[45] Under these circumstances, the obvious question arises: is a two-state solution—the State of Israel and a State of Palestine—or one state for two peoples, when the clear majority of Palestinians favor Hamas, realistic at the present time or in the foreseeable future?

Perhaps the most blatant example of Palestine Authority lethal intentions was shown in the seizure by the Israeli naval commando team Shayetet 13 in the Red Sea on January 3, 2002, at the height of the Second Intifada, of the *Karine A*. The ship carried fifty-five tons of high-grade Iranian weapons for the PA, ultimately to be delivered to the Gaza Strip. The cargo also included long-range rockets and high explosives that would have upgraded the capabilities of the Palestinian terrorist organizations and seriously escalated the campaign against Israel. The Iranian Islamic Revolutionary Guard Corps transferred the weapons from Kish Island, off the Iranian coast, to the hold of the *Karine A*. Worth over $15 million, the arms were purchased with money that came from international aid to the PA, The affair, widely publicized in the world media, had far-reaching political consequences: US President George W. Bush's administration called for Arafat, who denied any link to the affair despite unequivocal Israeli proof to the contrary, to be replaced by a different Palestinian leader. The *Karine A* was a turning point in the American administration's political strategy regarding the Israeli-Palestinian conflict.[46]

On October 19, 2023, *Reuters* reported that Khaled Mashal in Doha had declared to the Al-Arabiya television channel that Hamas "has what it needs to empty" the Israeli prisons of all the Palestinian captives there. Hamas, like other factions, had long called for the release of the roughly 6,000 Palestinians in Israeli prisons. He added that the Russians "sacrificed thirty million people in World War II in order to be liberated from Hitler's attack . . . The Palestinian people is like all the peoples, there is no people that is liberated without sacrifices."[47]

After the founding of Hamas in 1987, Mashaal had led the Kuwaiti branch of the organization. In 1992, he became a founding member of the Hamas politburo and its chairman. After Israel assassinated both Sheikh Ahmed Yassin and his successor, pediatrician Abdel Aziz al-Rantisi, in the spring of 2004, Mashal became the recognized head of Hamas. Under his leadership, Hamas stunned the world by winning a majority of the seats in the Palestinian legislative election in 2006. He stepped down as Hamas's politburo chairman at the end of his term limit in 2017.[48]

The IDF reiterated that it would act to free the hostages while eliminating Hamas. The captives, their exact whereabouts unknown, were believed to include nationals of many countries, including the United States, France, Thailand, and Germany; other countries had reported their citizens as missing. Soon after Mashaal's declaration, the spokesman of Hamas's armed wing, Abu Obeida, said in a video message that Hamas had "a group of detainees [sic] of different nationalities, these are our guests and we seek to protect them." He added, without elaborating further: "We will release detainees of different nationalities when circumstances on the ground allow." Another senior Hamas official, Mousa Mohammed Abu Marzouk, said on the same day that "foreign prisoners cannot be released due to the continued Israeli bombing of the Gaza Strip."[49]

IDF data published on October 19 revealed that, among the Israelis being held hostage by terrorists in the Gaza Strip, there were slightly under twenty children. Between ten to twenty of the captives were above the age of sixty. The majority were believed to be alive, but the terrorists had taken dead bodies as well. The number of individuals who were considered missing in action currently stood at over one hundred, in contrast to the approximately 3,000 who were unaccounted for on the first day of the war. The IDF estimated that the majority of the hostages were being held by Hamas, but some were held by the Palestinian Islamic Jihad, while others were kidnapped by mobs which apparently identified with Hamas.[50]

The IDF continued its effort to bring bodies from the field, with the assumption that there were still Israeli bodies not far from the Gaza border. Just the previous day, IDF forces had brought ninety bodies from near the Gazan territory, the majority of which were the bodies of terrorists. According to the IDF, the Red Cross and international organizations in the Gaza Strip were not answering calls to help. The commander of the intelligence apparatus for locating the POWs and MIAs, Maj. Gen. (res.) Nitsan Alon, stated: "My entire soul and mind are in this work, together with hundreds of people. We will not stop for a moment until we find every way to return our loved."[51]

Earlier that day, IDF Southern Command General, Maj. Gen. Yaron Finkelman, visiting troops near the Gaza border, told them that the expected ground offensive in the Gaza Strip would be "long and intense." "This war was forced on us, with a cruel enemy that harmed us greatly. But we stopped them . . . we are striking them heavily," he said. "The maneuver is going to move the fighting into their territory. We are going to beat them in their territory. the best of our commanders and soldiers are here." Finkelman added: "I greatly and completely believe in you. I believe in strength and thoroughness, and above all, everyone's spirit, which will lead us to victory."[52]

The battle order of one of the IDF division commanders ahead of the anticipated ground incursion into the Gaza Strip was revealed on October 19 by the Kan News Israeli TV station. The order stated: "You asked for hell— you'll get hell. We are in a war that was forced on us; we will move it to their territory. We are at war." The order continued: "This is our hour. The result: bodies of terrorists piled up in the streets and the enemy's infrastructure destroyed. The method: crush and conquer. We will fight and remain human beings, we are not them."[53]

The same day, Netanyahu met with combat soldiers from the 13th and 51st Battalions of the Golani Infantry Brigade in a staging area near the Gaza Strip. The soldiers affirmed their readiness for battle. In addition, he heard from IDF Ground Forces Commander Maj. Gen. Tami Yada'i about the fierce battles in which the battalions had been involved at the beginning of the war and their preparations for the future. "I am here with the warriors of the Golani Brigade, they come from every part of the country. They fought like lions, and they will continue to fight like lions," Netanyahu stated. He added: "We are going to win with all our might. The entire nation of Israel stands behind you, and we will deal a heavy blow to our enemies until we obtain victory. You heard me? Victory!"[54]

Israel had to deal a fatal blow to Hamas during the war in Gaza, declared former Shin Bet chief Yoram Cohen on October 19, because any other outcome would gravely put into question the possibility of reproducing Israeli deterrence. He added that Hamas had received a *fatwa* (religious ruling) from the late Sheikh Yusuf Qaradawi, then chairman of the International Union of Muslim Scholars, in which it was stated that in Israel's case there are no civilians. The venerated cleric argued that, since every citizen serves in the army in Israel, it was permissible to kill even a one- or two-year-old boy who will one day serve in those ranks—and he gave permission to kill Israeli women and children.[55]

A shocking discovery about the Hamas terrorists' use on October 7 of the synthetic amphetamine-type stimulant Captagon was reported the same day. The pills, clandestinely produced in southern Europe and trafficked through Turkey to consumer markets on the Arabian Peninsula, also known as "the cocaine for the poor," allowed the attackers to commit atrocities with a sense of calmness and indifference. Simultaneously, it kept them highly alert for extended periods and suppressed their appetite. Found to have been used by the Salafi jihadist group ISIS (the Islamic State of Iraq and Syria) terrorists in 2015, the group which beheaded thousands in Libya, Syria, and Iraq, as well as carried out lethal bombings in European cities, Captagon became a major source of income for Syria, long ago turned into another Iranian backyard, and was actively supported by Hezbollah.[56]

That day, Al-Arabiya Saudi network anchor Rasha Nabil questioned Mashal about the horrific massacre that the terrorist group had carried out in southern Israel. "You say that these acts of resistance are legitimate in your eyes, but the Western world has watched the crimes committed by Hamas against Israeli citizens on television," Nabil queried, "so much so that Hamas, and you who are responsible for explaining Hamas abroad, is beginning to be compared to ISIS." Mashaad responded: "Netanyahu invented this plot and the West, unfortunately, is conspiring with him." Two days later, notwithstanding the footage captured on GoPro and smartphone cameras during October 7 that were used by the very Hamas attackers and which they had proudly posted for viewers worldwide, the organization now denied that it had slaughtered Israeli citizens in that invasion. This was a war between armies, it claimed.[57]

Israeli authorities had said from the beginning that they were prepared to fight this war on multiple fronts. With dozens of rockets and missile from Hamas and Hezbollah continuing to rain down on its citizens, Hamas still hoping for "the unity of the battlefields," the IDF evacuated 30,000 citizens from the south and 40,000 from the north. Two weeks into the war, the IDF had also arrested 727 wanted Palestinians in the West Bank, more than 480 of them affiliated with Hamas. (By October 26, the numbers would rise to 930 and 608, respectively.)[58] In the early morning of October 14, in what may have been the first jet fighter attack in the West Bank in twenty years, the IDF bombed a tunnel under the Ayoub al-Ansari Mosque in Jenin, where Hamas and PIJ groups, who had murdered a number of Israelis in recent months, were planning "an imminent" terror attack. As the IDF pursued its steady aerial campaign against Hamas targets in Gaza, aided by the first usage of the precision "Iron Sting" mortar, and responded by tank fire to Hezbollah missiles, the military command also approved the distribution by the Samaria Regional Council of 300 assault rifles to civilian security teams in the northern West Bank.[59]

According to the IDF, some 750,000 residents of northern Gaza had heeded its warnings by then and, defying Hamas, left for the south. That left in the Israeli command's judgment between 300,000 and 400,000 in the

140-square-mile Gaza Strip, one of the most densely populated areas of the world.[60] Between August 15–22, 2005, Israel's unilateral withdrawal plan of expelling twenty-one Jewish communities in the Gaza Strip (known in Israel as Gush Katif) and four in North Samaria, affecting more than 9,000 Jewish citizens, had been carried out against determined domestic opposition. The advocates of the plan, put forward by Prime Minister Ariel Sharon, contended that it would improve Israel's security and international status in the absence of peace negotiations with the Palestinians. Yet Palestinians proceeded immediately to loot and destroy the 3,000 Israeli greenhouses left in the Strip, which were to be a key part of the future Gazan economy—a possible Singapore of the future. Over the next six months, terrorist groups fired some 1,000 rockets and mortar shells into Israel.[61] Once Hamas forcibly seized control of Gaza in June 2007, a constant, steady barrage of improvised Qasam rockets and then heavy rockets fell on Israel's southern cities and towns. Hamas leader Sinwar would boast in 2019 that his organization used irrigation pipes left in Gaza after the Israeli withdrawal in order to manufacture rockets.[62]

Not deterred by Israel's heavy blow against Hezbollah and Lebanon in 2006, Hamas continued launching tens of thousands of rockets against Israel. The IDF thus became embroiled in Operation Cast Lead (December 2008), Operation Pillar of Defense (2012) with its first use of the highly effective Iron Dome anti-ballistic-missile system, and Operation Protective Edge (July 2014), each marked by intensive aerial strikes against Hamas military and political targets.[63] Sixty-seven Israeli soldiers and six civilians were killed in Operation Protective Edge, with Israeli estimates of 1,598 Palestinian fatalities (of which seventy-five percent were combatants), making 2014 the year with the highest number of casualties in the Gaza Strip during all the years of conflict between Israel and the Palestinians. In addition, the recognition that Israel received from the international community for the 2005 disengagement faded with the years, while hostile criticism and political activity in the context of the Gaza Strip increased. This included the ill-fated effort on May 31, 2010, of IDF commandos to halt the *Mavi Marmara*, the flagship of the Gaza Freedom Flotilla which pro-Palestinian activists had aimed to break Israel's naval blockade of Gaza (installed to curb the Hamas rocket attacks), and some UN investigative commissions.[64]

Gaza proved to be the "leitmotif" of Michael Oren's tenure as Israel's ambassador to the United States (2009–2013). Taking up great swaths of his time, that conundrum created friction with President Barack Obama, who insisted that Israel submit to an investigation of the flotilla incident and criticized Jerusalem for the Shalit deal. Aside from Obama's adopting the Arab narrative when speaking of "a new beginning" at Cairo University on June 4,

2009, linking the State of Israel's legitimization to the Holocaust, calling for a Palestinian state alongside Israel, and not accepting "the legitimacy of continued Israeli settlements," the White House also held up the resupply of vital munitions to the IDF. On more than one occasion, the Washington-Jerusalem alliance's very fabric, opening to deep rifts, seemed close to unraveling. Hamas's getting Israel to fire back and kill innocent civilians (regularly used by Hamas as human shields), played up for media worldwide, the UN, and the International Criminal Court, was aimed to "whittle away" at Israel's international legitimacy. Once again assailed, this time in Operation Pillar of Defense, for acting disproportionally and firing randomly with airstrikes against Hamas and the Palestinian Islamic Jihad, US and international pressure again compelled Israel to accept a cease-fire. Gaza was once more devastated, but Hamas was still standing and free to rearm again.[65]

Operation Guardian of the Walls (May 2021) was yet another rerun of the 2008, 2012, and 2014 conflicts. Beginning with a Hamas barrage of rockets fired at Jerusalem, Israel's capital, Hamas and the Palestinian Islamic Jihad fired almost 4,000 rockets at Israel over the course of the next twelve days; approximately 680 of these misfired and fell within the Gaza Strip, causing Palestinian casualties. The IDF succeeded in blowing up some sixty miles of Hamas tunnels, struck over 1,500 targets, and killed hundreds of terrorist operatives. The Iron Dome Aerial Defense System successfully intercepted ninety percent of the rockets fired indiscriminately at Israeli civilians.[66]

The magnitude and brutality of the slaughter of October 7, 2023, however, unprovoked and unprecedented in Israel's history, demanded far more from the Jewish State. Now deeply traumatized Israelis had to gather all their forces to contend with Hamas's genocidal threat, convinced that they faced an existential security crisis to be unequivocally resolved and this enemy obliterated—whatever the cost. After the awakening that Saturday morning to radical Islamist hate, there could be no compromise with the rampage of pure, absolute evil.

Endnotes

1 Jewish News Syndicate (JNS), Sept. 1, 2024; David Grossman, interview with Daniel Gordis, *Israel from the Inside*, podcast, Nov. 19, 2023.
2 *Times of Israel*, Oct. 17, 2023. The accounts of the Hamas attack on October 7, 2023, are drawn from coverage the next day and after in the *New York Times, Washington Post, Wall St. Journal*, JNS, *Times of Israel, Jerusalem Post*, World Israel News, Al-Jazeera, Reuters, IDF News, and *Haaretz*. The use of poisonous gas was reported by JNS, Dec. 15, 2023. Seven other IDF field operation young women were kidnapped from Nahal Oz; one was rescued, one died in captivity. The female surveillance operators there kept broadcasting rather than attempt to flee. The testimony on May 12, 2024, at Midreshet Lindenbaum (Jerusalem) of

Ariella Ruback, a "spotter" at the Kisufim army base—where thirty-two died on October 7. Also see Samuel Forey, "Hamas Attack: October 7, a Day of Hell on Earth in Israel," *Le Monde*, October 30, 2023; https://www.lemonde.fr/en/international/article/2023/10/30/hamas-attack-october-7-a-day-of-hell-on-earth-in-israel_6213560_4.html; Patrick Kingsley and Ronen Bergman, "The Secrets Hamas Knew About Israel's Military," *New York Times*, October 13, 2023, https://www.nytimes.com/2023/10/13/world/middleeast/hamas-israel-attack-gaza.html; Bari Weiss, "When People Tell You Who They Are, Believe Them," *Free Press*, Oct. 10, 2023. The updated number of 253 hostages taken to Gaza (not 240, as reported for some time) was reported in the *Jerusalem Post*, Feb. 25, 2024.

3   "Israel Defense Forces: Israeli Casualties in Battle (1860–Present)," Jewish Virtual Library, https://www.jewishvirtuallibrary.org/israeli-casualties-in-battle-1860-present.

4   While some modern Muslims explain *jihad* in a spiritual sense of moral striving, most of the fourteen centuries of recorded Muslim history interpreted it, and certainly so in the contemporary world, to mean "armed struggle for the defense or advancement of Muslim power." Muslim tradition views the world as divided between the House of Islam (*Dar al-Islam*) and the House of War (*Dar al-Harb*)—the latter the rest of the world inhabited and ruled by infidels. The presumption is that the duty of *jihad* will continue until all the world either adopts the Muslim faith or submits to Muslim rule. Bernard Lewis, *The Crisis of Islam: Holy War and Unholy Terror* (New York: Modern Library, 2003), chap. 2; Gilles Kepel, *Jihad: The Trail of Political Islam*, trans. Anthony F. Roberts (Cambridge, MA: Belknap Press/Harvard University Press, 2002).

5   *Wall St. Journal*, Nov. 10, 2023; Keshet 12 News, Nov. 27, 2023; World Israel News, Feb. 4, 2024; CBS News, Oct. 11, 2023.

6   In 1989, Yassin was arrested by Israel and sentenced to life imprisonment for ordering killings of alleged Palestinian collaborators. In 1997, Yassin was released from Israeli prison as part of an arrangement with Jordan following a failed assassination attempt in Jordan of Hamas leader Khaled Mashal by the Israeli Mossad. Yassin was released in exchange for two Mossad agents who had been arrested by Jordanian authorities on the condition that he refrained from continuing to call for suicide bombings against Israel. He did not. Yassin was killed in an Israeli air attack on March 22, 2004, while he was being wheeled out of an early morning prayer session in Gaza City. Yassin and his bodyguards were killed instantly, along with nine bystanders. Another twelve people were injured in the operation, including two of Yassin's sons. Abdel Aziz al-Rantisi, Yassin's deputy, became the Hamas leader after his assassination, but was also killed shortly thereafter.

7   The baseless charge that Jews planned to destroy the Al-Aqsa Mosque and replace it with a Third Holy Temple began with the Grand Mufti of Jerusalem, Haj Amin al-Husseini, in 1921 and 1929, leading to the murder of scores of Jews. In 1990, it developed into the October riots, which led to the deaths of seventeen Muslims and many wounded on both sides. In 1996, Yasser Arafat and the Palestinian Authority accused Israel of endangering the Mosque, sparking riots during which seventeen IDF soldiers and about 100 Palestinians were killed. Ariel Sharon's visit to the Temple Mount in September 2000, a few months before he became prime minister, was used by Arafat as an excuse to launch the Second Intifada, also known as the Al-Aqsa Intifada. Gil Hoffman, "Is the Media about to Ignite World War III?," *Jerusalem Post Magazine*, Mar. 2, 2024.

8   David Remnick, "In the Cities of Killing," *New Yorker*, Oct. 28, 2023. The Colombian-Lebanese national Samuel Salman El Reda, who helped coordinate the deadly attack on the Jewish community center in Argentina, is still at large. He then went on to recruit, train, and manage Hezbollah operatives, send them to Panama, Peru, and Thailand to gather explosive chemicals and look for future appropriate targets. He is believed to be in Lebanon. In 2019, the State Department offered a $7 million reward for information leading to his arrest. The US Justice Department recently submitted an indictment to Manhattan's Federal Court, possibly spurred to action by the Argentine government in June issuing an international

9. arrest warrant for both El Reda and his brother, José, for allegedly plotting the attack on the Israeli Embassy in Buenos Aires in 1992. World Israel News, Dec. 21, 2023. Also see Matthew Leavitt, *Hezbollah: The Global Footprint of Lebanon's Party of God* (London: Hurst, 2013).
9. AJC Global Voice, Oct. 15, 2023; CBS News, Oct. 26, 2023; TV7 Israel News, Jan. 5, 2022.
10. Judith Miller, "Saving Sinwar," *Tablet*, Mar. 19, 2024; *Times of Israel*, May 11, 2017, and May 6, 2022. Netanyahu said the deal struck "the right balance" between Israeli security risks and the imperative of returning Shalit "to his family and people." In a televised address from Tel Nof Airbase after he greeted Shalit, Netanyahu stated, "Today we are all united in joy and in pain." *Washington Post*, Oct. 11, 2011; *New York Times*, Oct. 18, 2011.
11. CNN Newsroom Live, Oct. 17, 2023; Jo Becker and Adam Sella, "The Hamas Chief and the Israeli Who Saved His Life," *New York Times*, May 26, 2024; Miller, "Saving Sinwar," *Tablet*, Mar. 19, 2024; David Remnick, "Notes from the Underground," *New Yorker*, Aug. 3, 2024.
12. Dov Lieber and David S. Cloud, "Hamas Fighters' Orders: 'Kill as Many People as Possible,'" *Wall St. Journal*, Oct. 14, 2023, https://www.wsj.com/world/middle-east/hamas-fighters-orders-kill-as-many-people-as-possible-2a6abff8. Fox News, Oct. 20, 2023.
13. Formerly the Palestinian National Liberation Movement, Fatah was founded in 1959 by members of the Palestinian diaspora, principally by professionals working in the Persian Gulf States who had studied in Cairo or Beirut and had been refugees in Gaza. The founders included Yasser Arafat, then head of the General Union of Palestinian Students at Cairo University. According to the BBC, "Mr. Arafat took over as chairman of the executive committee of the PLO (Palestine Liberation Organization) in 1969, a year that Fatah is recorded to have carried out 2,432 guerrilla attacks on Israel." Fatah had been closely identified with the leadership of its chairman, Arafat, until his death in 2004, when Faruq al-Kaddoumi constitutionally succeeded him to the position of Fatah Chairman and continued in that position until 2009, when Mahmoud Abbas, president of the Palestinian Authority, was elected chairman. Said Aburish, *Arafat, From Defender to Dictator* (New York: Bloomsbury, 1998); BBC News, Aug. 4, 2009; Helga Baumgarten, "The Three Faces/Phases of Palestinian Nationalism, 1948–2005," *Journal of Palestine Studies* 34, no. 4 (2005): 25–48; Grant Rumley and Amir Tibon, *The Last Palestinian: The Rise and Reign of Mahmud Abbas* (Amherst, MA: Prometheus, 2017).
14. Beverley Milton-Edwards and Stephen Farrell, *Hamas, The Islamic Resistance Movement* (New York: Polity Press, 2010); Matthew Levitt, *Hamas: Politics, Charity and Terrorism in the Service of Jihad* (Washngton, D.C.: Washington Institute for Near East Policy, 2006).
15. *Wall St. Journal*, Oct. 8, 2023; Tony Badran, "Iran Sponsored the October 7 Massacre. America Paid for It," *Tablet*, Dec. 14, 2023.
16. *Washington Post*, Oct. 16, 2023; *Haaretz*, Mar. 22, 2024. A routine inspection of Israel Defense Forces posts along the Gaza border carried out seventy-two hours before Hamas's October 7 onslaught showed a severe lack of preparedness, Channel 12 reported months later. According to the Israeli broadcaster, only the Yiftah outpost near the seaside Zikim training base managed to get a passing mark on the October 4 audit. JNS, May 3, 2024.
17. David M. Weinberg, "Long Wars Ahead for the IDF," *Jerusalem Post*, Apr. 26, 2024. For the strategic recommendations by Shamir and Hecht regarding future IDF responses in light of the Hamas attack on October 7, 2023, see BESA Center report, Apr. 21, 2024, no. 2,277. The BESA Center (the Begin-Sadat Center for Strategic Studies) is affiliated with Bar-Ilan University in Ramat Gan, Israel.
18. Leavitt, *Hezbollah*.
19. BBC News, May 1, 2017.
20. Seth J. Franztman, "Liberman to 'Post': Israel's Overconfidence Led to Hamas's Massacre," *Jerusalem Post Magazine*, Nov. 10, 2023.
21. David Remnick, "The Price of Netanyahu's Ambition," *New Yorker*, January 14, 2024.
22. World Israel News, Jan. 16, 2024.

23 *Jerusalem Post*, Feb. 26, 2024. For additional incorrect assessments, as well as that some major IDF officials were "left out of the loop" about reports of an imminent Hamas attack, see Ynet, Nov. 29, 2023.

24 Thirty people were killed and 140 injured—twenty of them seriously—in a suicide bombing in the Park Hotel in the coastal city of Netanya on the evening of March 27, 2002, in the midst of the Passover holiday seder with 250 guests. Hamas claimed responsibility for the attack. The terrorist was identified as twenty-five-year-old Abdel-Basset Odeh, a member of the Hamas Izz ad-Din al-Qassam Brigades, from the West Bank city of Tulkarm. The next day, Prime Minister Ariel Sharon's government mobilized infantry and tank reserves and launched an invasion of West Bank cities in Operation Defensive Shield. Troops placed Arafat under siege in his government building in Ramallah, where he remained until shortly before his death. The West Bank security barrier was built. A year later, on April 14, the four Palestinian Hamas terrorists who planned the Park Hotel Passover massacre in Netanya were sentenced to twenty-nine life terms and another twenty years in prison. A year after that, the terrorist attacks had all but ceased. "Passover Suicide Bombing at Park Hotel in Netanya," Ministry of Foreign Affairs, Mar. 27, 2002, https://www.gov.il/en/pages/passover-suicide-bombing-at-park-hotel-in-netanya; Matti Friedman, "Ten Years after Passover Blast, Survivors Return to Park Hotel," *Jerusalem Post*, Mar. 27, 2012.

25 NBC News, Oct. 17, 2011; NPR, Aug. 22, 2014. Naftali Frankel, Gilad Shaar, and Eyal Yifrach were kidnapped on June 10 near the Gush Etzion junction while hitchhiking back from their religious schools. Their bodies were found almost three weeks later, buried in a shallow grave under rocks in a valley close to the southern city of Hebron. Hamas at first denied any role in their murder, but senior commander Saleh Arouri told a conference in Turkey on August 20, 2014, that operatives of Hamas's military wing, the al-Qassam Brigades, carried out what he described as aa "heroic operation" with the broader goal of sparking a new Palestinian uprising and hoping Hamas could exchange the youths for Palestinian prisoners held by Israel. NPR, Aug. 22, 2014.

26 The Abraham Accords declaration begins as follows: "We, the undersigned, recognize the importance of maintaining and strengthening peace in the Middle East and around the world based on mutual understanding and coexistence, as well as respect for human dignity and freedom, including religious freedom." Having secured the historic agreement, President Donald Trump hosted the signing on the Truman Balcony of the White House, Netanyahu standing on his right, together with Bahraini foreign minister Abdullatif bin Rashid Al-Zayani and Emirati foreign minister Abdullah bin Zayed Al-Nahyan. Not long thereafter, Morocco (December 22, 2020) and Sudan (January 6, 2021) endorsed the Accords. In exchange for Morocco's recognition of Israeli sovereignty, the United States recognized Moroccan sovereignty over Western Sahara.

27 AP News, Dec. 20, 2021; *Times of Israel*, Oct. 8, 2023.

28 "Remembering Pearl Harbor: A Pearl Harbor Fact Sheet," United States Census Bureau, https://www.census.gov/history/pdf/pearl-harbor-fact-sheet-1.pdf.

29 Peter L. Bergen, "September 11 Attacks," *Britannica, History and Society*. Al-Qaeda, founded by Osama bin Laden, began as a network to support Muslims fighting against the Soviet Union in Afghanistan in the 1980s. When the Soviets withdrew in 1989, the organization dispersed but continued to oppose as a "holy war" what its leaders considered corrupt Islamic regimes and especially the US presence in Islamic lands. Numerous terrorist attacks before the September 11 attack against the United States were the destruction of the American embassies in Nairobi, Kenya and Tanzania, and of the US warship *USS Cole* in Aden, Yemen. On May 2, 2011, bin Laden was killed by US military forces in Abbottabad, Pakistan.

30 Robert Satloff, "Why 10/7 Was Worse for Israel Than 9/11 Was for America," Washington Institute, Oct. 15, 2023.

31 Amotz Asa-El, "We Shall Overcome," *Jerusalem Post*, Oct. 13, 2023.

32 Ariella Marsden, "Who Is Taking Responsibility for Hamas' Attack on Israel?," *Jerusalem Post*, Oct. 18, 2023; Israel National News, Oct. 18, 2023.
33 *Times of Israel*, Oct. 8, 2023; *Guardian*, Oct. 10, 2023.
34 CBS, Oct. 16, 2023.
35 CNN, Oct. 9, 2023.
36 Reuters, Oct. 14, 2023; AP News, Oct. 11, 2023.
37 *Jerusalem Post*, Oct. 16, 2023.
38 Jewish Telegraphic Agency, Apr. 18, 1974, and May 5, 2011; "Ma'alot" and Golda Meir Knesset speech, May 30, 1974, https://jewish virtuallibrary.com.org.
39 *Times of Israel*, Oct. 17, 2023.
40 Linda Dayan, "For Hamas, The Gaza Hospital Tragedy is a Narrative Victory," *Haaretz*, Oct. 18, 2023; *Times of Israel*, Oct. 19, 2023; Yossi Klein Halevi, "Why is Israel Being Blamed for the Hamas Massacre?," *Times of Israel*, Oct. 25, 2023.
41 CNN, Oct. 13, 2023; *Times of Israel*, Oct. 17, 2023.
42 PBS, Oct. 19, 2023; *Times of Israel*, Oct. 19, 2023.
43 *Times of Israel*, Oct. 7, 2023; BBC, Sept. 7, 2023.
44 *Jerusalem Post*, May 31, 2021.
45 *Jerusalem Post*, June 20, 2021, and Jan. 30, 2022; Yossi Kuperwasser, *Incentivizing Terrorism: Palestinian Authority Allocations to Terrorists and their Families* (Jerusalem: Jerusalem Center for Public Affairs, 2017).
46 Amos Gilboa, *Drama in the Red Sea*, Meir Amit Intelligence and Terrorism Center, Oct. 15, 2017.
47 Reuters, Oct. 19, 2023; Palestinian Watch, Oct. 19, 2023, video cited in United with Israel, Dec. 8, 2023.
48 "Khalid Mishal: The Making of a Palestinian Islamic Leader Interviewed by Mouin Rabbani," *Journal of Palestine Studies* 37, no. 3, part 1 (Spring 2008): 59–73.
49 Reuters, Oct. 16–17, 2023.
50 *Times of Israel*, Oct. 19, 2023.
51 *Haaretz*, Oct. 19, 2023.
52 *Times of Israel*, Oct. 19, 2023.
53 *Kan News*, Oct. 19, 2023.
54 JNS, Oct. 19, 2023.
55 Israel National News, Oct. 20, 2023; "Yusuf al-Qaradawi, the Muslim Scholar Who Influenced Millions," Al-Jazeera, Sept. 27, 2022, https://www.aljazeera.com/news/2022/9/27/yusuf-al-qaradawi-the-muslim-scholar-who-influenced-millions.
56 Foundation for Defense of Democracies, Oct. 21, 2023; Judy Siegel-Itzkovich, "Amphetamines Emboldening Hamas," *Jerusalem Post Magazine*, Oct. 27, 2023.
57 *Times of Israel*, Oct. 20–21, 2023.
58 *Times of Israel*, Oct. 22 and 26, 2023.
59 *Times of Israel*, Oct. 22 and 24, 2023.
60 *Times of Israel*, Oct. 26, 2023.
61 "Evacuation of Israeli Civilians from the Gaza Strip Completed," Ministry of Foreign Affairs, Aug. 22, 2005, https://www.gov.il/en/pages/evacuation-of-israeli-civilians-from-the-gaza-strip-completed-22-aug-2005.
62 Israel National News, Nov. 16, 2019.
63 The Hebrew names of these three operations were *Mivtza Oferet Yetzuka* (2008), *Mivtza Amud Anan* (2012), and *Mivtza Tzuk Eitan* (2014).
64 Shmuel Even, "'The Decision that Changed History': Ten Years since the Disengagement from the Gaza Strip," *Strategic Assessment* 18, no. 2 (July 2015): 73–88.
65 Michael Oren, *Ally: My Journey across the American-Israeli Divide* (New York: Random House, 2016).
66 "Operation Guardian of the Walls," IDF News, June 14, 2021, https://www.idf.il. In Hebrew, the military operation in 2021 was called *Mivtza Shomer HaChomot*.

CHAPTER 2

Boots on the Ground in Gaza

The information war to influence world public opinion did not let up and grew more vitriolic. As the third week of what Israel called Operation Swords of Iron (Mivtza Charavot Barzel) began, the IDF, for the first time in its history, released a graphic video (including in Arabic to the Muslim world) documenting the Hamas's acts of massacre on October 7, 2023. Health authorities under Hamas control in Gaza countered with an announcement that Israeli air strikes in the space of two weeks had killed at least 5,300 people and wounded more than 13,000. As for the West Bank, the Palestinian Authority (PA) health ministry declared that at least ninety Palestinians had been killed by Israeli forces and settlers since October 7.[1]

On October 20, Hamas released to Israeli custody two American hostages, ailing mother Judith Ra'anan and her teenage daughter Natalie. They had been visiting relatives at Nahal Oz, just yards from Gaza, where the attackers, as elsewhere, started fires to smoke people from their safe rooms; more than 100 Israelis were murdered in that kibbutz. While US President Biden thanked the Qatari government for its mediation effort in this regard, Hamas spokesman Abu Obeida announced that this was done "for humanitarian reasons, and to prove to the American people and the world that the claims made by Biden and his fascist administration are false and baseless." Deeming the taking of hostages "a war crime under international law," Tirana Hassan, executive director of the NGO Human Rights Watch, declared that Hamas and Palestinian Islamic Jihad "should immediately and unconditionally release all detained civilians."[2]

Meanwhile, the first twenty trucks carrying medicines, food, and water were allowed into the Gaza enclave through the Rafah Crossing, a fraction of the quantity needed, with more than one hundred additional ones standing on the Egyptian side of that entry. Biden responded: "We will continue to work with all parties to keep the Rafah Crossing in operation to enable the continued movement of aid that is imperative to the welfare of the people of Gaza, and to continue working to protect civilians, consistent with obligations under international humanitarian law" and "without diversion by Hamas."[3]

Speaking that day near the northern border with Oz Commando Brigade and Maglan Unit Commando soldiers, Netanyahu hailed their stalwart battles against Hamas and Hezbollah, and declared that should the latter enter the war, it would "long for the Second Lebanon War" and would be "making the mistake of its life." Meeting with the Air Force command two days later, Defense Minister Yoav Gallant stated that the war might take even three months, but in the end joint aerial and ground attack must be "the last maneuver in Gaza, for the simple reason that after it there will not be a Hamas."[4]

A poll commissioned by the Israel Victory Project at this time demonstrated that 70 percent of Israeli Jewish adult respondents endorsed the proposition that the primary objective of Operation Swords of Iron should be "to eliminate Hamas." When given the option of launching a ground operation in Gaza to eradicate Hamas or avoiding a ground operation and finding another way to deal with that terrorist group, 68 percent chose the former and 25 percent the latter solution. Forty-three percent responded that Israel must consider the perspectives of allies, particularly the United States, on security matters, while 55 percent responded that Israel must ignore external demands and make its own security decisions. When asked "Who, in your opinion, should rule Gaza after the overthrow of the Hamas regime?," 24 percent said Israel, 24 percent said "New leadership in Gaza," 22 percent replied "The Palestinian Authority," and 19 percent chose "Arab nations." When asked, "If Saudi Arabia demands significant concessions to the Palestinian Authority by Israel as the price for formal ties, should Israel agree to these?" 72 percent of the Israeli public said no, whereas 21 percent said yes.[5]

Two flash surveys conducted by the Israel Democracy Institute during the second week of the Hamas-initiated war against the Jewish State, reported in JNS on October 23, showed a 13.5 percentage point rise in optimism (65.5 percent) compared to June of 2023 (52 percent). Among Jewish Israelis, increases in optimism were seen across the ideological spectrum—left, right, and center—while levels of optimism among Israeli Arabs remained stable at around 36 percent. The increase in optimism came as trust in the government hit historic lows, falling for Jewish Israelis from 28 percent in June to 20.5 percent in October. Right-wing Jewish Israelis' trust in the government saw a drop from 42 percent in June to 31 percent. Left-wing and centrist Israelis' trust level was already low, but the 18 percent in October represented the lowest percentage since the Israel Democracy Institute had started measuring trust in institutions in 2003. While trust in the government decreased, trust in the Israel

Defense Forces, police and media had increased among Jewish Israelis since June, with the IDF remaining highly rated at 87 percent compared to 85.5 percent in June.[6]

It quickly became clear that Arab-Israeli members of Knesset, strongly against the Hamas onslaught, spoke for a clear majority of Israel's Arabs. Once the brutality of Hamas's incursion into Israel became clear, Mansour Abbas, leader of the Islamic party Ra'am, wrote to his 300,000 followers on social media this: "I call on Arab citizens and all Arab and Jewish citizens to maintain restraint and behave responsibly and patiently, and to maintain law and order." Referring to the "unfortunate, tragic, and reprehensible events" still in progress, he also called on the leadership of the Palestinian factions in Gaza to "release the captives in your hands. Islamic values command us not to imprison women, children, and the elderly." A little later, when Hamas leaders began calling on Israel's Arab citizens to join the fight, Arab Knesset member Ayman Odeh responded angrily. In a media interview, he declared: "Any call for militant actions and igniting a war between Arab citizens and Jews inside Israel is something we will not accept." At the same time, the Israeli-Arab intellectual camp and spiritual *mullah* leaders maintained a deafening silence.[7]

A poll by the Agam Institute in Israel found that eighty per cent of Arab Israelis opposed Hamas's attack. Even Ahmed Tibi, leader of the Ta'al party and an advisor to the late PA president Yasser Arafat, declared in the Knesset on October 20 that "human morality is not selective. There is no half-morality. Murder of children is murder of children." Jerusalem-based Palestinian activist Bassem Eid released a video damning Hamas as "a criminal gang that only cares about increasing its own power," and ending with "Israel uses rockets to defend its people. Hamas uses people to defend its rockets."[8]

Arab profiles in courage emerged on that cursed day, what many called "the "Black Sabbath" of October 7, 2023. The Bedouin bus driver Youssef El Zaidneh is credited with saving thirty Israeli youngsters at the Nova music festival. As shown in the video "Have You Seen the Horizon Lately?," Hamed Alkarnawi and three family members from the Bedouin city of Rahat together with Aya Meidan of Kibbutz Be'eri, where 97 of 1,100 residents were killed and two dozen taken hostage, rescued under fire some forty young people at that festival. Twenty-three-year-old paramedic Awad Darawshe, who chose not to abandon wounded Jewish patients while working there with Yossi Ambulances (a division of United Hatzalah), was killed by Hamas gunmen. Twenty-five-year-old Amer Odeh Abu Sabila was killed while trying to save the two daughters of Dolev and Odaya Swisa near the police station in Sderot.[9]

Israelis coping with anxiety and stress were offered a few options. Natal, the country's Trauma and Resiliency Center, offered a zoom session for English speakers. For parents with children on the war fronts, EMDR Israel made consultations available at no charge. A volunteer effort, under the slogan "The World Has to Know," began to collect eye-witness testimony from survivors of the Hamas slaughter, making use of translators with knowledge of Japanese, English, German, Arabic, Spanish, and French.[10]

On the evening of October 20, the Israeli Philharmonic Orchestra gave a special concert, broadcast live from Tel Aviv's Heichal HaTarbut. Following the national anthem *Hatikva*, with the musicians standing in their places, Paul Ben Haim's *Fanfare to Israel* and Beethoven's *Eroica* symphony then filled out the program. Seats in the theatre—all empty—displayed a separate photograph for each hostage with one word: "KIDNAPPED."

Just before performing the *Eroica*, conductor Lahav Shani spoke in Hebrew of "these dark days." He began recalling to listeners near and far the unfathomable brutality of Hamas in the October 7 attack, the incredible bravery of civilians and soldiers against the slaughter, and the solidarity in all parts of Israeli society that offered "a point of light." As he saw it, the citizenry's resourcefulness and the spirit of volunteerism, together with the desire to help one another, "inspires us with hope." Shani ended by quoting in English a sentence from Leonard Bernstein's response sixty years ago, one day after the American Jew had conducted the New York Philharmonic Orchestra in a performance of Gustav Mahler's Second Symphony, *The Resurrection*, following the assassination of President John F. Kennedy: "Our music will never again be quite the same. This will be our reply to violence: to make music more intensely, more beautifully, more devotedly than ever before."[11]

Two days later, the IDF discovered that Hamas sought to create chemical weapons and implement their use among the civilian population. The source of the document was an Al-Qaeda manual dated 2003, indicating both the connection between the two Islamic terrorist organizations and Hamas's intention to use chemical weapons in order to cause mass casualties—as ISIS had planned in the past. Among the contents of the USB were precise instructions for preparing a device for dispersing cyanide agents. Presenting this evidence to the public, Israeli President Yitzhak Herzog then said the following:

> What we went through is evil. We have to uproot it, and when you uproot evil, we see people supporting evil, you see them in demonstrations in London or anywhere else in the world. Why are you supporting evil? What's the story? Do you really believe

that human beings need to be tortured? Civilians, pregnant women? Old people with dementia with the caretakers with their medication, people who have done only good?[12]

In the meantime, the IDF's Yahalom Engineering Unit, after taking an active part in combat over the first two weeks of the war, focused on recovering explosives and collecting Hamas weapons left in Israeli territory. For example, in the area of Kisufim, a children's school bag was found containing a remotely activated explosive device weighing about seven kilograms. As part of the unit's operational activity, over 1,000 weapons of various types, approximately 2,000 grenades, 1,000 RPG rockets of various types, and 1,200 explosive devices were collected to date.[13]

On October 23, the same day that an additional fourteen trucks loaded with humanitarian aid entered Gaza, Galei Tzahal, the IDF radio station, reported that Washington informed Israel that it intended to send additional American forces to the Middle East, ahead of the expected ground incursion, due to concerns that Iranian attacks against US forces in the area would increase. Israeli sources clarified that this was not the only reason for the delay. Among the other reasons were increasing the forces' operational preparedness and an attempt to do as much as possible—including, potentially, prisoner swaps—to free the hostages prior to a ground incursion. The sources also said that Israel had a clear interest in the United States sending additional forces to the region, since it would help the shared effort to fight off attacks on the various fronts which might escalate tensions during the next stages of the war.[14]

Iran stepped up its threats against Israel. IRGC deputy commander-in-chief Ali Fadavi warned that "if it is necessary" and the order is given, Iran would strike the northern city of Haifa "without hesitation." He also claimed that the IDF was lying about Israel's Iron Dome air defense system's highly successful interception rate, claiming it to be just thirty per cent against enemy rockets. "America created Israel for its security, and if it feels insecure, it will easily sacrifice it," Fadavi added. Tasnim News in Tehran reported that Foreign Minister Amin-Abdollahian "discussed and exchanged opinions" with Hamas's Ismail Haniyeh on the latest developments related to "the continuous aggression of the Zionist regime in the Gaza Strip." They spoke about "all the ways to stop the brutal crimes committed by the enemy in Gaza."[15]

Maj.-Gen. (res.) Yaakov Amidror, former head of Israel's National Security Council (2011–2013), would have none of this. Ground forces would have to be brought in to eliminate Hamas's military capability, he insisted in an interview with the *Jerusalem Post* on October 20, however much it would be a very complex operation. "Quite a few losses" would ensue, but Israel had "no choice." As for the humanitarian angle, he observed, the British did not ask themselves any questions when they bombed Germany in World War II, nor when recently giving weapons to the Ukrainians about the Russian cities being hit by the ammunition that the West provided. (He could have added the joint Anglo-American air forces' fire-bombing of Dresden on February 13–15, 1945.) With Hamas using Palestinians in Gaza as human shields and doing everything to harm our citizens, Amidror concluded, Israel had to "behave as in war, and in war we do not worry about the needs of the enemy population. Don't abuse it, and try not to hurt it, but in the end the aim should be clear."[16]

Nitzana Darshan Leitner, founder and president of the Israeli NGO Shurat HaDin Law Center, filed a complaint ("communication") with the Chief Prosecutor of the International Criminal Court (ICC), urging Karim A. A. Kahn to carry out a criminal investigation against the Hamas and Palestinian Islamic Jihad leaders who had planned and executed the brutal massacre in Israeli villages and towns on October 7, 2023. Shurat HaDin also demanded that the Prosecutor urgently issue international arrest warrants against the terrorist leaders. It blamed the two organizations for committing grave War Crimes and Crimes against Humanity during the "Sukkot Massacre" of October 7, attributing to them more than twenty-six different counts of violations of the 2015 "Rome Statute"—the constitution of the ICC—and in complete violation of the Geneva Conventions. In her words, "since the Holocaust, we have not seen such a terrible carnage against Jews." "The ICC," she added, "itself bears responsibility for the carnage. From the beginning, it has acted prejudicially and proved completely biased against Israel." From 2014 onwards, Shurat HaDin had filed "numerous complaints to the ICC Prosecutor. All were ignored. Only anti-Israel complaints got any attention." She closed: "If the ICC ignores this massacre, it has no right to exist."[17]

Amnesty International argued, *per contra*, that the ICC had to investigate Israel's continued deadly aerial bombings against Palestinians in Gaza "as war crimes." The UK-based rights group claimed that it had "documented unlawful Israeli attacks, including indiscriminate attacks," and described Israel's actions on Gaza as a "cataclysmic assault." Its researchers had spoken with survivors and eyewitnesses, analyzed satellite imagery, and verified photos and videos to investigate air bombardments carried out by Israeli forces on October 7–12. "Testimonies from eyewitnesses and survivors highlighted, again and again, how Israeli attacks decimated Palestinian families, causing such destruction that surviving relatives have little but rubble to remember their loved ones by," declared Agnès Callamard, Amnesty International's Secretary General.[18]

Come October 23, the IDF's air and ground forces had increased their joint training of varying scenarios for the upcoming invasion of Gaza. Despite an extensive delay of the invasion into the third week of the war, all signals from top IDF officials that Monday indicated that the invasion was not a question of if, but a question of when. IDF sources declared that the Iron Dome's success in intercepting rockets had given Israel more time to work with in order to select whatever moment its political echelon chose to invade. According to the IDF, both mandatory service and reservist soldiers remained in a state of high motivation, and the current drills were high-quality interweaving of infantry, tanks, artillery, and aerial forces. In addition to ongoing training, the IDF announced that it had handed out another 10,000 bulletproof vests to reservists, although it was unclear what the pace would be and if there would be enough for all 360,000 reservists (taking into account that many reservists were not in combat or not in the infantry).[19]

A ground invasion of Gaza loomed. Airstrikes were ramped up in the northern part of the Strip to ensure a safer entry for Israeli forces. Dozens of Hamas members were killed, including two Nukhba members and Mohammed Qatmash, whom the Israeli military said was responsible for rocket fire from the central part of Gaza. Further, the IDF conducted a first operation just across the Gaza border fence near the southern community of Kisufim, looking for bodies of missing Israelis and to clear the area for the ground offensive. On October 23, Kibbutz Nir Eliyahu's nineteen-year-old Cpl. Tamir Barak of the Combat Engineering Corps was killed and three others hurt near the border from a Hamas anti-tank guided missile. Israeli troops responded by shelling the terror cell. Elsewhere, in addition to the evacuation of 24,000 residents from Kiryat Shmona in the north and twenty-eight border-area villages during the past week, the Defense Ministry now added fourteen more communities to the evacuation roster.[20]

Photos of those Israelis abducted or missing were placed on all vacant seats in a special cargo El Al flight from New York to Tel Aviv. Overnight on October 24, Hamas released "on humanitarian grounds" another two hostages, Israelis Yocheved Lifschitz (85) and Nurit Cooper (79) through the mediation efforts of Egypt and Qatar. Their husbands remained in captivity. The older of the two grandmothers, together with husband Oded in Kibbutz Nir Oz, where of 427 people 40 were murdered and 79 abducted in the Hamas attack, had for more than a decade helped sick Palestinians in Gaza get from the Erez border crossing to Israeli hospitals for treatment. Invading Nir Oz, the terrorists had first set fire to all the cars so that no one could escape, then sabotaged the water supply so that residents could not put out the flames. The orgy of cruelty, including plunder and burning of houses, then began.[21]

The same day, Andrew Tobin revealed in the *Washington Free Beacon* that, while heavily armed Hamas terrorists in uniform carried out the massacre on October 7, a mob of Palestinian civilians, "ordinary Gazans" in everyday clothing, spontaneously joined in. Videos, eyewitness, and confirmation by IDF spokesman Jonathan Conricus corroborated that young men, some armed with knives, joined by teenagers, a few young boys, and older males and some women, including individuals who had worked in these kibbutzim, created a second wave of carnage. Their looting, burning, raping, killing, and kidnapping hostages rivaled the Hamas atrocities. Laughing and religious rallying cries of "*Allahu Akbar*" ("God is most great") were heard regularly. Videos also showed Palestinians cheering, hitting, and spitting on the raped, half-naked body of the twenty-three-year-old Shani Louk as the dead woman was paraded on a pick-up truck like a trophy through Gaza. The body of this Israeli of German parentage, along with those of Itzhak Gelerenter (53) and Amit Buskila (28), would be found in Gaza on May 17, 2024, in a joint IDF-Shin Bet operation prompted by intelligence that emerged from interrogations of Palestinians detained there. The three Israelis had been at the Nova rave and ran to the Mefalsim Junction, where they were murdered by Hamas terrorists.[22]

Survivors of the murderous attack, most formerly to be found on Israel's political left and longtime peace activists such as mayor of the Eshkol Regional Council Gadi Yarkoni, who lost both legs in a mortar attack during the country's 2014 Gaza war and survived in his house's safe room in Kibbutz Nirim on October 7, now arrived at a new consensus: "Coexistence is dead, and Gaza must be crushed." Kibbutz Be'eri's Yaniv Hegyi, chairman of the Kibbutz Movement leadership who was involved over the years in initiatives to foster dialogue and ties with the residents of Gaza, also came to a radical shift in thought: "After what happened, I understood once and for all it is either us or them." He had no desire for revenge. "I just don't want them to be here anymore. They educate their children to hate from infancy."[23]

Hamas leaders publicly expressed a willingness to accept heavy losses—potentially including the deaths of many Gazan civilians living under Hamas rule. "Will we have to pay a price? Yes, and we are ready to pay it," Ghazi Hamad, a member of the Hamas politburo, told Beirut's LCBI television in an interview aired on October 24. "We are called a nation of martyrs, and we are proud to sacrifice martyrs."[24]

Meanwhile, the IDF continued to plan how to deal with the Hamas network of 1,300 tunnels, spanning approximately five hundred kilometers in total, with some located many meters underground. Apart from the underground facility network of North Korea, Hamas operated what is estimated to be the world's largest tunnel network known as "the Gaza Metro," built with 50,000 tons of cement that Israel had approved passage into the Strip for hospitals, schools, and housing. In East Jerusalem, Border Police arrested five Arabs who took part in violent riots, while thirty-two wanted terrorists were arrested in the West Bank by the IDF and the Shin Bet. "Our fighters are prepared and determined," IDF spokesperson Hagari stated in an address to the nation the next morning, saying, "Long weeks of fighting lie ahead, we will act at the most appropriate time" in the army's invasion of Gaza to combat Hamas.[25]

Global attention focused on the plight of the close to 5,000 Palestinians in Gaza who had been killed due to IDF aerial bombing of the Strip and the failed Palestinian rocket launches. Humanitarian aid trucks entered Gaza through Egypt's Rafah Crossing for the third successive day on October 23 as the European Union foreign ministers discussed in Luxembourg the need for a pause in the fighting between the IDF and Hamas. "Now, the most important thing is for humanitarian support to go into Gaza," European Union foreign envoy Josep Borrell told reporters on arrival in Luxembourg.[26]

While some families of the Israeli hostages arrived at the United Nations to seek the release of their loved ones, UN Secretary-General António Guterres accused Israel of violating international law in its retaliation against Hamas, and called for an immediate truce that would leave the terrorist organization in power. On October 24, just when French President Emmanuel Macron called during a brief visit to Israel for an international coalition against Hamas, Guterres declared in a UN Security Council meeting devoted to the Gaza conflict that he had "condemned unequivocally the horrifying and unprecedented October 7 act of terror by Hamas in Israel," its launching of rockets against civilian targets and the taking of hostages. Yet the attack "did not appear in a vacuum," the Palestinian people having been subjected to fifty-six years of "suffocating occupation," their lands "steadily devoured by settlements and plagued by violence, their economies stifled, their people displaced, and their homes demolished. Their hopes for a political solution to their plight have been vanishing." Guterres closed: "To ease epic suffering, make the delivery of aid easier and safer, and facilitate the release of hostages, I reiterate my appeal for an immediate humanitarian ceasefire."[27]

The Israeli ambassador to the UN, Gilad Erdan, lost no time in responding. Guterres's "shocking speech" while rockets were being fired at all of Israel, he began, proved "conclusively, beyond any doubt, that the Secretary-General is completely disconnected from the reality in our region and that he views the massacre committed by Nazi [sic] Hamas terrorists in a distorted and immoral manner." To declare that the attacks by Hamas did not happen in a vacuum "expressed an understanding for terrorism and murder. It's really unfathomable. It's truly sad [sic] that the head of an organization that arose after the Holocaust holds such horrible views. A tragedy!" Benny Gantz, the National Unity Party opposition leader and former Defense Minister, now serving with Netanyahu and Gallant in Israel's new wartime security cabinet, went further: "The days when the UN Secretary-General supports terrorism are dark days for the world. There is no way to justify a massacre of innocent civilians. Anyone who is not on the right side of history will be judged by it. Anyone who justifies terrorism is not fit to speak for the world." Israeli Foreign Minister Eli Cohen announced that he would boycott Guterres and refuse to meet with him, saying that "after October 7 there is no room for a balanced approach. Hamas must be erased from the world!"[28]

Jordan's foreign minister countered in that session that Israel "appeared" to be above international law, and he urged an end to "double standards" in dealing with the Gaza conflict. In remarks after the United Nations Security Council meeting that did not call for an end to hostilities, Ayman Safadi added that the international community had an obligation to end Israel's war "against Palestinians" in Gaza.[29]

For his part, Iran's UN ambassador, Amir Saeid Iravani, criticized Antony Blinken, after the US Secretary of State warned Iran or its proxies against attacking US personnel. Speaking in the Security Council, he warned: "Don't throw fuel on the fire." Responding to Blinken directly, Iravani claimed that the Secretary of State had attempted to wrongly blame Iran for the Israel-Hamas conflict, and he added that Tehran categorically rejected his "groundless allegations." "Our commitment to regional peace and stability remains unwavering," Iravani declared: "The U.S. has further exacerbated the conflict by overtly aligning itself with the aggressor at the expense of the innocent Palestinian population." Iran's Supreme Leader, Ayatollah Ali Khamenei, repeated his original denial of any Iranian involvement in the Hamas attack.[30]

The same day, senior Hamas leader Mashal said that the Israeli civilians whom Hamas had abducted on October 7 would be freed if Israel stopped attacking targets in Gaza associated with Hamas. In an interview with the UK's Sky News, he declared that civilians were not killed by its military wing al-Qassam Brigades, and that any Israeli civilian deaths that had been caused by Hamas were not intended (sic!). Mashaal refused to refer to the civilians taken to Gaza as "hostages," and claimed that at least twenty-two of those captured were killed by Israeli airstrikes on Gaza. "If Netanyahu was keen on their safety, if the Europeans and the Americans are keen on their safety," he declared, "let them force Israel to stop its aggression, to stop this genocide, these brutal war crimes that are committed every day." "Let them stop this aggression and you will find the mediators like Qatar and Egypt and some Arab countries and others will find a way to have them released and we will send them to their homes."[31]

This Reuters report came the same day that Chief of Staff Halevi stated that "the IDF is ready for maneuvering, and we will make a decision together with the political echelon regarding the essence and timing of the next step," the ground assault into Gaza. "At this stage there are tactical and strategic considerations that allow us more time to improve and use every minute to be even more prepared. On the other hand, every minute that passes on the other side, we attack the enemy more, kill his operatives, kill his commanders, destroy his infrastructure, and gather more intelligence for what's to come." The goals of the war as defined for us by the Israeli government remained "the dissolution of Hamas, the restoration of security to the residents of Israel, and an utmost effort to free the kidnapped and return them home." Halevi went on: "We will never forget the children who were murdered, the women who were separated from their husbands, and the atrocities. We are taking these images with us to the battlefield, we are determined, and we will do it like warriors. We also remember and fight mainly because we know there is a purpose—this is our country, our home, and we will defend it in any way." Ending, he stressed that "this war has one address—the leadership of Hamas and everyone who acted under their command, they will pay the price for what they carried out."[32]

However, a day before Meshaal's interview, two Israeli officials had told the US news website Axios that Israel was willing to delay the invasion into Gaza in order to allow talks on Hamas's releasing a large number of hostages. Israel told Egyptian mediators that Hamas had to release all its women and children hostages for any kind of deal, the report said. The next day, the IDF dropped leaflets in the Gaza Strip stating that Palestinian civilians who had information on any hostages would be rewarded with cash and safety if they disclosed the details. It urged Gazan civilians to contact them through WhatsApp, Telegram, or through a secured line, for those in fear of repercussions by Hamas.[33]

On October 23, following several hours of quiet, Hamas resumed massive rocket fire on Tel Aviv, and on Israel's center and south. Ten terrorists were killed in waters off the shore of the southern Gaza border town of Zikim after attempting to infiltrate into Israel. The IDF struck infrastructure belonging to the Syrian Army, including mortar launchers, in response to rocket fire earlier in the evening toward Israel. Syrian media reported that the strikes targeted a radar site near Qarfa in the Daraa region of southern Syria and warehouses of the 12th Armored Brigade in Izraa in Daraa. Early the next morning, four Palestinians were killed and eleven others were injured in a strike conducted by the IDF in the Jenin refugee camp. The IDF announced that the drone strike was carried out after armed terrorists had fired and threw explosives at Israeli forces operating there. At least one of those killed in the strike was a member of the Palestinian Islamic Jihad.[34]

Iran-backed militias across the region upped their threats against Israel and the United States with several rocket and drone attacks targeting American forces in Syria and Iraq. Alwiyat al-Waad al-Haq, an Iran-backed militia believed to be linked to the Iraqi Kataib Hezbollah militia, threatened to target bases where American forces were housed in Kuwait and the United Arab Emirates in response to the Hamas-Israel war and "after the persistence of the Zionist entity and its supporters in exterminating our people in steadfast Palestine." That militia had claimed attacks against Gulf states in the past, although most drone and missile attacks in recent years toward Saudi Arabia and the United Arab Emirates (UAE) had been claimed by the Iran-backed Houthi militia in Yemen, which also threatened to enter Hamas's war against Israel. The *USS Carney* shot down four Houthi missiles over the Red Sea, while the fifth missile was shot down by Saudi Arabia in order to protect its airspace.[35]

Two dozen American military personnel were wounded the previous week in a series of drone attacks at US bases in Iraq and Syria, US Central Command (CENTCOM) told NBC News on October 23. Pentagon Press Secretary Air Force Brig. Gen. Pat Ryder stated that, on October 17–24, US and coalition forces had been attacked at least ten times in Iraq and three times in Syria by suicide drones and rockets. The Pentagon also announced on October 24 that a squadron of F-16 fighter jets had arrived in the US CENTCOM area of responsibility in light of the increased tensions in the Middle East. The United States sent a THAAD battery and Patriot missile battalions to the region as well.[36]

The United States will provide Israel with Iron Dome air defense systems from its stocks, a senior defense official said the same Tuesday. The escalation of US support came after the Biden administration's announcement the previous week that it would send Israel interceptor missiles which could be fired from its existing Iron Dome systems. White House National Security Council spokesman John Kirby declared that "a cease-fire right now really only benefits Hamas," although he added that the United States did support temporary "humanitarian pauses" to help get aid in, and civilians out, of Gaza. "That is not the same as saying a cease-fire," Kirby told reporters, adding that the difference was "a question of duration and scope and size."[37]

And the total of victims on both sides continued to mount. On day eighteen of the war, Palestinian authorities stated that Israeli strikes had killed at least 5,791 people in Gaza and wounded more than 16,200. Israeli authorities announced that more than 1,400 people had been murdered in Israel and more than 5,400 injured since the Hamas attack on October 7. At least thirty-two US nationals, they added, were among those killed.[38]

Turkish President Recep Tayyip Erdoğan, in a charged speech to his party's lawmakers in parliament on October 25, declared that Hamas was "a liberation group" waging a battle to protect its land. He urged an immediate cease-fire, said that Muslim countries must act together for lasting peace, and called on world powers to pressure Israel to halt attacks. The Rafah border gate must be kept open for humanitarian aid and prisoner exchanges should be concluded urgently. Calling on the Palestinian people to unite for a two-state solution, he suggested that Arab states should provide moral and financial support for this. Italy's deputy prime minister, Antonio Tajani, condemned the words of Erdoğan about Hamas, defining them as "grave and disgusting."[39]

That day, the *Wall Street Journal*, citing American and Israeli officials, reported that Israel had agreed to a US request to delay its expected ground offensive in the Gaza Strip so that air defenses could be put in place to protect American troops in the region. According to this report, the Pentagon was scrambling to deploy nearly a dozen air-defense systems to the region, including for US troops serving in Iraq, Syria, Kuwait, Jordan, Saudi Arabia, and the UAE, to protect them from missiles and rockets. Israel was also taking into account in its war planning the effort to supply humanitarian aid to civilians inside Gaza, as well as diplomatic efforts to free more of the hostages held by Hamas. US officials stated that their troops were of paramount concern, since the military command believed that American forces would be targeted by various militant groups once the IDF incursion into Gaza began. According to these sources, thirteen attacks using drones and missiles had already occurred in Iraq and Syria, resulting in the death of one American contractor and the destruction of a US drone. At least two dozen troops were injured in Syria and another ten in Iraq, nearly all of them minor.[40]

In the same issue, the *Wall Street Journal* reported that in the weeks leading up to October 7, some 500 members of Hamas and Palestinian Islamic Jihad "received specialized combat training in Iran." The training was overseen by officers of the Quds Force, the external operations arm of Iran's Islamic Revolutionary Guard Corps. "Senior Palestinian officials and Iranian Brig. Gen. Esmail Qaani, the head of the Quds Force, also attended." Oddly, the Biden administration's spokespeople continued to claim that "a growing body of evidence" existed showing that "neither Hezbollah nor Iran helped plan such a major attack by Hamas."[41]

That Wednesday night, Biden and Netanyahu held yet another telephone conversation, where the American president discussed ongoing US support for the continuous flow of humanitarian support to the civilian population in Gaza, and he welcomed efforts to increase this support over the coming period. Biden reiterated that Israel "has every right and responsibility to defend its citizens from terrorism and to do so in a manner consistent with international humanitarian law." According to the White House release, he also noted the importance of focusing on what would come after this crisis to include "a pathway for a permanent peace" between Israelis and Palestinians, "emphasizing that Hamas does not represent the Palestinian people or their legitimate aspirations." To a reporter's question, Biden expressed "no confidence" in the Hamas-run Gaza Health Ministry's claim of over 6,500 dead. Speaking the same evening to the Israeli public, Netanyahu emphasized that the elimination of Hamas remained Israel's overriding objective, with investigations to follow thereafter of accountability for the initial military/intelligence failure of October 7. For the first time since that tragic day, he included himself among those who would have to "provide answers" for the disaster.[42]

British Defense Secretary Grant Shapps also defended Israel's "right to go after" the Hamas terrorists. A cease-fire he thought "untenable," but then added that "a pause" could "assist with the international humanitarian situation." While noting Israeli wounded from the war to have passed 5,400, the IDF did accede to an additional convoy of fourteen trucks bearing food, water, and medicines to reach Gaza, for a total of seventy-four since the war began. It continued to deny fuel deliveries, however, showing aerial footage that Hamas storage tanks contained 500,000 liters of fuel which had been intended for the use of the Gazan population.[43]

The United States and Russia faced off at a meeting of the UN Security Council on October 25, with each vetoing resolutions on the Hamas-Israel war put forward by the other. Russia and China accused the United States of being out of step with global sentiment by not calling for an explicit cease-fire. President Biden's administration continued to reject such calls, although Secretary of State Blinken said the previous day that the United States supported the idea of "humanitarian pauses" in the fighting. "In charges and countercharges reminiscent of Cold War debates and more recent discord over Ukraine," wrote senior national security correspondent for the *Washington Post* Karen DeYoung, Moscow and Washington charged each other with bad faith, political posturing and pushing their own positions on other council members without consultation. The principal difference between the competing resolutions was Washington's call for "all measures, specifically to include humanitarian pauses," to allow aid to flow into Gaza—a position it had rejected as recently as the previous week and with no specific mention of ongoing Israeli airstrikes—against Moscow's call for a complete cease-fire. Both the US and Russian resolutions condemned Hamas and called for the immediate release of its Israeli and foreign hostages inside Gaza. Both also called for a long-term resolution of the Israeli-Palestinian struggle in accordance with previous UN resolutions mandating a "two-state solution."[44]

Hamas had its advocates within its clerical world. Gaza Islamic University professor Saleh al-Raqab, a former minister in the Hamas government of religious affairs and endowments, expressed his prayerful hope in an article on October 8 that Allah would enable the Hamas attackers "to kill the soldiers of the Jews, destroy the weapons of the Jews, and capture Jewish soldiers. O Allah, destroy the Jews completely. Paralyze their limbs and freeze the blood in their veins." On October 21, the Istanbul-based Palestine Scholars Association in the Diaspora published a *fatwa* permitting *jihad* against the Zionists as "one of the main obligations of our religion," with the stated goal being to free the Al-Aqsa Mosque and repel Zionists from "the Islamic country of Palestine." That *fatwa* ruling quoted verse 5.82 from the Qur'an, that stated "You will find that the most bitter enemies of Muslims are the Jews and the polytheists." In another *fatwa*, it lashed out at Muslim countries that had normalized relations with Israel, stipulating that normalization agreements were void and entailed no obligations.[45]

As the war entered its third week, the stance of the major political adversaries sharpened. Moscow received a Hamas delegation that wished to thank Russian President Vladimir Putin for his support, while Foreign Minister Wang Yi of China declared Israel's actions "beyond the scope of self-defense"—without naming Hamas in his comments. On the other side of the widening divide, the United States and Qatar, which had agreed two weeks earlier not to release to Tehran the $6 billion in Iranian assets frozen in sanctions by the administration of President Donald Trump, now announced that Qatar would "revisit" its relationship with Hamas once the crisis of the hostages were successfully resolved. Biden and Macron separately pushed for a two-state solution after the end of the Gaza war. The US House of Representatives, by a vote of 412–10, passed a resolution standing with Israel "as it defends itself against the barbaric war launched by Hamas and other terrorists," and prepared to assist Israel "with emergency resupply and other security, diplomatic, and intelligence support." Givati Brigade infantry and Israeli tanks briefly entered Gaza, the IDF saying that the raid was in preparation for the "next stage of combat" in invading the enclave, and adding that it had struck more than 7,000 Hamas targets in Gaza since October 7.[46]

The war grinded on. On October 26, the European Council called for "corridors and pauses" for humanitarian aid in the Gaza Strip, while also once again condemning Hamas for its terrorist attacks against Israel, its use of civilians as human shields "a particularly deplorable atrocity." The foreign ministers of the United Arab Emirates, Jordan, Bahrain, Saudi Arabia, Oman, Qatar, Kuwait, Egypt, and Morocco condemned the targeting of civilians and violations of international law in Gaza. US jet fighter airstrikes on October 26 against two facilities in eastern Syria used by Iran's IRGC and other groups it supported came after a week in which American and coalition troops had been attacked at least nineteen times in Iraq and in Syria by Iran-backed forces.[47]

That evening, even as Israel announced that 310 IDF soldiers had died in the war, IDF jets killed Shadi Barud, the Deputy Head of Hamas's Intelligence Directorate, who was responsible for planning the October 7 massacre together with Yahya Sinwar. A heavy barrage of Hamas rockets shook Central Israel, with red sirens sounded in Tel Aviv, Petach Tikva, and a few other cities. By then, the IDF had arrested around 1,000 Palestinians in the West Bank, 660 affiliated with Hamas. In Moscow, Hamas officials in Russia declared that no release of hostages could occur until a cease-fire was in place. President Biden on Thursday reiterated his commitment to secure the release of all the hostages being held by Hamas in the Gaza Strip: "We will not stop until we get them home."[48]

Paying tribute to the hostages, two singers from the Israeli Opera offered a rendition of "Bring Him Home" from the timeless Broadway musical *Les Misérables*. In a video that went viral, mezzo-soprano Anat Czarny and baritone Oded Reich performed in an empty theater in Tel Aviv. The video also showed short clips of some of the children who were kidnapped and held in Gaza, along with captions like "first time saying my name," and "first time meeting my brother."[49]

On October 27, Hezbollah Secretary-General Hassan Nasrallah made a public announcement for the first time since the outbreak of the war, together with Hamas deputy leader Saleh al-Arouri and leader of the Palestinian Islamic Jihad, Ziyad al-Nakhalah. Nasrallah also sent a letter to the units of his organization stating that every terrorist killed from October 7 should be given the title "Martyr on the way to Jerusalem." After this tripartite meeting of the leaders of the terrorist organizations, Hezbollah announced that a discussion was held on the ways "to achieve the real victory of the resistance in Gaza and Palestine and to stop the aggression in Gaza and the West Bank." The three also said that they would continue "the constant coordination and monitoring of all developments on a daily and regular basis." Six days earlier, the Islamic Republic-affiliated Press TV had reported that Nasrallah met with Amir-Abdollahian in

Beirut, where they, along with leaders of Hamas and Palestinian Islamic Jihad, emphasized the need for the "liberation of Palestine from Israeli occupation."[50]

That evening, the IDF launched a large-scale ground and naval incursion into Gaza with two large divisions, the 36th and the 162nd. Just before leading the charge with their sixty-ton Merkava IV tanks, the commander of Brigade 401's 46th Battalion made the Sabbath evening *kiddush* and stated that his soldiers "shall never forget what happened here in Israel on October 7 and that we cannot let history repeat itself." Aided by airstrikes, army forces destroyed additional Hamas targets, what Defense Minister Gallant called "a new phase," and the IDF warned northern Gaza residents that the area was now "a battlefield." In interrogation, a Hamas prisoner confirmed the IDF's contention that a number of "underground levels" of Shifa Hospital in Gaza City were chosen to serve as the group's main headquarters, believing that Israel would not target Gaza's largest hospital.[51]

In central London, 100,000 pro-Palestinian demonstrators marched under signs "Free Palestine" to demand the UK government call for a cease-fire. Similar Gaza-support rallies were held in Germany, Indonesia, Pakistan, France, Italy, Norway, and Switzerland. As more international voices and a UN majority vote (the Jordan-sponsored resolution did not mention Hamas) called for a humanitarian truce in Gaza, eighty-four aid trucks had entered the Strip via the Rafah crossing to date. Meeting with families of Israelis abducted to Gaza, Netanyahu stated that the government's efforts to rescue the hostages continued "all the time." Rocket barrages targeted northern and southern Israel throughout the day. The United States deployed its second aircraft carrier strike group, the USS *Eisenhower*, in the Mediterranean, further bolstering its military presence amid concerns of an escalating conflict with Iran and Hezbollah.[52]

On October 28, hours after the IDF's ground invasion of Gaza had begun, the Israeli government's war cabinet decided to allow the opening of an additional water line to the southern Gaza Strip. Claiming that the decision would give legitimacy to the continuation of the military operation in the northern area, it added that on the day after the war Israel would be completely disconnected from the Strip. While Hamas worked to prevent civilians from moving to the south, this move was meant to give a message to residents to leave for that safer area, to distance themselves from the battlefields, and to go to places where they could find humanitarian needs such as water. In the meanwhile, Israel's National Center of Forensic Medicine continued to grapple with its most profound challenge ever: identifying as quickly as possible a vast number of bodies from the October 7 deadly infiltration, some in a state that made identification extremely difficult.[53]

The same day, in the latest warning issued by the Islamic Republic since the start of the Hamas-Israel conflict, Iranian President Ebrahim Raisi said that Israel's ongoing bombardment of Gaza "may force everyone" to act. "The crimes of the Zionist regime have crossed the red lines, and this may force everyone to take action," Raisi wrote on X (formerly the Twitter social networking site). "Washington asks us to not do anything, but they keep giving widespread support to Israel." In fact, a US Marine rapid response force moved toward the eastern Mediterranean Sea, two officials told CNN on Sunday, amid concerns over the war in Gaza broadening into a regional conflict. The 26th Marine Expeditionary Unit, aboard the *USS Bataan* amphibious assault ship, which had been operating in the waters of the Middle East in recent weeks, began making its way toward the Suez Canal late the previous week. In Istanbul, President Erdoğan, addressing several thousand people on the eve of the Turkish Republic's centenary, accused Israel of committing war crimes and denounced it as "an occupier, an invader."[54]

In Makhachkala, the capital of the republic of Dagestan in southern Russia with a population of 3.2 million, Muslim rioters came to the international airport in order to harm Jewish Israelis. The crowds of this predominantly Muslim region, which has approximately 1,200 Jews, waited for an Israeli flight that was supposed to arrive and checked vehicles leaving the airport to try and find Israeli or Jewish passengers. Footage from the scene showed crowds shouting "*Allahu Akbar*," and also antisemitic chants. The flight, which took off from Ben Gurion International Airport in Israel and was scheduled to land in Makhachkala, was rerouted and landed at a different airport.[55]

Earlier that day, more than 3,500 pro-Palestinian protesters shut down the Brooklyn Bridge during a march from Brooklyn to Manhattan, demanding an end to "Zionist genocide" and calling for "Free Palestine" with placards reading "By any means necessary." This and similar mass demonstrations did not call for Hamas to stop firing rockets at Israelis, and none pleaded for the immediate release of the captives held by Hamas in Gaza or condemned the barbarity of Hamas's invasion three weeks earlier.[56]

On October 29, according to the IDF, rockets were launched from Lebanon to the upper and western Galilee several times, setting off sirens in towns including Kiryat Shmona, Nahariya, Shlomi, Tuba-Zangariyye, Rosh Pina, Ayelet HaShahar, and Hatzor HaGlilit. The IDF said that it had struck two Hezbollah terror cells in southern Lebanon preparing to carry out anti-tank guided missile attacks against northern Israel. It declared that six Israeli soldiers, at least forty-eight Hezbollah gunmen, and eight Palestinian gunmen had been killed in the recent exchanges. Amidst the repeated attacks from Lebanon, the military evacuated forty-two border communities and the city of Kiryat

Shmona. In all, some 200,000 Israelis had been displaced from the south and the north since the war began. Facing the grave threat of Hamas tunnels, the IDF's highly advanced AI-led target bank helped soldiers target and destroy 150 of them in one day. As for humanitarian aid to Gaza, thirty-three trucks entered the Strip, the largest number to date.[57]

The fourth week of the war began with sirens sounding in the Israeli border area near Gaza, in Be'er Sheva, and nearby Ofakim, as well as in Jerusalem and surrounding towns. Thousands who attended the funeral in Har Herzl of Armored Corps reservist Sgt.-Maj. Yinon Fleischman of the 71st Battalion, whose tank flipped over in northern Israel, dropped to the ground for cover. The IDF, while reaching the main Gaza highway, Salah al-Din Road, that goes north and south through the twenty-five-mile enclave, also rescued female soldier nineteen-year-old Pvt. Ori Megidish of Kiryat Gat, the first person abducted in the Hamas attack, near the Al-Shati refugee camp not far from Shifa Hospital, Hamas's headquarters. Gaza witnessed fierce clashes as Israeli forces expanded their offensive with troops backed by tanks, air and artillery strikes, killing scores of Hamas gunmen. Germany called on Israel to protect Palestinians in the West Bank; IDF spokesperson Hagari declared that the international community bore responsibility for the safe return of the Gaza hostages. Hagari also said that the IDF was continuing to operate against terrorists in Judea and Samaria, and that over 700 Hamas operatives had been arrested in that region since the start of hostilities.

The twenty-fifth day of the war witnessed a growth in the intensity of the IDF's military operations in Gaza. While red sirens warning of incoming Hamas and Hezbollah rockets and missiles reverberated across central Israel, as well as cities in the south and north, Israeli troops engaged in fierce battles deep in Gaza itself. Along with the IDF reporting dozens of Hamas terrorists killed, including top commanders, 300 additional targets were struck overnight. A Houthi surface-to-surface missile attack on the resort town of Eilat near the Red Sea was foiled in the morning, the IDF using the Arrow aerial defense system for the first time. Israeli UN envoy Gilad Erdan announced that until the UN condemned Hamas for its barbaric assault on Israeli civilians, he and his team would as a "symbol of pride" don the yellow star, which the Nazi regime had compelled Jews to wear, along with the words "Never again."[58]

Sending a message to the soldiers with boots on the ground in Gaza, IDF Southern Commanding Officer Finkelman declared that the fighting would be long and hard, yet "we have one goal—victory!" Rejecting a cease-fire as "surrender to Hamas, to terrorism," Netanyahu declared to foreign journalists that "today we draw a line between the forces of civilization and the forces of barbarism. It is a time for everyone to decide where they stand." FBI Director

Christopher A. Wray stated during a hearing of the Senate Homeland Security and Government Affairs Committee that Hamas posed the greatest domestic threat which the United States had faced since ISIS, and that while Jews accounted for less than two percent of the population, around sixty percent of religious-based hate crimes targeted Jews. Testifying before the same hearing, Secretary Blinken agreed with Netanyahu's stand "at this time" because such a cease-fire would "simply consolidate what Hamas has been able to do and allow it to remain where it is and potentially allow it to repeat."[59]

That night, the IDF announced the deaths of Sergeants Ro'i Wolf and Lavi Lipshitz of the Givati Brigade, both twenty years old, the first two to be killed in the northern Gaza campaign. Thirteen additional soldiers were named some hours later, including Givati Second Lieutenant Pedaya Mark, whose father was murdered in a shooting attack by a Hamas operative on Route 60 near the Hebron Hills on July 1, 2016, and whose cousin, Elhanan Kalmanson, was killed in the first days of fighting in the south. For its part, the Gaza Health Ministry announced that more than 8,000 Palestinians had died from Israeli air attacks.[60]

And the hostages held by Hamas? Their fate continued to remain unknown. For their families, a paralyzing awareness that time might be running out was palpable. Of the thirty-two child hostages, the youngest was Kfir Bibas, who had just started crawling and was now ten months old, from Nir Oz. His father Yarden, mother Shiri, and four-year-old brother Ariel were somewhere in Gaza. The mother's parents had been burned alive by the terrorist invaders, whose attackers killed or kidnapped one in four of those living in that kibbutz on October 7. In some cases, three generations were held in Hamas's vast warren of terror tunnels, their condition a mystery.[61]

During the Yom Kippur War of 1973, 314 Israelis had been held hostage by Egypt and Syria.[62] But those were soldiers, trained for such a scenario and better prepared for the brutal conditions of life in captivity. Furthermore, Hamas with its uncompromising jihadist ideology differed markedly from those enemies of the past. As the last day of October drew to a close, no definitive end to the war appeared in sight.

Endnotes

1. CBS, Oct. 26. 2023; UN News, Oct. 23, 2023; AP, 22, 2023.
2. *Times of Israel*, Oct. 21, 2023; BBC, Oct. 21, 2023; Human Rights Watch, Oct. 21, 2023.
3. Reuters, Oct. 21, 2023; CNN, Oct. 21, 2023.
4. JNS, Oct. 22, 2023; *Times of Israel*, Oct. 22, 2023.
5. *Jerusalem Post*, Oct. 23, 2023.
6. JNS, Oct. 23, 2023.
7. *Times of Israel*, Oct. 30, 2023; *Jerusalem Post*, Oct. 24, 2023.

8   Ela Levy-Weinrib, "A Turning Point for Arab Israelis," *Globes*, Oct. 22, 2023; Fox News, Oct. 12, 2023.
9   Jewish Telegraphic Agency, Oct.19, 2023; *Times of Israel*, Nov. 5, 2023; AP, Oct. 15, 2023; *Times of Israel*, Oct. 7, 2023; *New York Times*, Dec. 23, 2023. After the close of Yom Kippur on October 5, 1946, the Jewish Agency set up overnight "eleven points"—new settlements (later kibbutzim) with 400 settlers to establish a Zionist presence in the northern Negev. This unprecedented operation was achieved in response to the US-UK Morrison-Grady plan of July 31, 1946, that had cut off the Negev from the proposed semi-autonomous Jewish and Arab states in Palestine under British trusteeship and forbade Jewish settlement there. See Monty Noam Penkower, *Palestine to Israel: Mandate to State, 1945–1948*, vol. 1: *Rebellion Launched* (New York: Touro University Press, 2019), chap. 4. The eleven were Be'eri, Kedma, Gal On, Shoval, Tekuma, Mishmar HaNegev, Nevatim, Hatzerim, Urim, Nirim, and Kfar Darom. Yosef Avidar, *On the Way to Tzahal. Memories* (Hebrew) (Tel Aviv: Ministry of Defense, 1977), chap. 15. Kfar Darom was dismantled as part of the Israeli unilateral disengagement of all military forces and settlements from the Gaza Strip on August 15, 2005.
10 For more information about Natal and EMDR, see their respective websites, https://il.natal.org.il/ and https://wwww.emdr-Israel.org. For survivor stories, see the Instagram account october7_survivor_stories and the website https://www.october7.org.
11 *Algemeiner*, Oct. 27, 2023.
12 Government Press Office, Oct. 23, 2023, https://www.gov.il-news.
13 *Times of Israel*, Oct. 22, 2023.
14 Abdul Raouf Arnaout, "Ground Attack on Gaza Delayed until Arrival of More American Forces: Israeli Army," Anadolu Agency, Oct. 23, 2023, https://www.aa.com.tr/en/middle-east/ground-attack-on-gaza-delayed-until-arrival-of-more-american-forces-israeli-army/3029777.
15 *Jerusalem Post*, Oct. 23, 2023; Foundation for Defense of Democracies, Oct. 24, 2023, https//www.fdd.org.
16 *Jerusalem Post*, Oct. 20, 2023.
17 Israel National News, Oct. 23, 2023.
18 Amnesty.org, Oct. 20, 2023.
19 *Jerusalem Post*, Oct. 23, 2023.
20 *The Week*, Oct. 22, 2023, https://newsbeezer.com; *Times of Israel*, Oct. 22–23, 2023.
21 *Jerusalem Post*, Oct. 24, 2023; *Wall St. Journal*, Oct. 23, 2023; *Israel 21c 16* (2023), https://www.Israel21c.org; *Haaretz*, Apr. 24, 2024. An endless pile of cars, a large number completely burnt, were brought to Kfar Aza. Many of the vehicles in what became known as the "car graveyard" contained remnants of those who had tried to escape Hamas's attack on the Nova music festival. They were subject to deadly ambushes across Road 232, popularly nicknamed "The Death Road." *Jerusalem Post Magazine*, Mar. 1, 2024.
22 *Washington Free Beacon*, Oct. 24, 2023; Free Beacon, LiveJournal, Oct. 24, 2023, https://free-beacom.livejournal.com; *Haaretz*, May 17, 2024. A freelance photojournalist, Ali Mahmud, contributed to the Associated Press (AP) winning first place for the Team Picture Story of the Year in March 2024 for taking a photograph of Shani Louk's corpse as Hamas terrorists were driving it away on October 7, alluding to the photographer's knowledge of the attack beforehand. According to the Pictures of the Year program's website, the category "recognizes the collaborative effort of a photography staff covering a single topic or news story. It is a narrative picture story that consists of images taken as part of a team effort to cover a single issue or news story." *Jerusalem Post*, Mar. 28, 2024.
23 Free Beacon, Oct. 24, 2023, https://freebeacon.com-national-security; *Times of Israel*, Nov. 8, 2023.
24 LCBI interview, Oct. 24, 2023.
25 *Jerusalem Post*, Oct. 24, 2023.
26 CNN, Oct. 24, 2023; *Jerusalem Post*, Oct. 23, 2023.
27 Israel National News, Oct. 24, 2023; Reuters, Oct. 24, 2023.

28 Fox News, Oct. 24, 2023; Israel National News, Oct. 24, 2023.
29 Reuters, Oct. 24, 2023.
30 Reuters, Oct. 24, 2023; *Times of Israel*, Oct. 10, 2023.
31 Sky News, Oct. 24, 2023.
32 Reuters, Oct. 24, 2023.
33 Axios, Oct. 24, 2023, https://www.axios.com; *Guardian*, Oct. 25, 2023.
34 *Jerusalem Post*, Oct. 24–25, 2023.
35 *Jerusalem Post*, Oct. 24, 2023; ABC News, Oct. 20, 2023; Israel National News, Oct. 25, 2023.
36 NBC News, Oct. 23, 2023; US Department of Defense, Oct. 24, 2023, https://www.defense.gov.
37 Reuters, Oct. 19, 2023; *New York Times*, Oct. 23, 2023.
38 Al-Jazeera, Oct. 25, 2023; *Washington Post*, Oct. 25, 2023. The IDF would later revise the number of Israelis killed in the Hamas attack of October 7, 2023, from 1,400 to 1,200. *New York Times*, Nov. 11, 2023.
39 *Wall St. Journal*, Oct. 26, 2023; Ynet, Oct. 25, 2023.
40 *Wall St. Journal*, Oct. 25, 2023.
41 *Wall St. Journal*, Oct. 25, 2023; Tony Badran, "Iran Sponsored the October 7 Massacre. America Paid for It," *Tablet*, Dec. 14, 2023.
42 The White House, Oct. 25, 2023, https//www.whitehouse.gov; Israeli Ministry of Foreign Affairs, Oct. 25, 2023, https://www.gov.il.
43 Sky News, Oct. 25, 2023; *Times of Israel*, Oct. 24, 2023.
44 Karen DeYoung, "U.S., Russia Veto Each Other's UN Resolutions on Israel-Gaza War," *Washington Post*, Oct. 25, 2023.
45 *Times of Israel*, Oct. 26, 2023. The Arabic word *fatwa* can mean "explanation" or "clarification." It refers, in simple terms, to an edict or ruling by a recognized religious authority on a point of Islamic law. The Qur'an is the sacred scripture of Islam. According to conventional Islamic belief, it was revealed by the angel Gabriel to the Prophet Muhammad in the West Arabian towns Mecca and Medina beginning in 610 and ending with Muhammad's death in 632 CE.
46 *Times of Israel*, Oct. 26, 2023; *Haaretz*, Oct. 26, 2023; *Washington Post*, Oct. 20, 2023; *Times of Israel*, Oct. 26, 2023.
47 France 24, Oct. 26, 2023; *The Guardian*, Oct. 27, 2023; CNN. Nov. 9, 2023.
48 *Times of Israel*, Oct. 26, 2023; *Jerusalem Post*, Oct. 26, 2023; Politico, Oct. 27, 2023, htttps://www.politico.eu; CNN, Oct. 26, 2023.
49 *Jerusalem Post*, Oct. 26, 2023.
50 BBC, Nov. 1, 2023; FDD, Nov. 2, 2023.
51 *Jerusalem Post*, Feb. 8, 2024; *Haaretz*, Oct. 28, 2023; *Guardian*, Oct. 31, 2023.
52 *Times of Israel*, Oct. 28, 2023; *Haaretz*, Oct. 28, 2023; USNI News, Oct. 28, 2023.
53 Israel National News, Oct. 29, 2023; *Haaretz*, Oct. 29, 2023.
54 *Times of Israel*, Oct. 29, 2023; CNN, Oct. 29, 2023; *Le Monde*, Oct. 30, 2023.
55 *Jerusalem Post*, Oct. 29, 2023.
56 *New York Post*, Oct. 28, 2023.
57 *Times of Israel*, Oct. 22, 29–30, 2023; Ynet, Nov. 3, 2023.
58 *Haaretz*, Oct. 31, 2023; *Times of Israel*, Oct. 31 and Nov. 1, 2023; *National Herald*, Oct. 31, 2023.
59 Ynet, Oct. 31, 2023; *Times of Israel*, Oct. 30, 2023; Reuters, Oct. 31, 2023.
60 Ynet, Nov. 1, 2023; *Jerusalem Post*, Nov. 1, 2023; AP News, Oct. 29, 2023.
61 *Times of Israel*, Oct. 25, 2023.
62 *Haaretz*, July 12, 2006.

CHAPTER 3

The War Grinds On

November opened with intensified Israeli airstrikes on northern Gaza, notably two in Jabaliya, the Strip's largest "refugee camp," leaving dozens of civilians dead and injured. The IDF claimed, in turn, that approximately fifty terrorists were killed in this underground military stronghold, and that at least fifty-five Hamas leaders, including the head of its anti-tank fire against Israel, Muhammad Asar, had been "eliminated" in the war to date. Hamas official Ghazi Hamad, interviewed on the Lebanese news outlet LBCI, stood firm: "We will repeat the October 7 attack time and again until Israel is annihilated. We are victims—everything we do is justified." The Israeli civilian casualties of October 7 were, he maintained, the result of "unexpected complications on the ground."[1]

Some tens of thousands of Hamas and Palestinian Islamic Jihad forces remained in Gaza, with the number of Palestinians who had left for the south, now over one million, giving the IDF a freer hand to act. At the same time, the *Jerusalem Post* heard from military sources that the combined stages of the current all-out invasion and expected "later stages of insurgency and lower-grade fighting" would take several months. As for the West Bank, the IDF said that it had arrested forty-six people during raids overnight, thirty of whom it declared were members of Hamas. Overall, it had arrested 1,180 people in the West Bank since October 7, of whom 740 were suspected of having Hamas ties.[2]

The toll on Israel to this point in the war had been very heavy. In addition to the horrific murder of civilians and the hostages kidnapped on October 7, 394 members of Israel's security forces had been killed since the Hamas invasion, including from the Shin Bet and police officers—many on October 7 alone. An additional 712 soldiers were recognized as disabled due to their injuries. Thousands were injured on October 7, from lightly to critically. About 125,000 people, having been evacuated from almost 100 Gaza and Lebanon border communities, were hosted in hotels and guest houses. And the number of administrative detention of Palestinians had spiked since October 7 to 2,070 (up from 1,319 before the Hamas assault), bringing the total of "security prisoners" to 6,704. Not since the First Intifada had there been this many Palestinians in administrative detention.[3]

Thanks to a deal brokered between Egypt, Israel, and Hamas, at least 320 foreign passport holders left Gaza for Egypt via the Rafah Crossing. Seventy-six critically injured Palestinians and their families entered Egypt, while 500 foreign passport holders were expected to be allowed out of the Strip in the coming days. The limited evacuations were not expected to lead to an extended, unlimited opening of the crossing, however.[4]

On the diplomatic front, Jordan's foreign ministry recalled home its ambassador to Israel, saying that he would only return to Tel Aviv if Israel halted its war on the Gaza enclave and ended "the humanitarian crisis it has caused." Bolivia cut its ties with Israel, accusing Jerusalem of "crimes against humanity." Expressing "high esteem" for this official move, leftist governments in Chile and Colombia recalled their envoys to the Jewish State in protest of Israeli military operations in its war against Hamas. "As an occupying power," declared Russian UN representative Vasily Nebenzya before the Security Council, Israel did not have the right to defend itself "as confirmed by the advisory opinion of the International Court of Justice handed down in 2004." Its security "can only be fully guaranteed if we resolve the Palestinian issue on the basis of relevant UN Security Council resolutions." He ended: "The Jewish people suffered persecution for many centuries and the Jewish people should know better than anyone that the suffering of ordinary people, innocent lives lost in the name of blind retribution, will neither restore justice, nor bring the dead back to life, nor console their families." Germany's interior minister, on the other hand, announced a complete ban on all future activities of Hamas as "a terrorist organization whose aim is to destroy the State of Israel."[5]

On November 2, IDF spokesman Daniel Hagari announced that its forces had completely surrounded Gaza City, the center of Hamas activity. Nineteen of its soldiers had fallen in Gaza since the ground invasion began one week earlier, for a total of 339 killed overall. The IDF's Helicopter 669 Search and Rescue Unit evacuated from Gaza about 260 wounded, several in critical condition. In fierce fighting, soldiers from the 13th Battalion of the Golani Brigade and armored troops from the 53rd Battalion prevailed overnight against a number of Hamas squads inside the Strip, even as Hamas tunnels were "neutralized" with explosives. The UAE warned that there was a real risk of a regional spillover from the Hamas-Israel war in Gaza, adding that it was working "relentlessly" to secure a humanitarian cease-fire. Secretary Blinken arrived in Israel on Friday, seeking to push "for humanitarian pauses" to let more Palestinian civilians leave Gaza. The same day, as a convoy of 102 humanitarian aid trucks entered Gaza, the number of Israelis returning from abroad since October 7 to aid in the nation's war effort reached 300,000.[6]

The Gaza Health Ministry declared, in unconfirmed reports and not distinguishing between Hamas and civilians, that more than 9,500 Palestinians had been killed to date. Over a third of Gaza's thirty-five hospitals were not functioning. Among the victims of Israeli unrelenting air strikes, as reported in *Haaretz* on November 2, was the entire twenty-three-member family of Gazan journalist Ahmed Alnaouq, the twenty-nine-year-old who four years earlier co-founded the Facebook page "Across the Wall," where Israelis had read personal stories in Hebrew of daily life by average Gazans. On October 28, Ahmed's post from the United Kingdom about all his dead loved ones in Gaza, noting that he had "written countless messages to Israelis for peace and a just future over the years," ended thus: "Sadly, for this reason, posts to this page will stop for the time being." Responded a shaken Yuval Abraham, the Israeli co-founder of the page: "I don't know ... if we'll be able to build that bridge" after the war. He concluded: "We, as Israelis, cannot have security if Palestinians don't have freedom."[7]

At the same time, when the IDF Arabic spokesperson announced two days later that the Salah al-Din route in Gaza would be available between 1:00 p.m. to 4:00 p.m. for the 400,000 residents still in northern Gaza to move southwards for their safety, Hamas terrorists fired mortars and anti-tank missiles at Israeli troops who had arrived and operated to open the route. In addition to ammunition being embedded in hospitals, mosques, homes, youth centers, schools, and kindergartens, rocket launchers were found in playgrounds and near children's pools. A senior White House official declared that Hamas also tried to smuggle fighters among the Palestine wounded and foreign nationals in ambulances headed for Egypt, delaying efforts at further evacuation.[8]

One day after Hezbollah Secretary-General Nasrallah emerged from hiding to speak publicly in Beirut for the first time since October 7, hailing the "Palestinian operation" against Israel, characterized "as fragile as a spider web" needing American and Western support, and warning that expanding the "Lebanese front" was "a real possibility," Saudi Prince Abdul Rahman bin Mosaad al-Saud sharply lashed out in response. The missiles and massive weapons in Hezbollah's possession, he declared, "have nothing to do with supporting the Palestinian cause." Its continued policy is only "a means of implementing Iran's agenda in the region." "All illusions based on loud slogans and resonant speeches," he ended, "should fall" with Nasrallah.[9]

Reacting to the Saudi prince's remarks, IDF spokesman Maj. Doron Spielman labeled Hamas's terror attacks on Israel a "cult of death." This brought to mind Haniyah's declaration over Al-Aqsa TV on July 30, 2014, upon becoming the new head of Hamas: "We love death like our enemies love life! We love Martyrdom the way in which [Hamas] leaders died." In like vein, Hamas Chief of Staff Mohammad Deif's statement during the war, recorded by Palestinian Media Watch, announced: "Today you [Israelis] are fighting divine soldiers, who love death for Allah like you love life, and who compete among themselves for Martyrdom like you flee from death."[10] How does one respond to this genocidal, theocratic death cult?

Entering the fifth week of the war, the IDF stated that more than 2,500 Hamas terror targets had been struck since the ground invasion, and that 345 of its soldiers had died. Red alert sirens and constant rocket fire against Israel from Hamas and Hezbollah continued. Israeli forces and Palestinian terrorists clashed in Jenin, Nablus, and Tulkarm, as well as elsewhere throughout the West Bank. Still, even as the war intensified, the IDF reopened the Salah al-Din evacuation corridor for Gazan civilians to go south, urging them in Arabic not to be used any longer as human shields by Hamas in the north.[11]

At home, thousands of people gathered at the recently renamed Hostages Square opposite the Tel Aviv Museum on Saturday night to show support for the families of those kidnapped by Hamas. Shortly after the rally, remaining participants, including families of some of the hostages, were forced to scramble for cover as rockets were launched from Gaza at Tel Aviv and surrounding areas, a reminder of the war still raging in the south. In Jerusalem and elsewhere, hundreds renewed protests against Netanyahu, who had spoken with the president of the International Red Cross to demand the immediate release of those abducted on October 7, accusing the prime minister of mishandling the war and hostage negotiations and calling for his resignation.[12]

In Gaza, taking control of a Hamas military compound in the Strip on the night of November 5, Israeli forces also struck over 450 enemy targets from the air and the sea. Fighter jets killed additional Hamas terrorists and commanders, including Jamal Mussa, who was responsible for the special security operations in the organization. The next night, officers from the Jerusalem District Police and Border Police (*Mishmar HaGvul*), in a special operation in the Shuafat neighborhood in Jerusalem and Anata on the outskirts of the city, arrested twenty-three suspects for their alleged involvement in violent riots and attempts to harm security personnel.[13]

Meanwhile, the Biden administration, according to a *New York Times* report, sent warnings to Iran and Hezbollah that Washington was preparing for military intervention if they launched an attack against Israel. The United States also issued an unusual announcement that an Ohio-class nuclear submarine had arrived in the operational area of its Central Command and showed a photograph of its passing through the Suez Canal on Monday. This signaled an important addition to the American deterrence force in the region, and the ability to attack if necessary. Further, the Pentagon confirmed that the United States was conducting unarmed drone flights over Gaza to aid efforts to locate the hostages.[14]

The Israeli military carried out a series of significant air strikes against Hamas on Sunday evening, following the earlier arrival of Israeli forces on the enclave's coast. IDF spokesperson Hagari described the strikes as extensive, targeting both above ground and underground infrastructure. This offensive led to a communications blackout in Gaza throughout the night. A fighter jet killed the commander of Hamas's Deir al-Balah Battalion in the Central Camps Brigade, Wael Asefa. who, together with other commanders of this brigade, was responsible for sending Hamas elite Nukhba terrorists into Israeli territory on October 7. He had been involved in the incitement and promotion of terrorist attacks against Israeli civilians and IDF soldiers for decades and, following the massacre, had planned additional terrorist attacks. The IDF also reported on November 6 that Israeli troops had encircled Gaza City and divided the besieged coastal territory into North and South Gaza, marking a significant stage in Israel's military operation. It again informed the Palestinians in the north that they could safely depart between 10 a.m. and 2 p.m. via a designated humanitarian corridor to the south. As for the West Bank, almost forty suspects, some allied with Hamas, were arrested, and a terrorist cell in Tulkarm "eliminated."[15]

Biden's view of postwar rule in Gaza was clear. A long-term Israeli security presence could not be there nor could there be forced displacement of Palestinians from Gaza. Lastly, there must not be a continuous siege on the Strip. For their part, thirty-five Jewish and Arab peace and human rights advocates in Israel called for a cease-fire in Gaza, the release of Israelis kidnapped by Hamas, and a political and diplomatic solution to the conflict. They offered no suggestions for ending the month-old war. Secretary Blinken left the region, his second trip since October 7, without a combat pause.[16]

Hamas took its war to Jerusalem. Before being shot to death by police officers, a sixteen-year-old male from Issawiya fatally stabbed Border Police Sgt. Ross Elisheva Lubin, a twenty-year-old Lone Soldier from Atlanta who had helped prevent a fatal Hamas incursion into Kibbutz Sa'ad, her adoptive home, on the morning of October 7, outside the Shalem police station on Salah al-Din Street in the Old City. "Generations dreamed of reaching Jerusalem," she had told a US audience: "We have the privilege to defend her." Lubin's murder brought the toll of police officers killed from October 7 onwards to fifty-nine.[17]

On a separate front, more than thirty global antisemitism envoys released a statement calling on countries worldwide to step up support amid mounting Jew-hatred. For his part, Lt. Genl. Ingo Gerhartz, commander of the German air force, donated a pint of blood for the IDF at Sheba Tel HaShomer Medical Center while the attending nurse wrapped herself in an Israeli flag. The UN Security Council, however, failed again to agree upon a resolution on the Hamas-Israel war.[18]

Israelis across the country observed a minute of silence at 11 a.m. on Tuesday morning to commemorate the victims of Hamas's October 7 massacre, one month (the traditional period called *shloshim*) after the deadly onslaught. The minute of silence on that national day of mourning marked the start of memorial ceremonies across the country, but unlike Holocaust Remembrance Day and Memorial Day, it was not accompanied by a siren. Following the silence, flags across Israel were lowered to half-staff and mourners, wracked by grief, sang the national anthem, *Hatikva*. Prior to Tuesday's memorial events, a Defense Ministry ceremony was held on Monday night in the State Hall of Remembrance at Har Herzl, Israel's largest military cemetery, where, surrounded by candles, the newly engraved names of 349 people murdered on October 7, soldiers, police officers, Shin Bet operatives. and civilian security team members who died defending communities in the south, were unveiled on the walls.

With 1,400 candles illuminating the darkness of evening, prayers were said at the Western Wall in Jerusalem for the return of the hostages and missing persons, for the State of Israel, and for the IDF. Some families of the hostages lit a "torch of life," which will be passed across a number of nations until all the hostages would be returned and the torch then brought back to that holy place, and they called on the world to unite against Hamas and its crimes. A bi-partisan group of members of the US House of Representatives, holding memorial candles that night in Washington, D.C., commemorated "the tragic loss of life in Israel at the hands of Hamas terrorists" on October 7, called for the immediate release of those still held hostage, and declared that they stood "united with Israel against Hamas." "Hamas actually does have genocidal intentions against the people of Israel. They would like to see it "wiped off the map, they said so," National Security Council (NSC) spokesperson John Kirby told reporters in Washington on Tuesday. "That is what is at stake here," he stressed.[19]

The faces of the hostages imprisoned in Gaza were projected across the walls of Jerusalem's Old City. A joined memorial rally and protest was held in Jerusalem at 7:30 p.m., led by bereaved families. The group planned to establish a permanent camp outside of the Knesset, where participants will demand the resignation of Prime Minister Netanyahu and the dissolution of his government. Even a columnist for the once lock-step pro-Netanyahu newspaper *Yisrael Hayom*, in an impassioned plea, called on him to "lead us to victory and then go."[20]

That day, Israel's army, with a pincer movement coming from the north and the south, reached the heart of Gaza and took aim at Hamas's final defenses. The IDF exchanged heavy fire with Hamas fighters on the outskirts of the Al-Shati refugee camp and targets near the Al-Quds hospital in Gaza City. Under world scrutiny over Gaza, Israeli officials pointed to the civilian toll of US wars, saying that it was impossible to defeat Hamas without killing innocents, a lesson they argued Americans and their allies should understand. In an attempt to lower the number of civilian casualties in the Strip, reported the *Wall Street Journal*, the United States would deliver $320 million worth of precision bombs to Israel.[21]

Heavy rocket fire from Gaza into Israel persisted, while a growing number of Gazans, holding white flags, headed southwards. Ninety-three aid trucks entered Gaza in the last twenty-four hours, bringing the total since October 21 to 569. In the north of Israel, at least twenty rockets were fired from Hezbollah in the latest rocket barrage. IDF forces retaliated by striking terrorist targets in Lebanon.[22]

On November 8, Blinken called on Israel not to reoccupy the Gaza Strip once its war with Hamas ended. Speaking to reporters after G7 foreign ministers-held talks in Japan, Blinken listed what he said was needed in order to create "durable peace and security": "The United States believes key elements should include: no forcible displacement of Palestinians from Gaza, not now, not after the war; no use of Gaza as a platform for terrorism or other violent attacks; no reoccupation of Gaza after the conflict ends." He added that other conditions included no "attempt to blockade or besiege Gaza" or any "reduction in the territory of Gaza," together with "Palestinian-led governance and Gaza unified with the West Bank under the Palestinian Authority." Asked about Netanyahu's comments, Blinken allowed that "there may be a need for some transition period." He did not know what an "alternative mechanism" for Gaza would be. Whatever the decision, he stressed, "we need to replace the Hamas regime and ensure security" for Israel's citizens.[23]

The punishing Israeli attacks on the Gaza Strip did not let up. According to an analysis of satellite imagery reported in the *New York Times*, roughly a third of all buildings in northern Gaza were damaged or destroyed. Israel rejected, however, both a cease-fire and a humanitarian pause without the return of the hostages. For the first time since the 1982 First Lebanon War, an entire IDF army division (the 262nd) maneuvered in enemy territory. It captured the Beit Hanoun area in northern Gaza, from which a terrorist battalion had come to murder and kidnap in Kibbutz Erez, Moshav Netiv HaAsara, and Sderot, and since the beginning of the fighting had killed hundreds of Hamas operatives, including senior members, in Beit Hanoun and Jabaliya. The IDF also reported that Mohsen Abu Zina, the head of Hamas's weapons manufacturing department in the Gaza Strip, was killed in an Israeli Air Force (IAF) strike. Another strike eliminated Ibrahim Abu-Maghsib, head of Hamas's Anti-Tank Missile Unit in the Central Camps Brigade. Yet, in an interview with the *New York Times*, Hamas leader Khalil Al-Hayya asserted that his organization considered the October 7 attack a success, asserting that the Palestinian issue was back on the table "and now no one in the region is experiencing calm."[24]

The costs of war mounted. According to the Israeli Health Ministry, of the over 7,000 people wounded in the country since October 7, 342 remain hospitalized, of whom 51 were in serious condition. Israeli police declared that they had managed to verify the identity of 843 victims of the Hamas massacre in the southern border communities. For its part, the Gaza Health Ministry reported that more than 10,569 Palestinians had been killed to date. In the West Bank, 163 Palestinians had been killed by Israeli forces. Overnight, the IDF made forty arrests in that area, half of whom were Hamas members.[25]

The same day, Riyadh's investment minister remarked that Saudi-Israel normalization "remains on the table" despite the war with Hamas in Gaza. His comment caused little surprise, given that Saudi Arabia, the United Arab Emirates (UAE), Bahrain, Egypt, and Jordan view Hamas as posing a threat to their national security. Khalid Al-Falih, speaking at the Bloomberg New Economy Forum in Singapore, reiterated Riyadh's stance that a diplomatic rapprochement with Jerusalem was "contingent on a pathway to a peaceful resolution of the Palestinian question." In his words, "That was on the table—it remains on the table, and obviously the setback over the last month has clarified why Saudi Arabia was so adamant that resolution of the Palestinian conflict has to be part of a broader normalization in the Middle East."[26]

What of an end to the fighting? Palestinian terrorists in the Gaza Strip had fired more than 9,500 rockets at Israeli territory since Hamas launched its multi-pronged attack on the Jewish State one month ago, and launching did not stop. Nor did missiles from Hezbollah, whose cell in Brazil, with Iranian funding, had planned an attack against Jewish and Israeli targets but was thwarted by Israel's Mossad spy agency and Brazilian Federal Police. The IDF came out with a statement about their forces' readiness for a prolonged engagement, with preparations underway for a "winter war" in Gaza. As military spokespeople set expectations for an extended conflict, the hope for a swift resolution faded, with indications that the hostilities could well continue into the colder months, possibly until late December or even beyond.[27]

On the afternoon of November 8, speaking in Tel Aviv to journalists, Gantz had observed that "on the question of the operation's length there are no limitations." "The war here is for our existence and for Zionism, and so I can't provide an estimate of the length of each stage in the war and the fighting that will ensue after. We can't retreat from our strategic objective," Gantz replied to a questioner, adding that Hamas threatened "Zionist and democratic concepts." As for casualties, Israel Police said that 845 murdered civilians (not including soldiers) on October 7 had been identified so far; the Gaza Health Ministry reported that at least 10,812 Palestinians had been killed, including 4,412 children, since the war began.[28]

The next day, PA Prime Minister Mohammad Ibrahim Shtayyeh declared that Israel's goal of Hamas's elimination "will not happen," because the group is "also an idea," rather than just a military organization, even as IDF chief commander Halevi declared that the Palestinian Authority was working extensively every day to prevent pro-Hamas demonstrations in the West Bank. Thirty-nine Israeli soldiers had died in the war to date, the army revealed. Twelve Palestinian terrorists were killed in armed clashes with the IDF in Jenin, multiple drone strikes accompanying the fighting. Since the beginning of the war, the IDF had arrested more than 1,430 suspects in the West Bank, over 900 of whom were affiliated with Hamas.[29]

At a humanitarian conference about Gaza, held in Paris, United Nations officials expressed their concerns. The conflict in Gaza "is a wildfire" that could spread across the region, UN aid chief Martin Griffiths declared on November 9, adding that allowing the situation to continue in Gaza would be a "travesty." "The United Nations cannot be part of a unilateral proposal to push Palestinians into so-called safe zones," he remarked at the start of the deliberations. Philippe Lazzarini, chief of the UN Relief and Works Agency (UNRWA), mandated by the UN to serve "Palestine refugees" and which has supported multiple generations (5.9 million individuals are considered eligible today) with health, education, and social assistance, expressed his worry about the spillover risk of the situation in Gaza. He added that the West Bank "is boiling." At the same meeting, Egyptian Foreign Minister Sameh Hassan Shoukry charged that what Israel was doing went beyond self-defense, and he rejected any attempt to displace Palestinians from Gaza. *None* of the other twenty nations in the Arab world offered to open their doors to Palestinians in dire need or to administer Gaza after the war.[30]

Israel agreed to a daily four-hour pause in the fighting in northern Gaza, the White House said on Thursday, as Palestinian Islamic Jihad published a video of two of the hostages it indicated it could be willing to release. "We've been told by the Israelis that there will be no military operations in these areas over the duration of the pause and that this process is starting today," the NSC spokesperson John Kirby said. The pauses, which would be announced three hours in advance, emerged out of discussions between American and Israeli officials in recent days, including talks which Biden had with Netanyahu. The pauses would allow people to flee along two humanitarian corridors and were significant first steps, Kirby explained. Biden on Thursday went further, telling reporters that he had sought a pause much longer than that to get hostages being held by Hamas out to freedom.[31]

That evening, to mark the eighty-fifth anniversary of the Nazi *Kristallnacht*, prelude to the Holocaust, German Chancellor Olaf Scholz pledged before Berlin's Beth Zion synagogue, which had been targeted with two Molotov cocktails the previous month, to protect the country's 200,000 Jews against a "shameful" upsurge in antisemitism in the wake of the Hamas-Israel war. "There are parallels between the mentality of radical Islamists who want the extermination of Israel and the Jews, and those on the far right who despise our culture of Shoah remembrance." Essentially, he said, "this is about keeping the promise given again and again in the decades since 1945 . . . the promise 'never again.'" Scholz ended: "We will not be intimidated – that is also one of the lessons of the historic pogrom experience from November 9, 1938." The Brandenburg Gate was lit up with a Star of David and a message against antisemitism: "*Nie wieder ist jetzt!*" ("Never again is now!").[32]

The next day, the office of Iranian Supreme Leader Ayatollah Ali Khamenei published a hitherto unseen video of a May 1998 meeting in Tehran between Khamenei and Hamas founder Sheikh Ahmad Yassin. Believing that Hamas was "fighting on the frontline of the war between Islam and unbelief, and the war between truth and falsehood," Khamenei had declared that Iran would fight the "usurping" Zionist government and "that cancerous growth that they have planted in the Islamic lands," certain of future victory. Thanking his host and the opportunity to be "in the land of the Islamic Revolution," Yassin had replied that Hamas needed the support of everyone in all the Arab and Islamic lands to be able to strengthen the Islamic ranks and help the Palestinian people "so that they can stand firmly and strongly in confronting the Zionist-U.S. aggressions, God willing." He concluded thus: "We won't relinquish even a bit or a handspan of the territory of our homeland. We will remain committed to Islam. We will continue to be fighters who either achieve victory or are martyred, God willing, so that Al-Quds [Jerusalem] and the Al-Aqsa Mosque, the first *qibla* [the direction of Mecca to which Muslims turn in prayer] of the Muslims, are freed."[33]

Over the weekend, forces of the IDF eliminated a significant number of members of the Hamas Nukhba force who had taken part in the systematic massacre of October 7. Among the terrorists killed were Ahmed Musa, commander of the Nukhba force, and Amr Alhandi, the commander of a platoon in the force. Musa was one of the commanders of the raids on the Zikim military base and Kibbutz Zikim. In recent days, he had led offensive activity against IDF forces in Gaza. In addition, the head of the Hamas Northern Gaza Strip Brigade's Sniping Army, Mohammed Kahlout, was eliminated. The IDF also killed Ahmed Siam, a company commander of Hamas's Naser Radwan Company, the terrorist responsible for holding approximately 1,000 Gazan residents hostage in Gaza's Rantisi Children's Hospital, preventing them from evacuating south to safety. Hamas terrorists had opened fire on soldiers as they were facilitating the evacuation of the civilians. The troops returned fire and killed the attackers. Since the beginning of ground operations in Gaza, the IAF, with the assistance and direction of the ground forces, had struck approximately 5,000 targets in the Gaza Strip to counter threats in real time.[34]

IDF spokesman Hagari declared that ground forces, with air and naval support, were "deepening" operations in Gaza City's Al-Shati refugee camp, attacking terrorists who were choosing to fight from close to Al-Shifa Hospital. The IDF would continue to allow patients and staff at Gaza's hospitals, and all noncombatants in northern Gaza, to evacuate to the south, he said, and had spoken to staff at Al-Shifa to stress this. In the West Bank, nineteen suspects were arrested, nine associated with Hamas. Up north, intensive rocket and anti-tank missile attacks from Hezbollah continued to rain down on Israel; IDF artillery and tank fire retaliated by targeting launch locations. While more than 300,000 marched in London support of the Palestinians and denounced the civilian death toll in Gaza, thousands rallied in Tel Aviv's renamed Hostage Square to call for the release of the hostages in Gaza without further delay. The next big move from the Families Forum, its members living in a nightmarish state of limbo regarding the hostages, was to bring a lawsuit against senior Hamas officials. Included in the projected lawsuit would be articles of prosecution such as war crimes, genocide, and crimes against humanity.[35]

At this point in time, 870 of the more than 1,200 Israelis murdered in the October 7 massacre had been identified. The painstaking, exhausting task undertaken every day at the Abu Kabir Forensic Institute in Tel Aviv, working on body parts, dismembered limbs, and flesh, collected by the voluntary ZAKA (Disaster Victim Identification) organization, which operates according to

Orthodox Jewish law, was made more excruciating because victims were brutally mutilated and often burned. The air, reported Maayan Hoffman in the *Jerusalem Post Magazine* on November 10, was thick with the acrid blend of death, formaldehyde, and the lingering scent of cleaning products. The "odor of tragedy" was inescapable. Her earlier visit to the butchery that struck Israeli communities in the south, and especially upon later viewing the IDF film designed to convey the horrors of the massacre, led Hoffman to one conclusion; "Our ability to live in Israel is at stake; the ground upon which we walked—upon which we walk—trembled on October 7 and still trembles today."[36]

The same day, according to Israeli TV Channel 12 Arab affairs analyst Ehud Ya'ari, most of the nations present at the Arab League and the Organization of Islamic Cooperation meeting in Riyadh sought to include in the meeting's closing statement five additional clauses that were rejected by Israel's Arab peace partners and some others. The rejected demands were to prevent the transfer of US military equipment to Israel from American bases in the region; to freeze all diplomatic and economic contacts with Israel; to threaten to use oil as a means of leverage; to bar flights to and from Israel through Arab states' airspace; and to dispatch a joint delegation to the United States, Europe, and Russia to push for a cease-fire. The countries that rejected these demands were Saudi Arabia, the UAE, Bahrain, Sudan, Morocco, Mauritania, Djibouti, Jordan, and Egypt. All present called for an immediate end to military operations in Gaza, whose Health Ministry claimed that 11,078 people had been killed as of Friday, forty percent of them children, and urged the International Criminal Court (ICC) to investigate "war crimes and crimes against humanity that Israel is committing" in the Palestinian territories, according to a final communiqué.[37]

As Israel entered its sixth week of war, IDF troops continued to kill terrorists in close-quarter combat and to direct aircraft to strike Hamas terrorist infrastructure, weapons depots, observation posts, and command and control centers in the Gaza Strip. Its soldiers began operating in the Al-Shati refugee camp in the northern area, continuing to find arms caches in schools, mosques, and homes. Hamas confiscated three hundred liters of diesel fuel that were brought into the Shifa Hospital by the IDF in agreement with the hospital administrators. On the northern front, stepped-up heavy mortar attacks from Lebanon, injuring twenty-three soldiers in one day, brought Israeli retaliation on Hezbollah firing positions. In Jerusalem, the Israeli cabinet allocated funds for the protection of seventy percent of the hospital beds in the country, as well as all the beds in the blood banks and dialysis centers.[38]

Yossi Klein Halevi understandably wrote on November 12 that "the trauma of aloneness" had returned to world Jewry, finding itself at "a moral disconnect" with much of the international community. Anti-Israel rallies sprang up across the West where the slaughtered were branded the criminal. In like vein, Bret Stephens, contributing an Opinion piece in the *New York Times* five days earlier, had advised America's Jews that "in the long run we are alone."[39]

Still, sparks of light did appear for what Halevi had termed "the lonely people of history." Europe's leaders, including German Chancellor Scholz and the prime ministers of Spain, Denmark, Romania, and Malta issued a joint statement supporting Israel's right to defend itself and urging Hamas to release the hostages kidnapped from Israel. A Bayern Munich soccer game featured families of the hostages in Gaza; Sydney's famed Bondi Beach had individual chairs with a photograph of each hostage. The popular German Vice-Chancellor Robert Habeck, head of the Green Party, berated fellow progressives for their hateful anti-Zionism, and declared that "Hamas must be destroyed because it is destroying the process of peace in the Middle East." Over 180,000 rallied in Paris, and thousands more in seventy cities across the country, against a surge of anti-Jewish incidents in France, with 500,000 Jews the largest Jewish community in Europe.[40]

The International Christian Embassy Jerusalem (ICEJ) declared that it would plant a red tulip for each human being killed in the Hamas attack on October 7. Two days before that savage assault, an ICEJ group of 700 Christian pilgrims had replanted a section of the Be'eri Forest that had been burned over in recent years by Hamas arsonists launching incendiary kites and balloons from Gaza. (Over 130 members of Kibbutz Be'eri were massacred, and an unknown number taken as hostages to Gaza.) The ICEJ had also been the first organization to start putting mobile bomb shelters in the south, almost 150, and to deliver firefighting equipment to stop the balloon fires. "We're going to stay with this nation," said spokesperson David Parsons, "and help do what is necessary to bring peace and security to the whole region."[41]

Echoing the twenty-seven European Union nations' joint condemnation of Hamas on November 13 for what they described as the use of hospitals and civilians as "human shields" in the war against Israel, US National Security Adviser Jake Sullivan told CNN that Hamas used hospitals as "human shields" during the conflict. In addition, the Pentagon on Sunday announced new airstrikes on Iranian facilities in Syria that officials said were linked to recent attacks targeting US troops there and in Iraq, causing fatalities among proxy fighters backed by Tehran. The operation marked an important escalation by the Biden administration.[42]

Yet, only one day later the same administration extended a sanctions waiver to allow Iran to access upwards of $10 billion in electricity revenue once held in escrow in Iraq. The waiver allowed Baghdad to continue purchasing electricity from Iran and, in a change from past policy, for Iran to convert its revenue into euros and draw on the money for budget imports out of Iraq and Oman. The new waiver extended for 120 days a US waiver first issued in July that gave Iran access to the $10 billion in electricity revenue held in escrow in Iraq. It remained unclear whether Iran had spent any of the $10 billion since July.

The July waiver came as part of an unacknowledged nuclear understanding between the United States and Iran, evading the congressional review requirement of the 2015 Iran Nuclear Agreement Review Act. Weeks later, the administration had agreed to release another $6 billion in Iranian funds frozen in South Korea as part of a deal to secure the release of Tehran's American hostages. According to the Associated Press, US officials insisted that Iran could only spend the released funds on humanitarian purchases, including food, medicine, medical equipment, and agricultural goods. However, opponents of the waiver noted that money is fungible, and that the waiver would allow the Iran regime to free up funds to continue arming its anti-United States and anti-Israel proxies.[43]

The war in Gaza appeared far from over. For the first time since the start of the conflict, the IDF that Monday provided its official estimates of the size and make-up of what Hamas's forces were on the eve of the war which started on October 7. Its attacks had broken the effectiveness of ten out of twenty-four Hamas battalions, declared the military. According to the IDF, Hamas began the war with 30,000 men who were split into five regional brigades, which themselves split into 24 battalions, which themselves split into 140 companies. Each battalion had around 1,000 plus men. The IDF stated that it had struck numerous sites including some 300 terrorist tunnel shafts, since it began its invasion of Gaza. It had "eliminated" (miliary jargon for killed) Yaakub A'ashur, head of the anti-tank system in the Khan Younis Brigade, Mohammed Khamis Dababash, former Hamas director of military intelligence among other roles, and other officials. However, multiple top IDF sources expressed doubt about Hamas being close to "breaking," even as top political and army officials had stated publicly two days ago that Hamas had "lost control" of northern Gaza.[44]

Seven months earlier, Iranian President Ebrahim Raisi had delivered an unprecedented speech to an annual pro-Palestinian Arab rally in the Gaza Strip on Al-Quds Day. "The initiative to self-determination is today in the hands of the Palestinian fighters," Raisi said, dismissing the Palestinian Authority headed by Mahmoud Abbas, which had been at odds with Hamas since 2007. During the ceremony, leader of Hamas in Gaza Sinwar celebrated the fact that terrorists in southern Lebanon, Gaza, and Syria had fired rockets into Israeli territory, describing the attacks as a response to the police raid on the Al-Aqsa Mosque.[45]

As for the United States's intervention, Iranian Foreign Ministry spokesperson Nasser Kanaani warned on November 14 that the continuation of Washington's support for "Zionist crimes" and its opposition to a cease-fire might lead to the expansion of the war to additional fronts. The United States, he said, must understand that what will prevent the expansion of the war or the entry of additional elements into the war is an immediate cessation of "the massacres and the war against the residents of Gaza, the lifting of the humanitarian blockade from Gaza, and the immediate withdrawal of the Zionist forces from the area." Kanaani added that the only solution which Tehran advocated was the establishment of *one* unified Palestinian state from the Mediterranean Sea to the Jordan River and holding a referendum in which the real Palestinian residents in "Palestine" and abroad will participate. He thus affirmed the chant by pro-Palestinian demonstrators abroad, "From the river to the sea, Palestine will be free"—echoing the Hamas charter of 2017 regarding the Land of Palestine—to mean free of Jews. This ethnic cleansing recalled the *Judenrein* ("free of Jews") ideology of Adolf Hitler's Third Reich—denying the Jews' right to their ancestral homeland.[46]

Palestinians appeared much less divided than the rest of the world regarding the war and its aftermath. A November 14 poll by Birzeit University's Arab World for Research and Development firm near Ramallah found that Palestinians living in the West Bank overwhelmingly answered that they supported the Hamas attack on October 7 "extremely" or "somewhat" by 83.1 percent. Those living in the Gaza Strip responded in that manner by 63.6 percent. The support for a single Palestinian state "from the river to the sea" drew 77.7 percent of respondents from those living in the West Bank and 70.4 percent from those living in Gaza. Only 5.4 percent said that they would support "one state for two peoples." The majority felt that the current war was between "Israel and Palestinians in general" (63.6 percent), with a further 9.4 percent stating that they saw this as a war between "the Western world and the Arab world."[47]

The shadow of war did not stop hundreds of Ethiopian Jews from gathering at Jerusalem's Haas Promenade (the *Tayelet*) overlooking the Old City to celebrate Sigd, the holiday coming fifty days after Yom Kippur and begun hundreds of years ago to mark their community's yearning to return to Israel and affirm their connection to its capital. Earlier in the year, Netanyahu's coalition government had approved a plan to extend its scheme to integrate citizens of Ethiopian descent, numbering around 160,000, or almost two percent of the country's population. The goals were to include continuing to integrate Ethiopian Israelis into military service, close the income gap, and increase trust between that community and the government.[48]

What of Gaza after the war? Speaking in Riyadh at an Arab summit, Jordan's King Abdullah II bin al-Hussein rejected any plans by Israel to occupy parts of Gaza or create security zones within the enclave, remarking that the root cause of the crisis was Israel's denial of Palestinians' "legitimate rights." A two-state solution (he did not provide details) for Israelis and Palestinians was the Hashemite monarch's proposal as "a victory for humanity." At a Congressional hearing on November 1, Secretary Blinken had floated that a "revitalized" Palestinian Authority might oversee Gaza following the conflict's end. Yet, after Israel unilaterally withdrew from Gaza in 2005, the PA had failed to maintain power or order, or to bring any peace or growth there. Moreover, its "pay for slay" program and its children's textbooks that glorify the prospect of Israel's destruction foster and furthers violence. Had Blinken heard any Palestinian leader say they were willing to live in peace with a Jewish State? Even deep into the fighting, when the extent of the Hamas atrocities of October 7 was known, officials of the Fatah party, which dominates the PA, continued to refer to the slaughter as "the heroic operation."[49] The great challenge of Gaza's future remained.

On the other hand, Israeli Knesset members of opposing parties Danny Danon and Ram Ben-Barak, the former Israeli ambassador to the UN and the former deputy director of the Mossad respectively, proposed in a *Wall Street Journal* op-ed that Europe and the United States should offer a haven for Gaza residents who sought relocation. These countries had done so for refugees in the past, they observed, and now could provide one-time financial packages to help with relocation and acclimation to new communities. They had a "moral imperative to demonstrate compassion," the pair concluded, and help Gazans attain a more prosperous future, thereby "alleviating a humanitarian crisis." No positive response followed, however. In the meantime, the IDF spokesperson to Arabic media, Avichay Adraee, announced on Tuesday morning that the evacuation corridor along Salah al-Din Street to southern Gaza would be open and safe from 9 a.m. until 4 p.m. as it had been nearly every day in recent weeks, also allowing exit from area hospitals to safety.[50]

On the afternoon of November 14, nearly 300,000 rallied on the Washington, D.C.'s National Mall in supporting Israel and the immediate release of Hamas's hostages, as well as against the surge of antisemitism across the country. Holding aloft posters "Let our people go," "From the river to the sea Israel will forever be" and "Kidnapped" with photographs of individual hostages, American Jews and their supporters at this largest pro-Israel event in US history presented a united front which excluded the radical leftist anti-Zionist groups Jewish Voice for Peace and IfNotNow. Bi-partisan spokespersons from the US Senate and House of Representatives joined legendary Soviet "refusenik" Natan Sharansky and US Ambassador Deborah Lipstadt, Special Envoy to Monitor and Combat Antisemitism, together with family members of the hostages, in asserting Israel's right to defend itself from Hamas and destroy that jihadist organization. Three ZAKA volunteers, their yellow vests quickly recognized by the massive crowd, received thunderous applause for their heroism in giving dignity to Israel's dead.

Israeli President Herzog, speaking live from Jerusalem's Western Wall, the most sacred Jewish site in the world, reminded his listeners that Jews coming out of the Auschwitz death camp and embracing the restored Jewish State on May 14, 1948, had vowed "never again." After the largest massacre since the Holocaust of Jews on October 7, he went on, we must cry out in unison: "Never again is now!" The "moral clarity and bold actions" of President Biden and our American allies, Herzog asserted, demonstrated the depth of the US-Israel alliance, "which is stronger than ever before." Israel will heal, will rise again, and rebuild, he asserted: *Am Yisrael chai!* ("The People of Israel lives!"). Paraphrasing the prophecy of Zecharya (8:4–5), Herzog declared that boys and girls will once again play in the streets of Be'eri and Sderot, and the elderly shall sit peacefully by the walkways of Nahal Oz and Ofakim. He concluded: "And when the sounds of life and laughter return to the villages, the kibbutzim and the cities, our constant yearning for peace will return as well."[51]

Six thousand miles away from the rally, Israeli forces entered Al-Shifa Hospital in Gaza City's northern exclusive Rimal neighborhood to conduct what the Israeli military said was a "precise and targeted" operation against Hamas, with the expressed intent "that no harm is caused to the civilians being used by Hamas as human shields." With minimal loss of life, they found, as had been uncovered earlier in the Rantisi Children's Hospital, substantial caches of Hamas weapons—some hidden in infant incubators, intelligence reports, and military infrastructure. At the same time, the army announced that incubators, baby food, and medical supplies brought into Gaza by IDF tanks had arrived in Al-Shifa, and that the Israeli medical teams and Arabic speakers were ensuring that the supplies reached those in need. Overnight in the West Bank, where firebombs and explosives were thrown at IDF soldiers, security forces killed seven terrorists and arrested thirty-three wanted persons.[52]

Foreign Minister Eli Cohen declared that Israel will not reopen its two Gaza crossings, Kerem Shalom and Erez, after the war even once the hostages were released. At the press conference, Cohen declared that he favored a plan now under serious discussion by which goods would enter and exit Gaza via a newly established sea route between the enclave and Cyprus. On the evening of November 16, the IDF announced that its 603rd Combat Engineering

Battalion had extracted the body of sixty-five-year-old Yehudit Weiss, the Israeli mother of five and a cancer patient taken hostage by Hamas on October 7, from a structure adjacent to Al-Shifa Hospital that included Kalashnikov AK-47 assault rifles and RPGs (Rocket Propelled Grenades). Her husband, whom everyone called Shmulik, had been dragged from a safe room and murdered in their Kibbutz Be'eri home. The next day, the body of nineteen-year-old Corporal Noa Marciano of Modi'in, who earlier appeared alive in a video aired by Hamas, was extracted near that hospital and transferred to Israel for burial.[53]

The United States conducted its own airstrikes against Iran-linked targets in Syria that week. Unlike the previous strikes which hit empty buildings, this third set killed about six or seven fighters. They were retaliation for fifty-six attacks on US positions in Iraq and Syria by Iranian proxies which had wounded fifty-nine American military personnel since October 7, twenty-seven suffering traumatic brain injuries. US Defense Secretary Lloyd Austin emphasized that the strikes were not connected to Israel's ongoing war against Hamas in the Gaza Strip. "These narrowly tailored strikes in self-defense," he declared, "were intended solely to protect and defend U.S. personnel in Iraq and Syria ... and do not constitute a shift in our approach to the Israel-Hamas conflict." "We continue," he concluded, "to urge all state and non-state entities not to take action that would escalate into a broader regional conflict." At the same time, a US Navy warship shot down in the Red Sea a drone launched by the militant Shi'a Houthi movement, led by Abdul Malik al-Houthi, from northern Yemen towards Israel on November 15.[54]

The American air attacks showed that the Gaza war was part of a broader regional confrontation between Tehran and Washington. The concern that the Houthis' joining the war against Israel would also affect other countries in the region was validated following an incident in the Jazan province of Saudi Arabia, on Yemen's northern border, in which four Saudi soldiers were killed in clashes with Yemini militia fighters. Riyadh faced a particularly complex dilemma: it was in its fundamental interests to hurt Hamas and deny Iran's "axis of resistance" any accomplishments, but Saudi Arabia clearly preferred to remain outside the conflict. Understanding this, Iran and the Houthis were trying to exacerbate the dilemma confronting Riyadh.[55]

On November 16, even as the IDF took control of the Gaza port which Hamas had used as a training facility for its naval commandos to infiltrate into Israel, Kan 11 TV reported that Jerusalem sent a message by way of the White House advisor for Middle East affairs, Brett McGurk, that it would agree to a deal in which an international force would rule the Gaza Strip after the war. According to the report, Israeli officials who met with McGurk expressed their consent to the idea, and emphasized that the Palestinian Authority, in its current state, would not be able to rule the Gaza Strip. McGurk requested an explanation as to Netanyahu's statement that Israel would retain security control of Gaza following the war, and it was explained to him that such an arrangement would resemble the current situation in Judea and Samaria. They emphasized that Israel had no intention of taking civil control of the Gaza Strip or creating Jewish towns within it. The same day, the PA's Bethlehem Municipality wrote on Facebook that Christmas decorations installed several years ago in the city's neighborhoods and all festive appearances would be removed "in honor of the martyrs and in solidarity with our people in Gaza."[56]

That weekend, Israeli soldiers began operating in the Al-Shati refugee camp, killing numerous terrorists while securing in the face of Hamas fire an evacuation route for civilians there. Separately, a total of 129,000 liters of fuel with Israel's consent entered the Gaza Strip, where the Health Ministry claimed that more than 11,500 Palestinians had been killed. While sirens were heard in northern and central Israel, the IDF attacked Hezbollah positions in Lebanon multiple times in response to a massive mortar barrage. In the West Bank, the IDF killed five Hamas operatives and arrested six during a raid in Jenin. Concurrently, an estimated 20,000 marchers reached Jerusalem from Tel Aviv after five days under the slogan "We are going to bring them back," wishing to meet Netanyahu and the other war cabinet ministers.[57]

Israel's opposition to a cease-fire and insistence that it be able to finish the job and destroy Hamas was most eloquently expressed by Yechiel Leiter, Netanyahu's former bureau chief, at the funeral of his son, Moshe Leiter, who was killed in Gaza a week earlier. Reading out a letter which he had written to the White House occupant, a fellow native of Scranton, Pennsylvania, Leiter said: "Stand back, Mr. President. Don't pressure us. Let us do what we know how to do, indeed what we must do, to defeat evil. This is a war of light against darkness, of truth against lies, of civility against murderous barbarism."[58]

As if in reply, Biden's *Wall Street Journal* op-ed on November 18, wishing Gaza and the West Bank "to be reunited under a single governance structure, ultimately under a revitalized Palestinian Authority as we all work toward a two-state solution," made his stance clear: "If Hamas cared at all for Palestinian lives, it would release all the hostages, give up arms, and surrender the leaders and those responsible for October 7. As long as Hamas clings to its ideology of destruction, a cease-fire is not peace.... An outcome that leaves Hamas in control of Gaza would once more perpetuate its hate and deny Palestinian civilians the chance to build something better for themselves."[59]

As the seventh week of the war began, the IDF increased its military offensive in southern Gaza while announcing that sixty-one of its soldiers had died since mounting the Israeli ground attack. For its part, the Palestinian Authority's Foreign Ministry posted an official notice on November 19 blaming Israel for the deaths of those killed at the Supernova music festival on October 7: "According to Arabic media, a preliminary investigation by the Israel Police indicates that Israeli helicopters bombed the Israeli civilians present at the festival and that the Israeli Air Force is responsible for the widespread destruction in the region." (A few hours later this post was deleted, the PA stating that President Abbas had not approved it.) In a speech at an Islamic Revolutionary Guard Corps aerospace force center in Tehran, Iranian Supreme Leader Khamenei went further: "The defeat of the Zionist regime in Gaza is a fact."[60]

On the other hand, McGurk, Biden's main adviser on the Middle East, declared that there would not be a "significant pause" in the Hamas-Israel war until all women and children held by terror groups in Gaza were freed, aligning the administration with Israel's position. Even as a fifty-five-meter-long Hamas tunnel was found ten meters under the Al-Shifa Hospital, and surveillance cameras showed hostages being brought here on October 7, the IDF oversaw the safe transfer of twenty-eight premature babies to be evacuated by the UN from Gaza's main hospital and head for Egypt.[61]

The IDF reported on November 20 that it had killed another three Hamas commanders in Gaza and destroyed a weapons warehouse. In the West Bank, six terrorists were taken into custody, bringing the total since the beginning of the war to 1,850 suspects, of whom approximately 1,100 belonged to Hamas. From Lebanon, twenty-five launches were detected, and sirens sounded in northern Israel. Israeli women championed their own cause, a campaign to break global silence on Hamas's sexual violence during the October infiltration assault. And on World Children's Day, the Israeli Association for Early Childhood declared that lack of action by UN members to secure the release of some forty children and babies held by terror groups added to their suffering.[62]

The same day, a delegation of envoys from Saudi Arabia, Jordan, Egypt, Indonesia, and the Palestinian Authority visited Beijing on the first leg of a tour to world capitals urging an end to the hostilities in Gaza. Foreign Minister Wang Yi told the group that "we have always firmly safeguarded the legitimate rights and interests of Arab (and) Islamic countries and have always firmly supported the just cause of the Palestinian people." While China had been quick to denounce Israel over its settlements in the West Bank, it did not criticize Hamas's murderous rampage on October 7. *Per contra*, US National Security Council spokesperson Kirby told reporters in Washington that while "there are too many civilian casualties" in Gaza, "Israel is not trying to wipe the Palestinian people or Gaza "off the map." Israel "is trying to defend itself against a genocidal terrorist threat."[63]

Israeli Intelligence Minister Gila Gamliel's opinion article, which appeared in the *Jerusalem Post*, calling on Western countries to take in residents of Gaza who wish to leave, prompted clarification from the government's embassy in Washington, D.C., that she "is not a member of the war cabinet." Tragically, the IDF had just recovered the body of twenty-two-year-old Felix Mtenga, a Tanzanian student who was studying agriculture and working at Kibbutz Nir Oz's dairy farm on October 7. In Gaza, the supplies to establish a field hospital, accompanied by 170 personnel and 40 trucks of medical aid, entered the Strip. In Israel, through the newly created Tekuma Authority, it was announced that the Gaza border communities devastated in Hamas's October 7 massacre were to receive a government subsidy of $308 million for rebuilding, developing, and strengthening their homes. A government committee on Monday also earmarked $13.4 million for constructing additional bomb shelters in Bedouin towns across the Negev, as well as for satellite internet devices to facilitate connectivity and remote learning in protected spaces.[64]

As for the hostages still held underground in Gaza, on November 21 Israel agreed to a condition laid out by Hamas leader Sinwar to halt Israeli UAV drones in the Strip's airspace for six hours on each day of the cease-fire in exchange for the release of some of the captives and significant amounts of fuel to Gaza. This included the release of fifty Israeli children and women during a four-day cease-fire and the possibility of it being extended if Hamas located additional women and children held by other terrorist groups, with ten freed for each additional day of the cease-fire. The deal, opposed only by the right-wing Otzma Yehudit ("Jewish Strength") members of the coalition government, had the support of the IDF, Shin Bet, and the Mossad, and included the release of about 140 security prisoners from Israeli prisons. Israel insisted that prisoners convicted of murder not be included in the list of those released.[65]

For Vladimir Putin, Israel's war against Hamas offered an opportunity to escalate what he has cast as an existential battle with the West for a new world order that would end US dominance in favor of a multilateral system which he believed was already taking shape. Russia's leader waited three days before commenting on the Hamas massacre of Israelis, then blamed Washington. "I think that many will agree with me that this is a clear example of the failed policy in the Middle East of the United States, which tried to monopolize the settlement process," he told Iraq's Prime Minister Mohammed Shia' Al-Sudani. Six more days passed before Putin spoke to Netanyahu to offer his condolences for the slaughter. Forging ties with Iran and favoring the Palestinian cause would augment Russia's alliances with the Arab world along with China and North Korea as a new axis against the West and its support for Ukraine. Understandably, US officials feared that Iran was preparing to provide Russia with advanced short-range ballistic missiles for its military campaign against Ukraine begun on February 24, 2022, the largest attack on a European country since World War II.[66]

The State of Israel faced additional challenges. The Regavim organization warned that the PA had built 18,899 illegal buildings in Area C (under Israel's full control) on the Judea and Samaria border, purposely right up to the Green Line that had served as Israel's *de facto* borders until the Six Day War, which could turn into a front-line terrorist outpost in seconds. Further, the White House declared that the mercenary Wagner Group, at the direction of the Russian government, planned to provide an air defense system to Hezbollah or to the regime in Tehran. And in a separate development related to preserving the sanctity of those murdered by Hamas on October 7, 2023, for the first time since the establishment of the State of Israel ZAKA decided to bury more than one hundred vehicles with the approval of the Military Rabbinate and the Chief Rabbinate. Israel Hasid, a spokesperson for ZAKA Tel Aviv, observed: "These are vehicles that have become contaminated with ashes or blood, making it impossible to completely cleanse them."[67]

In a Tuesday press call, US National Security Council spokesman Kirby declared that the United States will not support Israel "moving forward with operations in the south absent a clearly articulated plan for how they're going to protect the lives of the hundreds of thousands of people" there. It was "even more incumbent" on Israel to "protect those civilians who moved at their urging." At the same time, he told Jewish community leaders the next day that after the truce "the fight is not over. The war is not over. The threat that Hamas poses is still real and still viable to the Israeli people," The United States, he added, will "continue to make sure that we're giving [Israel] the tools the capabilities the weapons systems that they need to continue to go after Hamas."[68]

With Hamas not providing information in full about the hostages for release or giving the International Red Cross access to the remaining hostages, the four-day cease-fire that was to commence on Thursday at 10:00 a.m. was delayed to the next day. At that point, the IDF announced that its soldiers had exposed and destroyed approximately 400 terror tunnel shafts in Gaza. Rocket barrages from Hezbollah, the heaviest since the war began, intensified towards the Upper and Western Galilee regions. For its part, the *USS Thomas Hudner* shot down multiple attack drones launched by the Iran-backed Houthi militia in Yemen over the Red Sea early Thursday morning.[69]

The IDF struck some 300 Hamas targets before the expected cease-fire, while Netanyahu announced at a joint press conference in Tel Aviv with War Cabinet members Gallant and Gantz present that he had instructed the Mossad to target the heads of Hamas "wherever they are." In the rival camp, the spokesman for Hamas's military-wing Izz ad-Din al-Qassam Brigades, Abu Obaidah ibn al-Jarrah, said this in a video speech aired by Al-Jazeera TV: "We call for escalation of the confrontation with the occupation throughout the West Bank and all resistance fronts."

Separately, the newly opened National Library of Israel, across from the Knesset in Jerusalem, mounted an exhibit "Each Hostage Has a Story." Dozens of black chairs, placed in the middle of the reading hall, carried a photograph of one of the captives and a book specifically chosen for that individual so that others could get to know them better and understand who they are.[70]

The Israeli public's top priority in the Gaza war was to bring home the hostages rather than to destroy Hamas, according to a poll by Hebrew University of Jerusalem researchers. A plurality of Israeli Jews, forty-six percent, ranked the return of the 239 hostages held in the Gaza Strip as the most important military objective of the war. Thirty-four percent said that the war was primarily about incapacitating Hamas. Israel's Jewish majority had become increasingly willing to make "painful concessions" to secure the release of the hostages, the poll also found. Sixty-one percent of the respondents declared that the country must do so, compared to just twenty-one percent six weeks earlier. At the same time, a recent poll by Israeli Channel 12 TV found that forty-four percent of respondents supported rebuilding Israeli settlements in Gaza, while thirty-nine per cent objected. A majority of respondents favored full Israeli control of the territory, reversing Israel's 2005 withdrawal.[71]

On Friday, after forty-nine days in captivity, four children, three mothers, and six elderly women were released by Hamas in exchange for thirty-nine Palestinian security prisoners. Ten Thais and one Filipino were freed in a separate deal. US President Biden stated that Americans had another reason to be thankful on this Thanksgiving holiday following the release of these hostages, but in an apparent echo of Israel's position he added that the agreement showed that the terror group would only "respond to pressure." When asked whether he had pressured Netanyahu to set a timeline for the end of the war, Biden replied that he had encouraged the Israeli prime minister "to focus on trying to reduce the number of casualties while he is attempting to eliminate Hamas, which is the legitimate objective." Egypt's President Abdel Fattah El-Sisi, who with Qatar had brokered the exchange, called for the establishment of a demilitarized Palestinian state with international intervention.[72]

IDF chief commander Halevi noted that the Israeli military was using the four-day truce in Gaza to "learn, prepare ourselves and our capabilities better" ahead of the continued fighting. "We are also resting," he said, adding that "we will resume our immediate dismantling of Hamas and maneuvers in the Strip, also to apply heavy pressure to bring as many hostages home" as possible. "We have a duty," he emphasized, "to battle and risk our lives so that the hostages could return to live safely in Israel." On a separate note, the IDF declared that the hearts, lungs, livers, and kidneys of five regular and reserve soldiers who had died in combat gave twenty-five people a new lease on life during the dark days of war.[73]

On Saturday night, Hamas released seven children and six female Israeli hostages and four Thais in exchange for thirty-nine Palestinian prisoners, women and teenage males arrested for "security offenses," including stabbings, shootings, and the transfer of explosives. For his part, Netanyahu pledged to Qatar that Israel will not target Hamas leaders living in that country.[74]

It was evident that Hamas was targeting the West Bank in the wake of the hostage and cease-fire deal. The prize for Hamas had already been obtained in images of Palestinian prisoners released amid Hamas flags flying in places like Beitunia in the West Bank near Ramallah. This was one of the Hamas goals all along since October 7. It was also likely the goal of the Hamas leadership abroad, in Qatar, and of Hamas backers in Iran, Turkey, and other countries. This came in the context of an aging Palestinian Authority leadership and the erosion in security in the northern West Bank over the past year. Palestinian Islamic Jihad and other armed gangs had also succeeded in spreading instability in Jenin, Nablus, Tulkarm, and other areas. This forced the IDF to launch increased raids in Jenin in 2022.[75]

On Saturday, thirteen Israeli hostages were released, including nine-year-old Emily Hand, who Irish Prime Minster Leo Varadkar claimed was "lost" rather than kidnapped by Hamas, and four Thais. On Sunday, fourteen were set free—including one in life-threatening condition and four-year-old Avigail Idan, the only US citizen freed, who saw her parents killed on October 7—and three Thai nationals. Of the thirty-nine Palestinian prisoners released each day, the youngest sixteen years old, all had been convicted or charged of violent crimes, many of terror crimes. Moreover, Hamas had violated the truce agreement by separating children from mothers, not permitting Red Cross visits to hostages in contravention of international law, and listing eleven rather than the regular thirteen for the fourth release. Yet, overlooking this and rather than speak against the Hamas horrendous attack, Jibril Rajoub, a senior official in the Palestinian Authority's ruling Fatah faction, said over the weekend that the October 7 massacre was carried out "in the context of the defensive war our people are waging."[76]

On Monday, November 27, the last day of the truce, Hamas released nine children and two women, with a two-day extension of the truce declared. It was also revealed that some forty Israelis were being held captive by the Palestinian Islamic Jihad and other groups; that Hamas was holding onto the bodies of three IDF soldiers who had been killed on October 7; and that children were forced to see videos of the October 7 slaughter with guns pointed at them if they cried. In addition, Eugene Kontorovich and Itamar Marcus reported in the *Wall St. Journal* that Palestinian Authority-controlled Fatah terrorists from Fatah's Al-Aqsa Martyrs Brigades terror group posted videos of its members in Gaza participating in Hamas's October 7 attack. Fatah terrorists killed, tortured, and kidnapped Israelis, and took videos of their actions.[77] Could the PA, which had never condemned the massacre, be relied upon to serve as a counterweight to Hamas after the war?

On Tuesday, while ten Israeli women, one a teenager, and two Thai nationals were released from Gaza, Hamas violated the cease-fire agreement. Israeli forces in the northern Gaza Strip were targeted by explosive devices and gunfire, breaching the agreed-upon terms and resulting in several IDF soldiers sustaining light injuries. At the same time, a senior US administration official, briefing reporters, said that President Biden and others in his government have "reinforced in very clear language with the government of Israel" that the "conduct of the Israeli campaign, when it moves to the south, must be done in a way that is to a maximum extent not designed to produce significant further displacement of persons."[78]

Wednesday saw the release by Hamas and the Palestinian Islamic Jihad of four Thai nationals and twelve Israelis, including two with dual Israeli-Russian citizenship in gratitude to Putin "for his support in the Palestinian struggle." At the same time, the Israeli delegation to the UN in Geneva condemned the Palestinian Authority delegation for falsely presenting in a photographic exhibit an Israeli boy, five-year-old Ido Avigal, who was killed in a Hamas rocket attack on Sderot in 2021, as an Arab child who was murdered by the IDF in Gaza. Israeli forces killed the three terrorists who had violated the cease-fire the day before and Mohammad Zubeidi, the commander of the Palestinian Islamic Jihad in Jenin. That evening, the cornerstone for a new settlement was laid in the south near Gaza, named Ofir in memory of Ofir Leibstein, the regional council head of Sha'ar HaNegev and the first Israeli who was killed on October 7. Netanyahu, present at the ceremony, announced that "we will build and continue to build here and everywhere in Eretz Israel."⁷⁹

On the last day of November, Hamas eventually released six Israeli women and two female teenagers. This led to the joint agreement for an additional one-day extension of the truce, with many Israelis and foreigners still held captive in Gaza. Egyptian officials said that the deal was expected to involve the release of another ten hostages, mostly women and children, a statement which Israel did not confirm. This did not prevent two brothers from Jerusalem's Arab neighborhood of Sur Baher, affiliated with Hamas and who had served jail time for acts of terror, from murdering in a shooting attack that morning three Israelis (one in advanced pregnancy) and injuring eight, innocents then waiting in a bus stop at the entrance to Jerusalem, before being killed by soldiers and a civilian. With Hamas taking responsibility for the attack, War Cabinet Minister Gantz declared this act proof of the necessity for war against the "murderous terror" throughout the country.⁸⁰ What this might entail for the future remained shrouded in uncertainty.

Endnotes

1 TPS, Nov. 1, 2023; Reuters, Nov. 1, 2023; *Haaretz*, Nov. 1, 2023.
2 *Jerusalem Post*, Nov. 1, 2023; *Haaretz*, Nov. 2, 2023.
3 *Jerusalem Post*, Nov. 2, 2023.
4 BBC, Nov. 1, 2023.
5 Al-Jazeera, Nov. 1, 2023; *Washington Post*, Nov. 1, 2023; *Buenos Aires Times*, Nov. 1, 2023; *Times of Israel*, Nov. 2, 2023.
6 *Times of Israel*, Nov. 3, 5, and 13, 2023; *Jerusalem Post*, Nov. 3, 2023; Reuters, Nov. 3, 2023.
7 Al-Jazeera, Nov. 4, 2023; BMJ, Nov. 13, 2023; *Haaretz*, Nov. 2, 2023.
8 CNN, Nov. 4, 2023; *Jerusalem Post*, Nov. 5, 2023; *Times of Israel*, Nov. 4, 2023.
9 Times of Israel, Nov. 3, 2023; All Arab News, Nov. 5, 2023.
10 Fox News, Nov. 4, 2023; Palestinian Watch, July 31, 2014.
11 *Jewish Chronicle*, Nov. 5, 2023; FDD, Nov. 6, 2023.
12 MAKI, Nov. 5, 2023; *Times of Israel*, Nov. 5, 2023.
13 PBS, Nov. 6, 2023; *Jerusalem Post*, Nov. 6, 2023; Israel National News, Nov. 6, 2023.
14 *Jerusalem Post*, Nov. 6, 2023; Al-Jazeera, Nov. 6, 2023.
15 *Times of Israel*, Nov. 6, 2023; Ynet, Nov. 6, 2023; CNBC, Nov. 7, 2023; FDD, Nov. 6, 2023.
16 Al-Jazeera, Nov. 7, 2023; *Haaretz*, Nov. 6, 2023.
17 Israel National News, Nov. 6, 2023; Ynet, Nov. 6, 2023.
18 *Times of Israel*, Nov. 7, 2023.
19 *Times of Israel*, Nov. 7, 2023; *Jerusalem Post*, Nov. 7, 2023.
20 *Haaretz*, Nov. 7, 2023.
21 *Times of Israel*, Nov. 10, 2023; *New York Times*, Nov. 7, 2023; CNN, Nov. 6, 2023.
22 Al-Jazeera, Nov. 7, 2023; *Times of Israel*, Nov. 7, 2023.
23 BBC, Nov. 8, 2023; AP News, Nov. 9, 2023.
24 NPR, Nov. 9, 2023; *Times of Israel*, Nov. 8, 2023; JNS, Nov. 7, 2023; *New York Times*, Nov. 9, 2023.
25 *Times of Israel*, Nov. 7 and 11, 2023; Al-Jazeera, Nov. 8, 2023; Reuters, Nov. 10, 2023.

26 BNN Bloomberg, Nov. 7, 2023.
27 JNS, Nov. 7, 2023; Reuters, Nov. 8, 2023; *Jerusalem Post*, Nov. 6, 2023. Hillel Kuttler, "Arise and Build," *Tablet*, Dec. 18, 2023. The CIA and the Mossad had cooperated in the assassination on February 12, 2008, of Imad Mughniyah, Hezbollah's international operations chief, with a car bomb. *Washington Post*, Jan. 30, 2015.
28 *Times of Israel*, Nov. 8, 2023; *Haaretz*, Nov. 9, 2023; France 24, Nov. 9, 2023.
29 *Times of Israel*, Nov. 9, 2023; *Haaretz*, Nov. 9, 2023; *Times of Israel*, Nov. 9, 2023.
30 CNBC, Nov. 9, 2023; Reuters, Nov. 9, 2023; UNRWA, Nov. 9, 2023, https://www.unrwa.org.
31 *Jerusalem Post*, Nov. 9, 2023; Reuters, Nov. 9, 2023.
32 *Times of Israel*, Nov. 9, 2023. *Kristallnacht* (the "Night of Broken Glass") took its name from the shattered glass that littered the streets after the destruction of Jewish businesses, homes, and synagogues in the Nazi pogroms unleashed against the Jewish population of Germany and recently incorporated territories during the night of November 9–10, 1938. During the pogrom, some 30,000 Jewish men were rounded up and taken to concentration camps, the first time a mass arrest of this kind had occurred against Jews. The Nazi regime then ordered the Jewish community to pay a one billion Reichsmark "atonement tax" and created under Adolf Eichmann a central office for future Jewish emigration. See Karl Schleunes, *The Twisted Road to Auschwitz: Nazi Policy toward German Jews, 1933–1939* (Urbana: University of Illinois Press, 1971).
33 MEMRI report, Nov. 13, 2023, https://www.memri.org.
34 Israel National News, Nov. 10, 2023; *Times of Israel*, Nov. 10, 2023; FDD, Nov. 13, 2023.
35 *Times of Israel*, Nov. 11, 2023; *Le Monde*, Nov. 25, 2023; *Jerusalem Post*, Nov. 12, 2023.
36 Maayan Hoffman, "Is This What Hell Looks like?," *Jerusalem Post Magazine*, Nov. 10, 2023.
37 *Times of Israel*, Nov. 11, 2023.
38 Israel National News, Nov. 12, 2023; *Jerusalem Post*, Nov. 13, 2023.
39 Yossi Klein Halevi, "The Lonely People of History," *Times of Israel*, Nov. 12, 2023; Bret Stephens, "For America's Jews Every Day Must Be Oct. 8," *New York Times*, Nov. 7, 2023.
40 *Jerusalem Post*, Nov. 13, 2023; *Times of Israel*, Nov. 4, 2023; France 24, Nov. 12, 2023.
41 *Jerusalem Post*, Nov. 9, 2023.
42 *Times of Israel*, Nov. 13, 2023; Reuters, Nov. 12, 2023.
43 FDD, Nov. 15, 2023.
44 *Jerusalem Post*, Nov. 13, 2023.
45 Israel National News, Apr. 15, 2023.
46 Aawsat, Nov. 14, 2023, https://english.aawsat.com.
47 i24 News, Nov. 16, 2023.
48 *Jerusalem Post*, Nov. 13, 2023; JNS, July 18, 2023.
49 Reuters, Nov. 13, 2023; *Jerusalem Post*, Nov. 11 and 27, 2023.
50 *Wall St. Journal*, Nov. 13, 2023; *Jerusalem Post*, Nov. 14, 2023; Seth J. Frantzman, "This Man is Israel's Face and Voice to the Arabic-Speaking World," *Jerusalem Post Magazine*," Feb. 2, 2024.
51 *Times of Israel*, Nov. 15, 2023; *Jewish Chronicle*, Nov. 14, 2023.
52 *Times of Israel*, Nov. 15, 2023; Reuters, Nov. 15, 2023;
53 *Jerusalem Post*, Nov. 14, 2023; *Times of Israel*, Nov. 16, 2023; *Haaretz*, Nov. 17, 2023.
54 BBC, Nov. 13, 2023; *Times of Israel*, Oct. 27, 2023; AP News, Nov. 15, 2023. The Houthis (or, more precisely, the Houthi movement, which was named after its founder, Hussein al-Houthi) are an extremist Shi'a Islamist movement that wrested control of the mountainous region of Yemen from the previous pro-Western government by capturing the capital city of Sana'a in 2015. Following this coup, the Houthi movement proclaimed itself the legal government of the entire country. Its flag features a five-line slogan: "God is great, death to America, death to Israel, a curse upon the Jews, victory to Islam." It is hardly surprising that the ayatollahs of the Islamic Republic of Iran embraced the Houthi movement from the day

of its establishment in 2004 and have supported it ever since with ample funds and arms. Uzi Rubin, "The Yemeni Houthi Missile Arsenal and the Threat to Israel," BESA Center Perspectives Paper no. 2,260, Feb. 1, 2024.

55 INSSS, Nov. 8, 2023, https://www.insss.org.il.
56 KAN 11 TV, Nov. 16, 2023; *Jerusalem Post*, Nov. 16, 2023.
57 IDF Press Release, Nov. 12, 2023; CNBC, Nov. 17, 2023; *Times of Israel*, Nov. 14 and 17, 2023;
58 *Jerusalem Post*, Nov. 14, 2023.
59 *Wall St. Journal*, Nov. 18, 2023.
60 *Times of Israel*, Nov. 19, 2023.
61 *Times of Israel*, Nov. 19, 2023; Reuters, Nov. 20, 2023.
62 *Times of Israel*, Nov. 20–21, 2023; Israel National News, Nov. 20, 2023; Ynet, Nov. 21, 2023.
63 Reuters, Nov. 20, 2023; *Times of Israel*, Nov. 20, 2023.
64 *Haaretz*, Nov. 21, 2023; *Times of Israel*, Nov. 20, 2023; Matzav, Nov. 20, 2023, https://matzav.com; *Jewish Chronicle*, Nov. 20, 2023.
65 *Jerusalem Post*, Nov. 21, 2023; *Times of Israel*, Nov. 21, 2023.
66 Reuters, Nov. 17, 2023; *Time*, Dec. 5, 2023; *Wall St. Journal*, Nov. 22, 2023.
67 Israel National News, Nov. 22, 2023; *Barron's*, Nov. 22, 2023; *Jerusalem Post*, Nov. 21, 2023.
68 *Newsweek*, Nov. 21, 2023.
69 IDF Press Release, Nov. 22, 2023; CNN, Nov. 23, 2023.
70 *Times of Israel*, Nov. 23, 2023; Ynet, Nov. 23, 2023.
71 Free Beacon, Nov. 23, 2023, https://freebeacon.com; *Times of Israel*, Nov. 18, 2023.
72 The White House, Nov. 24, 2023, https://www.whitehouse.gov; Anadolu Ajansi, Nov. 22, 2023, https://www.aa.com.tr.
73 *Jerusalem Post*, Nov. 24, 2023; *Times of Israel*, Nov. 25, 2023.
74 *New York Times*, Nov. 28, 2023; *Jerusalem Post*, Nov. 27, 2023;
75 FDD, Nov. 26, 2023; *Jerusalem Post*, Nov. 26, 2023.
76 *Haaretz*, Nov. 26–27, 2023; CNN, Nov. 29, 2023; JNS, Nov. 26, 2023.
77 Reuters, Nov. 27, 2023; *Times of Israel*, Nov. 28, 2023; *Guardian*, Nov. 28, 2023.
78 *Haaretz*, Nov. 28, 2023; *Times of Israel*, Nov. 28, 2023; France 24, Nov. 28, 2023.
79 *Times of Israel*, Nov. 29, 2023; Israel National News, Nov. 29, 2023; *Times of Israel*, Oct. 7, 2023.
80 *Times of Israel*, Nov. 30, 2023; *Guardian*, Dec. 1, 2023.

CHAPTER 4

... and On

As of 5:48 on Friday morning, December 1, 2023, Hamas broke the latest truce agreement by firing six barrages of rockets towards Israeli communities on the Gaza border. Just after 7:00 a.m., Israel announced that, following Hamas's violation of the cease-fire and renewal of rocket fire, "the IDF has resumed combat against the Hamas terrorist organization in the Gaza Strip." "IDF fighter jets are currently striking Hamas terror targets in the Gaza Strip," the statement added. Prime Minister Netanyahu's office announced that with the renewal of the war, including Hamas's reneging on its pledge to release all the female hostages, Jerusalem remained committed to achieving "the goals of the war: to release our hostages, eliminate Hamas, and ensure that Gaza will never again present a threat to Israel's citizens."[1]

The end to the week-long cease-fire on day fifty-six of the Hamas-Israel war, with 113 abductees released, brought a harrowing sense of darkness regarding the 137 remaining hostages. The day before, senior Hamas spokesman Ghazi Hamad had said in a CBS interview that it was "not important" how many hostages were still alive. Hamas had kidnapped babies to "pressure" Israel, to tell the Israeli government that "you pushed us to hell." The Bibas family, including ten-month-old Kfir Bibas and his four-year-old brother Ariel, Hamad added, "paid the price because of the occupation." A few days earlier, the IDF stressed that it had not yet been able to confirm Hamas's claim that the boys and their mother, Shiri, were killed after being kidnapped on October 7.[2]

Two new revelations on Hamas's methodical planning were cause for wonder. A blueprint reviewed by the *New York Times* laid out the plan for the Hamas massacre. Israeli officials, who had received the document more than a year ago, dismissed it as aspirational and ignored specific warnings. Codenamed "Jericho Wall" by Israeli authorities, it described the assault design and how Hamas would overwhelm the fortifications around the Gaza border, take over Israeli cities, and destroy the Jewish State's military bases. Hamas's extensive planning for the October 7 assault also emerged from IDF interviews with child hostages, who were repeatedly given drugs and shuffled from one location to another in the tunnels before their release. Earlier, each child seized was placed on a motorcycle. One leg was positioned against the bike's exhaust pipe, causing burns as a means of identification. The kidnappers would recognize that the children "belonged" to them by a specific sign in case they escaped their guards.[3]

That Friday, the IDF carried out strikes from air, land, and sea against four hundred terror targets in Gaza, more than fifty of these near Khan Younis, and thwarted terror cells in the southern and northern parts of the Strip. The next day, Deputy Hamas chief Saleh Al-Arouri told the pan-Arab Al-Jazeera TV that no more prisoners would be exchanged with Israel until there was a cease-fire in Gaza. Al-Arouri said that the hostages still being held captive by Hamas were Israeli soldiers and civilian men who had previously served in the Israeli army, who would not be freed unless there was a cease-fire and all Palestinian detainees were also released. "Let the war take its course. This decision is final. We will not compromise on it," he declared.[4]

On Saturday, along with heavy strikes on Khan Younis, IAF fighter jets eliminated Wessam Farhi Farhat, Hamas's Shejaiya Battalion commander since 2010. He had most recently taken part in the planning of the October 7 massacre, during which he directed Hamas elite Nukhba operatives to infiltrate Kibbutz Nahal Oz and IDF post. The next day, it eliminated Haitham Khuwajari, commander of Hamas's Shati Battalion who oversaw raids into Israeli territory on October 7. The IDF also announced that it had found over 800 tunnel shafts in Gaza since the start of the war, many located in civilian areas, and destroyed 500. For the first time, Shin Bet director Ronen Bar spoke at length of his responsibility for the October 7 debacle and said that his organization intended to eliminate Hamas "anywhere"—"this is our Munich."[5]

Come Monday, many IDF tanks rolled towards Khan Younis, ramping up the army's offensive against Hamas in the southern part of the Gaza Strip. It continued to advise civilians to leave the area beforehand, the IDF's published online map drawing praise from NSC spokesperson Kirby: "'There's not a whole lot of modern militaries that would do that." Yet nearly one-third of Israeli Arabs, in a recent Tel Aviv University poll, denied that Hamas intentionally targeted women and children on October 7; 44 percent of Israeli Arabs did not feel that Israel's response to the Hamas attack was justified, while 36 percent believed that both Israel and Hamas shared responsibility for the outbreak of war, At the same time, Israeli citizenship (33 percent) slightly edged Arab identity (32 percent) as the two most dominant components of Arab personal identity, with 8 percent saying Palestinian identity was the dominant component.[6]

As for the 17–20 women and children still held hostage in Gaza, US State Department Spokesman Matthew Miller told reporters in Washington that the hostage deal between Israel and Hamas partially fell apart last week because Hamas wanted to prevent the remaining Israeli women it held in Gaza from talking about their time in custody. Still, the *Washington Post,* following Reuters and the Associated Press (AP), stated that Israel and Hamas exchanged "captives," seeming to equate innocent kidnapped civilians and Arab prisoners convicted of terrorism. Moreover, the hostages, unlike the prisoners in Israeli jails, were threatened with death, suffered sexual assault, women and children placed in cages, men beaten with electric cables, given little food and water, and denied life-saving medicines.[7]

At this point, Alex Joffe and Asaf Romirowsky observed in examining "the red-green alliance" between the far left and jihadist Islamic radicals, Hamas, winning in the West, had so far effectively galvanized massive anti-Israel demonstrations in the United States, Australia, and Western Europe. While the IDF had staged a remarkably effective counterattack and was winning in Gaza, the fruits of decades of Muslim immigration, legal and illegal, into Europe were now fully revealed. In the United States, the linkages among the Council on American-Islamic Relations, American Muslims for Palestine, Students for Justice in Palestine, the Muslim Students Association, and the Palestinian Youth Movement pointed to domestic elements implacably opposed to Israel that took advantage of American tolerance, albeit crying "Islamophobia" at every opportunity when criticized. The red components, the dizzying array of seemingly disparate entities from the Democratic Socialists of America, Just Stop Oil, Black Lives Matter, IfNotNow, Jewish Voice for Peace, and more, had been responsible for putting bodies into American streets. All were funded by the same array of far-left foundations and dark-money bundlers with the support of "human rights" nongovernmental organizations. All acted as "foot soldiers," increasingly for one another's causes, and all were increasingly violent. They were all part of the same broad movement—anti-American, anti-Israel, and anti-Western.[8]

On December 6, Israel's diaspora affairs minister, Amichai Chikli, sent personal letters to ten European leaders and some European Union (EU) representatives, which included evidence of the terrorist activity of Hamas activists and operatives of the Popular Front for the Liberation of Palestine (PFLP) in major cities across the continent. "Weeks have passed since the barbarism that Hamas committed against infants, children, the elderly, and thousands of Israeli citizens. This is not the time for ambiguity. I want to clarify this unequivocally. Hamas has proven that their goal is to kill Jews everywhere," Chikli wrote.

"Since the massacre, calls for violence against Jews worldwide have increased by 120 percent—a shocking statistic. Unfortunately, Hamas's bloodlust is not limited to Israel and Jews but also extends to Europe and Christians. I want to remind you that in the past, Hamas members expressed the Islamic intention to conquer Europe."

Certain examples presented in Chikli's letters included Mohammed Ahmed Hanon, whose Charity Association for Palestine Support transferred funds to Hamas from Italy. Amin Abu Rashad, arrested by Israel in 2003 on suspicion of transferring millions of euros from Europe to Hamas through seemingly charitable associations, had praised the "hands" that carried out stabbing attacks in Jerusalem in the early wave of knife terrorism against Israelis in October 2015. Muhammad Suwala (Abu Obada), a member of Hamas's military wing in the West Bank and the political bureau, was currently residing in the United Kingdom. Another was Mohand Halabi, who murdered Rabbi Nehemia Lavi and Aharon Bennett in Jerusalem, and seriously wounded Bennett's wife and two-year-old son during his attack in October 2015. Khaled Barakat, a senior member of the PFLP, headed the NGO Samidoun Palestinian Prisoner Solidarity Network, operating in many European and North American countries, and was involved in establishing military cells and promoting terrorist activity in Israel and abroad. Tzur Bar-Oz, head of Research and Foreign Relations at Chikli's ministry, concluded: We hope that the leaders of the countries realize what Hamas is, and that "these are extreme people who pose a threat to citizens worldwide, not just Jews and not just in Israel."[9]

And the conflict wore on. Palestinian terrorists fired more than 11,500 rockets towards Israeli territory since Hamas launched its war against the Jewish State on October 7, stated the Israeli Foreign Ministry. The IDF tightened its encirclement of Khan Younis, the last Hamas stronghold, often in heavy hand-to-hand combat in the most intensive fighting of the war so far. In response to repeated attacks from Lebanon, in addition to striking some 250 targets across Gaza in one day, Israeli Air Force (IAF) fighter jets struck on Tuesday numerous assets belonging to Hezbollah. In Qalqilya, Israeli security forces killed two terrorists and wounded several others, and arrested twenty-nine across the West Bank, for a total of 2,150 since the war began. As for Iran, human rights groups charged that Tehran used the world's preoccupation with the war in Gaza as a cover to exact revenge on dissidents and execute more than 127 Iranian citizens, including women and children, without due judicial process.[10]

By December 7, the IDF had broken through the Hamas defensive lines in Jibaliya, Shuja'iya, and Khan Younis. At the urging of Washington, the Israeli War Cabinet approved the amount of fuel to enter Gaza. Hamas official

Haniyeh repeated his organization's preparedness to negotiate over hostage release only after a halt to the fighting. Invoking the rare use of paragraph 99 in the UN Charter, Secretary-General Guterrez called on the Security Council to press for an immediate cease-fire on humanitarian grounds because of "the threat to peace and security in the world." Israeli UN Ambassador Erdan and Foreign Minister Cohen immediately called for his resignation. After the presidents of Harvard, MIT, and the University of Pennsylvania, asked before a special Congressional hearing of the House Education Committee if calls for the genocide of Jews violated their respective schools' code of conduct as to bullying and harassment, responded that the answer "depends on the context" or only if it "rises to the level of incitement to violence," the White House spokesman Andrew Bates responded that such calls "are monstrous"; Yad Vashem stated that it was "extremely alarmed" at the academics' position. Secretary of State Blinken declared that Israel "is taking important steps to better protect civilians." The age of retirement for Israelis serving in reserves and active duty would be temporarily raised by one year to maintain the IDF's operational preparedness during wartime, KAN News 12 reported.[11]

Meeting in Geneva, the G7 (Canada, France, Germany, Italy, Japan, the United Kingdom, and the United States) and the European Union condemned the Hamas attack of October 7 on Israel and emphasized a sovereign state's right to defend itself in accordance with international law "as it seeks to prevent a recurrence of these traumatic events." Hamas, they went on, "offers nothing but suffering to the Palestinian people," and "we will continue to coordinate our efforts to isolate Hamas and ensure it cannot threaten Israel." The leaders called for the release of the remaining hostages and on Iran to stop providing support for Hamas, Hezbollah, and the Houthis. Finally, they urged that every effort be made to ensure humanitarian aid to civilians in Gaza, and that the G7 would provide more than $600 million, some of which the United Nations Relief and Works Agency (UNRWA) would distribute.[12]

By the end of the sixty-second day of the war, dozens of Hamas in the northern Gaza city of Jabaliya had surrendered after losing contact with the terrorist group's leadership, the largest number since the conflict began. Five IDF soldiers were killed on that December 7, for a total of 87 to date since the ground invasion; the Gaza Health Ministry declared that 17,177 Palestinians had been killed and 46,000 wounded since the start of the war. With rockets continuing against Israel from the south and the north, Netanyahu stated that if Hezbollah launched an all-out war against Israel, "then it will single-handedly turn Beirut and southern Lebanon . . . into Gaza [City] and Khan Younis." Overnight, twenty-one suspects were arrested in the West Bank, where much war material was uncovered. For its part, the United States resumed unarmed drone flights over Gaza to support hostage recovery efforts, according to the Pentagon; Hamas still held 138 captives, including 8 Americans.[13]

As the war entered its tenth week, IDF ground, aerial, and naval forces struck over 250 terror targets in Gaza. For the first time since the start of the fighting, the IDF Artillery Corps began operating inside the Gaza Strip and not merely on the border with Gaza. In Cyprus, local security agencies and the Mossad foiled a plan by Iranian terrorists to carry out attacks against Israeli and Jewish targets. At President Biden's instruction, the United States vetoed a UN Security Council demand for a cease-fire. Blinken determined on December 9 that an emergency existed to fast-track the sale of $106 million in roughly 14,000 tank shells to Israel, the same time that Israel's National Security Advisor Tzahi Hanegbi told Channel 12 that the Biden administration had not set a deadline for the IDF to end its military campaign to oust Hamas from Gaza. According to top defense officials, Israel's war in Gaza could finish by February, although a Hamas insurgency was expected to last between three and nine months. At the same time, Israeli security sources said that the IDF was unable to create new conditions for another hostage release deal. They noted that although fifty percent of Hamas's battalion commanders had been killed, militants from more junior ranks were taking their place, thus limiting the impact on Hamas' fighting capacities.[14]

On December 10, for the first time since the beginning of the war, the IDF released comprehensive figures of those wounded from the battles in the Gaza Strip, revealing how many soldiers had been injured in the line of duty. Since the beginning of the war, 1,593 combat soldiers had been injured, 559 of these since the ground invasion—255 of them seriously. Another 446 were moderately injured and 892 lightly injured. The IAF's tactical search and rescue unit, Unit 669, together with doctors and paramedics, continued their rescue operations from Gaza. Over the past week, helicopter crews of the search and rescue helicopter squadrons (Yanshuf and Yas'ur), combat soldiers and doctors of Unit 669, along with the medical forces and paramedics on the ground, had carried out approximately sixty evacuations of wounded soldiers from combat zones, providing advanced and life-saving medical treatment. A total of approximately 300 helicopter evacuations had taken place, in which about 600 wounded were evacuated since the beginning of the war.[15]

In the nine weeks since Hamas launched its cross-border attack on the northwestern Negev, IAF jets had struck more than 22,000 terrorist targets in the Gaza Strip. After Hamas violated the cease-fire-for-hostages deal on December 1, the IAF carried out strikes on more than 3,500 terrorist targets in the coastal enclave. The IDF announced that 430 soldiers had been killed since October 7, 104 of these since the ground war began. For its part, the Health Ministry in Gaza declared that 18,000 Palestinians had been killed and 49,500 wounded since the war erupted. In a statement published by Al-Jazeera on Sunday night, Hamas propaganda chief Abu Obeida claimed that "the enemy is still receiving blows from us, and what is coming is greater." The remaining hostages would only be released "on our terms," he vowed. Across the West Bank, Israeli security forces arrested eighteen suspects overnight Sunday, five of them Hamas militants.[16]

Hamas is an "essential part of the Palestinian political mosaic," Palestinian Authority Prime Minister Mohammad Shtayyeh told world leaders gathered in Qatar on Sunday, adding that Israel's goal of eliminating the Islamist terror group is "unacceptable" to Ramallah, the PA headquarters. "We want a situation in which Palestinians are united. . . . I think it is time that Hamas call the Palestinian president and tell him we're all united behind you, and you are the legitimate authority of the Palestinian people and we are ready to engage," Shtayyeh stated. At the same Doha Forum, Iran foreign minister Hossein Amir-Abdollahian, warning that continuation of the war in Gaza would lead to a "regional explosion," reiterated his country's proposal that a referendum be held to determine the fate of Palestine, with only descendants of those who lived there prior to 1948 being permitted to vote.[17]

Two days earlier, American news site *Politico* had reported that President Biden gave Israel until the end of the year to wrap up operations. However, the report was quickly walked back, with a US National Security Council spokesperson responding: "These are Israeli military operations and the Israelis will decide their course. We will continue to support Israel's efforts to defend itself from Hamas terrorists." Reiterating this stand, Secretary Blinken said during an interview with Jake Tapper of CNN on Sunday that Israel would decide when to end its war against Hamas. "We have these discussions with Israel, including about the duration as well as how it's prosecuting this campaign against Hamas. These are decisions for Israel to make," he declared. As if to confirm American continued support, the Pentagon announced that the Biden administration approved the sale of 14,000 rounds of tank ammunition to Israel for about $106.5 million. A State Department release repeated the point: "The United States is committed to the security of Israel, and it is vital to U.S. national interests to assist Israel to develop and maintain a strong and ready self-defense capability. This proposed sale is consistent with those objectives."[18]

One hundred trucks of humanitarian aid reached Gaza on Sunday via the Rafah Crossing, twenty percent of the number that entered the Strip daily before

October 7. The Israeli Defense ministerial body responsible for Palestinian civilian affairs accused the United Nations of not doing enough to process humanitarian aid into Gaza and charged that the world body was responsible for supplies not reaching the Strip at a fast enough pace. "We have expanded our capabilities to conduct inspections for the aid delivered into Gaza. Kerem Shalom is to be opened, so the number of inspections will double. But the aid keeps waiting at the entrance of Rafah," the Coordination of Government Activities in the Territories (COGAT) wrote on X (formerly Twitter). In a bid to facilitate an increase in the number of aid trucks that could enter Gaza each day, Israel had announced last week that it would open the Kerem Shalom Crossing with Gaza for the inspection of humanitarian aid trucks before they entered Gaza through Egypt's Rafah Crossing. "The UN must do better—the aid is there, and the people need it," the statement added.[19]

Two months after the deadly Hamas attack, signs of life slowly returned to Kibbutz Be'eri, one of the hardest hit on that holiday weekend. Its printing press, the kibbutz's main source of income, which escaped damage due to being nearly empty at the time of the assault, was abuzz with activity. The opening of the printing press one week after October 7 was "a very symbolic move to show residents of the community and the whole border area that there is a rebirth," said Ben Sochman, manager of the site and whose mother, Tamar, was shot dead outside her home by the terrorists that Sabbath morning. "Our hope," he added, "is that out of all this pain, there can be some growth." Three hundred of the 350 printing press workers were already back at their jobs, many commuting from their temporary homes in Dead Sea hotels or elsewhere for work. A hardcore group of scores of young kibbutz members returned home, braving the booms of artillery explosions from the IDF tanks fighting nearby and the continuing if dwindling number of rocket attacks from Gaza as the war entered its third month. "We are here," read the huge sign on the water tower opposite the newly reopened kibbutz secretariat and dining hall. Chanuka candles were lit on some of the window frames of the demolished, blackened homes, their light shining in the dark night.[20]

By contrast, shops, schools, and government offices were shut across the West Bank and East Jerusalem on December 11, as Palestinians staged a general strike protesting Israel's war on Hamas in the Gaza Strip. Activists called for a strike in solidarity with the territory covering businesses, public workers and education. Many Palestinians took part and rallies were staged in the West Bank, according to Essam Abu Baker, coordinator of Palestinian factions in Ramallah. He described the protest as part of a global effort to put pressure on Israel to stop the war, reporting strikes taking place in parts of Jordan and

Lebanon, too. "The strike today is not only in solidarity with Gaza, but also against the United States which used its veto in the Security Council against a truce," Abu Baker explained.²¹

Meeting that evening with leaders of the communities of southern Israel in Ashkelon, Minister Benny Gantz declared that "the military operation is expanding and intensifying in southern and northern Gaza, and also in the north against Hezbollah, which is being removed from the border and suffering losses." He added that the Hamas leadership at this point had "lost control" over a large part of the territory, and that the military apparatus was being "thoroughly dismantled" so that it could never be assembled again. As to Gaza's future, Gantz emphasized that "we will hold the territories in the Gaza Strip for a long period of time, we will act militarily wherever a Hamas member raises his head or his weapon, and we will make sure that the IDF soldiers can be seen from the windows of the houses of the residents in the south." Our operation, he concluded, "is aimed at continuing the dismantling of Hamas, the return of the hostages, and enabling the return of some residents to their homes in a process that will begin in the coming weeks and under the direction of the IDF."²²

As for the West Bank, Defense Minister Gallant declared that "the arena is secondary to the main effort we are conducting in the Gaza Strip. Similar to what is happening in the north, we have no interest in escalation." Yet, in the nine weeks since Hamas launched its cross-border attack from the Gaza Strip, data published by Israeli TV Channel 14 News counted 1,388 attacks in that volatile area, including 569 cases of rock-throwing, 287 attacks with explosives, 143 Molotov cocktail assaults and 70 terrorist shootings. Three Israelis—a civilian, a soldier, and a Border Police officer—were murdered in Judea and Samaria since October 7, and at least fifty-two Israelis sustained injuries. The report said that sixteen people were wounded by rock-throwing, ten sustained gunshot wounds, eight were violently attacked by Palestinians, and two were injured in a car-ramming attack. At least fifteen members of the security forces were wounded during counterterrorism raids in Judea and Samaria, while one Israeli was moderately injured as he neutralized a Palestinian terrorist. In the first six months of 2023, Rescuers without Borders (Hatzalah Judea and Samaria) recorded a total of 3,640 acts of terrorism throughout all of Israel. Palestinian terrorists killed 28 people and wounded 362 others between January 1 and July 1, 2023, the emergency service said.²³

Speaking at a Chanuka reception in the East Room of the White House on the evening of December 11 to a packed crowd of some 800, including Holocaust survivors, Biden called a "surge of antisemitism" around the globe "sickening" while drawing applause for his administration's efforts to rush more humanitarian aid to Gaza. "We continue to provide military assistance until they get rid of Hamas, but we have to be careful," Biden said of US support for Israel in the war: "The whole world, public opinion can shift overnight. We can't let that happen." He then went on: "As I said after the [October 7] attack, my commitment to the safety of the Jewish people, and the security of Israel, its right to exist as an independent Jewish state, is unshakeable." "You don't have to be a Jew to be a Zionist. I am a Zionist," echoing comments he had made in the wake of October 7. "Were there no Israel, there would not be a Jew in the world who is safe," he added. As for the remaining hostages being held by Hamas, the Chief Executive declared "we're not going to stop until we get every one of them home"; he had spent "countless hours" on the issue himself. Yet the very next day, Biden said that Israel's governing coalition needed to 'change", and that the Jewish State was losing international support due to its "indiscriminate bombing" in Gaza.[24]

The IDF suffered heavy losses that evening. Nine soldiers from the elite Golani Brigade, including a colonel and a lieutenant colonel, were killed in an ambush in the Hamas stronghold of Shejaiya in northern Gaza. Another soldier was killed in a separate incident in northern Gaza, for a total of 115 killed in the six weeks since the start of the ground operation. For comparison's sake, 95 American soldiers were killed in six weeks during the Second Battle of Fallujah in November-December 2004, the bloodiest US engagement of the Iraq War. What occurred on that soon dubbed "Black Tuesday" in Gaza led a research fellow at the Jerusalem Institute for Strategy and Security, echoing the more militant mood of many Israelis, to advocate that the IDF shift from aspiring to be "the most moral military in the world," as well as complying with demands from Washington to minimize harm to non-combatants, to adopting a strategy of preemptively destroying every building in a densely populated area strewn with explosive charges, ambushes, and anti-tank launches before sending in ground forces. At this point, it appeared that the end to the war in Gaza was not in sight, Gallant telling US National Security Council Advisor Sullivan that Israel needed "more than several months to destroy Hamas."[25]

In addition, Hamas's $2.5 billion budget reflected considerable strength. According to a study in *Haaretz*, that included $1.1 billion from the Palestinian Authority, $365 million from taxes, $360 million from Qatar, $325 million from UNRWA, $125 million from Iran, and $100 million from "charity organizations." On December 14, while the IDF distributed flyers offering $400,000 for information leading to the location of Hamas leader Sinwar and large sums for other leaders, eight IDF soldiers were seriously wounded in southern Gaza and evacuated to hospital care. The Mossad announced that, thanks to its efforts, seven Hamas operatives were arrested in Denmark for plotting an attack on Jews. In addition, the Shin Bet said that it had thwarted multiple Iranian attempts to recruit Israelis online to carry out "hostile missions." Clearly, Hamas was still a formidable foe with a significant war chest even as its fierce war with Israel continued. Stripping the organization of its wealth would be a formidable task.[26]

In a major thirty-hour counterterror raid on December 12, continuing well into the next day, Israeli security forces operating in the Samaria city of Jenin detained hundreds of Palestinian suspects. IDF soldiers, officers from the Israel Border Police, and Shin Bet members searched more than 400 buildings and confiscated weapons, large amounts of ammunition, explosives, and other military equipment. Troops also uncovered and destroyed seven bomb laboratories, more than ten tunnel shafts, and five "war rooms" used by terrorists in Jenin's "refugee camp" to monitor IDF counterterrorism activities. Two drone strikes were also carried out. Ten armed Palestinians were killed and several wounded; seven IDF soldiers were lightly wounded in the raid. Since the beginning of the war, more than 2,200 wanted suspects had been arrested throughout Judea and Samaria and the Jordan Valley, at least 1,190 of whom are associated with Hamas.[27]

And the death tolls continued to rise. As of mid-December, Israel had lost 445 soldiers since the Gaza war began, 119 of whom were killed during the ground invasion. The number of wounded came to 1,740, including dozens in critical condition. Tragically, during Gaza battles the IDF killed three male hostages who had escaped Hamas captivity, mistakenly thinking them terrorists. The Gaza Health Ministry claimed that 18,787 Palestinians had been killed since the beginning of the war, with 50,897 wounded. Yet Israel's citizenry was united as perhaps no other time in its history of armed conflicts since the 1948 War of Independence, best seen by the unbreakable spirit and patriotism of its younger generation of soldiers committed to the longevity of the State of Israel.

On the other side, a recent poll taken by the Palestinian Center for Policy Survey and Research found that almost seventy-five percent of Palestinians believed that the Hamas attack on October 7 was "correct" given its outcome so far. The ensuing Gaza war had lifted support for the Islamist group both there and in the West Bank, where it had more than tripled and which witnessed the highest levels of violence in years between IDF soldiers and Palestinians living there. Mahmoud Abbas's popularity had plummeted given widespread accusations of Palestinian Authority corruption and inefficiency, and amidst an almost decade-long impasse in US-sponsored negotiations on the creation of a Palestinian state alongside Israel.[28]

Now is not the time for a two-state solution, Israeli President Herzog told the Associated Press in a December 14 interview. "Why? Because there is an emotional chapter here that must be dealt with. My nation is bereaving [*sic*]. My nation is in trauma." Politicians across Israel's political spectrum, from Prime Minister Netanyahu to opposition leader Yair Lapid, had come out against handing the Gaza Strip over to the Palestinian Authority—a move advocated by the United States as a first step towards a two-state solution. "In order to get back to the idea of dividing the land, of negotiating peace or talking to the Palestinians, etc., one has to deal first and foremost with the emotional trauma that we are going through and the need and demand for [a] full sense of security for all people," he said. Herzog once led Israel's Labor Party, which called for a two-state solution, but following the October 7 carnage by Hamas such a position had become politically untenable, particularly as the PA had allocated $3 million for slain Hamas terrorists as part of its "pay-for-slay" program while its Fatah party boasted of members taking part in the attack.[29]

After the Netanyahu cabinet voted on December 15 to reopen its Kerem Shalom Crossing for humanitarian aid to be able to enter Gaza directly through Israel for the first time since the outbreak of the war, two American and Israeli officials told the Times of Israel that the Biden administration had set its sights on its next ask from Israel: to allow commercial goods into the Strip. "The Israelis understand that the more aid that gets in, the more time they'll have to continue operations in Gaza," the US official said. As for the IDF's tragic error in killing three hostages, a "heartbroken" Minister Gantz declared that "our responsibility is to win this war, and part of that victory will be bringing the hostages home. We'll do everything we can to bring them back alive. Everything," he vowed. The mayor of the Bedouin town of Rahat reacted thus: "Such bitter news: Bedouins and Jews were taken hostage together, managed to flee together in an effort to continue their lives—and ended their lives together in this very tragic event," Ata Abu Madighem told Army Radio. In Hostages Square, a public plaza in front of the Tel Aviv Museum of Art, thousands protested overnight into Saturday for a new deal with Hamas to secure the release of all 129 remaining hostages.[30]

Meanwhile, the Houthis' threat from Yemen gained in force. The US Navy destroyer *USS Carney* shot down fourteen Houthi drones in the Red Sea on December 16. Swiss-based MSC (Mediterranean Shipping Co.), the world's biggest container shipping company, said that it would stop plying these waters after an attack on one of its ships. After similar announcements from Maersk, CMA, CGM, and Hapag-Lloyd, four of the five largest global shipping companies now diverted shipping routes due to Houthi attacks. (BP followed two days later.) Houthi official Ali Al-Qahoum announced that the group, whose official slogan is "death to America, death to Israel, curse the Jews," "will not abandon the Palestinian cause regardless of any US, Israeli, or Western threats." In response, US Secretary of Defense Lloyd Austin and his UK counterpart, Grant Shapps, discussed "the ongoing threat to civilians and global shipping" posed by Houthi attacks, according to the Pentagon. Egyptian air defenses shot down a suspected drone off the Red Sea coast near Dahab on Egypt's eastern Sinai coast. Washington wanted the "broadest possible" maritime coalition to protect ships in the Red Sea and signal to the Houthis that attacks would not be tolerated, US Special Envoy for Yemen Tim Lenderking told Reuters. The proposed multinational naval force would face "extraordinary problems," responded Iranian Defense Minister Mohammad Reza Ashtiani, and nobody "can make a move in a region where we have predominance."[31]

A video clip from the Gaza battlefront made its way around Israeli social media at this time. It was 2 a.m. and Israeli soldiers noticed some suspicious movements on the horizon in the Zeitoun neighborhood. In a time of war, that would generally mean to open fire. But the IDF, being the IDF, waited and then noticed that it was a child, a four-year-old girl. She was walking around aimlessly without shoes and with multiple wounds. The IDF soldiers took her to the field doctor, treated her wounds, and then brought her to the humanitarian corridor in an attempt to locate her family and care for her. It turned out that the child was sent by Hamas into the heart of a war zone to see if the Israeli soldiers were up and alert. At thirty-five seconds into the video, a soldier's sigh could be heard. As Daniel Gordis put it, "no other response really makes any sense. What is there to say about 'human beings' who would use a young girl that way?" This story never made it to the world press.[32]

On the afternoon of December 18, one day after the IDF revealed the largest-ever Hamas attack tunnel discovered—2.5 miles long, 10 feet wide, and 165 feet deep running from the Jabaliya refugee camp close to the Erez border crossing with Israel, Netanyahu met with US Secretary of Defense Austin at the Kirya military base in the center of Tel Aviv, first declaring: "We're fighting a war of civilization against barbarism." He expressed again Israel's commitment to achieve total victory against Hamas, adding that in many ways it was America's war "because you are leading the forces of civilization in the world." This was a battle against the Iranian axis of terror, he added, which was now threatening to close the maritime Strait of Bab-el-Mandeb, a direct challenge to the freedom of navigation of the entire world.

Responding, Austin said that America's commitment to Israel "is unshakeable." "I know that Israel is a small, tight-knit country, and I know that all Israelis were touched by the vast evil committed by Hamas," he said. "I'm here to mourn with you for the innocent souls taken from you on October 7. I'm also here to stand alongside the families of those still missing in Gaza, including U.S. citizens." The US Defense Secretary described the task force that the United States was leading in the Red Sea to protect freedom of navigation from Iran and its Houthi proxy, a crucial step given that more than 20,000 ships transited the Red Sea every year, and he demanded an end to "Iran's support for Houthi attacks on commercial vessels." Earlier, the Pentagon had announced that the Secretary would also discuss "steps Israel is taking to mitigate civilian harm," and what were to be "the next steps in the conflict after an eventual cessation of high-intensity ground operations and airstrikes."[33]

That last statement appeared to echo Biden's reply five days earlier if he wanted Israel to scale back or tone down its attacks on Gaza by the end of the year. "I want them to be focused on how to save civilian lives, not stop going after Hamas, but be more careful," the US president replied. Biden's comments came after four senior US officials confirmed that his administration had asked Israel to end the large-scale campaign against Hamas and move to a more targeted operation by the end of 2023. The American plan for the second stage of the operation involved extensive use of special forces to conduct precise raids inside Gaza and at locating and eliminating Hamas leaders, rescuing hostages, and continuing to destroy the prolific network of terror tunnels which the organization had built. The calls for a change in tactics came on the background of Defense Minister Gallant's recent announcement, during a meeting with NSC advisor Sullivan, that the war would take several more months. The same American officials, speaking on condition of anonymity, said that Biden was calling for the large-scale ground campaign to end within three weeks, or soon after. They likewise emphasized that there was no instruction or demand by Washington to make the transition.[34]

Meeting with Austin on December 18, Gallant declared for the first time that parts of Gaza were already close to being able to transition to a "day after" status even as other parts might remain in intensive conflict for an extended period. Although he declined to say where, his statement came only hours after the IDF announced that Division 252 had "completed its mission" in the northern Beit Hanoun area of Gaza, with IDF sources telling the *Jerusalem Post* that many of the reservists involved would now get to go home. Despite the United States' concern about the rising Palestinian civilian casualties in Gaza, including Biden having warned on December 12 of Israel losing global support over "indiscriminate" bombing there and Austin having cautioned on December 2 that harm to civilians would "replace a tactical victory with a strategic defeat," Austin now declared that Jerusalem faced "an incredibly complex battlespace."

While Austin continued to urge Israel to improve, he voiced being impressed that lessons which Israel had learned from its operations in northern Gaza were already being implemented in southern Gaza to reduce civilian casualties. Although calling to increase humanitarian aid entering the Strip, he declined to set any timeline on the ongoing Israeli operation. The main open disagreement between the two sides remained regarding the plan for "the day after," with Austin insisting on the two-state solution and Gallant alluding to developing new relations with groups of Gazans not connected to Hamas who could help manage the Strip after the war ended.[35]

The same day, a *Wall Street Journal* editorial charged that Israeli concessions to operate in Gaza according to the Biden administration's demands to minimize civilian losses were endangering IDF lives. "Israel fights on because it has no other choice if it wants to survive as a state. But many nations see these U.N. votes as consequence-free gestures for peace or solidarity. That a cease-fire now would mean a Hamas victory and the death of Israeli deterrence, bringing on the next massacre and the next war, doesn't concern them." The IDF, it went on, "was now telegraphing its attacks to the enemy so that civilians can flee, and it was using a smaller force with less reliance on air power and artillery. As a result, Israel is taking more casualties. The rising fatality rate is noticed in Israel, if nowhere else." Civilian casualties in Gaza "were tragic, but they were mainly a result of Hamas's way of embedding in what should be safe civilian spaces." The newspaper's pointed critique ended thus: "Israel has no good choices here, but America does. The President can focus on supporting a U.S. ally in vanquishing a genocidal enemy."[36]

The next day, Austin, who said that Israel has "a moral duty" to protect Gaza civilians as the IDF attacked more hospitals, announced a new international mission to protect commercial ships transiting the Red Sea that had come under attack by drones and ballistic missiles fired from Houthi-controlled areas of Yemen. The United Kingdom, Bahrain, Canada, France, Italy, Netherlands, Norway, Seychelles, and Spain would join the United States in the new mission. Several other countries also agreed to be involved in the operation but preferred not to be publicly named. In response, top Houthi negotiator Mohammed Abdelsalam told Reuters on Tuesday that the Iran-aligned Houthis would not change their stance on the Gaza conflict due to the establishment of a multinational naval alliance to safeguard shipping in the Red Sea. The naval alliance led by the United States was "essentially unnecessary," he declared, adding that all the waters adjacent to Yemen were safe except for Israeli ships, or ships heading to Israel, because of the "unjust aggressive war on Palestine."[37]

The Hamas tsunami of radical Islamist evil, which crashed down on Israel seventy-four days ago, already showed its marked impact across the Jewish State's domestic scene. Well over 100,000 residents from the north and south were forced to move, evacuees living temporarily in hotels. The country's freed child hostages were haunted by the anguish of captivity in Gaza. Doctors related that children released in negotiations spoke in whispers, suffered sleeplessness, and in some cases regressed developmentally. Rape victims remained traumatized. 129 hostages remained in captivity—probably not all of them alive. As the eleventh week of the war began, the IDF death toll since the ground invasion was launched had reached 129 soldiers. 2,816 soldiers began treatment at the Defense Ministry's Rehabilitation Department since the war broke out, and 18 percent had mental health difficulties and PTSD.

Politically, Israelis were abandoning the left-over security concerns after October 7. Disenchanted by the prospect for peace following Hamas's devastating terrorist attack, and embracing a rare, broad consensus of support for the war to eradicate any possible threat of Hamas in the future, Israelis were becoming more conservative in their politics. The tourist industry showed a state of collapse, with a ninety percent drop in visitors in November. The economy suffered greatly, the government losing an equivalent of $2.5 billion a month, with the cost of the conflict probably running to at least 27 billion shekels, or 1.5 percent of Israel's Gross National Product. Israeli stocks on the main market index in Tel Aviv were down 15 percent in dollar terms, equivalent to $25 billion. Israel's war with Hamas in Gaza would likely cost it at least another 50 billion shekels ($14 billion) in 2024 and result in a near-tripling of its budget deficit, the Finance Ministry said, projecting that fighting would last through February.[38]

Gaza's economy, crumbling for years, was being "pounded to dust" by the war. Last year, eighty percent of the population relied on international aid, according to a United Nations estimate. Some 1.5 million people had been displaced, according to the United Nations. The UN Development Program published a report in December estimating that sixty-one percent of jobs in Gaza had been lost, along with $857 million of economic activity, setting the economy back "by many years." At least sixty-six percent of jobs had been lost in Gaza since the Hamas-Israel conflict erupted in October, the International Labor Organization (ILO) said on December 20. Some Palestinian officials put the economic cost of Israel's ground operation in Gaza in 2014 at more than $6 billion. The Palestine Economic Policy Research Institute estimated the same month that the cost of rebuilding this IAF "cratered landscape" could reach $20 billion over the next five years. Gaza's economy could shrink by thirty to seventy percent, said Anas Iqtait, an expert on Middle Eastern economies at Australian National University, and he concluded thus: "The only way for the economy to recover, if at all, is through extensive international intervention."[39]

In Gaza, Al-Jazeera and AP reported on December 19 that at least 29 Palestinians were killed in an Israeli air strike in a residential area of Rafah in the southernmost part, while 13 people were killed and 75 injured in an Israeli attack in the Jabaliya refugee camp. According to the Gaza Health Ministry, 19,453 Palestinians had been killed and 52,286 wounded since the beginning of the war. The UN estimated that thousands more lay buried under the rubble of Gaza. More than one million displaced Palestinians crammed into Rafah on Gaza's border with Egypt in order to escape Israeli bombardments farther north despite fears that they would also not be safe there. Hamas reiterated its position, "categorically rejecting holding any form of negotiations over a prisoner exchange" amid the ongoing Israeli military operation in Gaza. "We are, however, open to any initiative that contributes to ending the aggression on our people and opening the crossings to bring in aid and provide relief to the Palestinian people," the terror group declared. Hamas also conditioned a deal on Israel withdrawing troops from the Strip. Both conditions were non-starters for Israel.[40]

All the while, Hezbollah increased its missile barrages on Israel's northern front, creating havoc, raising red sirens, forcing 80,000 residents to abandon their homes, and killing a number of IDF soldiers and civilians. This steady attack in its undeclared war with Israel ran counter to UN Resolution 1701, passed by the Security Council at the end of the Second Lebanon War in 2006 during which Hezbollah fired about 4,000 rockets into Israel and killed 110 IDF soldiers and 44 Israeli civilians, which called for a permanent cease-fire and a zone "between the Blue Line and the Litani River" free of "any armed personnel, assets, and weapons other than those of the Government of Lebanon." Remaining in southern Lebanon and continually ignoring multiple resolutions by the Council to disarm, Hezbollah's leaders also violated UN Resolution 1559 (2004) and the Lebanese Taif Agreement (1989), which called for the disbanding and disarmament of all Lebanese and non-Lebanese militias. The Alexandroni Brigade, one of Israel's oldest infantry units and targeted by Hezbollah over the last two months, partnered with the 8th Armored Reserve Tank Unit after October 7 to prepare for actual combat with the Iran-backed enemy.[41]

French President Macron recently sent a message to Lebanon pushing for a diplomatic solution to distance Hezbollah from the border with Israel, warning that "the rules of the game that existed before October 7 are not the rules of the game today. We are in a different reality, and you need to understand that the situation has changed." French Minister for Europe and Foreign Affairs Catherine Colonna arrived in Israel on December 17 and met with Foreign Minister Cohen, who stressed that "only the implementation of Resolution 1701 and the distancing of Hezbollah terrorists north of the Litani River will prevent war in Lebanon." Gantz called on her to distance Hezbollah from the border, in accordance with the United Nations decision. He also warned that if this did not happen, Israel would do it herself, emphasizing "we are ready for a diplomatic solution, but we are also preparing for a military operation." Colonna also used her visit to criticize the accelerated Jewish settlement construction in Judea and Samaria and charged that "action will be taken" against "settlers depriving Palestinians of their rights and their land." Stating that too many civilians were being killed in Gaza, she called for an "immediate and durable truce," but Cohen responded that this would be a gift to Hamas. He repeated Jerusalem's position that there would be no cease-fire, but declared that France could play an important role in preventing the escalation of regional tensions, adding that while Israel "has no intention to start another front" on its northern border with Lebanon, it would do "whatever it takes" to protect Israeli citizens.[42]

A total of approximately 8,000 Palestinian Authority Arabs were allowed to enter Israel for work purposes, even though the government's ministers vehemently opposed such a move, according to a morning report on December 20 by Israeli TV's *Kan Reshet Bet*. The workers, who represented about twenty percent of the usual number of PA Arabs allowed into pre-1967 Israel, were allowed to return to their places of employment despite the fact that the political echelon had not approved the move. The workers in question were mostly employed in large industrial areas, such as Barkan and Mishor Adumim, and in larger cities such as Ariel. The report added that the approval followed requests by Israeli employers to the IDF. The brigade commanders in the relevant areas, along with border security in the Jerusalem area, approved security measures for the duration of the workers' employment. The report noted that the IDF's Central Command was in charge of the matter and did not need approval from the political echelon in order to make decisions. It also noted that only about 5,000 PA Arabs, or five percent of the previous workforce, had worked in pre-1967 Israel; the rest were employed in Jewish areas of Judea and Samaria. The group of workers included only those employed in essential industries, such as hospitals and cemeteries. Earlier this month, a discussion was held on the matter, with the defense echelon claiming that another battlefront would develop in Judea and Samaria if the PA Arabs continued to be denied entry to Jewish towns in Judea and Samaria and to pre-1967 Israel.[43]

During a year-in-review press briefing at the State Department on December 20, Blinken said that Hamas should be removed from power when the conflict in Gaza ended. "Everyone would like to see this conflict end as quickly as possible, but if it ends with Hamas remaining in place and having the capacity and the stated intent to repeat October 7 again and again and again, that's not in the interest of Israel," he stated. "It's not in the interest of the region," he added. "It's not in the interest of the world." It is "striking" that amid all of the international demands for a cease-fire there is virtually no pressure being put upon Hamas to stop using human shields or to end the conflict, which it could do immediately by surrendering, Blinken added. "How can it be that there are no demands made of the aggressor and only demands made of the victim?" the US Secretary of State asked. "It would be good if there was a strong international voice pressing Hamas to do what's necessary to end this, and again, that could be tomorrow." He reiterated the Biden administration's position that Israel had a right to self-defense, but also said that the United States wanted to see Israel shift to a more targeted phase of combat, with fewer Palestinian civilian casualties. Blinken also noted ongoing negotiations over a United Arab Emirates-proposed resolution in the UN Security Council that called for additional aid to be delivered to Gaza with ships and aircraft, in addition to the current convoys of trucks.[44]

The next day, however, Sami Abu Zuhri, a senior Hamas official and spokesman for the organization, said that the terror group's leadership was steadfast in its decision to insist on a cease-fire in Gaza before holding negotiations on a new prisoner swap, which would see innocent Israeli hostages freed in exchange for convicted terrorists. Speaking to Al-Araby Al-Jadeed, Abu Zuhri declared that Israel's statements on a new deal to free hostages were made due to internal Israeli needs. Quoting senior sources in the various terror groups in Gaza, the newspaper also reported that Israel had offered a one-week cease-fire, while the terror groups rejected this offer and demanded a permanent cease-fire. The sources also said that any Israeli proposal which did not include a long-lasting cease-fire was worthless, and statements in Israel and the United States regarding progress on a new deal only aimed to show their populations that there were efforts being made to return the hostages. Meanwhile, Hamas leader Haniyeh traveled to Cairo for the purpose of discussing a new prisoner exchange. According to reports, Hamas was demanding the release of several high-ranking terrorists, including Marwan Barghouti, who headed the Fatah party's military arm during the Second Intifada; Popular Front for the

Liberation of Palestine leader Ahmad Saadat; and Abbas Al-Sayed, who had orchestrated the Park Hotel bombing attack in Netanya by Hamas during a Passover Seder on March 27, 2002, which killed 30 and injured 140 Israelis, and other terror attacks.[45]

The same day, while the IDF announced that the number of wounded soldiers since October 7 stood at 1,929, the military's Arabic spokesperson Avichay Adraee wrote on X that the IDF had successfully liquidated four out of seven senior Hamas brigade commanders, and he warned the remaining commanders to lay down weapons and surrender to Israeli forces in Gaza. Even as a heavy barrage of Hamas and Hezbollah missiles struck Israel, the IDF took over the senior Hamas leaders' quarters (Palestine Square) in Rimal, Gaza's most prosperous neighborhood. Soldiers for the Yahalom special operations unit of the IDF's Combat Engineering Corps, along with troops from the 401st Brigade combat team, which worked with the air forces' Shaldag Unit and the 13th Squadron, destroyed the web of tunnels there. The IDF also announced that, with the Golani, 188th Armored, Bislamach, and Paratrooper Brigade Battle Teams, it had gained control of the neighborhood of Shejaiya in eastern Gaza City. Earlier, soldiers in the 99th Division, together with the 179th and 646th Brigades, killed hundreds of Hamas operatives, located many weapons, and destroyed tunnel shafts. Terrorists who had participated in the October 7 attack were arrested. According to the announcement, forces of the 36th Division, in close-quarters combat, achieved an "operational hold" in the neighborhood, and the army would continue to hold the area and carry out "targeted operations."[46]

The White House declared that 200 humanitarian aid trucks had entered battered Gaza in the last twenty-four hours. Yet, across Gaza, residents were struggling to find food and clean water. Over a quarter of Gaza's population faced starvation, the World Food Program said. The enclave's disintegrating healthcare system was incapable of coping with the flow of sick and injured people. According to the Gaza Health Ministry, 20,000 had been killed in the Strip since the war began. The *Wall Street Journal* reported that voiced criticism of Hamas was getting louder and spreading, with more Gazans holding it responsible for provoking Israel's wrath and failing to shield the population from a humanitarian crisis. (Hamas had also not built any bomb shelters for Gazans nor allowed them into Hamas's vast tunnel system during IDF airstrikes.) "There is more questioning of the decision to go to war," said Khalil Shikaki, director of the Palestinian Center for Policy and Survey Research think tank and a professor of political science based in Ramallah. Mkhaimar Abusada, a political scientist at Gaza's Al-Azhar University, expressed this observation: "There is a lot of criticism among Palestinians that the October 7 attack—the killing of Israeli civilians, women and children—was a strategic mistake that provoked Israel into the current war."[47]

On December 22, the IDF declared that 139 soldiers had fallen in battle since the ground operation had begun. The previous evening, Netanyahu had rejected outright Abu Zuhri's conditions, saying in a video broadcast that "we are fighting until victory." He went on: "We will not stop the war until we achieve all of its goals—completing the elimination of Hamas and releasing all of our hostages. The choice I propose to Hamas is very simple: Surrender or die. They do not have—and will not have—any other choice. And after we eliminate Hamas, I will use all my power to ensure that Gaza never again threatens Israel—neither Hamastan nor Fatahstan." The IDF called on residents of the Al-Bureij refugee camp in the central Gaza Strip and nearby neighborhoods to immediately evacuate to shelters in the southern city of Dir al-Balah. IDF spokesperson in Arabic, Adraee, also announced a temporary cease-fire in western Rafah from 10:00 a.m. to 2:00 p.m., to facilitate the passage of supplies for humanitarian needs.[48]

On Friday night, IDF spokesman Hagari declared, "A UN resolution passed a few hours ago and was adopted by the Security Council. It includes a demand for the unconditional, immediate release of the hostages held by Hamas and to allow humanitarian access to address their medical needs. We call on the international community and international organizations to enforce this resolution." Hamas quickly responded: "During the past five days, the US administration has worked hard to empty this resolution of its essence, and to issue it in this weak formula . . . it defies the will of the international community and the United Nations General Assembly in stopping Israel's aggression against our defenseless Palestinian people." Riyad Mansour, the Palestinian Authority's representative to the UN, said that the resolution was "a step in the right direction," but called for an immediate cease-fire. The Secretary-General of the Arab League, Ahmed Aboul Gheit, criticized the UN vote as overdue and inadequate over its exclusion of a call for a ceasefire, providing Israel with "a license to kill." Israeli UN Ambassador Erdan, while appreciating that the resolution "maintains Israel's security authority to monitor and inspect aid entering Gaza," noted that the Security Council had not yet condemned the October 7 massacre. An earlier resolution, opposed by Israel with US backing, had called for "an immediate humanitarian ceasefire." The ultimate resolution, including the call for urgent steps "to create the conditions for a sustainable cessation of hostilities," was approved by a vote of thirteen with abstentions from both the United States and Russia.[49]

On December 23, an Israeli fighter jet killed Hassan Atrash, the individual responsible for the trade, production, and equipping of the military arm of Hamas. He also had taken part in the smuggling of weapons from various countries into the Gaza Strip and the West Bank. Five more Israeli soldiers died in Gaza over the weekend. More than 200 Palestinian Islamic Jihad terrorist operatives apprehended by the IDF and the ISA (Shin Bet) in the Gaza Strip during the last week were taken for further questioning in Israel. Within a week, the IDF and ISA caught hundreds of suspects involved in terrorist activities in the Gaza Strip. Some of the operatives voluntarily turned themselves in and were transferred by field interrogators from Unit 504 in the Intelligence Directorate and the ISA. Overall, more than 700 operatives from terrorist organizations in the Gaza Strip had been taken for further questioning thus far. The same day, Hezbollah reported the death of its 122nd fighter from IDF fire since the start of the conflict between the two sides, but the Israeli estimate was that the number was much higher.[50]

An exclusive in the *Wall Street Journal* that day reported that Biden had urged Netanyahu to cancel a pre-emptive strike against Hezbollah forces in Lebanon days after Hamas's October 7 assault on southern Israel, warning that such an attack could spark a wider regional war. Israel had intelligence—which the United States deemed unreliable—that Hezbollah attackers were preparing to cross the border as part of a multipronged attack, pushing some of Israel's more hawkish officials to the brink. Israeli warplanes were in the air awaiting orders when Biden spoke to Netanyahu on October 11 and told him to halt and think through the consequences of such an action. After six hours of back-and-forth telephone calls and meetings, the Israeli officials agreed to stand down. The conversation between Biden and other US officials and Netanyahu and his war cabinet set a pattern of White House efforts to guard against any expansion of the conflict that could draw in the United States.

The situation remained tense, with Hezbollah having hit Israel more than 200 times in attacks that killed ten people, including seven Israeli soldiers, according to data compiled by the Armed Conflict Location and Event Data Project. Israel responded with nearly 1,000 strikes inside southern Lebanon that had killed more than 120 Hezbollah fighters and 10 Lebanese civilians. As for the threat to Red Sea shipping, Washington declassified information showing Tehran "deeply involved" in those attacks, but it held off on redesignating Houthis as a terror group.[51]

As the war entered its twelfth week, the IDF death toll since the ground offensive began reached 154, with 1,988 Israeli soldiers wounded in combat since October 7. Suicide belts for children were found in a northern Gaza medical clinic, as well as a weapons compound with mortar shells and grenades embedded inside a civilian building. Addressing his government cabinet one day after fourteen soldiers fell in battle and thirty-six were wounded in Gaza on December 22–23, Netanyahu declared that he had told Biden the previous night that "we will fight until absolute victory—however long that takes. The U.S. understands this." The IDF's General Staff representative in the Cabinet, General Eliezer Toledano, told the cabinet that "this war will continue for several long months. We will need to manage an economy of ammunition, but the goal is the eventual destruction of Hamas," of whose members the IDF had killed close to 8,000. The Gaza Health Ministry said on Sunday that at least 166 Gazans had been killed in the past 24 hours in the Strip, during which the IDF attacked 200 targets in the Strip, raising the death toll to 20,424 since October 7. The IDF and the Israel Air Force completed their attack on a series of Hezbollah targets in Lebanon, hitting terrorist infrastructures, military buildings, and missile launch positions. Iran joined the Houthi attacks on ships by carrying out a long-range drone attack on a chemical tanker in the Indian Ocean, thereby creating an arc of drone threats that stretched from Yemen to Chabahar in Iran, near the border with Pakistan.[52]

Israel's Chief Ashkenazi Rabbi David Lau called on Pope Francis to retract his charge that the IDF was engaging in terrorism just like Hamas. That accusation, repeated by the Archbishop of Canterbury Justin Welby and the Latin Patriarch of Jerusalem Pierbattista Pizzaballa, was followed by the incendiary allegation—unsubstantiated—that the IDF shot and murdered two Christian women on the grounds of a Catholic church in Gaza's Rimal neighborhood. The old Christian doctrine that Jews were damned for rejecting Jesus, given new life by Palestinian Christian "liberation theology" which (falsely) states that the Palestinian Arabs were the original possessors of the Land of Israel, now connected to the fiction trumpeted by Father Naim Ateek of the Sabeel Ecumenical Liberation Theology Center in Jerusalem that the descendants of the "Palestinian" Jesus (in reality a Galilean Jew) were again being crucified by the Jews in Israel. Their liberation would require the dissolution of the Jewish State. Echoing the ancient Christian calumny that the Jews are killers motivated by revenge and blood lust, concluded journalist Melanie Phillips, "the Christian church is once again tragically turning on its Jewish parent while embracing its Islamic assassin."[53]

On December 25, Hamas leader Yahya Sinwar spoke out for the first time since Hamas savagely attacked Israel, clarifying that a prisoner swap to free the hostages was not on the table at present. In a message sent to Hamas leaders outside Gaza, Sinwar clarified that Izz ad-Din al-Qassam, Hamas's military arm, would not submit to the "conditions of the occupation." According to the report on Al-Jazeera, Sinwar expressed his "appreciation" for the residents of Gaza and the fact that "they sacrifice themselves and express courage and solidarity." He also wrote that the Hamas troops were waging an "unprecedented battle against the forces of the Israeli occupation," and stressed the high number of Israeli casualties. "One-third of them were killed, another third were injured, and a third are disabled forever," he said, claiming that 5,000 soldiers and commanders were attacked and 750 vehicles lost. According to Sinwar, also reported in the Houthi's media al-Masirah, Hamas's army had "destroyed the occupation's army," and was "on the way to crushing them—and we will not cave to their conditions."[54]

However greatly removed this defiant stance was from reality, Hamas continued to hold ground with 10,000 or more operatives as it apparently sought to create an underground kind of guerilla war in Gaza. That would mean a more complex battlefield and less contact with the enemy. The Israeli military said that it could take months to assert control over a key city in southern Gaza, as Hamas guerrilla tactics were causing casualties to mount among Israeli troops. At least sixteen Israeli soldiers were killed across Gaza over the past three days, bringing the Israeli ground op death total to 156. The military focused on killing Hamas's leaders and dismantling its extensive tunnel network, where some bodies of hostages were found. The IDF announced that it had dismantled a large, underground tunnel complex that served as Hamas's northern command headquarters. Fighting continued in the southern Hamas stronghold of Khan Younis, where the IDF believed the terrorist leadership was hiding. For their part, Hamas and the Palestinian Islamic Jihad rejected an Egyptian proposal that they relinquish power in the Gaza Strip in return for a permanent cease-fire. Up north in Israel, roads and towns near the Lebanese border were closed to civilian traffic on Monday morning until further notice, due to escalating tensions between Israel and Hezbollah. As workers were called up to fight or become jobless, the country's economy was expected to shrink two percent.[55]

Haaretz reported on Monday that the IDF Gaza Division's operations officer, Lt. Col. Sahar Fogel, had been unhappy about the Nova Music Festival being held on October 7 so close to the Strip, and his concerns were supported by other officers. The worries reportedly did not stem from fears of a terrorist incursion, but rather the threat of rocket and mortar fire from Gaza. Despite his objections, Fogel was told to approve the music festival, the report said, detailing concerns of legal difficulties if the festival were not approved, as well as a request to combine the authorization with that of the smaller trance Psyduck

Music Festival, held nearby on October 5–6. A special alert area was established in the Iron Dome system, known as a "polygon," to give extra protection to the festival venue. However, the report said, security forces were aware that safe spaces could not be provided for the thousands of partygoers. The Eshkol Regional Council also opposed the rave, believing that it would be a public nuisance.[56]

The same day, Netanyahu laid out in the *Wall Street Journal* Israel's conditions for "the day after" the current war. These included the demilitarization of the Gaza Strip, the destruction of Hamas, and the de-radicalization of the Palestinian Arab population. "Among other things," he went on, "this will require establishing a temporary security zone on the perimeter of Gaza and an inspection mechanism on the border between Gaza and Egypt that meets Israel's security needs and prevents smuggling of weapons into the territory." Netanyahu referred to the Abraham Accords, the peace deals Israel had signed with the United Arab Emirates, Bahrain, Morocco, and Sudan in 2020—with Saudi Arabia's tacit approval, and the transformations of defeated Germany and Japan after World War Two as successful examples of how nations and populations had been deradicalized as Gaza must be. Once the three desiderata were achieved, he concluded, "Gaza can be rebuilt and the prospects of a broader peace in the Middle East will become a reality."[57]

Defense Minister Gallant declared on the morning of December 26 that the IDF was fighting already in six of seven fronts in "a multi-front war" against different adversaries: Gaza; Lebanon; Syria; Judea and Samaria; Iraq; Yemen; and Iran. From the war's commencement, 2,450 wanted suspects had been arrested in the West Bank and the Jordan Valley, some 1,210 associated with Hamas. As for Hezbollah, the United States and France did not support Israel's need to push that terrorist group's armed forces deeper into Lebanon. Iran, clearly the puppet master of much of the regional conflict, threatened that "the usurper and savage Zionist regime will pay" for the IAF-strike killing in Damascus of Sayyed Reza Mousavi, a senior commander in the Islamic Revolutionary Guard Corps in charge of arming both Syria and Hezbollah with Iranian weapons. "This action is another sign of frustration, helplessness, and inability of the occupying Zionist regime," said President Raisi. In Iraq, the United States struck Iran-backed groups during a round of retaliation for a series of assaults, including a drone attack that injured three American soldiers. The Gaza Health Ministry claimed totals to date of 20,424 killed and 54,036 wounded in the war. Concurrently, as Palestinian civilians were trying to get food and basic supplies from humanitarian aid trucks, Hamas started firing into the crowd in an attempt to dispel them and take the shipments for themselves. The shooting resulted in the killing of a Palestinian boy, which prompted rioting in neighborhoods all around Gaza and a Hamas police station being set on fire.[58]

IDF Chief-of-Staff Halevi declared the same day that it could even take months to arrest or kill Hamas's top leaders and "many months" to finish fighting Hamas. Recognizing that the broader diplomatic and political context would not allow a full all-out war for that long, he said that the IDF would adjust itself to different intensity levels of fighting as needed. The IDF chief also stated that Israel would need new security mechanisms and tactics even after the different levels of fighting became less intense to ensure long-term security for Israeli residents in the South. Further cause for concern was the declaration by the International Atomic Energy Agency that Iran had reversed a slowdown in the rate at which it was enriching uranium to up to sixty percent purity (close to weapons grade), returning to a rate of around nine kilograms a month from the reduced rate of three kilograms, which "greatly concerned" the United States.[59]

More than ten thousand parents of IDF soldiers signed a letter to Netanyahu, arranged by the March of Mothers of Combat Soldiers' movement and the Torat Lechima organization, demanding that he end the humanitarian aid to Gaza. "Our heroic sons are fighting with strength and bravery, as we taught them, against a Nazi enemy in Gaza and on all other fronts. We demand not to endanger them needlessly," the letter began. Their plea went on: "Stop the Hamas truck convoys. We demand that buildings be collapsed, hospitals (terrorist command centers) schools (which teach incitement and antisemitism) and any enemy building, and not to send our sons into dangerous alleys. The most humanitarian thing possible is to kill the enemy." The IDF named 165 soldiers who made the ultimate price fighting terror since the ground invasion of Gaza; the Gaza Health Ministry declared that the death toll reached 21,110. Hamas denied Iran's claim that the October 7 massacre was retaliation for the IDF's proving intelligence which had led to the American assassination by drones on January 3, 2020, of senior Iranian military commander General Qassem Soleimani, saying that its actions were a "response from the Palestinian resistance" to Israel's "occupation and aggression against the Palestinian people and holy sites," including the Al-Aqsa Mosque. While it was highly implausible that Tehran and Hezbollah proxy did not know beforehand of the attack, Hamas's denial reflected the terrorist organization's wish to show its decisive leadership.[60]

On December 27, Turkish President Erdoğan told his Justice and Development Party (AKP) members that the world had "watched Israel's Nazi camps." He went on: "They talk about Hitler in a strange way; what is the difference between them and Hitler? They will make us miss Hitler even more.

Netanyahu committed one of the greatest atrocities of this century in Gaza and has already put his name down in history as the butcher of Gaza." Erdoğan's solution? "The independent state of Palestine should be established on the basis of the 1967 borders, with East Jerusalem as its capital." "The voice that stands with the oppressed is the voice of the Muslim Turks," he concluded. Netanyahu responded to these remarks: "Erdoğan, who is carrying out a genocide of the Kurds, who holds a world record in jailing journalists who oppose his regime, is the last one who can preach morals." The prime minister added: "The IDF is the most moral army in the world, which is fighting and eliminating the most despicable and cruel terror organization in the world, Hamas-ISIS, which carried out crimes against humanity and which Erdoğan praises and hosts its leaders."[61]

That day, the IDF attacked 200 targets across the Strip, expanding the ground offensive into Gaza's central urban camps. The IDF admitted and expressed regret that a Christmas eve airstrike on central Gaza's Maghazi refugee camp, killing dozens of innocents, was an error caused by the type of weaponry "that did not match the nature of the mission." US forces intercepted twelve attack drones and five missiles in the southern Red Sea, launched over a ten-hour period by Houthi terrorists in Yemen. Lobby 1701, a group representing some 60,000 evacuees from northern Israel, urged the Biden administration to back a military campaign to push Hezbollah away from the border. The group was named after the UN Security Council Resolution that ended the 2006 Second Lebanon War and mandated that the Iranian terrorist proxy stay north of the Litani River, which is around 18 miles from the Israeli border.[62]

Hamas leader Mashal extended a hand to Palestinian Authority chief Abbas's ruling Fatah faction on Wednesday, telling France's *Le Figaro* newspaper that the terror group was willing to consider joining a PA-led governing body for the Gaza Strip, Judea and Samaria. "Sooner or later, the United States will argue that Hamas is a reality and enjoys legitimacy among the people," Mashaal predicted. "We must learn from history. The Americans accepted the Taliban. [PLO founder] Yasser Arafat even won the Nobel Peace Prize." Hamas's October 7 assault in southwestern Israel "shocked world public opinion, and polls in the U.S. show increased support for the Palestinian cause," he continued, vowing that Hamas will not be destroyed as it "passed the credibility test" against Israel. "After three months of [Israeli] bombings, our rockets are still reaching Tel Aviv. The one who is worried is not the Palestinian side.... It is clear that we have losses, but they had no consequences for Hamas's military capabilities or command," declared Mashaal.[63]

In an interview with Egypt's *ON* television channel on Tuesday, Abbas had said that he hoped to work out a reconciliation deal with all Palestinian terrorist groups which were "present and absent" during unity talks held in late July, including Hamas and Palestinian Islamic Jihad. In the interview, Abbas's first media appearance since the October 7 attack, the Palestinian leader again failed to explicitly condemn Hamas's atrocities on the fateful Sabbath day. That massacre, *Le Figaro* reported, was planned in detail between three senior figures in Hamas, who shared the plan with other leaders just half an hour before it was executed. Osama Hamdan, the Hamas representative in Lebanon, only found out about the attack from the media, after the attack had already happened. Another senior figure, Saleh Al-Arouri, was told only thirty minutes before the attack, with the goal of allowing him to alert Hezbollah leader Nasrallah. Jibril Rajoub, Fatah Central Committee Secretary, echoed Abbas, declaring that the PA would refuse to rule Gaza without Hamas or the Palestinian Islamic Jihad, adding "Hamas is part of the fabric of our struggle."[64]

Israel's northern towns were rocked on December 28 by the heaviest Hezbollah barrages since the outbreak of the war. No injuries ensued, but buildings in largely evacuated Kiryat Shmona suffered damage as at least thirty-four rockets were fired from Lebanon. The previous day, IDF chief of staff Halevi approved operational plans at the military's Northern Command, which had responsibility for the Lebanese border, and warned of the need to "be ready to attack if required." In Gaza City, Israeli forces were active in recent days in the Daraj and Tuffah districts, battling that battalion of Hamas's Gaza City Brigade. It was just revealed that months before Hamas's October 7 onslaught, the Shin Bet security service had received intelligence from a reliable source in Gaza that Hamas was planning to carry out "a big move" shortly after the Jewish High Holy Days, but colleagues marked it as insignificant, concluding "if this really nears implementation, we'll receive additional intelligence" corroborating it. Now the IDF death toll since October 7 reached 500, of that figure 167 in Gaza, and the mounting tally of over 6,000 wounded troops presented a separate, hard challenge for Israel's health system.[65]

IDF troops located and destroyed tunnel shafts under Gaza's Al-Rantisi Children's Hospital and in the nearby high school connecting to a network of underground tunnels passing under the hospital, spanning several kilometers, and leading to strategic points in the heart of Gaza City. For the first time since the Israeli ground invasion began, soldiers of the 5th "Sharon" (Reserve) Infantry Brigade began destroying dozens of tunnel shafts and weaponry in Operation Oz and Nir in Khan Younis's Khirbat Ikhza'a, the base of many of the terrorists who attacked Kibbutz Nir Oz on October 7. Near the town of Otniel in the Hevron Hills, four were injured in a ramming attack; the terrorist was killed. Up north, a new poll conducted by Lazar Research showed that a clear majority of Israelis (sixty-eight percent) supported a military operation to remove Hezbollah from the Israel-Lebanon border. Just sixteen percent supported the current acceptance of the situation, while eighteen percent had no opinion on the matter.[66]

Day eighty-five of the war saw the IDF deepening its ground operation in southern Gaza and raiding Hamas military posts in the heart of the city of Khan Younis, including the organization's key intelligence war room. In response to aerial intrusions from Lebanon, the IDF said that fighter jets attacked infrastructure and terrorist units in the Hezbollah stronghold of Kfarkela. At least seven Iranian-linked militia were killed in an airstrike attributed to Israel near Aleppo in northwest Syria. Protests calling to oust Netanyahu and have "elections now" took place on Saturday night across Israel, including a Tel Aviv solidarity rally with the families of hostages still held in Gaza. Yet at a press conference in the IDF's Tel-Aviv headquarters, his plummeting popularity notwithstanding, the prime minister said he had no plans to resign and indicated that he intended to remain in power once the war ended, to ensure that Gaza was demilitarized and no new terror threat could emerge from there following Hamas's October 7 massacres.[67]

Approximately seventy percent of the homes in Gaza and half of its buildings had been damaged or destroyed by Israeli airstrikes, according to the *Wall Street Journal*. An investigation by the *New York Times*, whose horrific expose two days earlier had detailed Hamas's systematic sexual violence against Israeli women and girls on October 7 (already confirmed in November by Physicians for Human Rights Israel), revealed that on that day IDF troops were disorganized, relied on social media to choose targets, and had no battle plan for a large-scale Hamas invasion. The US State Department circumvented Congress (as it had on December 9) in approving a $147.5 million arms sale to Israel, saying that the proposed sale of 155-millimeter artillery shells and related equipment was consistent with Washington's commitment to Israel's security and efforts to help it "develop and maintain a strong and ready self-defense capability."[68]

On the last day of December 2023, responding to South Africa's demand that the International Court of Justice investigate Israel for genocide, Netanyahu declared that Israel's war against Hamas was "without peer" in justice and morality, and he asked: "Where were you when millions were killed in Syria, elsewhere?" Israeli investigators and prosecutors began building an indictment against captured Hamas terrorists similar to the one against the Nazi leader Adolf Eichmann for his central role in the Holocaust, a trial that would be the country's most significant since the early 1960s. Israel was prepared to let ships deliver aid to the war-ravaged Gaza Strip "immediately" as part of a proposed sea corridor from Cyprus, Israel's outgoing Foreign Minister Cohen said on Sunday. US naval helicopters sank three Houthi boats attempting to highjack a merchant vessel in the Red Sea. In the central West Bank, Israeli security forces arrested five suspects, confiscated weapons, and clashed with armed assailants during operations in the Nur Shams refugee camp near Tulkarm.[69]

Netanyahu vowed "absolute victory" over Hamas. What did that entail? At this point in time, day eighty-six since October 7, more than 500 IDF soldiers had been killed, of these, 172 since the ground invasion. Even as the IDF drew down on its reservist soldiers in Gaza's north, there were still seven brigades fighting in Khan Younis, up from an original four. 132 Israeli hostages remained in Gaza, probably not all of them alive; 200,000 Israelis living in the south and north had to abandon their homes. The Health Ministry in Gaza claimed that 21,822 Palestinians had been killed; 1.8 million had been displaced to the south. Although the chairman of the Christian Lebanese Forces, Samir Geagea, and Maronite Patriarch Bechara Boutros Al-Rahi criticized Hezbollah and demanded that it stop striking Israel due to a fear by citizens that they would pay the price for it, Hezbollah rockets, like Hamas operating from behind civilian populations, continued to harass Israel. Hezbollah's number two, Sheikh Naim Qassem, said Sunday that Israel "first must stop the Gaza war in order for the war in Lebanon to stop". The top Hamas leaders, Yahya Sinwar and Mohammed Deif, were still at large in Gaza, as were thousands of their fighters engaged in guerrilla combat. Israeli President Herzog, calling on world leaders as the year closed to demand and work for the immediate, unconditional release of all the hostages, concluded with a noble aspiration: "May the light dispel the darkness, and may the New Year bring peace, hope, and healing for all."[70] What force, in the end, would prevail?

Endnotes

1   CBS News, Dec. 1, 2023; France24, Dec. 2, 2023; *Wall St. Journal*, Dec. 21, 2023.
2   *Jerusalem Post*, Dec. 1, 2023.
3   *New York Times*, Dec. 1, 2023; 124 News, Nov. 30, 2023.
4   *National Post*, Nov. 30, 2023; Reuters, Dec. 2, 2023.
5   *Jerusalem Post*, Dec. 2, 2023; CNN, Dec. 4, 2023; Ynet, Dec. 5, 2023; i24 News, Dec. 3, 2023. The phrase "our Munich" alluded to the terrorist attack on September 5, 1972, against Israeli Olympic team members at the Summer Games in Munich, orchestrated by affiliates of the Palestinian militant group Black September, a Fatah offshoot. Eleven Israeli athletes were killed along with one Munich policeman, and five Black September terrorists lay dead. Three of the gunmen were captured. The *Britannica* online entry aptly concluded its summary of the rescue attempt thus: "With myriad failures in both planning and execution, the result was a disaster on virtually every level." "Munich Massacre," *Britannica, History and Society*. Israeli

Prime Minister Golda Meir responded by authorizing Operation Wrath of God, a covert assassination campaign by the Mossad against Black September operatives and organizers. After a series of spectacular operations cut a swathe through senior Palestinian leadership, that program was suspended in July 1973 when the assassination squad mistakenly killed an innocent man in Lillehammer, Norway. In 1977 Abu Daoud (Mohammed Daoud Odeh), the planner of the Munich attack and Fatah member, was arrested in France, but West Germany's extradition request was denied on a technicality, and he was released and flown to freedom in Algeria. In an interview with Al-Jazeera television in 1999 after publication of his memoir *Palestine, from Jerusalem to Munich*, he stated that "our aim was not civilians. We targeted athletes who in reality were Israeli officers and soldiers. Every person in Israel is a reservist." He died of illness in Damascus on July 3, 2010. France 24, July 3, 2010. Fifty years after the massacre, President Frank-Walter Steinmeier, addressing the victims' families on Berlin's Fürstenfeldbruck airfield, offered a solemn German apology for his country's "lack of protection" for the Israeli athletes and for the 'lack of trying to find explanations afterward." *New York Times*, Sept. 5, 2022.

6 *Jewish Chronicle*, Dec. 4, 2023; JNS, Dec. 3, 2023.
7 *Times of Israel*, Dec. 4, 2023; JNS, Dec. 4, 2023; *Jerusalem Post*, Dec. 4, 2023.
8 Alex Joffe and Asaf Romirowsky, "The Red-Green Alliance against the West," *Washington Examiner*, Dec. 1, 2023.
9 *Maariv*, Dec. 6, 2023.
10 JNS, Dec. 4, 2023; i24 News, Dec. 4, 2023; *Guardian*, Dec. 2, 2023.
11 Israel National News, Dec. 6–7, 2023; *Jerusalem Post*, Dec. 7, 2023. Soon after the pointed exchanges at the special Congressional hearing, the University of Pennsylvania President Elizabeth Magill, and the chairman of its board of trustees, Scott Bok, resigned following pressure from donors, politicians, and alumni. She continued to retain, at the same time, her tenured, full professorship in the university's law school.
12 JNS, Dec. 6, 2023.
13 *Haaretz*, Dec. 7, 2023.
14 *Jerusalem Post*, Dec. 10, 2023.
15 Israel National News, Dec. 10, 2023.
16 JNS, Dec. 10, 2023; IDF Press Release, Dec. 11, 2023; *Haaretz*, Dec. 10, 2023.
17 JNS, Dec. 10, 2023; Reuters, Dec. 11, 2023; *Jerusalem Post*, Dec 11, 2023.
18 JNS, Dec. 10, 2023.
19 *Times of Israel*, Dec. 11, 2023.
20 Etgar Lefkovits, "Border Kibbutz Rebuilds from the Ashes," JNS, Dec. 10, 2023.
21 *Times of Israel*, Dec. 11, 2023.
22 Israel National News, Dec. 11, 2023.
23 JNS, Dec. 11, 2023.
24 *Times of Israel*, Dec. 11–12, 2023. For a sharp critique by an historian of Biden's charge against the IDF airstrikes, see Michael Oren, "The US Charge of 'Indiscriminate Bombing' is over the Top," *Times of Israel*, Feb. 15, 2024.
25 *Haaretz*, Dec. 12, 2023; Omer Dostri, "Stop Being 'the Most Moral Military in the World'—Opinion," *Jerusalem Post*, Dec. 19, 2023.
26 *Haaretz*, Dec. 12 and 21, 2023; Israel National News, Dec. 14, 2023; *Times of Israel*, Dec. 17, 2023. One week later, the IDF announced that an airstrike in the middle of Rafah had killed Subhi Ferwana, a prominent financier who, together with his brother, had been involved over the past few years and during this war in the transfer of tens of millions of dollars to Hamas and its military wing in the Gaza Strip. Israel National News, Dec. 19, 2023.
27 JNS, Dec. 17, 2023.
28 *Haaretz*, Dec. 14, 2023; *Jerusalem Post*, Dec. 15, 2023.
29 JNS, Dec. 17, 2023.
30 *Times of Israel*, Dec. 15, 2023; *Haaretz*, Dec. 16, 2023.

31 *Haaretz*, Dec. 16, 2023; *Jerusalem Post*, Dec. 15, 2023. With some twelve percent of the oil and eight percent of the liquid gas traded worldwide in the first half of 2023 passing through the Red Sea, these oil companies' withdrawal from passage through that area coupled with recent Russian official statements that Moscow would decrease its daily manufacture by about 50,000 barrels, the price of oil increased by 2.5 percent. Bizportal, Dec. 18, 2023.
32 Daniell Gordis, "Israel from the Inside," Dec. 17, 2023. This was confirmed by IDF reservist and former CEO of the Yesha Council Yigal Dilmoni, who was present at the scene. Israel National News, Feb. 28, 2024.
33 *Times of Israel*, Dec. 17, 2023; Israel National News, Dec. 18, 2023. IDF troops had identified at this point about 1,500 Hamas tunnel shafts and underground passages, most found beneath schools, hospitals, mosques, UN facilities, and civilian institutions. Israel National News, Dec. 19, 2023.
34 Israel National News, Dec. 14, 2023.
35 *Jerusalem Post*, Dec. 18, 2023; ABC News, Dec. 12, 2023; Politico, Dec. 2, 2023; *Times of Israel*, Dec. 18, 2023.
36 *Wall St. Journal*, Dec. 18, 2023.
37 *Washington Post*, Dec. 19, 2023; AP News, Dec. 19, 2023; Reuters, Dec. 19, 2023. Also see David Levy, "The Influence of Sea Power in Iran's Proxy War. Part 2: U.S. Navy Operations and Options," BESA Center Perspectives Paper no. 2,245, Bar-Ilan University, Dec. 21, 2023.
38 *Wall St. Journal*, Dec. 19, 2023; *New York Times*, Dec. 19, 2023; JNS, Dec. 19, 2023; *Haaretz*, Dec. 19 and 25, 2023; i24 News, Dec. 18, 2023; Galit Altstein, "Israel's Economy Convulsed by the War with Hamas," Bloomberg, Oct. 30, 2023; *Haaretz*, Dec. 25, 2023.
39 Adam Taylor, "Gaza's Economy, Crumbling for Years, Is Being Pounded to Dust," *Washington Post*, Nov. 15, 2023; Reuters, Dec. 20, 2023; *Washington Post*, Dec. 23, 2023.
40 Al-Jazeera, Dec. 19, 2023; AP, Dec. 19, 2023; *Times of Israel*, Dec. 19, 2023.
41 IDF report, Jan. 29, 2015; Seth Frantzman, "Preparing for a Second Front," *Jerusalem Post Magazine*, Dec. 15, 2023.
42 Israel National News, Dec. 18, 2023; BBC, Dec. 17, 2023.
43 Israel National News, Dec. 20, 2023.
44 JNS, Dec. 20, 2023.
45 Israel National News, Dec. 21, 2023.
46 *Jerusalem Post*, Dec. 21, 2023.
47 *Haaretz*, Dec. 21, 2023; *Wall St. Journal*, Dec. 21, 2023; *Washington Post*, Dec. 22, 2023.
48 *Jerusalem Post*, Dec. 22, 2023; World Israel News, Dec. 21, 2023; *Haaretz*, Dec. 22, 2023.
49 Israel National News, Dec. 22, 2023; Reuters, Dec. 22, 2023; Times of Israel, Dec. 22, 2023.
50 Israel National News, Dec. 23, 2023; *Jerusalem Post*, Dec. 23, 2023.
51 *Wall St. Journal*, Dec. 23, 2023; Times of Israel, Dec. 23, 2023.
52 *Reuters*, Dec. 24, 2023; *Haaretz*, Dec. 24, 2023; *Jerusalem Post*, Dec. 24, 2023.
53 Israel National News, Dec. 24, 2023; *Jerusalem Post*, Dec. 24, 2023; JNS, Dec. 21, 2023.
54 Israel National News, Dec. 25, 2023.
55 *Jerusalem Post*, Dec. 25, 2023; *Wall St. Journal*, Dec. 24–25, 2023; Reuters, Dec. 25, 2023; *New York Times*, Dec. 25, 2023.
56 *Times of Israel*, Dec. 25, 2023.
57 *Wall St. Journal*, Dec. 25, 2023.
58 IDF Reports, Dec. 25–26, 2023; Israel National News, Dec. 26, 2023; *Jerusalem Post*, Dec. 26, 2023; *Haaretz*, Dec. 26, 2023; *New York Times*, Dec. 26, 2023; United with Israel, Dec. 25, 2023.
59 *Jerusalem Post*, Dec. 26, 2023; Reuters, Dec. 26, 2023; *Haaretz*, Dec. 26, 2023. The threat was no longer "just" possibly one Iranian nuclear weapon, but rather a potential arsenal of nuclear weapons. At its current rate, Iran could roughly produce enough uranium for a new nuclear weapon every four-and-half months if it decided to breakout over the nuclear

threshold. Yonah Jeremy Bob, "Iran's Latest Threat on Israel: An Arsenal of Nuclear Weapons—Analysis," *Jerusalem Post*, Dec. 27, 2023.
60 Israel National News, Dec. 26–27, 2023; *Haaretz*, Dec. 27, 2023; *Jerusalem Post*, Dec. 27–28, 2023.
61 Israel National News, Dec. 27, 2023.
62 Israel National News, Dec. 27, 2023; World Israel News, Dec. 27, 2023.
63 JNS, Dec. 27, 2023. The Taliban, founded by Mullah Omar and Abdul Ghani Baradaar, is a fundamentalist Sunni Islamist nationalist and pro-Pashtun movement founded in September 1994 in Kandahar, Afghanistan. This terrorist group ruled most of Afghanistan as the Islamic Emirate of Afghanistan from 1996 until October 2001. The Taliban, which rose from the ashes of Afghanistan's post-Soviet civil war, provided Al-Qaeda sanctuary for operations. Afghan commander Ahmad Shah Massoud was assassinated on September 9, 2001, by Al-Qaeda agents, two days before the 9/11 attacks on New York and Washington. Massoud had fought Soviet forces in Afghanistan in the 1980s and the Taliban and Al-Qaeda alliance in the following decade. Terrorism experts believe that his assassination assured Al-Qaeda leader Osama bin Laden protection by the Taliban after the 9/11 attacks. When on August 30, 2021, the United States completed a full withdrawal of troops from Afghanistan, bringing its twenty-year-long war, aided by the native Northern Alliance, against the Taliban to an end, the Taliban took over Kabul two weeks later. Its adherents advocate a strict interpretation of Qur'anic instruction and jurisprudence. In practice, that means often merciless policies on the treatment of women, political opponents of any type, and religious minorities. The Taliban government is still not formally recognized by any country. See Ahmed Rashid, *Taliban: Militant Islam, Oil and Fundamentalism in Central Asia* (New Haven: Yale Nota Bene Books, 2000).
64 JNS, Dec. 27, 2023; Israel National News, Dec. 28, 2023.
65 *Times of Israel*, Dec. 27–28, 2023; JNS, Dec. 28, 2023.
66 Ynet, Dec. 28, 2023; *Jerusalem Post*, Dec. 29, 2023; Israel National News, Dec. 29, 2023.
67 *Haaretz*, Dec. 30. 2023; *Times of Israel*, Dec. 30–31, 2023.
68 *Wall St. Journal*, Dec. 30, 2023; AP News, Dec. 6, 2023; *New York Times*, Dec. 28, 30, 2023; *Washington Post*, Dec. 30, 2023.
69 Israel National News, Dec. 31, 2023; *Jerusalem Post*, Dec. 31, 2023; Reuters. Dec. 31, 2023.
70 Israel National News, Dec. 31, 2023; *Jerusalem Post*, Dec. 31, 2023; *Haaretz*, Dec. 31, 2023; *New York Times*, Dec. 31, 2023; France 24, Dec. 31, 2023.

CHAPTER 5

Ring in the New Year

As revelers across the globe rang in New Year 2024 at midnight with spectacular fireworks, Hamas fired a heavy barrage of thirty rockets into central Israel and Tel Aviv on day eighty-seven of the war, sending Israel a message that the terrorist group was far from being defeated. While freed hostages returned to Kibbutz Be'eri for the first time, an IAF jet killed Adil Mismah, the Nukhba's Deir al-Balah Brigade commander who had led the attack on Kibbutz Kisufim and directed other Hamas terrorists to Be'eri and Kibbutz Nirim during the deadly incursion of October 7. An explosive device in the northern Gaza Strip killed IDF reservist twenty-four-year-old Sgt. 1st Class Amichai Yisrael Yehoshua Oster of the 5th Brigade's Battalion 7020, the first army casualty of 2024, and wounded another eleven soldiers, two of them seriously. In the largest tort claim ever filed in Israel against the state, some survivors of the Nova music festival slaughter near Kibbutz Re'im on what many called that "Black Sabbath" began preparing a lawsuit for damages of NIS 200 million against the IDF, Shin Bet, and the Israeli police, charging that the disaster could have been avoided at many points in time.[1]

At 6:45 p.m. that same evening, an unprecedented full panel of Israel's Supreme Court voted 8–7 to strike down a law that sought to limit the court's power over government decisions, legislation which had put the country on the brink of a constitutional crisis just before Israelis united behind the war effort in Gaza. Monday's ruling concerned the Reasonableness Standard Law, an amendment to Israel's Basic Law, that was pushed through the Knesset and passed by Netanyahu's coalition government in July. The contentious law had removed the right of Israel's highest court to block Knesset-passed laws or government decisions that the judges deemed "unreasonable." By striking it down, the court granted itself the authority to overrule Basic Laws, which serve as Israel's de facto constitution. It affirmed this power in a separate ruling, approved by a 12–3 majority.

Netanyahu's Likud Party was swift to condemn the court's decision, calling it "in opposition to the nation's desire for unity, especially in a time of war." Israeli Justice Minister Yariv Levin said that the ruling threatened the unity needed "so our troops can succeed at the front," and he pledged to pass the entire judicial overhaul package after the war ended. Adversaries who had protested the overhaul welcomed the ruling but refrained from public celebrations. Brothers in Arms, a group of reserve soldiers who had spearheaded opposition since 2023 to the overhaul, responded that its members "stand behind the independence of the Supreme Court, respect its ruling, and call all to abstain from division and hatred." "After October 7, Israel cannot return to the division and chasms between parts of the nation," they declared. While the ruling, striking down a quasi-constitutional Basic Law for the first time in the country's history, threatened to revive the deep political and social domestic strife generated for nine months by the amendment as part of judicial reform, Netanyahu did not say whether he would abide by the decision.[2]

The 460th Brigade secured control of terrorist infrastructure embedded inside the residence of Hamas's Northern Gaza Brigade commander, killed dozens of terrorist operatives in close-quarters combat, destroyed tunnel shafts, seized large quantities of weapons, and found intelligence material connecting the central Daraj Tuffah Mosque to the October 7 massacre. Hamas deputy head since 2017 Saleh Al-Arouri, a key target for Israel in the past year due to his central role in planning the October 7 slaughter, co-founder of its military wing, linked to the murder of three Israeli teen boys in 2014, and head of terrorist operations in the West Bank in recent years, was killed on January 2 along with at least six Hamas operatives in a drone strike in Beirut, which US officials and Hamas attributed to Israel. Hamas leader Ismail Haniyeh responded: "Just like the assassinations of Yassin and Rantisi, Al-Arouri's death won't stop the revolution." Parents of fallen IDF soldiers requested to meet US Secretary of State Blinken on his upcoming visit to Israel to express that stopping the war would be "a terrible mistake of historic proportions." "We are in the middle of World War III," declared Israeli Foreign Minister Israel Katz on his first day in office, "we are there for everyone" against "Iran-led radical Islam, whose tentacles are already in Europe."[3]

Elsewhere, the Israeli air force attacked Syrian army infrastructure in response to five rockets fired at the Golan Heights. Hamas's Haniyeh said that his organization had delivered its position on a cease-fire/hostage release deal to Qatar and Egypt which was based on "a complete cessation of the aggression," adding that "hostages will not be released except under the resistance's conditions." The US Sixth Fleet announced that the aircraft carrier *USS Gerald*

Ford, the world's largest warship, was returning from the eastern Mediterranean Sea after months of providing protection for Israel in the Red Sea to its home birth in Norfolk, Virginia. Navy officials added that the United States retained "extensive capability both in the Mediterranean and across the Middle East." A group of French students began circulating a petition, initiated by twenty-three-year-old Muslim student Hichem Mouttaki, to have the date of October 7 named the "World Day against Antisemitism." The much criticized president of Harvard University, Claudine Gay, citing "racial animus," resigned after only serving six months—a record—amid increasing allegations of extensive scholarly plagiarism and the backlash following comments to a Congressional committee last month about antisemitism on campus and her declining to state plainly that a call for genocide against Jews would violate the university's code of conduct.[4]

On January 3, the IDF continued uncovering tunnel shafts and anti-tank firing posts in the Khirbet Khuza'a area of the Gaza Strip, while Givati fighters in the Hamas stronghold of Khan Younis and the IAF's use of drones eliminated terrorists and munitions factories. US spy agencies verified Israeli claims that Hamas and another Palestinian terrorist group had used Shifa Hospital, the Strip's largest medical facility, as a command center and to hold hostages. The IDF published collated photos and videos showing Gaza children undergoing military training, posing with weapons, and even simulated drills in a mock tunnel. The Gaza Health Ministry said that 128 were killed and 61 injured in the last twenty-four hours. Israeli forces from the Shin Bet, Border Police, and the IDF launched a widespread operation in the Nur Shams refugee camp in the West Bank. The IDF announced that eighteen Palestinian terrorists had already been detained with six arrested since the operation was launched earlier in the morning. In addition, four terror suspects were arrested, and weaponry seized in Qalqilya.

Responding to the murder of Saleh Al-Arouri in Beirut, Iranian Foreign Office spokesperson Nasser Kanaani declared: "The martyr's blood will undoubtedly ignite another surge in the veins of resistance and the motivation to fight against the Zionist occupiers, not only in Palestine but also in the region and among all freedom-seekers worldwide." Hezbollah Secretary-General Nasrallah condemned the assassination as "flagrant Israeli aggression," and he declared that the Hamas attack of October 7 had "weakened Israel and put it on the path to extinction" while reiterating that Hezbollah was "unaware" the attack would occur. He added that, if Israel decided to wage war against Lebanon, "Lebanon's interest will be to go to war all the way, unrestrained." By contrast, Mossad chief David Barnea issued this warning: "Let every Arab mother know that if her son was a partner in the October 7 massacre, his blood is on his own head."

About fifty IDF reservists gathered in front of Netanyahu's office in Jerusalem to demand that the fighting in Gaza not stop until Hamas were defeated. Even as the toll of army soldiers killed in Gaza combat rose to 175, an Israel Democracy Institute poll found that seventy-five percent of Jewish Israelis rejected the Biden administration's demand to shift the war against Hamas to a new phase of targeted killings and less bombing in populated areas; fifty-six percent of Arab respondents said Israel should accede to US pressure. As for the threat of Hezbollah, which claimed that 140 of its fighters had been killed since the war began, the UN Interim Force in Lebanon, echoing French President Emmanuel Macron. called for restraints from all parties lest escalation occur in the region.[5]

On day ninety, the IDF announced that three Israelis missing since October 7 had been kidnapped to Gaza, bringing the total of remaining hostages to 136, and that IDF intel resulted in "widespread damage to our enemies, from Gaza to Iran." While IAF air strikes continued to pummel Khan Younis, the Gaza Health Ministry said that 22,438 Palestinians had been killed and 57,614 wounded since the war began. The International Court of Justice (ICJ) scheduled public hearings on January 11 and 12 for a case brought by South Africa alleging Israel was committing genocide in Gaza, leading US National Security Council spokesperson John Kirby to call the submission "meritless, counterproductive and completely without any basis in fact whatsoever." The United Arab Emirates defended its decision to normalize ties with Israel via the Abraham Accords, and stressed that it would not walk back its moves over the Gaza war.

Defense Minister Gallant told Amos Hochstein, President Biden's senior advisor leading efforts to avoid further escalation between Israel and Hezbollah, that "Israel would prefer to resolve the military conflict with Hezbollah through diplomatic means, but the time span for this is limited." Under intense domestic pressure, and facing effective Israeli air strikes, Hezbollah's Nasrallah used his recent speech to underscore the lack of desire for a major escalation at the present time, even as he championed ethnic cleansing by declaring that those Israelis with foreign passports should leave because the Land of Palestine belonged exclusively to the Palestinian people. Five people, including a Hezbollah regional commander, were killed in an Israeli airstrike on targets in southern Lebanon overnight. In the West Bank, Israeli forces searched houses in the Nur Shams refugee camp near the city of Tulkarm, detaining hundreds of people suspected of terrorist activities. According to the IDF, approximately

2,600 Palestinians had been arrested in the West Bank since the beginning of the war, including 1,300 who were Hamas-affiliated.[6]

Over the weekend, an IAF strike eliminated Commander Ismail Siraj and Deputy Commander Ahmed Wehbe of Hamas's Nuseirat Battalion, responsible for terror attacks on October 7, including against Kibbutz Be'eri, and involved in anti-tank missile and UAV fire targeting Israeli troops during the war. IDF spokesman Daniel Hagari said on Saturday that "Hamas's military framework in the northern Gaza Strip has been completely dismantled." A *Wall Street Journal* investigation revealed that Zaher Jabarin, operating from an Istanbul office Hamas's financial empire and its major financial ties to Iran, as well as co-founder with Al-Arouri of Hamas's military wing in the West Bank, had enabled the payment of weapons and fighters' wages for the October 7 onslaught. Nasrallah warned Israel in a second televised speech that Hezbollah would respond swiftly "on the battlefield" to the killing of Hamas deputy leader Al-Arouri. Retaliating to a massive volley of more than forty rockets from Lebanon, the IDF struck Hezbollah terror cells, military sites, and launch posts. Thousands of Israelis protested on Saturday night in Tel Aviv, Haifa, and near Netanyahu's private residence in Caesarea, calling for early elections and the prime minister's dismissal. Martin Griffiths, the UN humanitarian chief, described Gaza on Friday as "uninhabitable" three months into the war, and warned that famine was looming and a public health disaster unfolding.[7]

As the war entered its fourteenth week, the Gaza Health Ministry reported at least 113 killed, including journalist Ali Salem Abu Ajawa, grandson of Hamas founder Sheikh Yassin, and 250 others injured in the past twenty-four hours by Israeli airstrikes. While 198 humanitarian trucks entered Gaza throughout Sunday, Blinken warned that the war between Hamas and Israel could "metastasize" and threaten security in the wider Middle East. Eleven IDF soldiers were injured, one seriously, in fighting during the past day. Border Police nineteen-year-old Sgt. Shai Garmai was killed when an explosive device hit the military vehicle she was in during an overnight operation in the West Bank city of Jenin, with three other Border Police officers wounded, one of them seriously; eight Palestinians were killed in an Israeli airstrike there. The IDF announced that it found proof that Hamas, aided by Iran, had developed cruise missile capabilities. Kfir Brigade soldiers found a large cache of weapons hidden inside bags bearing the logo of UNRWA, the agency for Palestinian refugees in the Strip. UNRWA headquarters and educational facilities had been known to employ Hamas operatives as schoolteachers, the IDF noted, these buildings protected by international law while in fact funneling billions of dollars into the Hamas treasury.[8]

The *Washington Post* reported that US officials feared Netanyahu would try to expand the fighting against Hezbollah to maintain his political survival. That newspaper also reported that a new assessment by the US Defense Intelligence Agency suggested it would be difficult for the Israeli army to win a large-scale war against Hezbollah during the on-going fighting in Gaza. Israel and Egypt were negotiating the future of the narrow, fourteen kilometer-in-length Philadelphi Corridor between Egypt and Gaza that Israel said had been used by Hamas to smuggle weapons and fighters through underground tunnels and was key to destroying the militant group. Jordan's King Abdullah II warned Blinken of the "catastrophic consequences of the continuing war in Gaza" and called for "an end to the dire humanitarian crisis" in the coastal enclave. Blinken said that Saudi Crown Prince Mohammed bin Salman al-Saud remained interested in normalizing relations with Israel "but it will require that the conflict end in Gaza, and it will also clearly require that there be a practical pathway to a Palestinian state." "The year 2024 will be challenging," declared IDF chief Halevi. "We will be fighting in Gaza all year, that's for sure, and this will also hold the other arenas, certainly in Judea and Samaria, to a certain state of alertness."[9]

On Monday, IDF forces, of whom 176 soldiers had fallen in battle in Gaza since the ground operation began. struck some thirty "significant" targets across the Strip's southern city of Khan Younis. Intelligence revealed that Hamas possessed stockpiles of sophisticated Chinese-made weaponry, as well as armaments from North Korea. Red alert sirens were activated in Israeli southern communities as Hamas continued to launch rockets on the three-month anniversary of its massacre of October 7, 2023. In conversations with the IDF's Unit 504, which specializes in human intelligence, Gaza civilians revealed how Hamas regularly stole food and humanitarian aid from them, killed relatives, and took over their homes for military purposes. Throughout the West Bank, Israeli forces arrested seventeen terror suspects overnight and confiscated many weapons.[10]

The IDF confirmed that its air force's traffic control base at Mount Meron had been damaged by Hezbollah rocket fire on Saturday, but clarified that the air defense systems' operational preparedness was not harmed. In retaliation, ratcheting up cross-border tensions, an Israeli air strike on Khirbet Selm in southern Lebanon killed Wissam (Jawad) al-Tawil, senior commander in Hezbollah's elite Radwan field force who was responsible for the rocket that damaged Israel's Meron air force base. The IDF also eliminated Hassan Hakashah in Beit Jinn, Syria, the terrorist responsible for recent rocket launches by Hamas from Syria toward Israeli territory. Soldiers of the 188th and Golani Brigades, operating in the central Gaza Strip, uncovered the largest weapons-production facility since the beginning of the war in a tunnel thirty meters deep under the Al-Bureij refugee camp. It contained components for long-range rockets that could be fired from the Gaza Strip as far as northern Israel, as well as mortar shells, explosives, and ammunition.[11]

"I have been quietly working with the Israeli government to get them [to] reduce and significantly get out of Gaza," Biden said in what had been one of the US president's clearest statements to date expressing his desire for the Gaza war to end. He spoke after several protesters calling "ceasefire now" interrupted his remarks at the Mother Emanuel AME Church in Charleston, South Carolina. There will be a shift in the fighting in Gaza from the "intense maneuvering phase of the war" toward "different types of special operations" over a long period of time, Gallant told the *Wall Street Journal*, adding that Israel would not abandon its goal of destroying Hamas. Jordan's King Abdullah II said on Monday that Israel had created a whole generation of orphans in Gaza, where he said around over 30,000 people, mostly women and children, had been killed or were missing because of the conflict.[12]

On January 9, the IDF announced the death of six combat engineer reservists and three other soldiers, along with eight wounded, in three incidents, most from an unintended detonation by a tank of tunnel demolition explosives near the partially underground and overground rocket manufacturing factory uncovered at Al-Bureij in central Gaza. Givati troops found a large amount of weaponry in Khan Younis's Islamic University, while paratroopers (*tzanchanim*) of Battalion 101, in face-to-face combat, killed terrorists in one of that city's buildings. World Health Organization officials in Geneva voiced concern about the possible collapse of hospital provision in southern and central Gaza. Citing several military sources, World Israel News reported that the IDF knew the location of Sinwar, most likely in the tunnel network under Khan Unis, but was unable to strike because the Hamas chief was using some of the remaining hostages as human shields.[13]

Ali Hussein Barji, who was responsible for dozens of drone attacks on Israel, was killed along with two other Hezbollah operatives in a car blast in Lebanon. Hezbollah attempted by a UAV to attack the IDF Northern Command base in Tzfat (Safed). Naim Qassem, second-in-command of Hezbollah, said, "We do not want to expand the war, but if Israel does that, the response and clash will be unavoidable." An Israeli foreign ministry spokesperson clarified on X that Israel was not actively exploring the possibility of relocating Palestinians from the Gaza Strip to African countries, countering recent publications to that effect. The families of 132 Israeli hostages being held by Hamas held a march in an attempt to disrupt the transfer of aid to Gaza, calling on Israel to halt the flow of aid until their loved ones were freed. The procession tried to march from Kibbutz Magen to the Kerem Shalom Crossing, but since the armed conflict began civilian access to this area had been restricted as a war zone. Residents of the nearby towns and agricultural communities were evacuated, and police blocked the protestors' path.[14]

The same day, the *Washington Post* reported that, on the afternoon of October 11, a group of masked, armed Israelis, possibly from the hilltop outpost of Esh Kodesh half a mile to the south, struck the West Bank village of Qusra and killed three residents there. Seventeen-year-old Obada Saed Abu Srour, eldest of four children, was shot in the back, probably as he was running from gunfire. Muath Raed Odeh, twenty-nine and a new father, and twenty-year-old Musab Abdel Abu Rida also died. IDF soldiers and police were photographed at the scene of the deaths only after the outbreak ended, even though troops stationed at nearby military stations were within earshot of the gunfire. In the past, "price tag" attacks by extremist "hilltop youth" had uprooted olive groves, physically assaulted Palestinian farmers, and harassed others in the region. The Judea-Samaria settlement leadership and prominent Religious Zionist rabbis had "fiercely condemned" such actions of this small militant fringe. The army and Border Police told the newspaper that the incident was under "active investigation." Final judgment had to await their findings.[15]

Arriving at Ben-Gurión Airport for his fourth trip to Israel since the war started, Blinken presented a plan for Gaza's future to Israeli officials based on his recent meetings with rulers in Saudi Arabia, the United Arab Emirates, Qatar, Jordan, Greece, and Turkey before arriving in Israel. Ending the war, he posited, would give Jerusalem a chance to improve ties with Arab neighbors, relations that were notably warming before the October 7 assault. He reiterated a focus on the postwar rebuilding of Gaza, with non-Hamas Palestinians at the center, as a possible pathway to a future Palestinian state. Blinken did not, however, offer details on how Washington would overcome the sticking points that have bedeviled every previous US administration in forging a path to a Palestinian state. He also urged caution in Israel's response to the presence of Hezbollah forces in Lebanon.

US officials, reported the *Washington Post*, hoped that the actual start that month of troop reductions—the first since ground operations began—signaled that Israeli officials were finally bending to Washington lobbying, in addition to the economic strain of diverting tens of thousands of reservists from the workforce, to move from intense battles to more targeted operations. For the first time, military spokesperson Hagari confirmed to the *New York Times* that the IDF had done so, with fewer ground troops and air strikes needed, and would continue reducing the number of troops in Gaza.[16]

IDF operational activity in the areas of Al-Ma'azi in central Gaza and Khan Younis in the south continued since Tuesday, with over 150 targets hit, many weapons and tunnel shafts uncovered, and dozens of terrorists eliminated. The Mothers of Combat Soldiers Foundation, in a demonstration upon Blinken's arrival, unfurled huge signs with pictures of the children of senior US government and military officials dressed in IDF uniforms on the battlefield under the title: "Let our children fight as you would let your children fight." A secret Telegram channel consisting of 3,000 UNRWA teachers in Gaza filled with posts expressing support for the Hamas massacre on October 7 was exposed by a UN Watch report on Wednesday. Shortly after the massive infiltration into Israel had begun, members of the group had praised the perpetrators as "heroes," lauded the education received by the terrorists, shared images of dead or captured Israelis, and called for the execution of hostages. White House NSC spokesperson Kirby said that Washington still did not "support a cease-fire at this time" because "we don't believe that benefits anybody but Hamas. We continue to support humanitarian pauses." The United States and United Kingdom shot down twenty-one drones in the Red Sea, the largest Houthi attack to date, but held back from attacking Houthi bases fearing a wider conflict in the region with other Iranian-backed groups.[17]

The *Asharq Al-Awsat* newspaper, citing senior Hamas officials, reported that the idea to infiltrate Israeli communities near the Gaza border was thought about and preparations for it began before Operation Protective Edge in 2014, but it was put on hold when the war started. The planning was renewed two years ago following Operation Guardian of the Walls. For two years, thousands of terrorists underwent specialized training and tests. The report also stated that the decision regarding the timing of the attack was known only by five individuals: Hamas leader in Gaza, Yahya Sinwar, his brother Muhammad, the leader of Hamas's military wing, Muhammad Deif, and two additional senior officials. The battalion commanders played their role in preparing their selected forces for the mission, while Ayman Siam, commander of the missile unit in the Gaza Strip, received special instructions to prepare to launch hundreds of missiles coinciding with the start of the attack. The sources explained that the date of October 7 was determined following field reports from monitoring units that confirmed complete silence on the border. Then, on Friday, the five officials decided that the most appropriate time was Saturday morning, an official holiday in Israel. At midnight on the 7th, they gave the order to prepare, so the field commanders and fighters of the Nukhba elite forces received instructions and began to move until the dawn hours, and then the operation began.[18]

Beyond the Gaza war, Hezbollah was believed to be the first to use precise anti-tank missiles to target civilian structures. Dozens of Israeli buildings had taken direct hits, and now even towns that were not evacuated were within firing range. Iran, reported Sky News, developed a new attack drone, the Shahed-107, for Russia in its war against Ukraine and was close to providing Moscow with surface-to-surface missiles. The Shahed-107 was an "explosive and reconnaissance" UAV with the technology to seek out high-value battlefield targets, such as British and American multiple-launch rocket systems used by Ukrainian forces. Tehran had been accused by Ukraine and its allies of supplying Russia with one-way attack drones, including the Shahed-131 and Shahed-136, referred to as "suicide drones" because they flew into targets and exploded on impact.[19]

Scores of Palestinians were leaving the Gaza Strip through its southern border by paying up to $10,000 to "brokers" with alleged links to Egyptian intelligence, reported *The Guardian*. Jordan and Egypt had repeatedly made clear that they would not accept any Palestinians from the Strip, declaring it a "red line." "There will be no refugees in Jordan and no refugees in Egypt," King Abdullah II said following a meeting with German Chancellor Olaf Scholz in mid-October. Egyptian security sources had likewise dismissed proposals to allow Gazans fleeing the conflict to enter that country, with one saying they would not allow safe corridors so as to protect "the right of Palestinians to hold on to their cause and their land."[20]

After two weeks of intensive fighting, soldiers of the IDF's 5th Brigade gained control over the southern Gaza town of Khirbat Ikhza'a, which had served as the staging area from which Hamas attacked the kibbutzim of Nir Oz, Nirim, and Ein HaShlosha on October 7. At least one-third of the 136 hostages still in the Hamas terror group's custody in Gaza were at imminent risk of death, suffering from chronic diseases that needed immediate treatment, declared a report by the Hostages and Missing Persons Families Forum. Former PA Ambassador Osama Al-Ali, with sharp criticism of Hamas leader Haniyah "happy and carefree" in Qatar, voiced unexpected opinions on Al-Arabiya Network in urging Hamas to release the remaining Israeli hostages and bring an end to the suffering of the Gazan people. Iran's Supreme Leader Ayatollah Ali Khamenei tweeted on X in Hebrew and English that "the crimes of the Zionist regime" will not be forgotten even after it "is destroyed by the grace of God." He then declared, "after nearly 100 days, the Palestinian Resistance is still alive, energetic, and well-prepared while the Zionist regime is tired, abased, regretful, and has been marked as a criminal."[21]

On Thursday, Israel Police and the Shin Bet foiled terror attacks planned by two East Jerusalem Arab residents in support of ISIS, whose suicide bombers from Afghanistan had killed almost 100 Iranians during a memorial service for IRGC head Qassem Soleimani memorial in Tehran yesterday. At least seven people in Kiryat Shmona were wounded after Hezbollah fired a barrage of rockets on Israel's north, which also caused electricity shortages there and in the Upper Galilee. Offering a pathway to a Palestinian state was the best way to stabilize the wider region and isolate Iran and its proxies, Blinken declared before returning to the United States from his latest frenetic regional tour over the Gaza war. He added that Washington "is focused on making sure the West Bank does not explode."[22]

Expressing support for South Africa's accusation at The Hague that Israel was guilty of genocide, Hamas claimed it legitimate "to stop the occupation's aggression" against "our Palestinian people in the Gaza Strip." Dozens of Palestinians gathered in front of the statue of Nelson Mandela in the West Bank city of Ramallah to thank South Africa for bringing a genocide case against Israel over its war with Hamas, *Per contra*, in a post on X, the Israeli Foreign Ministry called the case "one of the greatest shows of hypocrisy in history." The US State Department declared that the petition's allegations against Israel were "unfounded," adding "it is those who are violently attacking Israel who continue to openly call for the annihilation of Israel and the mass murder of Jews."[23]

Using the information collected by IDF troops on the ground and analysis of the tunnels exposed by the armed forces up to then, the Intelligence Directorate revealed that over 6,000 tons of concrete and 1,800 tons of metal had been used to build hundreds of kilometers of underground infrastructure, at a total cost of tens of millions of dollars. "Instead of investing in civilian infrastructure and development to benefit the residents of the Gaza Strip, Hamas used vast quantities of money and resources over many years to build a vast underground tunnel network used for its deadly terrorist activity," the IDF Spokespersons' Unit noted.[24]

That night, US and UK military forces, with Australian, Bahraini, Canadian, and Dutch support, struck more than a dozen targets in Yemen associated with the Houthis. President Biden announced that the strikes were "in direct response to unprecedented Houthi attacks against international maritime vessels in the Red Sea, including the use of anti-ship ballistic missiles for the first time in history." "More than 2,000 ships have been forced to divert thousands of miles to avoid the Red Sea, which can cause weeks of delays in product shipping times," he added, noting that on January 9, Houthis launched their largest attack to date—"directly targeting American ships." The attack was the first acknowledged US airstrike in Yemen since 2020.[25]

Come Friday morning, the IDF reported that its forces had eliminated dozens of terrorists during operations in Khan Younis and Maghazi, including commanders in Hamas's elite Nukhba Force involved in the October 7 onslaught. The IDF also said that it destroyed two central Gaza sites with dozens of rocket launchers, some of which were loaded and ready for use, and that Israel's air force attacked a Hamas command center in central Gaza. A terrorist squad from the Arab town Idna attacked the West Bank settlement of Adora on the Sabbath; the three infiltrators were killed. In a recent video, founder in 1982 of Hezbollah Subhi Al-Tufayli claimed "it is Egypt that's besieging Gaza and starving its children." He called for the fall of Egyptian President El-Sisi and trial for the "thieving Zionist criminal lowlifes," referring to Egyptian army generals. Al-Tufayli also criticized the Jordanian regime, urging accountability for King Abdullah II. US Lt. General Douglas Sims told reporters that twenty-eight targets had been hit in Red Sea strikes, adding "we have degraded [the Houthis'] capability" to carry out attacks. In response, Tehran warned that this would fuel "insecurity and instability" in the region, and its UN ambassador declared that the United States and its allies had "single-handedly" triggered the spillover of conflict to the entire region in the wake of the strikes.[26]

A tunnel was recreated in Tel Aviv's Hostages Square to raise awareness of the plight of the Hamas-held hostages after 100 days in captivity. The US Central Intelligence Agency (CIA) set up a new task force in the wake of the October 7 assault that was gathering intelligence on the location of senior leaders of the terror group and the hostages it was holding in Gaza, and sharing the information with Israel, the *New York Times* reported. Thousands gathered in Jerusalem at the Western Wall Plaza in prayer, "impoverished, broken, and in pain," for the soldiers and remaining hostages' safe return home. Initiated by the country's chief rabbis, pauses punctuated by shofar blasts, it drew a mix of religious and secular Israelis in a show of unity that had arisen across Israel during the past 100 days.[27]

As for ICJ deliberations at The Hague charging Israel with genocide in the Gaza Strip, lawyers for Israel argued that Hamas's "wholesale massacre, mutilation, rape, and abduction" three months earlier better fit the term genocide; that the breadth and methods of Israel's counterattacks did not deviate from the laws of war and instead showed that Israel, by allowing humanitarian aid into Gaza, warning civilians of impending attacks, and facilitating their evacuation, was not intent on killing Palestinians en masse. Moreover, they asserted, the case cheapened a term that had been coined by the Polish Jewish lawyer

Raphael Lemkin during the Holocaust to describe the systematic destruction of the Jewish people under Nazi German rule. Canadian and UK officials also rejected the premise of South Africa's case at the ICJ, and Berlin, warning against "political instrumentalization" of the UN Genocide Convention, announced that it would present its own arguments against that claim.[28]

A twenty-four-hour protest rally called "100 Days in Hell" was held in Tel-Aviv beginning on the cold, rainy late evening of January 13. It drew 125,000 to mark Hamas's war against Israel on October 7 by its methodical slaughter and kidnapping of hostages to Gaza, of whom an estimated 25 of 136 were believed to have died. Retail chains, restaurants, businesses, and law firms come to a standstill during a 100-minute labor strike to express solidarity with the hostages and their traumatized families. At 4 p.m. Jerusalem time on January 14, repeated in New York City, Berlin, Delhi, and Beijing, one million bells were rung to mark that dark passage of time. A ceremony on Jerusalem's Haas Promenade, overlooking the crenelated walls of the Old City, concluded with iconic musician Idan Reichel's song *Waiting* for the day when "there will be nothing to fear," the sounding of a shofar, and the Israeli national anthem *Hatikva*.

Three days earlier in New York City, in place of the weekly Friday morning gatherings outside the home of UN Secretary-General Guterres, 2,500 demonstrators at the UN's Dag Hammarskjöld Plaza had heard thirteen-year-old Hila Rotem Shoshani of Kibbutz Be'eri tell of her harrowing experience as a hostage until released in late November. Governor Kathy Hochul, who said that she had been devastated during her visit to Kfar Aza, joined in pleas to "Bring them home now!" and asked, "Where is the outrage?" Reflecting on how his entire nation responded to the "boiling and horrifying cauldron of terror" unleashed by Hamas 100 days ago, Israeli President Herzog lauded the bravery and heroic sacrifices in battle of "the Tik Tok generation" along with the trauma suffered by hostages and their families, certain that "our spirit will prevail."[29]

The IDF continued eliminating terrorists and rocket launchers in the Gaza Strip on January 14, while four terrorists were killed in a firefight along the Lebanese border. Forty-eight-year-old Barak Ayalon, a member of the local security response team, and his mother Meirav were killed when a Hezbollah anti-tank missile struck a house in Moshav Yuval in the Upper Galilee, bring the total number of Israelis killed in the northern cross-border clashes to fifteen, nine of them soldiers, since October 7; a similar attack at Moshav Beit Hillel injured eleven, among them eight soldiers. In recorded telephone calls with officers of the 504 Human Intelligence Unit, which the IDF released on Sunday, residents of Gaza called for Allah to curse Hamas and its leaders who lived abroad in luxury hotels, referred to them as "dogs" who should be killed.

COGAT (the Coordinator of the Government Activities in the Territories), a new IDF website revealing the scope of Israel's dedicated humanitarian aid efforts in Gaza, noted that, since the beginning of the war, 8,394 trucks and 153,580 tons of humanitarian aid had entered the Gaza Strip through the Kerem Shalom and Nitzana inspection points. Additional field hospitals were in the process of being set up and were expected to be operational in the coming days. Additional equipment and personnel for the field hospitals operating in the Gaza Strip had entered as well.[30]

Marking the dark milestone of 100 days, the IDF announced that 522 soldiers had been killed since October 7, 188 of these after the ground invasion into Gaza, with 2,536 wounded. About 9,000 Hamas fighters had been "neutralized" in Gaza, adding to the 1,000 terrorists confronted and killed within Israel on that fateful day. Some 30,000 target sites in Gaza were hit; 9,000 rockets were launched against Israel. Hezbollah, of whose military sites 750 had been hit and 170 fighters killed, had dispatched 2,000 rockets from Lebanon. *Haaretz* reported that 1,600 Israeli soldiers suffered from PTSD since the start of the war, with 90 discharged from service. As for the hostages still underground in Hamas's labyrinth of Gaza tunnels, Israel handed over to the International Red Cross a list of medicines to transfer to the remaining hostages. Among other items, anti-depressants and anxiety medications, sleeping pills—and food compounds for toddlers Kfir and Ariel Bibas—were on the list.[31]

For its part, the Hamas-controlled Gaza Health Ministry declared that a total of 23,968 Palestinians had been killed and 60,582 wounded since the war began. Half a million Gazans were suffering from acute hunger, according to a *Haaretz* report. While Hamas fought on, Hezbollah chief Nasrallah said on Sunday that his group would not stop fighting Israel and that "American aggression in the Red Sea" will turn it into "a battlefield." Iranian President Raisi declared that, "with their initiative, the Palestinians have raised the level of war from a fight using stones to a war using missiles and drones. We have also declared that we will support Palestine and the resistance groups." "Palestine has emerged victorious, and the Zionist regime and its allies have bitten the dust," he added. In Washington, pro-Palestinian protesters criticized Biden's policy on the Hamas-Israel war, and family members of Gazans told their stories. Demonstrators who breached the outer fence of the White House chanted "Intifada" and threw bottles at Secret Service agents posted there. Anti-Israel protesters reacted to the airstrikes against Yemen by gathering at Times Square in New York City, chanting: "UK and US go to hell."[32]

On day 101, soldiers from the IDF's 36th Company left for home after having played a significant part in killing hundreds of terrorists and destroying dozens of kilometers of Hamas tunnels during the last eighty-eight days in the northern regions of Gaza. In a combined car-ramming and stabbing attack for which Hamas claimed responsibility, a terrorist from Hebron and his nephew left one dead and eighteen wounded in the Israeli central city of Ra'anana before being captured. The IDF said it arrested nine members of a Hamas student cell hiding in a West Bank university. Security officials told reporters that the situation in that region was "on the verge of explosion," and cautioned that if Israel's political leadership did not make decisions offering an economic future to West Bank Palestinians, the risk of conflict would increase. Iran was using fake online profiles to gather intelligence in Israel, the Shin Bet said on Monday. An Israeli soccer player in Turkey was released from custody after being detained for showing in a game solidarity with the Israeli hostages. A Houthi missile on one US-owned commercial ship near Yemen and another targeting a Navy destroyer showed their attacks were becoming more widespread and indiscriminate. The state-owned Qatari oil company halted transit through the Red Sea, while the Houthis' chief negotiator said that attacks there would not stop until Israel ended the war in Gaza.[33]

On the evening of January 15, Iran struck sites in Syria and Iraqi Kurdistan, shutting down the airport in the latter region. Tehran claimed that the strikes targeted Islamic State and a "Mossad headquarters," respectively. The attacks on Iraq hit close to a US consulate, but no American forces or installations were harmed. The next day, rocket-alert red sirens sounded in western Negev communities as terrorists in the center of the Gaza Strip launched over 50 rockets into southern Israel. In response to October 7, the European Union added Hamas's Yahya Sinwar to its list of international terrorists, imposing sanctions on him. Arab countries were not keen to get involved in the rebuilding of Gaza if the Palestinian enclave will be "leveled" again in a few years, Blinken told CNBC, adding that the Palestinian statehood question needed to be addressed.[34]

At least 100 more miles of tunnels, between 350 to 435 miles, with close to 5,700 different tunnel shafts leading to the underground tunnel network, were now estimated to be under Gaza than Israel had previously estimated, according to a *New York Times* report. Over the past twenty-four hours, Brigade 401 struck some 100 rocket installations and 60 ready-to-launch rockets and killed dozens of terrorists in the city of Beit Lahiya in Gaza's north, close to the Israeli border. Aerial and artillery strikes were carried out deep in Lebanon's Wadi Saluki area, a focal point of Hezbollah's operations, while special ground forces destroyed a terror threat near the village of Ayta al-Sha'ab.[35]

"Incensed" survivors of the ravaged Gaza border kibbutzim gathered outside the Knesset to demand that the government resign. Forty-two massacre survivors of the Nova music festival on October 7 launched a $53 million lawsuit against Israel's security agencies. The first shipment of medication from Qatar landed at the El-Arish airport in Egypt on Wednesday morning. This was bought from France and would reportedly be sent to Egypt in two shipments before being transferred to Gaza. The agreement stated that proof must be provided to Israel that the medication reached the hostages. Senior Hamas official Musa Abu Marzouk declared that "the Red Cross submitted a request to provide medicine to Hamas prisoners of war [sic!], and there were 140 types of such medicine, so we set several conditions." These included "that in exchange for each package of medicine, one thousand packages must be provided for Gazans; the Red Cross would distribute the medicines in four hospitals covering all areas in the Gaza Strip, including medicine for the hostages; food and aid for the Strip had to be increased; and the Israeli army must be prevented from inspecting the drug shipments." At Netanyahu's last-minute order, Israeli officials at the Kerem Shalom Crossing inspected the medicine shipment for Gaza.[36]

During an operation in the Balata refugee camp in Nablus, the IDF and the Shin Bet eliminated with a drone strike the head of a terror cell, Amed Abdullah Abu-Shalal, as well as Bilal Nofal, a key Hamas operative responsible for interrogating individuals suspected of espionage against the terror organization in the southern Gaza Strip and playing a crucial role in advancing Hamas's research and development processes. Following the deadly ramming attack yesterday in Ra'anana, the secretariats of tens of towns in Judea and Samaria wrote to Gallant and Netanyahu demanding that equal restrictions be imposed for Palestinian Arab workers wishing to enter their towns to that of workers attempting to enter the rest of Israel. Between October 7 and January 15, Rescuers without Borders first responders had recorded more than 2,600 attacks targeting Israeli civilians and soldiers in Judea, Samaria, and the Jordan Valley regions. These figures did not include the hundreds of violent attacks on security personnel during counterterrorism operations in villages under the control of the Palestinian Authority. Palestinian terrorists in Judea and Samaria had killed five Israelis and wounded many others since October 7, according to Hatzalah.[37]

On January 18, Hostages Square lofted orange balloons to mark the first birthday of redheaded Kfir Bibas, the youngest person taken hostage during the October 7 attack, uncertain whether the family was alive. A group of relatives of hostages arrived at the Kerem Shalom Crossing to protest the transfer of humanitarian aid to Gaza and to prevent the trucks from entering. but were stopped by police. On the other side of the divide, hundreds chanting we must bring them home "alive and not in coffins," blocked the Ayalon Highway in

Tel-Aviv overnight. One bereaved father, revealing to the Israeli press that a Hamas attacker on October 7 had decapitated his soldier son and later tried to sell the head for $10,000, added that, "by a miracle," the head was eventually found by the army and returned to Israel for burial. While completing the destruction of the Hamas Central Camp Brigade's weapon production infrastructure, the IDF also found that the area near Salah al-Din Road consisted of weapons factories and lathes, both above and below ground, that were used to produce ammunition and weapons for Hamas. Army troops killed sixty terrorists over the past twenty-four hours, forty in Khan Younis, while Israeli security forces arrested fifteen terror suspects and killed eight more in a thirty-five-hour raid of Tulkarm.[38]

The United States launched another series of strikes against Houthi sites in Yemen after redesignating the group a terrorist organization. The other day, the Shell oil company suspended Red Sea shipments amid fears of additional Houthi attacks. Pakistan conducted retaliatory strikes against the portion of Baluchistan in Iran after Tehran missiles had fired on alleged Islamic State (ISIS) affiliates in its territory, as Iran had recently against such affiliates in Syria and an alleged but less credible "Mossad headquarters" in Iraqi Kurdistan. Hezbollah rebuffed top Biden adviser Amos Hochstein's initial proposal for reducing tensions with Israel, including pulling its militants further from the border, but remained open to US diplomacy to avoid war. Jordan's Prime Minister Bisher Al-Khasawneh said that peace with Israel was "a strategic choice" but the displacement of Palestinians posed an "existential threat" to his country. The US Senate, by a vote of 72–11, rejected a resolution advanced by Senator Bernie Sanders (Independent, Vermont) to force the State Department to freeze all US aid to Israel unless a report was produced within thirty days on potential Israeli human rights violations in Gaza. The defense for Israel argued at The Hague regarding the South African charge of carrying out genocide against Hamas, an accusation which *New York Times* columnist Bret Stephens called "a moral outrage," that the dire humanitarian situation in Gaza was the clear outcome of that terrorist group's brutal actions.[39]

President Biden informed reporters that Netanyahu told him in their telephone call on Saturday that he did not categorically oppose all two-state solutions. In Netanyahu's public response, he claimed he told Biden "Palestinian independence clashes with Israel's security need for control of Gaza." When asked two days earlier about the future of Israel's peace process with the Palestinians, Israeli President Herzog had declared "Israel has lost trust in the peace process." The IDF released photos of a drawing by five-year-old Emilia Aloni (who was released in a November exchange), found in a Khan Younis tunnel twenty meters underground "without daylight in dense air with little oxygen and terrible humidity that makes it difficult to breathe." Qatar said that medicines sent to Gaza "likely" reached the hostages but could not confirm. Rafael Grossi, director general of the International Atomic Energy Agency, the UN agency based in Vienna which had been struggling since 2021 to carry out controls on Iran's nuclear program, declared that Tehran was barely cooperating with his agency.[40]

A forty-five-hour IDF campaign in Tulkarm ended with many terrorists killed, 37 suspects arrested, and more than 400 explosives destroyed, along with five weapon-making factories and four lookout posts. Wael Abu-Fanounah, who was responsible for publishing videos of the Palestinian Islamic Jihad's rocket attacks against Israel, as well as the creation and distribution of documentation of the Israeli hostages, was killed in Gaza. Israel pounded targets across the Strip on Saturday while its planes dropped leaflets on Rafah, the southernmost city on the Strip, urging Palestinians seeking refuge there to help locate hostages held by Hamas. Five members of the Iranian Revolutionary Guard Corps were killed in an alleged Israeli air strike on Damascus, including the head of Iranian intelligence in Syria, a security source in the regional pro-Syrian alliance told Reuters. US Central Command forces conducted strikes against three Houthi anti-ship missiles that were aimed into the southern Red Sea and were prepared to launch. The European Council established a framework of restrictive measures that would allow the European Union to hold accountable any individual or entity who "supports, facilitates, or enables violent actions" by Hamas and the Palestinian Islamic Jihad.[41]

On January 21, Netanyahu rejected outright "the Hamas monsters' capitulation terms," which demanded, "in exchange for the release of our hostages, the end of the war, the withdrawal of our forces from Gaza, the release of the murders and rapists of the Nukhba, and leaving Hamas in place." He went on to explain: "Were we to agree to this our soldiers would have fallen in vain; we would not be able to ensure the security of our citizens; we would be unable to safely restore the evacuees to their homes; and the next October 7 would be only a question of time. I am not prepared to accept such a mortal blow to the security of Israel." The same day, the *Wall Street Journal*, citing estimates from US intelligence agencies, reported that Israel had eliminated twenty to thirty percent of Hamas's fighters in Gaza, and that Hamas still had enough munitions to continue fighting for months. Israel would escalate fighting with Hezbollah in the "next several weeks," Lebanese officials said, "if no deal were reached to distance the Iran-backed group from the border." One of the world's leading experts on nuclear weapons programs, American physicist David

Albright, issued a report stating that Iran's regime needed roughly a week to produce enough uranium for an atomic bomb, and after five months of producing weapon-grade uranium, it could have enough for twelve."[42]

The next day, as the IDF began operations in the south and west of Khan Younis while revealing cages where hostages had been kept in tunnels, Hamas released a memorandum claiming that the deadly attack on October 7 was to stop the "Judaization" of the West Bank and end the Gaza blockade. It denied all atrocities which it had committed—and publicly recorded—that fatal day. The timing of the document's release raised questions: Sources in Gaza, including those identifying with Hamas, said it was contending with criticism over the heavy price Gazans had paid since. Hamas leader Mashal rejected the two-state solution, emphasizing that the terrorist group's goal of replacing Israel with a Palestinian state was more attainable after October 7.[43]

According to a Palestinian Center for Policy and Survey Research (PCPSR) survey, over ninety percent of Palestinians polled believed that "Hamas did not commit the atrocities seen in the videos" on October 7 referring to attacks on civilians. That number rose to ninety-seven percent when only including West Bank residents, compared to eighty-three percent of Gazans. The dismissal of the incontrovertible evidence was mainly due to the purposeful lack of coverage in Palestinian and Arab media, said Khalil Shikaki, director of the PCPSR who conducted the poll. On Al-Jazeera and other networks, coverage feted Hamas or parroted its claims, justifying the October massacre as "self-defense" against "occupation" and claiming the United States complicit in Israeli actions.[44]

Families of the hostages pitched tents outside Netanyahu's home, demanding an immediate deal, while others disrupted a Knesset finance committee meeting. "You will not sit here while our children die," some screamed. Around 1,000 people whose loved ones were killed by Hamas at the Nova music festival on October 7 planted 200 seedlings with the Jewish National Fund in the scorched earth of the Kibbutz Re'im parking lot, hoping to bring new life to the scene of death and desecration, a few days before the Jewish holiday of Tu B'Shvat marking the Jewish new year for trees. A study published by the Tel-Hai Academic College and Eshkol East Galilee showed that about half of the residents evacuated from towns on the Israel-Lebanon border were afraid to return home. The study found that ninety percent of residents who remained in their homes planned to continue living in their towns on that border, compared to sixty percent of those who evacuated. At the same time, forty-eight percent of residents who remained in their homes following the start of the war reported post-traumatic symptoms. Israel was giving Hezbollah ten more days to move away from its border and then the IDF would significantly escalate its reactions to the terrorists' rain of rockets on Israel's north, the *Washington Post* reported. Lebanon's senior Druze leader, Walid Jumblatt, said talks with Nasrallah and parliament speaker Nabih Berri were underway to prevent an all-out war with Israel.[45]

That same afternoon, the IDF suffered the deadliest incident in Israel's war against Hamas with twenty-one reservists (*miluimnikim*) killed in Al-Muasi in central Gaza, three others in a separate engagement. Engineering forces of the 261st Brigade were booby trapping ten two-story buildings located 600 meters from the Gazan side of the border as others were securing the activity to carve out a wider buffer zone between Gaza and Israel. At around 4:00 p.m., a terrorist approached the scene after coming out of a tunnel shaft and fired an RPG type missile at a tank that secured the operation. Two soldiers were killed and two were wounded. At the same time, an anti-tank missile was fired at two buildings where dozens of soldiers were staying. The explosion of the missile in the building apparently caused the trap to explode and the buildings to collapse on the soldiers. This brought the total of fallen soldiers since the war's commencement to 556, 221 of them from the ground invasion of October 27 onwards. Israeli President Herzog wrote in response that "behind every name whose world has fallen apart—a family that we take to our hearts with sorrow and pain, and at the same time with pride—for the heroism of the generation." Sending his condolences, Defense Secretary Gallant ended with "This is a war that will determine the future of Israel for decades to come—the fall of the fighters is a requirement to achieve the goals of the war."[46]

The United States and Britain, with the support of Australia, Bahrain, Canada, and the Netherlands, carried out large-scale military strikes against eight military sites in Yemen controlled by Houthi militants. The strikes, the eighth in nearly two weeks, signaled that the Biden administration intended to wage a sustained and, at least for now, open-ended campaign against the Iran-backed group that had disrupted traffic in vital international sea lanes. Commanders from Iran's Islamic Revolutionary Guard Corps and Lebanon's Hezbollah were on the ground in Yemen helping to direct and oversee Houthi attacks on Red Sea shipping, four regional and two Iranian sources told Reuters. India deployed a growing number of warships to counter rebel attacks on commercial ships plying around the Middle East, while steering clear of joining the official US-led force in the Red Sea, as it looked to protect its ties with Iran.[47]

On Tuesday the IDF continued its major division-level new push since Monday in completely encircling western Khan Younis, maintaining the most intense fighting in Gaza since early December, with more than 100 Hamas terrorists killed in larger-than-usual organized battles and close-quarter combat. The Gaza Health Ministry declared that, in that twenty-four-hour period, 195 Palestinians were killed in Israeli airstrikes. IDF figures, showing a fuller picture than that offered in the *Wall Street Journal* of January 21, noted that 48–60 percent of Hamas's forces were out of commission—meaning either killed, wounded, or arrested. At the same time, the IDF killed around 3,500 in northern Gaza in the initial three weeks of the invasion but had only killed around 2,000 more in the last six weeks, indicating that elimination of Hamas forces had dropped steeply. Military journalist Yonah Jeremy Bob observed further that, besides removing Hamas forces from the battlefield, the IDF had also killed nineteen out of twenty-four battalion commanders. Yet not only were three of Hamas's five brigade commanders still at large, its entire high command was still operational, and with hostages close by in the tunnels to use as human shields.[48]

Overnight Monday, Israeli forces arrested eight wanted Palestinian terrorist suspects and seized weapons, cash, and bomb-making materials in counterterror raids across Judea and Samaria. Israeli security forces thwarted a Palestinian knifing attack outside Psagot in the Binyamin region of Samaria, shooting the suspect before he could cross the Jewish community's fence. Soldiers also confiscated tens of thousands of shekels in terror funds in operations in Hebron, while weapons were confiscated in Mazra'a, Khairbat al-Luz, and Dhahiriya. Former hostages testified before the Knesset that Hamas treated female hostages like "sex dolls," one noting that some were no longer getting periods, and she prayed that they would not become pregnant. Concurrently, the Tel Aviv Expo hosted a "recreation" of parts of the Nova Festival that ended so tragically on October 7. The powerful exhibition—showing the faces of the murdered young Israelis, displayed clothing, shoes, sunglasses, coke fridges, tent equipment, keys of cars (in which some victims were incinerated), notes to those killed—reminded the viewer of Holocaust memorials. Joining grief and hope, a sign had both 6:29, the minute the horror began, and the promise "We will dance again."[49]

Troops from the 7th Brigade killed many terrorists and, along with Yahalom forces of the Combat Engineering Corps, located numerous tunnel shafts in Khan Younis which led to a long tunnel route with a laboratory and a lathe for manufacturing rockets underground, the biggest lathe discovered so far in the southern Gaza Strip. Throughout the day, IDF troops and airstrikes attacked several Hezbollah targets in Lebanon. The US State Department offered a reward of up to $15 million dollars in its Rewards for Justice program regarding Iranian businessman Hossein Hatefi Ardakani, declaring that he "has helped the Iranian Revolutionary Guard Corps acquire sophisticated technology for weapons production." The United States had destroyed or degraded over twenty-five Houthi missile launch facilities and more than twenty missiles in Yemen since it started strikes in the country earlier this month, the Pentagon announced. UNRWA posted on X that over 570,000 people in Gaza faced "catastrophic" levels of hunger, and the agency called for a "critical increase" of humanitarian access to combat the growing risk of famine. Hamas rejected an Israeli proposal for a two-month cease-fire and exile for its Gaza leaders in exchange for the release of all hostages, a senior Egyptian official said.[50]

On day 110 of the war, the IDF, Shin Bet, Yamam National Counter-Terrorism Unit, and Border Police forces, operating for the last thirty-five hours in a counterterrorism operation in Tulkarm, killed at least eight terrorists, arrested fifteen suspects, seized numerous weapons, and destroyed an explosives factory. The IDF confirmed that it was considering distributing anti-tank missiles to the civilian emergency squads in towns in Judea and Samaria, allowing them to handle a situation in which terrorists attack in cars like the October 7th slaughter. Lt. Col. Avichay Adraee, the IDF's Arabic-language spokesman, published footage of a spontaneous anti-Hamas protest by dozens of children, which broke out in Gaza's central city of Deir al-Balah, calling for the release of the Israeli hostages to bring about an end to the Hamas-Israel war so they could return to their homes in the northern Strip. The protest came one day after another small demonstration against Hamas in the southern Gaza city of Rafah. "Will these cries and demands reach the hideouts of Hamas leaders?" Adraee asked on X.[51]

In a TV address reviewing recent IDF losses, Gantz declared that "our responsibility is to ensure that their sacrifices don't leave us with waves of memory but of action. May the lesson to those who hurt us be that we are more united and more determined than ever." Israel's Herzog, speaking at a special event marking the seventy-fifth anniversary of the Knesset, began by describing the mourning that had recently united the nation, noting that, along with deep sorrow, "we do not forget how proud we are of our children who fell in a war more just than any other." He concluded thus: "We cannot speak of unity without the Knesset being a central part of it and making a change of its own in the conversations here. This is our responsibility to the nation and the generation." A new display at Ben-Gurion International Airport reminded anyone leaving or entering Israel that more than 130 people remained in captivity in Gaza. Eight hundred "freedom tags" hanging against a glass wall were imprinted on the top half with *"Halev shelanu shavui b'Aza"* ("Our heart is captive in Gaza"). The lower half declared "Bring them home—now!"[52]

Sixty percent of Jewish Israelis opposed a deal that would see the remaining hostages returned in exchange for releasing all Palestinian security prisoners and an end to hostilities in Gaza, according to an Israel Democracy Institute survey. Broken down by political affiliation, 53 percent on the left would support such an agreement, as would 46 percent in the center and 24 percent on the right. Among Arab Israeli respondents, 78.5 percent would support such a deal. In this connection, hundreds of demonstrators, including evacuees and families of hostages, from the *Tzav* 9 ("Order 9") movement prevented dozens of humanitarian aid trucks from entering the Gaza Strip from Israel at the Kerem Shalom border crossing on Wednesday, demanding that "no aid goes through until the last of the abductees returns, no equipment be transferred to the enemy." (An Order 8 call-up notice is an order for the emergency mobilization of an IDF reserve soldier outside the framework of regular reserve duty.)[53]

Hearing reserve soldiers from the 969th Battalion of the Northern Brigade and the new armored unit "Phoenix" (assigned to repair tanks) said they would continue their duty until the IDF goals would be reached, Gallant declared, "This battle is a battle of national determination, it's not just who wins at a certain point, but rather the common will, that is national determination. We are being tested here both on military strength—security strength, but no less than this, on the moral might of the State of Israel. When I say moral strength I mean to say, what right do you have to stop when there are 136 hostages in Gaza?"[54]

On January 25, the IDF reported that its forces had killed dozens of terrorists in Khan Younis, as well as central and northern Gaza. The recent intensifying of attacks in Khan Younis also brought the average of firing Hamas rockets to an all-new low, something the IDF had not been able to do in around fifteen years of prior rounds of armed conflict. Yet the IDF's creating a one-kilometer buffer zone along the Philadelphi Corridor on the Gaza side of the border with Egypt risked a new rift with Washington, which had been vocal against any permanent change to Palestinian territory. An official French source, in agreement, said that the zone, intended to thwart terrorist infiltration into Israel, would make it difficult for the Palestinian Authority to control Gaza. UK Foreign Secretary David Cameron visited Israel to pressure Israeli officials to call for an immediate pause in fighting and to increase aid to Gaza, including delivery through the Ashdod port. Hamas "absolutely" rejected an offer by Israel to end the war on the condition that six senior leaders would be exiled from the Strip, Reuters reported. The Hamas-controlled Gaza Health Ministry said that a total of 25,700 Palestinians had been killed and 63,740 wounded since the war began. Senior Israeli officials estimated that Hamas earned $8–12 million a month through online donations, much of it through organizations posing as charities to help civilians in Gaza.⁵⁵

Arabs across the Middle East and North Africa overwhelmingly viewed Hamas's October 7 assault as a "legitimate resistance operation," according to a new survey of sixteen nations throughout the region conducted earlier in the month. A think tank funded by Qatar polled some 8,000 Arabs in Algeria, Egypt, Iraq, Jordan, Kuwait, Lebanon, Libya, Mauritania, Morocco, Oman, Qatar, Saudi Arabia, Sudan, Tunisia, Yemen, and the Palestinian Authority-controlled areas in Judea and Samaria. The Doha-based institute claimed that the surveyed individuals represented more than 95 percent of the Arab population in the region. Only 5 percent denounced Hamas's war crimes as an "illegitimate operation," while 3 percent said that it was a "legitimate resistance operation that involved heinous (unacceptable) or even criminal acts." The massacre received the highest support in Libya, Jordan, Tunisia, Morocco, and among Palestinians, with a staggering 0 percent of Judea and Samaria residents agreeing that the atrocities of October 7 were illegitimate. Most Arabs said they disapproved of recognizing the State of Israel, with 89 percent saying they would support rejecting or revoking such a move, up from 84 percent in 2022. Meanwhile, support for the recognition of the Jewish State was the highest in Sudan (14 percent), Lebanon (8 percent), and Morocco (7 percent).⁵⁶

Haaretz reported on January 25 that Israel and Hamas reached agreement on the basic principles for a thirty-five-day cease-fire, the release of all Israeli hostages and of an unspecified number of Palestinian prisoners and detainees from Israeli jails. Biden was dispatching CIA chief Bill Burns to Europe to meet with the head of the Mossad, Qatar's prime minister, and Egypt's intelligence chief to broker a truce. Ahead of the ICJ's interim ruling Friday, Israel sent the Court declassified documents to show the steps it was taking to minimize civilian casualties in Gaza. The IDF said it had expanded fighting in Khan Younis, destroying Hamas infrastructure and weapons caches during raids in the Al-Amal neighborhood. Hundreds of Palestinians protested in Khan Younis for Hamas and Israel to stop the war. Calls at the demonstration included: "Netanyahu and Sinwar: cease-fire" and "Stop the war! Stop the destruction!"⁵⁷

The IDF attacked a key Hezbollah-Iran airstrip at Kilat Jaber in southern Lebanon, only twenty kilometers from Israel, for launching aerial attacks against Israel in a major escalation between the sides. Iran's Guardian Council's decision the same week to disqualify virtually all "pragmatists" from public office in electing the next Assembly of Experts (likely to choose a successor to the ailing eighty-five-year-old Supreme Leader Khamenei) made ongoing conflict between Israel and Iran's proxies a virtual certainty, and war more likely than ever. Amid the ongoing war in Gaza, Israel signed a substantial arms deal with the United States, Channel 12 reported, including a fleet of F-35 fighter jets (25 planes), a fleet of F-15 AI jets (25 planes), and a fleet of Apache attack helicopters (at least 12), together with the delivery of thousands of munitions within the coming days.[58]

On Friday, the International Court of Justice's seventeen-member panel stopped short of ordering an immediate cease-fire or deciding that the Jewish State was committing genocide, but it did call for six urgent provisional measures to prevent acts of genocide taking place in Gaza. Only one justice, Julia Sebutinde of Uganda, rejected all the charges as unmerited "even on a prima-facie basis." Netanyahu noted that the decision "rightly rejected the outrageous demand to deny Israel the right to basic self-defense," but charged that the court's willingness to discuss the charge of genocide "is a mark of disgrace that will not be erased for generations." Herzog sought a historical context: "The very fact that the hearing at the court in The Hague was held on the eve of International Holocaust Remembrance Day, to judge whether the democratic, moral, and responsible State of Israel, which rose from the ashes of the Holocaust with the overwhelming support of the family of nations and its institutions was guilty of committing genocide, is a blood libel that undermines the very values on which this court was established." Senior Hamas official Sami Abu Zuhri, on the other hand, called this "an important development for isolating Israel and exposing its crimes."[59]

Almost at the same time, while Washington declared the genocide charge "unfounded," President Biden declared on International Holocaust Remembrance Day that, "without equivocation or exception, we must also forcefully push back against attempts to ignore, deny, distort, and revise history. This includes Holocaust denialism and efforts to minimize the horrors that Hamas perpetrated on October 7, especially its appalling and unforgiveable use of rape and sexual violence to terrorize victims." He concluded: "We hold the Jewish community and the people of Israel close in our hearts. We recommit to carrying forward the lessons of the *Shoah*, to fighting antisemitism and all forms of hate-fueled violence, and to bringing the hostages home. And we remember the enduring strength, spirit, and resilience of the Jewish people—even in the darkest of times."[60]

The United States, United Kingdom, Canada, Germany, France, Scotland, Austria, Italy, Iceland, Romania, Switzerland, Australia, New Zealand, Finland, the Netherlands, Latvia, Lithuania, Estonia, Sweden, Iceland, and Japan suspended funding to the UNWRA after viewing IDF evidence that twelve of its Palestinian employees had taken part in the October 7 onslaught. The UNWRA's commissioner general, Philippe Lazzarini, found this action "shocking". He went on to declare "this threatens humanitarian work in the whole region, especially in Gaza."[61]

Thousands protested in various demonstrations across Israel demanding the release of hostages, immediate elections, and the removal of Netanyahu. Israel's defense echelon estimated that Hamas's rocket supply had dwindled significantly, and currently stood at just a few hundred. The IDF published a recording of residents of the Gaza Strip evacuating from Khan Younis and chanting: "The people want to overthrow Hamas," and it opened a humanitarian corridor for residents to move away from areas of fighting to the town of Al-Mawasi in southwestern Gaza. According to IDF data, 37 soldiers were currently hospitalized in serious condition, another 249 soldiers in moderate condition, and another 101 in mild condition. Since the beginning of the ground operation in the Gaza Strip, 258 soldiers had been seriously injured. The Gaza Health Ministry claimed that at least 26,257 people had been killed since the beginning of the conflict in October and 64,797 people wounded.[62]

The IDF reported "intensive fighting" on January 28 in the Khan Younis area, which led to thousands of civilians fleeing the city towards Rafah on the Egyptian border. A few thousand activists meeting in Jerusalem's Binyenei HaUma called for Jewish resettlement in Gaza. Responding to an NBC report that the Biden administration was mulling slowing delivery of some weapons to Israel to press Netanyahu to scale back the offensive in Gaza, the White House announced there was no change to its Israel policy. Three US Army soldiers were killed and at least thirty-four service members injured in a drone attack on a small US military outpost in Jordan known as Tower 22 near the border with Syria, marking the first time American troops had been killed by enemy fire in the Middle East since the start of Israel's war with Hamas. According to officials, the drone was fired by Iranian-backed "militants" and appeared to come from Syria. "We will carry on their commitment to fight terrorism," Biden responded. "And have no doubt—we will hold all those responsible to account at a time and in a manner our choosing." While IDF jets, tanks, and artillery continued to strike Hezbollah military infrastructure, paratrooper and combat engineering forces carried out intensive training drills at the IDF's Northern Command, preparing troops for combat in densely populated urban areas, winter weather conditions, and in the northern terrain.[63]

The IDF declared on Monday that it was close to defeating Hamas in Khan Younis, Gaza's second largest city and the Hamas leadership's headquarters, with close to three of the four Khan Younis battalions already nearly beaten. Yet Minister Benny Gantz warned that the war against Hamas "could last a year, ten years, or even an entire generation," Channel 12 News quoted him as adding: "We have time to destroy Hamas. The hostages have no time—right now, that is the priority." Hamas reiterated its position that it would only release hostages if it were guaranteed an end to the Israeli offensive in Gaza and the IDF withdrew its forces from the Strip. Around ten percent (1,200) of UNRWA employees in Gaza had ties to Hamas and Palestinian Islamic Jihad, the *Wall Street Journal* reported, quoting intelligence sources. Nineteen terrorist suspects were arrested at night in Judea and Samaria, with explosives and much weaponry found in Jenin. The IDF thwarted a stabbing attack around Tekoa; a soldier was seriously wounded in Haifa after an axe-wielding terrorist rammed his vehicle at a group of soldiers near a naval base before he was killed. Israeli air strikes destroyed the Quds Force branch of the IRGC's Shi'ite stronghold in Damascus.[64]

"Incendiary and irresponsible," declared the United States and France in condemning the previous evening's conference in Jerusalem, which had been attended by eleven government ministers and fifteen coalition Knesset members, for the establishment of Israeli settlements in Gaza. Right-wing political leaders Finance Minister Bezalel Smotrich of the Religious Zionism Party and National Security Minister Itamar Ben-Gvir of Otzma Yehudit had joined in signing what was dubbed the "Covenant of Victory and Renewal of Settlement," Ben-Gvir telling the jubilant masses that it was "time to return home to Gush Katif." In response, Gallant told US officials that he would not allow for the reestablishment of Israeli settlements inside the Gaza Strip. The German Foreign Ministry announced that it rejected any consideration of Israeli resettlement of Gaza and the transfer, whether voluntary or forced, of the Palestinian population.[65]

White House NSC spokesperson Kirby, in an interview with Israel's Channel 12 News on the tensions between Netanyahu and Biden, said "We are still solidly behind our Israeli partners in their right and their responsibility to go after Hamas, which we recognize is a viable threat to the Israeli people, and so the support that we provide to Israel is going to continue." He noted that Israel had "relied less on air power and structured their ground operations in such a way to try to be more targeted and precise" in Gaza. There were 165 attacks on US troops in the Middle East since October 17, according to Department of Defense figures provided to the *Washington Post*, most in eastern Syria and Iraq. The Houthis in Yemen were prepared for a "long-term confrontation" with the United States and United Kingdom, according to a statement on Tuesday by the commander of the Houthi forces, Mohamed Al-Atifi.[66]

Troops of the 98th Division raided an underground tunnel twenty meters deep located under the Bani Suheila cemetery, where they unearthed the office of the Eastern Battalion commander of the Khan Younis Brigade, from where he directed the October 7 attacks. Israel's intelligence dossier on UNRWA included allegations against 190 employees, including teachers, who had doubled as Hamas or Palestinian Islamic Jihad terrorists. Israeli forces had so far killed or wounded at least half of Hamas's estimated 30,000 operatives in the Gaza Strip, Gallant stated. The IDF announced for the first time that it had flooded Hamas tunnels in an effort to destroy them. During a visit to a pre-military academy in the Samaria settlement of Eli, Netanyahu said the IDF would not leave Gaza as part of a hostage release deal, and that Israel did not intend to release thousands of terrorists. Israeli commandos entered a Jenin hospital in disguise as medical staff to kill three terrorists including Mohammad Jalamneh, a leader in Hamas's al-Qassam Brigades, whom the military said was planning to carry out an attack "in the immediate period."[67]

Day 117 of the war was dominated by reports of a new plan backed by Israel and the United States, reported in the *Washington Post*, calling for Hamas to release all civilian hostages being held inside Gaza in exchange for a six-week cease-fire. Israel would also remove troops from Gazan population centers, release Palestinian prisoners at an approximate ratio of three Palestinians for each hostage, and significantly increase humanitarian aid to Gaza. Further pauses would see captured soldiers released in exchange for additional Israeli concessions, and for the basis for a long-term plan for the future of the Gaza Strip. Israel agreed in principle to the plan, transmitting it to special summit meeting in Paris, and which was presented to Hamas by Egyptian mediators. Hamas acknowledged its receipt but had yet to present a formal response. Netanyahu's office released a statement insisting that the reports were incorrect: "The prime minister's position is consistent—the war will only end when all its goals are achieved, the IDF will not withdraw from the Strip and thousands of terrorists will not be released." The same day, the US House of Representatives, by a vote of 422–2, with 1 voting present, refused passports and visas to, as well as "the removal" of, anyone involved in the "horrific" Hamas October 7 massacre.[68]

The IDF persisted in its attacks against Hezbollah targets and Syrian army posts, as well as arresting fourteen Palestinian terrorist suspects in the West Bank. Yet, despite all of Israel's achievements to date against Hamas in Gaza, IDF sources were unsure if they would catch that organization's leadership and the hostages being held underground within Khan Younis. A rising number of military officials believed that some of Hamas's leaders and those abducted might now be Rafah, where there were close to 1.5 million Palestinian civilians to hide among. Action with ground troops in Rafah could take time and significant negotiations. Part of the tension with Egypt on that issue seemed to be that the Israeli government's preference to have control of the Philadelphi Corridor on the Gaza-Egypt border before any cease-fire with Hamas set off alarm bells in Cairo, with officials saying it would undermine the 1979 peace treaty. Additionally, another 105,000 Palestinian civilians had recently left Khan Younis for other safe zones, with around 20,000–30,000 remaining there. Further, about 2,000 Hamas operatives were still believed to be in northern Gaza among around 200,000 civilians. And the IDF death toll continued to rise, with four more soldiers in Gaza fallen that day bringing the total army losses since the outbreak of the war to 561, 224 of these since the ground offensive began.[69]

These harsh realities notwithstanding, Israel's citizenry remained steadfast, overwhelmingly committed to the slogan adopted one day after October 7, 2023: *b'yachad n'natzeiach* ("united, we will win"). The *Jerusalem Post* editorial on the last day of the month captured the mood of the populace, and particularly its faith in the IDF offensive. It singled out the recent, daring ten-minute commando raid that killed three terrorists in Jenin's Ibn Sina Hospital to foil an imminent Hamas attack, reflective of the army's retaining operational freedom to operate in the West Bank's Palestinian cities from Operation Defensive Shield (2002) onwards. The editorial concluded thus: "While the operation in the hospital has been shared with the public, the efforts to protect Israel occur 24/7 in thousands of ways that the public is not aware of. For that, we are eternally grateful to those who hold the line, day and night, and keep us safe so our state may prosper and grow."[70] Determined to live in security against enemies bent on their very destruction, and not wanting loved ones' ultimate sacrifice to have been in vain, the home front and its armed defenders pressed on.

Endnotes

1 *Jerusalem Post*, Jan. 1, 2024; IDF News Report, Jan. 1, 2024; *Haaretz*. Jan. 1, 2024; Israel National News, Jan. 1, 2024.
2 *Times of Israel*, Jan. 2, 2024; *Haaretz*, Jan. 1–3, 2024; *Washington Post*, Jan. 1, 2024.
3 Israel National News, Jan. 2, 2024; *Jerusalem Post*, Jan. 2, 2024. One of the terrorists killed along with Al-Arouri was Azzam Akre, who commanded Khalil Al-Kharaz. The latter directed Hamas terrorist forces in Lebanon until he was killed in November 2023. Al-Kharaz was a director of Hamas cells in Europe, including the one that was planning an attack on the Israeli embassy in Sweden. He also had made contact with the Danish street gang LTF ("Loyal to Familia"), banned in that country in 2021, which had plans to attack the Israeli embassy in Stockholm and secure drones for Hamas. World Israel News, Jan. 14, 2024.

4 *Haaretz*, Jan. 2, 2024; CNN, Jan. 2, 2024; World Israel News, Jan. 2, 2024; *New York Times*, Jan. 2, 2024.
5 *Jerusalem Post*, Jan. 3, 2024; *New York Times*, Jan. 2, 2024; *Haaretz*, Jan. 3, 2024; JNS, Jan. 2, 2024; Israel National News, Jan. 3, 2024.
6 *Jerusalem Post*, Jan. 4, 2024; *Haaretz*, Jan. 4, 2024; Times of Israel, Jan. 4, 2024; JNS, Jan. 4, 2024; United with Israel, Jan. 4, 2024.
7 *Haaretz*, Jan. 6, 2024; *Wall St. Journal*, Jan. 4, 2024; Israel National News, Jan. 5–7, 2024; *Jerusalem Post*, Jan. 6, 2024.
8 *Haaretz*, Jan. 7, 2024; Times of Israel, Jan. 7, 2024; *Wall St. Journal*, Jan. 7, 2024; *Jerusalem Post*, Jan. 7, 2024; Israel Video Network, Jan. 7, 2024.
9 *Washington Post*, Jan. 7, 2024; PBS News Hour. Jan. 8, 2024; Israel National News, Jan. 7–8, 2024.
10 *Jerusalem Post*, Jan. 8, 2024.
11 Israel National News, Jan. 8, 2024; *Jerusalem Post*, Jan. 8, 2024.
12 *Jerusalem Post*, Jan. 8, 2024; *Haaretz*, Jan. 8, 2024.
13 Israel National News, Jan. 9, 2024; Reuters, Jan. 9, 2024; World Israel News, Jan. 9, 2024.
14 *Jerusalem Post*, Jan. 9, 2024; Times of Israel, Jan. 9, 2024; JNS, Jan. 10, 2024.
15 *Washington Post*, Jan. 9, 2024; *New York Times*, Sept. 23, 2011; *Haaretz*, Oct. 3, 2008; Ynet, Sept. 19, 2011.
16 *Washington Post*, Jan. 9, 2024; *New York Times*, Jan. 9, 2024.
17 Israel National News, Jan. 10, 2024; *Haaretz*, Jan. 10, 2024.
18 Israel National News, Jan. 10, 2024; *Jerusalem Post*, Jan. 10, 2024; *Haaretz*, Jan. 10, 2024; *New York Times*, Jan. 10, 2024.
19 *Haaretz*, Jan. 10, 2024; *Jerusalem Post*, Jan. 10, 2024.
20 JNS, Jan. 10, 2024.
21 JNS, Jan. 10–11, 2024; United with Israel, Jan. 10, 2024.
22 Israel National News, Jan. 11, 2024; *Haaretz*, Jan. 11, 2024.
23 Times of Israel, Jan. 11, 2024; *Jerusalem Post*, Jan. 11, 2024.
24 Israel National News, Jan. 11, 2024.
25 *New York Times*, Jan. 12, 2024.
26 Times of Israel, Jan. 13. 2024; Israel National News, Jan. 12, 2024.
27 United with Israel, Jan. 11, 2024; *New York Times*, Jan. 12, 2024; *Times of Israel*, Jan. 14, 2024.
28 JTA, Jan. 12, 2024; *Haaretz*, Jan. 13, 2024. The Convention on the Prevention and Punishment of the Crime of Genocide, or the Genocide Convention, for which Lemkin campaigned vigorously, was the first human rights treaty adopted by the General Assembly of the United Nations on December 9, 1948, and ratified in 1951. It is an international treaty that criminalizes genocide and obligates state parties to pursue the enforcement of its prohibition. At present, there are 153 state parties to the Genocide Convention. Only three have been legally recognized—and led to trials—under the Convention: Rwanda in 1994, Bosnia in 1993 (and the 1995 Srebrenica massacre), and Cambodia under the 1975–1979 Pol Pot regime.
29 Israel National News, Jan. 14, 2024; *Washington Post*, Jan. 14, 2024. TikTok is a short-form video hosting service owned by Chinese Internet company ByteDance. It hosts user-submitted videos, which can range in duration from three seconds to ten minutes.
30 Israel National News, Jan. 14, 2024; *Forward*, Jan. 15, 2024; *Haaretz*, Jan. 14, 2024; *Jerusalem Post*, Jan. 14, 2024.
31 IDF News, Jan. 14, 2024; *Jerusalem Post*, Jan. 14, 2024; *Haaretz*, Jan. 3, 2024.
32 *Jerusalem Post*, Jan. 14, 2024; *Haaretz*, Jan. 14, 2024; *Washington Post*, Jan. 14, 2024; JNS, Jan. 14, 2024.
33 Israel National News, Jan. 15, 2024; *Jerusalem Post*, Jan. 15, 2024; *New York Times*, Jan. 15, 2024; *Wall St. Journal*, Jan. 15, 2024; *Haaretz*. Jan. 15, 2024.
34 JNS, Jan. 16, 2024; Israel National News, Jan. 16, 2024.

35 *New York Times*, Jan. 16, 2024; Israel National News, Jan. 16, 2024; *Jerusalem Post*, Jan. 16, 2024.
36 Israel National News, Jan. 16, 2024; *Jerusalem Post*, Jan. 17, 2024
37 Israel National News, Jan. 17, 2024; *Jerusalem Post*, Jan. 17, 2024.
38 *Forward*, Jan. 18, 2024; Israel National News, Jan. 18, 2024; *Haaretz*, Jan. 18, 2024; Times of Israel, Jan. 18, 2024; World Israel News, Jan. 18, 2024; JNS, Jan. 18, 2024.
39 World Israel News, Jan. 17, 2024; *Wall St. Journal*, Jan. 16, 2024; *Haaretz*, Jan. 17–18, 2024; Reuters, Jan. 16, 2024; Bret Stephens, "The Genocide Charge against Israel is a Moral Obscenity," *New York Times*, Jan. 16, 2024. For Sanders' earlier accusations against Israel and his opposition to helping Soviet Jews, see Rafael Medoff, "Bernie Sanders Abandons the Jews, Again," *Jewish Journal*, Jan. 17, 2024.
40 *Haaretz*, Jan 20, 2024; *Jerusalem Post*, Jan. 19, 2024.
41 IDF News, Jan. 19, 2024; Israel National News, Jan. 19–20, 2024; Reuters, Jan. 20, 2024.
42 Times of Israel, Jan. 21, 2024; *Jerusalem Post*, Jan. 21, 2024; *Wall St. Journal*, Jan 21, 2024; *Haaretz*, Jan. 21, 2024.
43 *Haaretz*, Jan. 22, 2024; World Israel News, Jan. 22, 2024; JNS, Jan. 22, 2024.
44 *Times of Israel*, Jan. 22, 2024; United with Israel, Jan. 23, 2024.
45 *Forward*, Jan. 22, 2024; Israel National News, Jan. 22, 2024; *Haaretz*, Jan. 22, 2024; *Times of Israel*, Jan. 22, 2024.
46 Israel National News, Jan. 23, 2024; *Jerusalem Post*, Jan. 23, 2024.
47 *New York Times*, Jan. 22, 2024; Reuters, Jan. 20, 2024; *Wall St. Journal*, Jan. 25, 2024.
48 *Jerusalem Post*, Jan. 22–23, 2024; *Haaretz*, Jan. 233, 2024.
49 JNS, Jan. 23, 2024; Daniel Gordis, *Israel from the Inside*, podcast, Jan. 23, 2024.
50 Israel National News, Jan. 23, 2024; *Jerusalem Post*, Jan. 23, 2024; Reuters, Jan. 23, 2024; *Haaretz*, Jan. 23, 2024; Times of Israel, Jan. 23, 2024.
51 Israel National News, Jan. 24, 2024; JNS, Jan. 24, 2024.
52 *Jerusalem Post*, Jan. 24, 2024.
53 JNS, Jan. 24, 2024.
54 Israel National News, Jan. 24, 2024.
55 Israel National News, Jan. 24, 2024; *Jerusalem Post*, Jan. 25, 2024; *Washington Post*, Jan. 25, 2024; *Haaretz*, Jan. 24–25, 2024.
56 JNS, Jan. 24, 2024.
57 *Haaretz*, Jan. 25, 2024; *Jerusalem Post*, Jan. 25, 2024.
58 *Jerusalem Post*, Jan. 25, 2024; Israel National News, Jan. 25, 2024.
59 *Washington Post*, Jan. 26, 2024; JNS, Jan. 29, 2024; Israel National News, Jan. 26, 2024. The six provisional measures. most of the court-mandated actions things Jerusalem was already doing, were: 1. for Israel to take "all measures" to prevent acts of genocide from taking place; 2. to ensure the IDF does not engage in any acts of genocide; 3. to prevent and punish public incitement to genocide, including by government and military officials; 4. to enable basic services and humanitarian aid to reach Gazan civilians; 5. to preserve evidence related to violations of Genocide Convention; 6. to submit a report to the ICJ within one month on all measures taken. Israeli security officials said that, due to the ICJ ruling, they would not allow blocking of humanitarian aid trucks via the Kerem Shalom Crossing. *Haaretz*, Jan. 27, 2024.
60 The White House, Jan. 26, 2024, https://www.whitehouse.gov. Since 2005, the UN General Assembly marked January 27, the day when the Soviet Red Army liberated the Auschwitz-Birkenau death camp in 1945, as International Holocaust Remembrance Day.
61 *Times of Israel*, Jan. 27, 2024.
62 Reuters, Jan. 27, 2024; Israel National News, Jan. 26, 2024; *Haaretz*, Jan. 27, 2024; VOA News, Jan. 27, 2024.
63 Israel National News, Jan. 28, 2024; *Washington Post*, Jan. 28, 2024; *Jerusalem Post*, Jan. 28, 2024.
64 *Jerusalem Post*, Jan. 29, 2024; Israel National News, Jan. 29, 2024; IDF News, Jan. 29, 2024.

65 *Haaretz*, Jan. 29, 2024; Times of Israel, Jan. 29, 2024.
66 Times of Israel, Jan. 30, 2024; *Washington Post*, Jan. 30, 2024; *New York Times*, Jan. 30, 2024.
67 *Jerusalem Post*, Jan. 30, 2024; World Israel News, Jan. 30, 2024; *Haaretz*, Jan. 30, 2024; Reuters, Jan. 30, 2024.
68 *Washington Post*, Jan. 31, 2024; *Times of Israel*, Jan. 31, 2024. The two negative votes were cast by Cori Bush (D., Missouri) and Rashida Tlaib (D., Michigan), the only Palestinian-American currently in Congress. In Tlaib's words, this "redundant bill," given existing legislation that prohibits entry to "participants in terrorism," was "just another GOP messaging bill being used to incite anti-Arab, anti-Palestinian, and anti-Muslim hatred that makes communities like ours unsafe." Delia Ramirez (D., Illinois) voted present.
69 *Haaretz*, Jan. 31, 2024; *Jerusalem Post*, Jan. 31, 2024; Times of Israel, Jan. 31, 2024.
70 *Jerusalem Post*, Jan. 31, 2024.

CHAPTER 6

From Khan Younis to Rafah

The first day of February opened with news that President Biden issued an unprecedented executive order to impose financial sanctions and visa restrictions on Jewish settlers who assault or intimidate Palestinians in the West Bank in the wake of Hamas's October 7 attack on southern Israel, naming four individuals whose US assets would be seized. "The United States has consistently opposed actions that undermine stability in the West Bank and the prospects of peace and security for Israelis and Palestinians alike. This includes attacks by Israeli settlers against Palestinians and Palestinian attacks against Israelis," according to the State Department. Netanyahu reacted by declaring that Israel "acts against all those who break the law everywhere, and therefore there is no room for exceptional measures." Israeli Finance Minister Smotrich defiantly responded: "The 'settler violence' campaign is an antisemitic lie that enemies of Israel disseminate with the goal of smearing the pioneering settlers and settlement enterprise, and to harm them and thus smear the entire State of Israel."[1]

As for the war in Gaza, Defense Minister Gallant said that after additional gains by the IDF in Khan Younis, 10,000 Hamas fighters had been killed and 10,000 wounded, with 224 the present number of IDF slain troops since the ground invasion. The 55th Brigade left Khan Younis after two months of operations there during which seventy tunnel shafts were dismantled and numerous terrorist operatives eliminated. Elisha Medan, a soldier in the reserves and son of Har Etzion Yeshiva Dean Rabbi Yaakov Medan, who was critically injured in a tunnel shaft explosion in Gaza and was recovering from his injuries and the loss of both legs, echoed the general sentiment of fellow combatants when he told a visiting Netanyahu: "It is important for us to know that my friends getting killed and my injury were not in vain. We are going to mow them down, defeat them, not give up, and not return to October 6th in any way—neither security-wise, nor in the separation we had in the nation." While an IDF spokesman called on terrorists in northern Gaza to surrender, rocket sirens sounded in locations across central Israel for the first time in nearly a month, The IDF's Home Front Command announced that it was easing restrictions in communities close to the border with Gaza and allowing educational institutions to open. The Hamas-controlled Gaza Health Ministry announced that at least 27,019 Palestinians had been killed and 66,139 wounded since the war began.[2]

Citing US officials, CBS News reported that the Biden administration had approved plans for many strikes in Iraq and Syria against multiple targets, including Iranian personnel and facilities. The United States believed the drone that killed three soldiers in Jordan on January 29 was Iranian-made. Iran's decision to to pull out senior IRGC commanders from Syria was driven partly by its aversion to being sucked directly into a conflict bubbling across the Mideast and partly fearing Israeli assassinations. The Israeli Defense Ministry's data showed that Iranian proxy Hezbollah's launch of well over 2,000 rockets, as well as dozens of anti-tank missiles and drones, hit 427 homes in Israel's north since the war began, with 80 of them sustaining direct hits. IDF chief Halevi, meeting with officers on the northern border, declared that citizens would be returned there only when security was restored in the area. IAF strikes were carried out in southern Lebanon after Hezbollah missile attacks on Metula and Kiryat Shmona.[3]

Over the weekend, IDF forces killed dozens of Hamas militants across the Strip. The 5th Brigade, IAF, and Yahalom Unit destroyed a tunnel shaft in north Gaza containing an underground elevator leading to a hideout room with much weaponry and documents. The IDF's Arabic-language spokesman shared videos "taken in Khan Younis in recent weeks" of Hamas operatives halting aid from reaching the Al-Amal Hospital area and preventing civilians from going on Israel's guaranteed humanitarian corridor in the direction of Rafah. Hamas's top leaders were arguing about the proposed cease-fire and hostage exchange deal, forcing it to be pushed off further and further, the *Wall Street Journal* revealed. Thousands in five major Israeli cities called for the return of the remaining hostages, Netanyahu's ouster, and immediate elections. The IDF claimed that since the war began it had attacked 3,400 Hezbollah targets and eliminated more than 200 of its combatants; Gallant said that even if a Gaza cease-fire took place, strikes on Hezbollah would continue. The IDF announced that in Judea and Samaria, army reservists carried out thousands of operations after October 7, arresting more terrorists than over the entire preceding year, "one of the reasons that the situation here has not yet exploded." British Foreign Secretary David Cameron said he told Netanyahu to "start talking about the things a Palestinian state can be, rather than the things it can't be," reiterating UK support for a two-state solution.[4]

On February 2, US forces dropped more than 125 precision munitions on eighty-five targets in Iraq and Syria belonging to Iran's IRGC Quds Force and its affiliated militia groups in retaliation for the deadly drone attack launched by Iran-backed groups against US troops in Jordan. CENTCOM said it would continue to take action and that Iran's Revolutionary Guard Corps and affiliated militias "continue to represent a direct threat to the stability of Iraq, the region, and the safety of Americans." The strikes overnight killed dozens of fighters and several civilians, according to statements from the Iraqi government, militia groups, and a local monitoring network on Saturday, in a first round of retaliatory action as the Biden administration sought to respond to the killing of three US soldiers without stoking regional conflict. The airstrikes were a show of force but, Biden choosing not to endorse Republican hawks' call to strike inside Iran or even Tehran, appeared to do little damage to direct Iranian assets in the region, instead largely targeting Iran's proxy forces. Iran's President Raisi said that Tehran would not start a war but will "respond strongly" to anyone who bullied it. Armed forces of the United States, the country which the late Supreme Leader of the Iranian Revolution Ayatollah Khomeini termed "the Great Satan," also shot down several Houthi drones over the Red Sea.[5]

With February 3, 2024, marking day 120 of the Hamas-Israel war, a new milestone was set as the conflict became Israel's longest open war since the 1948 twenty-month War of Independence.[6] Visiting the Tel Nof Airbase the next day, Gallant declared that every IAF strike in the Gaza Strip "pushes us forward, both to achieve our goal and to bring back the hostages," while in the north (which faced fifteen rockets the previous day) "the more we intensify our operational achievements, the greater the chance of reaching a situation where we are not forced to go to war. I repeat the slogan I saw at the entrance to the base—'No place is too far.'" As part of operations in western Khan Younis, the Givati Brigade conducted a targeted raid on the Al-Qadsia compound, which served as the main base of the Khan Younis Brigade and as a training facility for Hamas to train terrorists to carry out the October 7 massacre. Speaking to American media outlets, US NSC Advisor Jake Sullivan said, "No one wants the war to continue. But for this to happen, all the hostages need to come home and Hamas needs to no longer pose a threat to Israel." The United States and United Kingdom launched a third series of strikes against thirty-six Houthi targets in Yemen with the support of Australia, Bahrain, Canada, Denmark, the Netherlands, and New Zealand, US Secretary of Defense Austin announced. Continued US-British "aggression" in Yemen would not achieve their goals and would not affect Yemen's support for Gaza, a Houthi spokesperson responded.[7]

On Monday, Gallant said there was no place where Hamas could hide, including Rafah, the enemy's last refuge. He declared that the IDF had killed or seriously wounded more than half of Hamas's forces. In addition, he argued that the victory was larger at an organizational level, having taken apart eighteen of Hamas's twenty-four battalions. He added that three of four Khan Younis battalions had been taken apart, with the fourth in western Khan Younis on the verge of falling. Hundreds of Hamas fighters were killed and scores arrested by the 162nd Division, the IDF announced. At a meeting of his Likud party, Netanyahu said that "we must kill the Hamas's leadership" and emphasized that the war could not end before that happened, which he defined as taking "months and not years." While remarking that a Gaza hostage deal hinged now on Hamas, US NSC Advisor Sullivan stated that such a deal "is in the national security interest of the United States. And we're going to press for it relentlessly." Soldiers from the IDF, the Shin Bet, and Border Police arrested thirty-three wanted persons throughout the West Bank. As for the Houthi threat, UK Defense Secretary Grant Shapps said that recent strikes against that terrorist group "had a significant effect on degrading their capabilities," but did not stop it from continuing to attack vessels in the Red Sea.[8]

Egypt sent messages to Israel warning that an influx of refugees from Gaza to the Sinai Peninsula would endanger the peace agreement between the two countries. For this reason, as well, Cairo told Jerusalem that it vehemently opposed both an expansion of the fighting in Rafah and Israeli control of the Philadelphi Corridor. Yet a Hamas military brigade, with four battalions, was operating out of Rafah, and it had to be defeated to eliminate Hamas's military capabilities. Control of the Corridor was also necessary, the IDF argued, to prevent smuggling between Sinai and Gaza. It was estimated that there were dozens of smuggling tunnels in the Rafah area, including ones used in the October 7 onslaught, some of which were still in operation. Control of the Philadelphi Corridor, however, would require a long-term military presence, until a more permanent solution was found for the smuggling problem.[9]

IDF's 98th Division eliminated scores of terrorists and arrested about eighty suspects, among them perpetrators in the October 7 slaughter. Givati Brigade snipers killed more than fifteen Hamas fighters, while soldiers of the Nahal and 401 Brigades eliminated many terrorists in northern Gaza. A batch of IDF leaflets titled *Al-Waqea* ("Reality"), dropped on Monday over Rafah, where more than one million Gazan Palestinians were sheltering from war, offered no specific directions or warnings—raising fears among the civilian population about the Israeli military's plans. A broad black headline in that leaflet called on readers to "wake up. Hamas killed your children. They destroyed everything good." Speaking to IDF soldiers at the Armored Corps Memorial Site and Museum in Latrun, west of Jerusalem, Netanyahu declared "victory is essential because it ensures the security of Israel. Total victory is the only way in which we can ensure additional historic peace agreements, which await." A recent poll taken by the Tel-Aviv based Institute for National Security Studies found that sixty percent of Israelis wanted the war to continue at all costs, and only five percent supported the transfer of power in Gaza after the war to the Palestinian Authority (PA). Lebanese Foreign Minister Abdallah Bou Habib rejected an international proposal for Hezbollah to withdraw from Israel's northern border to eight to ten kilometers behind the Litani River, as set out under UN Security Council Resolution 1701. He characterized it as reflective of "half solutions that do not bring the desired peace and do not secure stability."[10]

Hamas's long-awaited answer on February 6 stated that it responded to the proposal agreed upon by Israel and the United States in "a positive spirit." In its view, that called for a full cease-fire ending the war, humanitarian aid, the rehabilitation of Gaza, the end of Israel's blockade, and the exchange of hostages and prisoners. Two days later, KAN News would report that Sinwar had lost contact with fellow terror leaders "ten days ago" and was not involved in that reply to the hostage deal and cease-fire proposal. The IDF thought that he and some of the remaining Hamas leaders were hiding in the vast tunnel system of Khan Younis, Sinwar's hometown. Israel pressed the United States and the UN to allow UNRWA to continue its role in supplying humanitarian aid to Gaza during the war. "There has been some movement," President Biden said, but added that Hamas's response "seems a little over the top."[11]

The *New York Times* reported that IDF intelligence now believed that 32 of the 136 hostages still being held by Hamas were dead, the majority killed on October 7, and that another 20 hostages were feared dead. An exclusive news story noted that Be'er Sheva's Seroka Medical Center was trying to save the life of a premature baby boy born to the niece of Hamas's Haniyeh, whose sisters, Israeli citizens, lived in the Bedouin town of Tel Sheva in the Negev. As for Iran, documents found by the IDF in Gaza revealed that between 2014 and 2020 Tehran gave Hamas and its leader Sinwar more than $150 million. Furthermore, a couple was sent by Iran to Stockholm as undercover agents with the goal of murdering Jewish citizens, *Radio Sweden* reported.[12]

A poll by the Israel Democracy Institute showed that about half of Israelis would oppose a deal to end the war if it included the establishment of a Palestinian state and peace agreements with Saudi Arabia and other Arab countries, with 36 percent in favor. A breakdown in that poll by nationality revealed that a majority of Jewish Israelis were opposed to the idea (59 percent, versus 29 percent who were in favor), while among Arab Israelis the picture was reversed (69 percent supported and only 10 percent opposed). Only 39 percent of Israelis said that the State of Israel was successfully ensuring their security, a rate like that in 2022 but representing a sharp decline from 76 percent in 2020 and 56 percent in 2021. A large majority of Israelis also believed that the next election should be held much earlier than the designated date in November 2026.[13]

In Gaza, the *Wall Street Journal* reported that the enclave's hospitals were overstretched and understaffed, leaving pregnant women without proper care. Women were giving birth in tents and public bathrooms. UNICEF, the UN's children's fund, described Gaza as the "most dangerous place in the world to be a child," saying that Israel's war against Hamas had turned the Strip into "a graveyard for thousands of children." Amid a deepening humanitarian crisis and warnings about the imminent risk of famine, UNICEF said that many children were malnourished and sick. At least 17,000 children in Gaza were unaccompanied or separated from their families, according to UNICEF estimates. Reflecting IDF bombing from the air, land and sea, satellite data showed that at least half of all the buildings in the enclave were likely to have been damaged or destroyed, according to American researchers. Some 1.7 million Gazans had fled their homes during the war, and most of them were in the south in huge tent cities. The Gaza Health Ministry announced that 27,585 Palestinians had been killed and 66,978 wounded in Israeli attacks on Gaza since October 7, women and children the most vulnerable by far.[14]

Hamas's three-stage cease-fire plan over 135 days, split into three 45-day phases that would lead to an end to the war, together with the release of more than 1,500 Palestinian prisoners, including 500 convicted of murder who were serving life or lengthy sentences, Netanyahu considered unrealistic and said that its conditions would "lead to another massacre." While hearing that the war cabinet was prepared to continue negotiations for an "acceptable" release of the hostages, a visiting Blinken stressed on February 7 the urgent need to de-escalate tensions in the West Bank and "prevent the conflict from expanding." In an interview with Sky News Arabia, Palestinian political analyst Zaid Alayoubi blasted Hamas and their stealing of humanitarian aid designated for the people. Operating throughout Khan Younis, scores of Hamas operatives were killed by the Paratroopers Brigade, Maglan reconnaissance units, Brigade 646, and Givati troops. Netanyahu confirmed to reporters that the IDF had been ordered to begin operating in Rafah, where Hamas police's special forces head, Majdi Abd el-A'el, was killed the same day. Twenty-one suspects were arrested in the West Bank overnight; Hezbollah said 184 of its fighters had been killed to date. The next day, along with the killing in a drone strike of senior Hezbollah regional military commander Abbas Muhammad al-Dabs ("Hajj Abdullah") in Nabatieh, the IDF announced that 228 soldiers had been killed and 1,314 wounded in Gaza Strip ground operations, figures that did not specify casualties from Khan Younis.[15]

In a press conference on Wednesday, Netanyahu charged that Biden's executive order to impose sanctions on four residents of Judea and Samaria accused of violence against Palestinian Arabs was "very severe and inappropriate," harming "an entire population of law-abiding citizens, among whom are soldiers who fell in the fight to eliminate Hamas." "If they were using it equally," he added, "they would have imposed sanctions on Palestinians as well." After spending over a week hearing and seeing testimony of Hamas's savage assaults especially directed at women on October 7, Pramila Patten, special representative of the UN secretary-general on sexual violence in conflict, concluded thus: "Only after I saw the IDF video of the atrocities did I understand the magnitude of the disaster that happened," adding that she had not slept since then. One hundred relatives of the forty-two French-Israeli victims of the Hamas attack of October 7 attended France's national memorial ceremony, the first in the world, held at the Elysee Palace in Paris. President Emmanuel Macron declared that "68 million French citizens are in mourning today." Meeting with Netanyahu, Argentina's newly elected President Javier Milei declared on his first overseas diplomatic trip that Buenos Aires intended to designate Hamas a terrorist organization and move the country's embassy to Jerusalem.[16]

"Israelis were dehumanized in the most horrific way" on October 7 and "the hostages have been dehumanized every day since, but that cannot be a license to dehumanize others," Blinken told reporters in Tel Aviv on February 8. "The U.S. has done more than any other country to support Israel's right to ensure that October 7 never happens again," but "the daily toll that [Israel's] military operations continue to take on innocent civilians remains too high. The overwhelming majority of people in Gaza had nothing to do with the attacks of October 7," he maintained. "While there are some clear nonstarters" in the Hamas reply, "it creates space for an agreement to be reached and we'll work at that relentlessly till we get there."

Netanyahu publicly disagreed, calling the Hamas demands "delusional," claiming that "total victory" over Hamas was "within touching distance," and promised the "eternal disarmament" of Gaza. He added that he was trying to recruit regional players to help with Gaza's future civil governance and vowed that UNRWA would be replaced. At the same time, he told Blinken that Israel would not begin operating in Rafah or the Philadelphi Corridor without full coordination with Egypt, while Gallant told the American visitor that Hamas's response had been formulated to ensure Israel's rejection, and the terrorists' position would prolong the war.[17]

Concurrently, citing six "Israeli officials and senior advisers," NBC reported that Israel would allow the exile of Sinwar from Gaza in exchange for the release of the remaining 136 hostages and the end of Hamas rule in the Strip. According to this report, Israeli officials had been discussing the idea since November of allowing him to leave just as Palestine Liberation Organization head Yasser Arafat had left Beirut with several hundred PLO fighters in 1982 after an agreement between the United States and some European governments guaranteed his safe passage by boat to Cyprus and ultimately Tunis. In Gaza, the IDF Commando Brigade, Paratrooper forces, Givati soldiers, and the 41st Brigade killed many terrorists, while IAF drone strikes continued against Hezbollah in southern Lebanon.[18]

The US military strike in Iraq on Wednesday, declared the Central Command, had killed Wissam Mohammed Abu Baqir Al-Saadi, who had overseen operations in Syria of the Iran-backed Kata'ib Hezbollah, the militia force responsible for the recent attack on a US base in Jordan. This did not mark the end of a series of retaliatory actions that Biden had authorized early last week, a senior administration official told CNN. Yet Iraqi Prime Minister Mohammed Shia' Al-Sudani soon accused the United States of violating his country's sovereignty, saying the strike would push Baghdad to terminate the mission of the US-led military coalition, formed in 2014 and including approximately 2,500 American troops, assisting local forces to prevent a resurgence of Islamic State of Iraq and Syria (ISIS) militants. Elsewhere in the war-torn region, the American base in the Al-Omar oil field in the Kurdish-controlled region of northeastern Syria, close to the city of Deir ez-Zur, was attacked by a "swarm of suicide drones" according to Egypt-based Bayan-gate news. That assault marked the second attack of its kind in the same week against US bases in the area.[19]

"I'm of the view, as you know, that the conduct of the [Israeli] response in Gaza, in the Gaza Strip, has been over the top," Biden told reporters at the White House on Thursday evening, adding that "There are a lot of innocent people who are starving. Lots of innocent people are in trouble and dying. And it's got to stop." He also issued a memorandum that night asking countries receiving US military funding to prove they were following international humanitarian and human rights laws. If reports of violations were found credible, defense articles or services could be suspended. The White House briefed Israeli officials on the memorandum, and they reiterated their willingness to provide these types of assurances. Moody's credit rating agency announced the next day that it was lowering Israel's credit rating from A1 to A2—the first rating downgrade in the country's history—and the country's growth outlook from "stable" to "negative." Catching officials in Jerusalem by surprise, although the ramifications were yet to be seen, it represented a strong blow to Israel's international image.[20]

The White House clarified the next day that Biden's criticism of Israel's military conduct in Gaza as "over the top" did not portend an upcoming policy change, the press secretary saying "the U.S. wants to see Hamas defeated," but Israel must do so while protecting civilians. Israel decided to reject most of Hamas's demands for a new hostage release deal, Israeli Channel 12 News reported, wishing to return to the framework of the understandings from the Paris talks, and excluding from the document all the demands of Hamas that were not related to the issue of the war, such as the Temple Mount in Jerusalem and the imprisonment conditions of the terrorists in Israeli prisons. Senior Hamas Nukhba Brigade Commander Abu al-Baraa told the Shin Bet during interrogations that he had a message for the remaining Hamas fighters: "I recommend everyone surrender, your fate is death." On Saturday, the IDF assassinated Hamas Police Intelligence Chief Ahmed al-Yaakobi, his deputy, Iman Rantisi, and Ibrahim Shatat, the Rafah Police appointee for aid distribution, in an IAF strike on a car in western Rafah.[21]

IDF forces also discovered that beneath UNRWA's central offices in northern Gaza's upscale Rimal neighborhood was a tunnel which shared electric infrastructure with Hamas forces, indicating that UNRWA's facilities supplied the tunnel with electricity. A data center and large quantities of weapons were found inside the rooms of the building, including rifles, ammunition, grenades, and explosives. Intelligence and documents discovered in the offices of UNRWA officials confirmed that the offices had in fact also been used by Hamas terrorists.[22]

Netanyahu ordered Israel's defense establishment to present plans to evacuate Gazan civilians from the Rafah area in the south of the Strip. A statement from his office declared "It is impossible to achieve the goal of the war of eliminating Hamas while leaving four Hamas battalions in Rafah," adding that such an operation "requires the evacuation of the civilian population from combat zones." An Israeli official cited in a CNN report said Netanyahu told the war cabinet that the operation in Rafah must end by Ramadan. IDF chief Halevi announced that the army's operation in Khan Younis, although "far from over," had achieved great success with at least 2,400 terrorists eliminated. The US State Department responded that an Israeli military operation in Rafah would be a humanitarian "disaster," as did UN officials, the foreign ministers of the United Kingdom, Germany, and the Netherlands, and Arab governments. Regarding the Moody downgrade credit rating, Netanyahu declared that it "is entirely due to the fact that we are at war. The rating will go back up as soon as we win the war—and we will win." *Per contra*, Israeli Opposition Leader Yair Lapid called the downgrade "additional proof that this government is not functioning properly and harming the public."[23]

In a telephone conversation with Netanyahu on February 10 that lasted about forty-five minutes, Biden reaffirmed "our shared goal to see Hamas defeated and to ensure the long-term security of Israel and its people." In addition, the two discussed ongoing efforts to secure the release of all remaining hostages held by Hamas as soon as possible and to increase the consistency of humanitarian assistance to Palestinian civilians, while Biden reiterated his view that a military operation in Rafah should not proceed without a "credible and executable plan for ensuring the safety of and support for the more than one million people sheltering there." The next day, declaring in an ABC interview that "victory is within reach," Netanyahu stated: "Those who say that under no circumstances should we enter Rafah are basically saying lose the war, keep Hamas there." This led to a *Washington Post* headline "Biden Moving Closer to a Breach with Netanyahu over War in Gaza." Egypt's Foreign Ministry warned Israel of "dire consequences" if the IDF assaulted Rafah, while cautioning Hamas it had only two weeks to reach a prisoner exchange agreement. According to the *Wall Street Journal*, should the terrorist organization fail to reach an agreement, Israel would begin a large-scale ground offensive into the Rafah region. Media further reported that Egypt was expanding its forces in northeast Sinai near the border with Gaza, in the last two weeks sending about forty tanks and armored personnel carriers there, to prevent thousands of Gazans from entering the area.[24]

The two-state solution. which the US president continued to advocate, increasingly appeared a chimera, however, especially to the southern kibbutz that was proportionately the hardest hit from Hamas's invasion on October 7. In speaking with members who lived through the butchery at Kibbutz Nir Oz, a *Wall St. Journal* reporter heard that the massacre "changed everything" for residents who once welcomed Palestinian fieldworkers into their homes. Speaking now fundamentally differently about the Palestinian and Gaza issues, residents who had grown wheat and potatoes, now living elsewhere as "internally displaced persons" (IDPs in refugee-speak), graphically recalled the eight hours during which Hamas fighters and some Palestinian civilians hunted down their Jewish prey, murdering forty-six human beings, and abducting seventy-one to Gaza. These innocent victims numbered more than one quarter of the people who lived there. Of around 150 modest homes, only four remained undamaged, flowers blooming alongside charred houses, no birds or bicycles or rosemary bushes—a reminder of a paradise lost. Amit Siman Tov, who survived in the family *mamad* (safe room) along with her husband and four children three separate raids on her house, the last by laying down urine-soaked sweatshirts at the foot of the door to stop smoke from seeping in when Hamas attackers set the building on fire, spoke for these survivors and most Israelis: "Our trust is gone. Completely lost."[25]

The morning of February 12 brought Israel's citizenry a rare moment of exhilaration in the war upon hearing that dozens of IAF strikes several hours earlier against Hamas's Shabura Battalion were a decisive deception that enabled IDF forces to rescue the Argentinian-born Fernando Marman (61) and Louis Noberto Har (70), both taken hostage in Kibbutz Nir Yitzhak on October 7, from an apartment in the heart of Rafah. A shocked Hamas, making no reference to the successful rescue mission, announced that at least sixty-seven were killed and dozens wounded amid heavy fire by "the Nazi occupation army's attack on the city of Rafah last night." Netanyahu saluted those who carried out the daring operation, writing on X "only the continuation of military pressure, until complete victory, will result in the release of all our hostages," and concluding "we will not miss any opportunity to bring them home." The Hostages and Missing Families Forum, which represented the relatives of most of those held in Gaza, welcomed the nighttime action, and called on the government to "exhaust every option" to secure the freedom of those still in captivity as "their lives are at risk with each passing moment." The same organization intended to file a lawsuit against Hamas at the International Criminal Court, with a delegation from the Forum set to head to The Hague on Wednesday, Ynet reported.[26]

During the same night, the IDF arrested seventeen wanted terrorists in Judea and Samaria. From the start of the war, more than 3,080 terrorists had been arrested in that area, the Jordan Valley, and central Israel, half of them Hamas operatives. The IDF announced that captured Hamas documents revealed Al-Jazeera journalist Mohamed Washah to also be a senior operative in the terrorist group's anti-tank forces and who did research for its air unit. Concomitantly, even as Israel's Institute for Forensic Medicine continued to inspect more than 350 bodies from Gaza for the purpose of examining whether the bodies of hostages were among them, the IDF delivered twenty oxygen tanks and medical supplies to the Al-Amal hospital in Khan Younis. Israeli President Herzog wrote a special op-ed in the *Wall Street Journal* charging that "The South African case, brought in support of Hamas, is a blood libel against the nation-state of the Jewish people." More worrisome for Jerusalem was a CBS News report that President Biden, during recent private conversations, some of them with campaign donors, had been vulgarly letting out his frustration with his failure to convince Israel to change its military tactics in Gaza. Citing five people directly familiar with his comments, the report claimed that he named Netanyahu as the primary obstacle, saying he was trying to get Israel to agree to a cease-fire, but Netanyahu is "giving him hell" and was impossible to deal with.[27]

On day 130 of the war, meeting with Biden at the White House for the first time since the war erupted, King Abdullah attacked the impact of Israel's "seventy years of occupation," and emphasized that the only solution to the violence was "a political horizon that leads to a just and comprehensive peace based on the two-state solution" with East Jerusalem as the Palestinian capital. "Continued escalations by extremist settlers in the West Bank and Jerusalem's holy sites and the expansion of illegal settlements will unleash chaos on the entire region," Jordan's monarch declared. The president announced in turn that the United States was working on a hostage deal that would include a six-week pause to the war. Axios reported that Netanyahu expressed displeasure during his telephone call with Biden two days earlier about the executive order to sanction four residents of Judea and Samaria over purported "settler violence," given the decrease for some time in the number of attacks against Palestinians living there. He stressed that his government had taken serious steps to tackle the violence, including issuing several administrative detention orders against Israelis. Finance Minister Smotrich's holding up a shipment of American flour to Gaza because it was intended for UNRWA further enraged Biden administration officials, who claimed that it violated a commitment given by Netanyahu to the president according to which all American aid would be allowed into the Strip.[28]

While Israel's Mossad chief David Barnea and Sinwar's deputy Khalil Al-Hayya arrived in Cairo for separate negotiations on a cease-fire and hostage release deal with Qatari and Egyptian mediators, the IDF recovered a Hamas video from October 10 of a healthy Sinwar seen with a wife and his children fleeing in a tunnel under Khan Younis while the war raged above. "The hunt will not stop until we capture him—alive or dead," said IDF spokesperson Hagari, adding "We are determined to capture him—and we will." Biden and Abdullah warned about Israel's planned invasion of Rafah, but the *Wall Street Journal* reported that Israel had recently shown Egypt a proposal to get civilians out of Gaza's most southern city ahead of the ground op against Hamas. This included a plan envisioning fifteen sites containing 25,000 tents each across Gaza, running from the southern edge of Gaza City down to the Al-Mawasi area north of Rafah.[29]

As for Israel's north, Reuters reported that France had proposed a cessation of the hostilities across the border with Lebanon by having Hezbollah withdraw to six miles from the border. In its place, Lebanon would send military units to the south of the country. Senior Hezbollah politician Hassan Fadlallah responded that the terror group would not discuss "any matter related to the situation in the south before the halt of the aggression on Gaza." Hezbollah's Nasrallah went further, saying his organization was "committed to fighting Israel until it is off the map." The French Foreign Ministry also announced that it would impose sanctions on twenty-eight Israeli settlers who had attacked Palestinian civilians in the West Bank.[30]

The same Tuesday, a joint operation of the Border Police, Shin Bet, and IDF arrested Omar Fayed, a senior Hamas military leader in Jenin, and overnight arrested eighteen wanted persons throughout Judea and Samaria. In the past month, a total of over 350 Hamas operatives were apprehended by the IDF and ISA, as well as over 120 Palestinian Islamic Jihad operatives. Overall, more than 500 terrorists were apprehended in the Gaza Strip and transferred to Israeli territory for further questioning. According to a report in *Yediot Achronot*, a company hired by the IDF Rehabilitation Department estimated that in the coming year, 12,500 disabled veterans would be registered, and the scope of requests was expected to reach 20,000. European Union High Representative for Foreign Affairs Josep Borrell suggested that the United States and other countries halt weapons shipments to Israel over allegations that "too many people are being killed" in the war against Hamas in the Gaza Strip. The *Daily Mail* reported that Iran was recruiting British Muslims for espionage activities targeting Jews and dissidents in the United Kingdom. Israeli ministers declared Francesca Albanese, the UN's special rapporteur on "the occupied Palestinian territories," persona non grata in Israel after she said that victims of Hamas's October 7 onslaught were not murdered for being Jews, but "in response to Israel's oppression."[31]

On February 14, IDF jet planes embarked on "widespread strikes" in Lebanon targeting Hezbollah command centers and other infrastructure after a Hezbollah Grad missile attack on an IDF base in Tzfat (Safed—not a border town like Kiryat Shmona) killed twenty-year-old St. Sgt. Omer Sarah Benjo of Moshav Ge'a and wounded eight, one of whom later died of his injuries. In Israel's eyes, this represented a serious escalation on the northern front. Speaking to mayors and leaders of local authorities in the area, IDF chief of staff Halevi said that there were "very great achievements" in hitting Hezbollah in

Lebanon, "but we continue to act. This is not the point to stop. There is still a long way to go and we will walk it together." The Israeli delegation returned from Cairo after reporting no breakthrough in the talks, the major bone of contention Hamas's insistence on a very large release of terrorist prisoners in Israeli jails. The hostage families slammed this decision as a "death sentence" for the captives in Gaza. The talks were extended for three days, a US official saying that the next two days of talks on a hostage release deal would involve lower-level officials, who would continue discussing a new framework for a deal. PA chairman Abbas called on Hamas to quickly reach a prisoner swap agreement, in order to "prevent deportation and suffering for the Palestinian nation, and in order to distance IDF forces from Rafah."[32]

Israel registered a protest with the Vatican after Pope Francis's deputy defined what was happening in Gaza as "carnage" resulting from a disproportionate Israeli military response to Hamas. "It is a deplorable statement. Judging the legitimacy of a war without taking into account all relevant circumstances and data inevitably leads to wrong conclusions," the Israeli embassy to the Holy See declared in a statement. A day earlier, Cardinal Secretary of State for the Vatican Pietro Parolin reiterated the "request that Israel's right to defense, which has been invoked to justify this operation, be proportional, and certainly with 30,000 deaths, it is not." "I believe we are all outraged by what is happening, by this carnage, but we must have the courage to move forward and not lose hope," Parolin said, adding that "we must find other ways to solve the problem of Gaza, the problem of Palestine."

French President Macron, in a phone call with Netanyahu, sounded a related note by expressing his firm opposition to a possible IDF military offensive in Rafah: "This could only lead to a humanitarian catastrophe of a new magnitude and to forced displacement of populations," he declared, "which would constitute violations of international human rights and bring additional risk of regional escalation."[33]

Tehran's Islamic Revolutionary Guard Corps (IRGC) celebrated "Guards Day," the anniversary of the Iranian Revolution forty-five years ago when secular Shah Mohammad Reza Pahlavi left the country and Shi'i Ayatollah Ruhollah Khomeini created a theocratic dictatorship, by blasting ballistic missiles at a simulated version of one of Israel's airbases. The simulation was performed as part of an overall show and celebration, shooting missiles from submarines and boats in a naval showcase. The replica model of the airbase was built in the Iranian desert, MEMRI (the Middle East Media Research Institute) reported. Iranian media declared that Israel's Palmachim Airbase was selected as it "is the main location of the F-35 fighter jets of the Zionist regime." Last month,

Netanyahu had announced from the Palmachim base that Israel would not hesitate to attack Iran. The IRGC reportedly used measurements of the area of the airbase to build their targets and size the new missiles. State media also reported that the Emad liquid fuel ballistic missiles were far more explosive and claimed that the missiles were able to destroy targets at 1700 kilometers within a small margin. IRGC commander-in-chief Hossein Salami boasted of the alleged success in launching long-range ballistic missiles from a warship for the first time, crowing "There will be no safe place for any power that wants to create insecurity for us."[34]

The families of the two hostages rescued from Gaza two days earlier said that their loved ones did not receive medications that Hamas and Qatar had promised would be delivered to the captives. This renewed calls within Israel to suspend humanitarian aid deliveries to the Strip. National Security Minister Itamar Ben-Gvir wrote a letter to Netanyahu calling for the suspension of aid transfers to Gaza until the well-being of the hostages was verified. The *Tzav 9* movement, which organized the demonstrations that blocked trucks at the Kerem Shalom and Nitzana Crossings carrying aid to the Gaza Strip, claimed on Wednesday that, at the beginning of the week, humanitarian aid trucks at the Kerem Shalom Crossing were found to be containing helmets and protective vests which were meant to reach Hamas. Seeing this as additional proof that the hundreds of trucks transferred daily ammunition and supplies to Hamas, "into the hands that are covered in our brothers' blood," it called on the entire public "to take the struggle to the next step and come with us to block the Hamas trucks with our bodies. No aid passes until the last hostage returns."[35]

The Biden administration, together with several Arab countries, was quickly advancing a plan for a timetable to create a Palestinian state the day after the war in Gaza ends, the *Washington Post* reported on February 15. According to the plan, which the newspaper called a "comprehensive plan for long-term peace between Israel and Palestinians," the timeline for the establishment of "Palestine" could be announced within the next several weeks. The plan was being advanced quickly due to the proposed temporary cessation of fire suggested in the prisoner swap deals placed on the negotiations table. The planners hoped that a cease-fire of at least six weeks would allow time to announce the plan to the public, recruit support, and take necessary steps towards creating a state; they hoped that an agreement could be reached before Ramadan began on March 10. One US official told the *Post* that "the key is the hostage deal." The *Washington Post* claimed that Israel was "the elephant in the room," since Israel would need to agree to withdraw "many, if not all, settler communities on the West Bank," as well as agree to the capital of "Palestine" being "East Jerusalem," reconstructing Gaza, and allowing security and governance agreements for an Arab state in Judea, Samaria, and Gaza. "The hope is that Israel would also be offered specific security guarantees and normalization with Saudi Arabia and other Arab states that would be hard to refuse," the newspaper added.[36]

"Biden-Netanyahu Relationship at Boiling Point as Rafah Invasion Looms," read a headline in the *Wall Street Journal* the same day, with the US administration acknowledging "a waning influence over its closest Middle East ally." The newspaper also reported that the White House was considering a series of legislative procedures against Israel to exert more pressure on Netanyahu. These included canceling decisions by the former Trump presidential administration to allow products made in Judea and Samaria to be labeled as "made in Israel," and another declaring that Israeli towns in Judea and Samaria did not violate international law.[37]

"A military operation into Rafah would be catastrophic," Prime Ministers Justin Trudeau of Canada, Anthony Albanese of Australia, and Christopher Luxon of New Zealand said Thursday in a joint statement. "We urge the Israeli government not to go down this path. There is simply nowhere else for civilians to go," they said, calling for an immediate humanitarian cease-fire. "Palestinian civilians cannot be made to pay the price of defeating Hamas," the prime ministers added. Thousands of Gazans were, indeed, evacuating Rafah as the IDF repeatedly put out warnings of imminent operations within Hamas's last stronghold. Gaza-based journalist Jehad Saftawi said that Hamas "used my family and hundreds of our neighbors as human shields. Hamas continues to hold the people of Gaza captive." Courageously posting this on X, he added "There should be no reconstruction of my family's home while a stockpile of weapons lies underneath."[38]

Vasfije Krasniqi Goodman, a Kosovo Albanian and a prominent advocate against wartime sexual violence, ended her week-long visit in Israel as a guest of Shurat HaDin, an Israeli women-led non-governmental organization founded in 2003 by attorney Nitzana Darshan-Leitner and dedicated to combatting terrorism and antisemitism. Her trip aimed to witness Hamas's atrocities, show solidarity with Israeli victims, and demand justice for victims of sexual assaults perpetrated in Israel by Hamas's elite Nukhba terrorists. In a separate effort, business executive Sheryl Sandberg, the former COO of Meta and founder of LeanIn.org, teamed up with the Israeli documentary maker Kastina Communications to make the documentary "Screams before Silence." To be released in April, it would give a voice to the women and girls who were raped, assaulted, and mutilated in a brutal campaign of gender-based violence by Hamas on October 7.[39]

The US House of Representatives passed a bipartisan resolution condemning Hamas terrorists' use of rape and sexual violence as weapons of war during—and since—the group's attacks in Israel on October 7, Fox News reported. The resolution, introduced by Rep. Lois Frankel (D., Florida) and endorsed by 200 co-sponsors from both sides of the aisle, passed in a vote of 418 to 0. Rep. Rashida Tlaib (D., Michigan), voted "present." Yet the United Nations Entity for Gender Equality and the Empowerment of Women (also known as UN-Women) released a statement on October 13, 2023, equating the Hamas brutalities with Israel's self-defense. Likewise, the UN Committee on the Elimination of Discrimination Against Women (CEDAW) neglected to explicitly condemn Hamas's atrocities. And the international #MeToo movement completely failed to mention Hamas—or the Israeli victims.[40]

More Israelis would choose to defeat Hamas over returning the hostages in a hypothetical scenario where Jerusalem was faced with the stark choice, according to the Jewish People Policy Institute (JPPI)'s monthly Israeli Society Index for February. Forty percent of the Israeli public prioritized toppling the terrorist group in Gaza at the expense of bringing the captives home, while 32 percent supported the return of the hostages and leaving Hamas in charge of the coastal enclave. Broken down by ethnicity, 47 percent of Israeli Jews chose winning the war compared to 25 percent who said returning the hostages was more important. Among Israeli Arabs, 61 percent prioritized returning the hostages over defeating Hamas.[41]

The IDF launched a targeted operation within Nasser Hospital in Khan Younis, apprehending Hamas terrorists and hearing that ten hostages had been held there. The IDF said it killed Ahmed Gul, a Hamas commander who participated in the October 7 massacre in Israel and who held hostage nineteen-year-old Cpl. Noa Marciano, who was killed in Gaza's Shifa Hospital. It also revealed that Ismail Abu Omar, an Al-Jazeera journalist wounded in an Israeli strike near the southern Gaza city of Rafah, served as a deputy company commander in Hamas's Khan Younis Battalion. "Voices from Gaza," a collection of interviews with Palestinians angry with Hamas that ordinarily would be omitted by Arab news outlets such as Al-Jazeera, which had glorified the October 7 "heroic" massacres and ongoing "resistance" to Israel, were aired thanks to the Center for Peace Communications in cooperation with The Free Press, a media company founded by former *New York Times* op-ed writer and editor Bari Weiss. Israeli forces arrested twenty-two people suspected of involvement in terrorist activities in the West bank over the last twenty-four hours. The IDF took credit in a rare instance for assassinating Hezbollah militant Ali Muhammad al-Dabas, also Hamas elite Radwan unit commander in charge of its Palestine portfolio and the mastermind behind the terrorist attack at the Megiddo Junction in Israel on March 13, 2023, his deputy Hassan Ibrahim Issa, and a third man six days earlier. That brought the terrorist group's losses to 202 fighters, without counting dozens more Hamas operatives killed in Lebanon.⁴²

Asked about the feasibility of Israel's military goal to eliminate Hamas and disallow the terrorist group from having any governing say in Gaza, UN Under-Secretary-General for Humanitarian Affairs and Emergency Relief Coordinator Martin Griffiths responded "Hamas is not a terrorist group for us, as you know, it is a political movement [sic!]. But I think it is very difficult to dislodge these groups without a negotiated solution which includes their aspirations." He explained: "I cannot think of an example offhand of a place where a victory through warfare has succeeded against a well-entrenched group, terrorist or otherwise." Speaking of Hamas's October 7 attack, Griffiths said he had "total understanding" of the "trauma" it had caused Israel, but that Israel would need to build a relationship with its neighbors regardless. He also claimed that the United Nations was struggling to get aid into Gaza, and that Palestinians had nowhere safe to evacuate to now that Israel had begun operations in Rafah. Gaza would need a new "Marshall Plan" to recover from the conflict between Israel and Hamas, a UN trade body official said on Thursday, adding that the damage from the conflict so far amounted to around $20 billion.⁴³

Coinciding with the IDF's announcement on February 16 that 235 soldiers had made the ultimate sacrifice to date fighting Hamas and Hezbollah, Netanyahu stated, following a war cabinet discussion of Biden's possible push for a Palestinian state, that "Israel outright rejects international dictates regarding a permanent arrangement with the Palestinians. Such an arrangement will be reached only through direct negotiations between the parties, without preconditions." Hamas turned down an Israeli offer to free all hostages taken into the Gaza Strip in exchange for the release of 1,500 Palestinians from Israeli prisons, Saudi media outlet Al-Arabiya reported. Egypt was constructing a wall along its border with the Gaza Strip in Rafah, where 1.3 million civilians were displaced because of the war. Egyptian officials told the *Wall Street Journal* that the wall, set to span eight square miles, was being developed because Cairo feared refugees from Gaza would flood into the country after Israel removed Hamas from power. While the IDF continued its successful killing operations against Hamas in Gaza, an Arab resident from Shuafat in East Jerusalem with Israeli residency killed two people and wounded four others in a shooting attack on Highway 40 near Bnei Re'em in southern Israel on Friday afternoon.⁴⁴

Up north, the relentless exchange of fire between Israeli forces and Hezbollah forced a surreal reality on residents of Israel's northernmost communities, many of whom remained displaced from their homes. Travelers on deserted roads consoled themselves with the knowledge that Hezbollah's anti-tank missile aiming systems had difficulty dealing with fast moving targets. Hezbollah fired the previous evening more than twenty-five missiles towards Israel's Kiryat Shmona, leading to material damage and power outage as several rockets dodged the Iron Dome defense system and fell inside the city. The IAF retaliated by pounding Hezbollah sites across the border in Lebanon. What Seth J. Frantzman called Israel's "dance of death" with Hezbollah now becoming "a dangerous chess game" once 80,000 Israelis had been evacuated from the north and Iran sought to unify various "arenas" against Israel, would these adversaries' "incrementalism" policy of limited attack and response work in Lebanon?[45]

Secretary Blinken declared at the sixtieth Munich Security Conference on February 17 that "an extraordinary opportunity" existed in the coming months for Israel to normalize ties with its Arab neighbors while also emphasizing the need for the creation of a Palestinian state. Meeting there with President Herzog, he reiterated Biden's emphasis in a telephone call with Netanyahu two days earlier that while Israel had the right to ensure the terrorist attacks of October 7 could never be repeated. the United States could not support a military ground operation in Rafah without "a credible and implementable plan for ensuring the safety of the more than one million people sheltering there."[46]

Herzog told the Munich gathering that Israel's security and Hamas's "eradication" were paramount, and that medications brought into the Gaza Strip for the hostages had not yet reached them. Netanyahu brought up the last point with visiting CIA director William Burns in Jerusalem, adding that Israel would not agree to more humanitarian gestures for Gaza "until we receive concrete proof that the hostages received the medicine that was sent to them." On the growing conflict in Israel's north, Israeli Foreign Minister Katz told the Security Conference "if a diplomatic solution is not found, Israel will be forced to remove Hezbollah from the border." For its part, Hamas suspended all Gaza cease-fire and hostage deal negotiations until humanitarian aid was brought into the northern part of the Strip, Al-Jazeera reported on Saturday a Hamas source saying: "Negotiations cannot be held while hunger is eating away at the Palestinian people."[47]

In Gaza, the Commando Brigade, naval force Shayetet 13, and additional special units continued to conduct a precise and limited operation against Hamas within the Nasser Hospital in Khan Younis. The activity conducted led to apprehending approximately 100 individuals suspected of terrorist activity and the killing of numerous terrorists around the area of the hospital. Stocks of medicines sent by private families, with the names of hostages, as well as many weapons were also found there sealed—*unused*. Arab media broadcast that near the Gaza Strip's border crossing with Egypt, riots took place after Muhammad Al-Araja, a Palestinian teen, tried with a group of people to grab items from a humanitarian aid shipment and was shot dead by Hamas police. Gallant told reporters that Israel had intelligence that more than thirty of UNRWA's employees actively participated in the October 7 murder spree, assisting in the kidnapping of civilians and soldiers. The *Washington Post* disclosed that UNWRA worker Faisal Ali Musalam Naami was seen on video "removing the limp body of an Israeli man shot at Kibbutz Be'eri and driving off with it." Following such reports, Finance Minister Smotrich decided to cancel the tax benefits extended to UNRWA.[48]

The fighting in Gaza would continue until the hostages were returned, war cabinet minister Gantz declared: "Even in the approaching month of Ramadan,[49] the firing can continue. Either our hostages will be returned, or we will expand the fighting to Rafah." At the same time, while thousands of demonstrators on Saturday night called for the prime minister's ouster, Netanyahu told a press conference the same night that a military operation there could only occur if safe areas for Gazans to enter from Rafah were made available. As for huge billboards, some paid for by Yom Kippur War veterans, and advertisements in major newspapers calling for early national elections rather than waiting until the government's official term was completed in November 2026, he advised not "getting involved in them now. It will immediately divide us, and this is what Hamas is waiting for." Poll results clearly favoring Gantz to replace him were dismissed as "a small minority who don't represent the majority of most Israelis. Most of the people want one thing: unity for the sake of victory!"[50]

Sharply responding to UN relief chief Griffiths's claim two days earlier that Hamas was "a political movement," Foreign Minister Katz tweeted "The United Nations reaches new lows every day," pointing to statements from Griffiths and Secretary-General Guterres. "We will eliminate Hamas with or without them," he pledged, adding "Jewish blood is not cheap." NSC spokesman Kirby, replying to a question on Griffiths's comments, put it more bluntly: "Hamas is a terrorist organization. We've said so. It is. It just is. You don't have to look any further than what they did on the seventh of October to see it in stark terms." He then remarked: "Take a look at their manifesto, even the one that was so-called watered down in 2017. There's no doubt that they just want to wipe out Israel off the face of the map. This is a terrorist organization. Pure and simple. Period."[51]

Netanyahu's governing coalition voted unanimously on Sunday, day 135 of the war, to oppose plans by some allies to recognize a Palestinian state without Israeli participation in talks, the resolution reading "Israel utterly rejects international diktats regarding a permanent settlement with the Palestinians." The cabinet did express a willingness to engage in direct negotiations with Palestinians, something that had not taken place in over a decade. The *Wall Street Journal* reported that the Biden administration was looking to financially prop up the Palestinian Authority amid warnings from officials in Ramallah that it was close to running out of money, potentially jeopardizing US hopes that the organization would be able to govern Gaza when Israel's war with Hamas ended. PA Prime Minister Mohammad Shtayyeh said that international leaders gathered for the Munich Security Conference should not continue focusing on the Hamas assault of October 7. He later clarified his remarks in an interview with Qatari's Al-Jazeera saying that "yes, October 7 is a major event," but "Palestinian suffering did not start on October 7. Palestinians have been suffering for the last 75 years . . . we need an end to the struggle. Don't deal with the cosmetics, you should deal with the roots of the problem, which is Israeli occupation."[52]

Minister Gantz told a delegation of the Conference of Presidents of the Major American Jewish Organizations after Sunday's coalition vote that Israel would expand its ground offensive into Rafah, "in coordination with our American and Egyptian partners to minimize civilian casualties," if the hostages held by Hamas were not released by Ramadan, to begin on March 10. Jordanian Foreign Minister Ayman Safadi blamed Netanyahu for failing to advance a cease-fire deal that would lead to a forty-five-day pause in fighting in exchange for the release of remaining hostages, while Egypt's foreign minister, Sameh Shoukry, warned that an Israeli offensive in Rafah would have "severe repercussions" on the crisis in Gaza and for Egypt's security. He also sharply criticized Hamas at the Munich Security Conference as "outside the Palestinian consensus, which recognizes Israel and wants to reach negotiations with it, because [Hamas] is not ready to give up its support for violence."[53]

While the IDF continued building a fortified road cutting the Gaza Strip into two parts to isolate the major terror center of Gaza City and the northern section from its center and south, the last of its reserve units that had first gone into Gaza were being pulled out. Gaza residents received messages in recent days calling on them in Arabic to provide the Israeli security forces with information about the hostages, promising a cash reward to anyone who would do so. The flyer read: "Let's create a better future together for both nations. Hamas and the other organizations have led you to hell."[54]

Netanyahu blasted left-wing Brazilian president Luiz Inácio Lula da Silva's comparing the IDF's campaign in Gaza to "when Hitler decided to kill the Jews" as crossing "a red line," his remarks a "trivialization of the Holocaust and an attempt to harm the Jewish people and Israel's right to defend itself." The Foreign Office declared him persona non grata; da Silva retaliated by recalling Brazil's ambassador to Israel "for consultations." He received the backing of his counterparts in Colombia and Bolivia, Gustavo Petro and Luis Arce, three days later, although Blinken made it clear to Brazil's leader in "a frank exchange" that Washington did not agree with his recent remarks about Israel's war in Gaza.[55]

Jerusalem expected intense fighting to continue in Gaza for another six to eight weeks, including in Rafah City, before scaling back the war effort, Reuters reported on Monday. "Military chiefs believe they can significantly damage Hamas's remaining capabilities in that time, paving the way for a shift to a lower-intensity phase of targeted airstrikes and special forces operations," the report stated. Since the war began, the IAF registered more than 186,000 flying hours striking over 31,000 targets, most of them in the Gaza Strip but also that very evening two weapon depots near Sidon, more than fifty kilometers from the Israel-Lebanon border. IDF forces found technological equipment made in Iran and China in the Hamas facility under the UNRWA headquarters in Gaza. Netanyahu urged the leaders of an American Jewish delegation to press Qatar, on which Hamas was dependent financially, to press Hamas, "because we want our hostages released." He added "I hope that we can achieve a deal soon, to release more of our hostages. But deal or no deal, we have to finish the job to get total victory."[56]

As for Judea and Samaria, where twenty-two terrorist suspects were arrested overnight, IDF data revealed that the number of terror attacks in that region over the course of 2023 was 350 percent higher than in 2022. The data showed that, over the course of 2023, there were 608 ramming, shooting, stabbing, and explosive device attacks, compared to 170 such attacks in 2022. Around 300 of the incidents were shooting attacks, the highest number since the Second Intifada. Northern Samaria was a hotbed of terror during that period, with over 50 of the shooting attacks originating from Jenin. Given the thirty-eight percent increase in the Jewish population there and the Jordan Valley over the past decade, Shlomo Ne'eman, the head of the Gush Etzion Regional Council and the Yesha Council, asked the government to approve another thousand housing units to meet the great demand. "The government of Israel and its leader must understand," he declared, "that we have reached the point at which the enemy should receive their answer not only in Gaza and Lebanon, but also in Judea and Samaria."[57]

Preparations for a ground op in Rafah would take weeks due to the need to evacuate civilians, IDF intelligence officials said, adding that they thought only some 100 hostages were still alive and held in extremely unhygienic conditions, which might prove to be life-threatening. Protesters blocked the Nitzana border crossing with Egypt once again in order to prevent the passage of humanitarian aid into the Strip, A spokesperson for Qatar's Foreign Ministry declared that Doha "categorically" rejected the "empty accusations" made by Netanyahu, who had called for Qatar to pressure Hamas to release the hostages, describing his comments as "nothing but a new attempt to stall and prolong the war" and blaming them on "the Israeli Prime Minister's personal political challenges." Following the United States, United Kingdom, and France, Spain announced it would unilaterally impose sanctions on violent Israeli settlers in the West Bank if its European Union partners failed to reach an agreement on the issue. Ireland's Foreign Minister, Micheál Martin, said he hoped to get unanimity from the EU regarding the sanctions, adding that the world was "shocked" at the level of the IDF's "inhumanity" within Gaza. At the International Court of Justice in The Hague, hearings began regarding Israel's "occupation of Palestinian territories," Palestinian Authority Foreign Minister Riyad Al-Maliki charging that Israel was committing genocide in Gaza and had enforced a policy of apartheid against Palestinians for years.[58]

Every EU nation except for Hungary signed a joint statement on February 19 calling for "an immediate humanitarian pause that would lead to a lasting cease-fire" in the Hamas-Israel war, "the unconditional release of all hostages," and that Israel should not take military action in Rafah which "would worsen an already catastrophic humanitarian situation." The next day, the United States cast the lone veto against the draft resolution put forward by Algeria at the UN Security Council and supported by thirteen nations (the United Kingdom abstained) that demanded an immediate cease-fire in the war in Gaza between Israel and Hamas. "We hope that the Council will adopt our proposed resolution so that we can reach a temporary ceasefire under which all the abductees will be released and humanitarian aid will be delivered to Palestinian citizens who desperately need it," declared Ambassador Linda Thomas Greenfield, adding "We should finally condemn Hamas for their horrible acts on October 7 that started the conflict. We are obliged to continue working on the proposal in the following days."[59]

In Gaza, Hamas declared that if restrictions were placed on the entry of worshippers to the Al-Aqsa Mosque during Ramadan, "it will blow up in the face of the occupation." Hamas also warned Israel against an "adventure in Rafah" and attacked Netanyahu for "arguing that the hostages can be released by force." Jerusalem denied a Saudi report that the Israeli defense establishment believed Hamas leader Sinwar, along with his brother Mohammed and other senior figures in the organization, had fled with some hostages to Egypt through tunnels between Rafah and Sinai. While NSC spokesperson Kirby told the press "We don't want to see a second front open up" between Hezbollah and Israel, Hassan Fadlallah, a member of Lebanon's parliament and senior Hezbollah official, told Al-Jazeera that everywhere in Israel was within range of Hezbollah missiles. Israel, he stated, "wants to apply military pressure to calm its residents who live in the north. From day one, threats to destroy Lebanon have been issued. Israel is not in a position to set conditions."

IDF chief Halevi said in a letter dispatched to commanders, "We are not on a killing, revenge, or a genocide spree. We have come to win and defeat a cruel enemy who deserves a bitter loss." He explained that the military still had a "long way ahead" in combat, with many challenges to come in the northern, central, and southern fronts. Halevi further added, "We will not allow the enemy accomplishments in the international arena. A true warrior is the one whose values do not alter in the face of a challenging reality."[60]

The Knesset, by a vote of 99–11 on February 21, approved the coalition government's decision that opposed any unilateral declaration of the establishment of a Palestinian state. IDF troops conducted a targeted raid in the Zeitoun area in northern Gaza, killing dozens of terrorists and locating numerous weapons; Givati troops also intensified their activities in Khan Younis. Residents of Jabaliya in the northern Gaza Strip and Rafah took to the streets that night to protest against Hamas leaders, Palestinian social networks showing residents shouting "We need food... Sinwar and Haniyeh, stay away from us, you thieves." Israeli TV's N12 reported that Sinwar was suffering from a complicated case of pneumonia, citing an anonymous Arab country which said it had heard the report from senior Hamas officials. That country had been in contact with the terror group, asking it to advance toward a cease-fire. Hamas subsequently responded that its situation was grave; it lacked ammunition, and its military structures were deteriorating.[61]

An Israeli political source told ABC News that Israel was preparing to reopen the Karni border crossing, closed as of 2011, to ease the entry of humanitarian supplies into the northern Gaza Strip. Northern Gaza had been isolated by the Israeli military and almost completely cut off from aid for weeks, according to the United Nations. Israel's military ordered two neighborhoods of Gaza City to evacuate amid signs of hunger and mounting desperation in the northern part of the enclave at a time when the focus of Israel's offensive had shifted south. The evacuations came as the World Food Program halted deliveries in the north on Tuesday, describing scenes of chaos as its teams faced looting, hungry crowds, and gunfire in recent days. In Jenin, Israeli forces killed three armed men overnight, including Aref Ali Al-Kaddoumi, who had served in Fatah's military wing, while arresting forty wanted individuals across the West Bank. Syria reported Israeli airstrikes on a residential area in Damascus, while Iran accused Israel of sabotaging that country's two major gas pipelines.[62]

The United States on Wednesday defended Israel's "decades-long occupation of the West Bank and East Jerusalem," arguing at the International Court of Justice that the October 7 Hamas-led brutal attack was a reminder of the threats facing the country and of its security needs, "and they persist." "Regrettably, those needs have been ignored by many of the participants in asserting how the court should consider the questions before it," Richard C. Visek said, referring to other countries' testimony in the hearings. Visek, the acting legal adviser at the US State Department, urged a fifteen-judge panel not to call for Israel's immediate withdrawal from these areas. He declared that only the establishment of an independent Palestinian state alongside Israel could bring about lasting peace. Israel had said it would not participate in the hearings, and sent a letter to the ICJ last year arguing that the focus of the proceedings failed to "recognize Israel's right and duty to protect its citizens" or its right to security. South Africa condemned Israel's policies against Palestinians, calling them "a more extreme form of apartheid," the race-based system of laws that had deprived Black South Africans for decades. Across the Atlantic, Biden was pushing the Republican-led House of Representatives to take up a bill, passed by a bipartisan Senate vote, which allotted $14 billion to Israel as part of a $95 billion foreign aid bill which intended the majority of the funds to Ukraine in its war against Russia.[63]

The IDF began clearing the Zeitoun neighborhood in northern Gaza of Hamas terrorists so that Israel could attempt a pilot project to bring Gazan civilians back to the area. Israel TV's Channel 12 News reported on February 22 that the plan was for a local Gazan group to run the neighborhood instead of Hamas. If this succeeded, those leaders would control the humanitarian aid brought into the neighborhood, distributing it to residents in place of the terror group which had thus far ruled northern Gaza. The IDF said it forcibly cleared a protest against the transfer of aid to Gaza at the Kerem Shalom Crossing, adding that one demonstrator suffered a light head injury. Israel's Defense Minister Gallant told visiting White House Mideast advisor Brett McGurk, who was spearheading hostage negotiations, that Israel's government "will expand the authority given to our hostage negotiators" while "preparing to continue intense ground operations" in Gaza. The United Kingdom was considering suspending arms export licenses to Israel if the IDF carried out a military operation in Rafah. War Cabinet Minister Gantz announced that a new hostage deal might be underway, but if no agreement were reached in three weeks, the IDF would operate in Rafah during the Muslim holy month of Ramadan. The Health Ministry in Gaza said that at least 29,410 Palestinians had been killed and 69,465 wounded since the war began.[64]

In the latest sign of Washington's isolation on the issue, the US opposition to an immediate cease-fire in Gaza came under repeated criticism during a two-day meeting in Rio de Janeiro of the chief diplomats of the world's twenty largest economies. Brazilian Foreign Minister Mauro Vieira, host of the G20 gathering, began the meeting by decrying the "paralysis" at the UN Security Council, where Washington had vetoed a third resolution for an immediate cease-fire in Gaza earlier in the week. "This state of inaction results in the loss of innocent lives," Vieira remarked. Almost all present agreed that a two-state solution was "the only answer" to the conflict. In the International Court of Justice, Irish and Jordanian officials declared that Israel's fifty-seven-year "occupation" had deprived Palestinians of their basic rights to a state, and they urged its judges to issue an advisory opinion rendering the situation illegal. At the same time, Biden wrote on social media platform X that the Palestinian people "are suffering as a result of Hamas' terrorism, and it does not represent the Palestinian people."[65]

A twenty-six-year-old Israeli was killed and eleven people were wounded, including a pregnant woman and two others in serious condition, in a shooting attack near the West Bank settlement of Ma'aleh Adumim on Thursday. Three terrorists from Bethlehem, arriving in two cars at a checkpoint near the settlement, opened fire on cars waiting in a traffic jam. Police shot the three assailants, killing two and wounding one. In response and with Netanyahu's participation, the Israeli ministers of defense, finance, and strategic affairs decided to convene the Supreme Planning Council in the Civil Administration to approve 3,000 housing units in Ma'aleh Adumim, Efrat, and Kedar in Judea and Samaria. Dozens of settlers from the West Bank settlement of Yitzhar threw stones and tried to torch several houses in the Palestinian village of Asira al-Qibliya; Israeli security forces were dispatched to the village, but no arrests were made. Israeli forces arrested seventeen wanted persons in the West Bank overnight into Thursday, the IDF said. As for the Hezbollah threat, four months after the cabinet decision to evacuate communities up to five kilometers from the border with Lebanon, purportedly for the safety and security of residents, the government now admitted that fourteen of those communities in the range of 2–3.5 kilometers from the border were emptied only for the IDF's "freedom of operation."[66]

Netanyahu on Thursday evening brought before the Political-Security Cabinet his proposal for the "day after" Hamas's defeat. The IDF would continue the war, it began, until Israel's goals were achieved: the destruction of the military capabilities and governmental infrastructure of Hamas and the Palestinian Islamic Jihad, the return of the hostages, and the prevention of a threat from the Gaza Strip for a lengthy period of time. In the interim period, Israel would maintain operational freedom of activity in the entire Gaza Strip, without a time limit, for the purpose of preventing the renewal of terrorism and thwarting threats from Gaza. Israel would maintain a "southern closure" on the Gaza-Egypt border to prevent the re-intensification of terrorist elements in the Strip. The "southern closure" would operate, as much as possible, in cooperation with Egypt and with the assistance of the United States and would be based on measures to prevent smuggling from Egypt both underground and above ground, including at the Rafah Crossing. Israel would have security control over the entire area west of the Jordan River, including what was called "the Gaza Envelope," to prevent the strengthening of terrorist elements in Judea, Samaria, and the Gaza Strip and to thwart threats against Israel. There would be a complete demilitarization in the Gaza Strip.

The civil administration and responsibility for public order in the Gaza Strip, Netanyahu's proposal continued, would be based on local officials with administrative experience, local entities not identified with countries or entities that support terrorism and would not receive payment from them. A comprehensive de-radicalization program would be promoted in all religious, educational, and welfare institutions in the Gaza Strip, as much as possible with the involvement and assistance of Arab countries. Israel would work to shut down UNRWA. The rehabilitation of the Strip would only be possible after the demilitarization was completed and the de-radicalization process began. The rehabilitation programs would be financed and led by countries that were acceptable to Israel.[67]

The next day, the Palestinian Authority and Hamas both denounced Netanyahu's proposal. "If the world wants security and stability in the region, it must end the Israeli occupation of Palestinian territories and recognize the independent Palestinian state with Jerusalem as its capital" and Gaza part of that state, said Nabil Abu Rudeineh, the spokesperson for PA chairman Abbas, as reported by Al-Jazeera. Senior Hamas official Osama Hamdan also lambasted Netanyahu's plan for postwar Gaza during a press conference in Beirut on Friday, declaring: "When it comes to the day after in the Gaza Strip, Netanyahu is presenting ideas which he knows fully well will never succeed," as quoted by Agence France-Presse. Hamas added that "an explosion is coming in response to any restrictions on the entry of Muslims to Al-Aqsa Mosque during the month of Ramadan." NSC spokesperson Kirby declared only that "the Palestinian people should have a voice and a vote . . . through a revitalized Palestinian Authority." Still, the deputy US representative at the UN, Robert Wood, declared that there could be no cease-fire between Israel and Hamas until the terror organization released the hostages in Gaza.[68]

At the same time, responding to the Israeli pronouncement of a considerable construction plan after the deadly attack near Ma'aleh Adumim on Thursday, the Biden administration declared that Israeli West Bank settlements were "inconsistent with international law," reversing the so-called Pompeo Doctrine, a claim made by President Trump's Secretary of State in 2020 that settlements were "not per se inconsistent with international law." Blinken declared that the decision was a return to "longstanding U.S. policy, under Republican and Democratic administrations alike."[69]

While the IDF continued its campaign over the weekend in Gaza, the West Bank, and the northern border, US-UK airstrikes hit eighteen targets across eight locations in Yemen associated with Houthi military facilities to counter more than sixty attacks the Iran-backed group had mounted against Red Sea vessels. Israeli Foreign Minister Katz warned in a letter to the UN Security Council that Iran had accelerated its shipments of weapons to Hezbollah through Syria since the war in Gaza began. Israel, he stressed, had an "inherent right . . . to defend its territory and its citizens," and in a post on X added, "Iran is the head of the snake. We will not be patient much longer for a diplomatic solution in the north. If the dramatic intelligence information we revealed to the Security Council does not bring about change, we will not hesitate to act." National Unity Party leader Gantz released a statement in which he promised that the war would expand farther into both Hamas and Hezbollah territory to ensure that Israelis could return home safely. As for the talks in Paris regarding the Israeli hostages kidnapped to Gaza by Hamas, Chief of Staff Halevi said that the continued war was the surest way to secure the hostages' release.[70]

On Sunday, Hamas spokesman Jihad Taha denied reports that it had discussed the issue of creating a technocratic government for the "Palestinian people" in the near future, claiming that the primary focus for Hamas now was stopping Israeli aggression. "Nobody in the whole world expected" the Israeli response after October 7 "to be so barbaric" (*sic*!), Hamas official Moussa Abu Marzouk told Egypt's Alghad TV, "and in such violation of all international laws, treaties, and norms, because, ultimately, the resistance fights soldiers. It is not fighting civilians with planes and tanks." As for Rafah, the White House clarified that President Biden had not seen or been briefed on any Israeli plans for a military operation there, including the evacuation of over a million displaced Palestinians.[71]

Concurrently, Gallant declared that if anyone thought that when Israel reached an agreement to release hostages in Gaza and the war stopped there temporarily, this would make things easier on the northern border "they are mistaken." "We will continue the fire and we will do so independently from the south, until we achieve our goals," he explained. "The goal is simple—to withdraw Hezbollah to where it should be—either via a [diplomatic] agreement, or we will do it by force." A hostage deal for the remaining 134 hostages out of the 253 seized on October 7 would delay the Rafah military operation, Netanyahu confirmed in a CBS interview on Sunday, but "total victory is our goal, and total victory is within reach. Not months away, weeks away once we begin the operation." As for the UN Human Rights Council's report calling for an arms embargo of Israel, Foreign Minister Katz tweeted thus: "Since the October 7 massacre, the UN has cooperated with Hamas terrorists and is trying to undermine Israel's right to defend itself and its citizens," adding that the world body had turned a blind eye to Israeli suffering, including sexual crimes, at the hands of Hamas.[72]

The Palestinian Authority's government resigned on Monday, an early step toward the overhauls which the United States and Middle Eastern powers saw as a condition for that body to take charge of Gaza after the war. The move fell short of changes Western and Arab governments had pressured the Authority to make, including replacing longtime career politicians with a technocratic team and for Abbas, the PA's aging and unpopular president who had not faced a ballot since he was elected in 2005 and was perceived by Palestinians as ineffective, corrupt, and too dependent on the goodwill of the United States and Jerusalem, to step aside and invest a new prime minister with some of the president's powers. "The next phase and its challenges require new political and governmental arrangements that take into consideration the new reality in Gaza, the national unity talks, and the urgency of reaching internal Palestinian reconciliation based on national interest," Prime Minister Shtayyeh said as he tendered his and his government's resignation. It would also necessitate, he added, "the extension of the PA's authority over the entire land, Palestine [sic]."[73]

Gallant met with the families of hostages, telling them that the defense establishment's position was that Gazan civilians would only be able to return to the northern Gaza Strip once all those kidnapped were repatriated to Israel. At the same time, bereaved families from the Heroism Forum came to a Knesset committee to demand that MKs authorize the continuation of fighting in Gaza. The war cabinet approved the direct entry of humanitarian aid into the northern Strip to prevent the looting of convoys by residents. Division 162, along with the Nahal Brigade's combat team and engineering forces, unearthed a ten-kilometer underground tunnel network that connected the north and south of the Gaza Strip. The IDF announced that twenty-two Hamas-affiliated suspects were arrested in the West Bank overnight, while confirming that the commander of the eastern region in Lebanon under Hezbollah's control, Hassan Hossein Salami, had been killed in an IAF airstrike. Hezbollah, for its part, claimed that it had retaliated against Israeli airstrikes deep in eastern Lebanon for the first time, near Baalbek sixty-two miles from the Israel-Lebanon border, by firing sixty rockets toward an IDF division command in northern Israel.[74]

Both Hamas and Israeli officials said they were unaware of any basis for Biden's optimistic remarks on Monday that a hostage-for-cease-fire agreement in Gaza was imminent. As to the president's charge in an evening NBC interview that if Israel "keeps up with this incredibly conservative government they have"—Ben-Gvir was specifically mentioned—"it would lose support from around the world," Netanyahu pointed the next day to a recent survey conducted within the United States by the Harris Poll and HarrisX showing that more than eighty percent of respondents supported Israel in the war and close to seventy percent said they believed that Israel was trying to avoid civilian casualties. For its part, Hamas declared that European leaders were partially responsible for not "preventing the criminal attack on Rafah." When asked on the whereabouts of Hamas leader Sinwar, IDF spokesperson Hagari simply responded: "We will get to him, dead or alive."[75]

Warning that Iran, Hezbollah, and Hamas were trying to use Ramadan to inflame the region to achieve another October 7 disaster against Israel, Defense Minister Gallant strongly opposed National Security Minister Ben-Gvir's push to reduce access to the Temple Mount for certain Israeli-Arabs or Palestinians during the Islamic holy month. In a separate, secret warning, the Shin Bet advised the Interior Ministry that criminal gangs had taken over or penetrated seven local authorities in the Israeli Arab community, could obtain weapons, and now held key positions there. The Israeli security agency cautioned that the gangs were attempting to influence the outcoming of Tuesday's local elections and therefore recommended postponing elections in those authorities. Shlomit Kalmanson, widow of husband Elchanan who died rescuing victims from Kibbutz Be'eri on October 7, addressed the Knesset House Committee as a member of the Heroism Forum, saying "the fighting must continue until Hamas is vanquished. This is how we will safely bring the kidnapped home," and "I am also sitting here on behalf of the murdered people from the Shalit deal."[76]

On Wednesday, while Hamas rejected the latest cease-fire proposal, political bureau head Haniyeh called on Palestinians in Jerusalem and the West Bank to barricade themselves at the Al-Aqsa Mosque on the first day of Ramadan. He added that "the world, especially the Arab states, must restrain the enemy and refuse to let them invade the city of Rafah." Iran gave Hezbollah the green light to escalate its attacks along Israel›s northern border, the *Arabic Post* reported, ordering it to launch a large-scale attack on Israel only after it "had become certain of Israel's intention" to carry out an invasion of the southern Gaza city of Rafah. Hezbollah's Nasrallah told Esmail Qaani, IRGC head and commander of its Al-Quds Force, that the attack was likely to be most likely in the month of Ramadan, or with Israel's invasion of Rafah, and he asked Qaani to give him "complete freedom in how he intends to attack." Israeli and American officials told Axios that the Biden administration gave Jerusalem until mid-March to sign a letter providing assurances that it would abide by international law while using US weapons and allow humanitarian aid into Gaza. As for the latter, the IDF said that 160 packages of food and medical equipment were airdropped into southern Gaza and the Jordanian field hospital in Khan Younis as part of an effort by Israel, the United States, UAE, Jordan, Egypt, and France.[77]

Pressures also mounted on Israel's domestic front, with Gallant calling that evening on the government to pass the Draft Law and to include the conscription of ultra-Orthodox (*hareidim*) young men into the IDF to achieve Israel's objectives in the war against Hamas. He warned that if the legislation did not have the support of the entire Cabinet, he would not support it. "The war has proved that everyone must go 'under the stretcher,'" the defense minister said during a press conference, characterizing the current period as "a time of war we have not known for 75 years." Gallant had recently conveyed to Netanyahu that on the issue of ultra-Orthodox conscription, he would support whatever Minister-without-Portfolio Gantz proposed. It was understood that, outraged over this decision, and in a conversation about Gallant with his confidants, Netanyahu threatened to delay passage of the law to extend the mandatory military service in the IDF for conscripted and reserved troops—a measure that was important for the army and Gallant. Netanyahu was angry that Gallant was essentially leaving him to deal alone with the *hareidi* parties (Shas and United Torah Judaism) on this matter, threatening his cabinet coalition. Separately, families of kidnapped Israelis held by Hamas in Gaza began a four-day march from the parking lot in Kibbutz Re'im, near the site of the Nova music festival massacre, to Jerusalem, calling for the release of the hostages after more than four months in captivity.[78]

The last day of February hinted at potential major changes in the Middle East. The announcement of a meeting between representatives of Hamas and Fatah in Moscow could have significant implications for Palestinian unity, the future of Gaza, and the regional balance of power. US State Department spokesman Matthew Miller demanded that Israel "facilitate access to the Temple Mount for peaceful worshippers during Ramadan, consistent with past practice," while CNN reported Washington's concern that Israel was preparing for a ground invasion into Lebanon at the end of spring or during the early summer if the negotiations with Hezbollah to move away from Israel's northern border would come to an impasse. This reflected what the *New York Times* characterized as "the essential tension" and "the disparity of visions" between Netanyahu and Biden, the first leader speaking of continued war, the second of a cease-fire that could lead to a broader realignment that would finally, peacefully, end the underlying conflict that had defined the Middle East for generations. UN High Commissioner for Human Rights Volker Turk declared on Thursday that war crimes had been committed by Israel and Hamas, calling for them to be investigated and for those responsible to be held accountable. New Zealand's Foreign Minister, Winston Peters, said "we can no longer distinguish between the military and political wings of Hamas" following October 7, but announced sanctions against "extremist Israeli settlers" as well.[79]

Other imponderables arose. What of an IDF ground invasion of Rafah? A lengthy *Wall Street Journal* analysis pointed out that while Israel was betting that its military could do sufficient physical damage to Hamas to win security for itself, outweighing the diplomatic cost of worldwide opprobrium, Hamas was betting that it could evade the Israelis' best efforts to crush it, allowing it to regenerate and claim a political triumph. The newspaper reported that Sinwar recently sent a message to Hamas senior leaders in Doha, declaring "Don't worry, we have the Israelis right where we want them," its al-Qassam Brigades were doing fine in the war "that Israel declared" (*sic*!), their fighters were ready for Israel's expected incursion into Rafah, and high numbers of Palestinian casualties (the Gaza health ministry reported 30,035 deaths to date—of which the IDF said more than one-third were Hamas operatives and that additional Palestinian civilians had been killed by 10–15 percent rocket misfires by Hamas) would increase international pressure on Israel to end the armed conflict, after which Sinwar would be able to come out of hiding and announce Hamas's victory and continued rule in Gaza. The fate of the Hamas-held Israeli hostages and of those yet to die on both sides was also enveloped in mystery. When, if at all, could one definitively declare "*finis*"?[80]

As for the major sponsor of terrorism worldwide, Iran made a concerted effort after heavy US airstrikes on February 2 against Iran-backed militias in Iraq and Syria to see that there were no further attacks by these groups on American bases there. Yet what of Tehran's subsequent responses in the region and across the globe, as well as its drive toward nuclear power and repeated threats to destroy Israel? Supreme Leader Ayatollah Khamenei tweeted his support for the deceased Aaron Bushnell, the twenty-five-year-old US Air Force cyber defense operations specialist who set himself alight in front of the Israeli Embassy in Washington on February 25 to protest with cries of "Free Palestine!" the IDF's military offensive in Gaza, posting this on X: "The West's disgraceful antihuman policies with regard to the genocide in Gaza have reached such a point that a US military officer sets himself on fire."[81] Iran's future stand and that of its Hezbollah proxy in Lebanon remained unsettled, as were Israel's military plans vis-à-vis its northern border and beyond. "It is not certain that everything is uncertain," observed the French philosopher and mathematician Blaise Pascal in his *Pensées* (1670), but clarity and conclusion on the Hamas-Israel war appeared as elusive as ever.

Endnotes

1. *Haaretz*, Feb. 1, 2024; *New York Times*, Feb. 1, 2024.
2. *Jerusalem Post*, Feb. 1, 2024; Israel National News, Feb. 1, 2024.
3. CBS News, Feb. 1, 2024; Reuters, Feb. 1, 2024; *Haaretz*, Feb. 1, 2024; IDF News, Feb. 1, 2024.
4. *Haaretz*, Feb. 2–3, 2024; Israel National News, Feb. 3, 2024; IDF News, Feb. 3, 2024; *Wall St. Journal*, Feb. 2, 2024.
5. *Washington Post*, Feb. 3, 2024; *New York Times*, Feb. 3, 2024. While there were at least 170 such Iranian attacks on US military bases in Syria and Iraq between October 7 and February 4, not one occurred since February 4. Max Boot, "In the Shadow War with Iran, Biden Just Scored an Unheralded Victory," *Washington Post*, Apr. 8, 2024.
6. The war was now longer than the First Lebanon War (1982—116 days); the Second Lebanon War (2006—34 days); the Yom Kippur War (1973—19 days); the Sinai Campaign (1956—8 days), and the Six Day War (1967—6 days).
7. *Jerusalem Post*, Feb. 4, 2024; Israel National News, Feb. 4, 2024; *Haaretz*, Feb. 4, 2024; *New York Times*, Feb. 4, 2024.
8. Israel National News, Feb. 5, 2024; *Haaretz*, Feb. 5, 2024; *Jerusalem Post*, Feb. 5, 2024.
9. Israel National News, Feb. 5, 2024.
10. JNS, Feb. 6, 2024; *Washington Post*, Feb. 6, 2024; *Jerusalem Post*, Feb. 6, 2024.
11. *Jerusalem Post*, Feb. 6, 2024; JNS, Feb. 6, 2024.
12. *New York Times*, Feb. 6, 2024; IDF News, Feb. 6, 2024; Israel National News, Feb. 6, 2024.
13. JNS, Feb. 6, 2024; *Haaretz*, Feb. 6, 2024.
14. *Wall St. Journal*, Feb. 6, 2024; *New York Times*, Feb. 4 and 6, 2024; *Haaretz*, Feb. 8, 2024; Al-Jazeera News, Feb. 6, 2024.

15 *Haaretz*, Feb. 7, 2024; IDF News, Feb. 7, 2024; Israel National News, Feb. 7, 2024; World Israel News, Feb. 7, 2024; *Jerusalem Post*, Feb. 7–8, 2024.
16 World Israel News, Feb. 7, 2024; Israel National News, Feb. 7, 2024; *Haaretz*, Feb. 7, 2024. The next day, with the families of hostages seated in the gallery, the council of Paris unanimously voted in favor of a resolution to grant honorary citizenship to all hostages. After the vote, council members stood and applauded the families. All party leaders, including the Communist Party and the Radical Party of the Left, voted in favor and demanded in their speeches the immediate release of all hostages. Israel National News, Feb. 8, 2024.
17 *Jerusalem Post*, Feb. 8, 2024; *Haaretz*, Feb. 8, 2024. When asked by a reporter to further explain what "total victory" meant in the current context, Netanyahu invoked a chilling metaphor, citing how one smashes glass "into small pieces, and then you continue to smash it into even smaller pieces and you continue hitting them." *Washington Post*, Feb. 9, 2024.
18 NBC News, Feb. 8, 2024; IDF News, Feb. 8, 2024.
19 Israel National News Feb 8, 2024; *Washington Post*, Feb. 8, 2024; *Wall St. Journal*, Feb. 8, 2024; *Jerusalem Post*, Feb. 8, 2024. ISIS is a Salafi-Jihadist militant movement, based on Sunni Islamist theology which interprets sacred Islamic texts in their most literal, traditional sense, that seeks to establish an Islamic caliphate in Iraq and Syria and to create a global Salafi-Jihadist movement. The ideological basis of the contemporary Salafi-Jihadist movement largely came from the teachings in the 1950s of the Islamist scholar Sayyid Qutb of Egypt that Muslims should wage armed *jihad* against the secular and Western-allied governments in the Arab world until the restoration of Islamic rule. Brian R. Farmer, *Understanding Radical Islam: Medieval Ideology in the Twenty-First Century* (New York: Peter Lang, 2007).
20 CNN, Feb. 8, 2024; *Jerusalem Post*, Feb. 10, 2024; *Haaretz*, Feb. 9, 2024.
21 *Haaretz*, Feb. 9–10, 2024; Israel National News, Feb. 10, 2024; IDF News, Feb. 10, 2024. The Temple Mount (*Har HaBayit*) plaza is built on top of a hill which according to Jewish tradition is identified as Mount Moriah—the most sacred place for the Jewish people, where the world was created and the binding of Isaac by his father Abraham, the first biblical patriarch, took place. The two Holy Temples, destroyed by the Babylonians (586 BCE) and the Romans (70 CE), were built here. One of its four retaining walls, which Jews called for centuries the Wailing Wall, is the Western Wall, used today for Jewish prayer and gatherings. Among Muslims, the Temple Mount is called *Haram al-Sharif* (the Noble Sanctuary). They believe it was here that the Prophet Muhammad ascended to the "Divine Presence" on the back of a winged horse-like creature, 'Al-Buraq—the Miraculous Night Journey, commemorated by the Dome of the Rock shrine. The Dome of the Rock (*Qubbat aṣ-Ṣakhra*) is an Islamic shrine at the center of the Al-Aqsa Mosque compound on the site of the Temple Mount. The mosque is the world›s oldest surviving work of Islamic architecture and the third holiest place in Islamic tradition, after Mecca and Medina in Saudi Arabia, which claims that it is from here that Muhammad ascended to heaven for one night.
22 *Jerusalem Post*, Feb. 9–10, 2024.
23 *Jerusalem Post*, Feb. 9, 2024.
24 *Jerusalem Post*, Feb. 11, 2024; Israel National News, Feb. 11, 2024; *Washington Post*, Feb. 11, 2024; *Haaretz*, Feb. 11, 2024. At a visit to the Yahalom Unit base on Sunday, Netanyahu was even more explicit, saying that the IDF had to have control of security "over all the territory west of the Jordan River, including the Gaza Strip." IDF News, Feb. 11, 2024.
25 Tunku Varadarajan, "Ghost Town on the Gaza Border," *Wall St. Journal*, Feb. 9, 2024.
26 Times of Israel, Feb. 12, 2024; *Haaretz*, Feb. 12, 2024; *Jerusalem Post*, Feb. 10, 2024.
27 IDF News, Feb. 12, 2024; *Times of Israel*, Feb. 9, 2024; Israel National News, Feb. 12, 2024. The blood libel, the superstitious accusation that Jews ritually sacrifice Christian children at Passover to obtain blood for unleavened bread (*matza*), began in Norwich, England (1144), and continued through the centuries. After the Hamas October 7 massacre, it resurfaced in cartoons and social media posts accusing Israel of stealing organs from Palestinians killed in Gaza. Anti-Defamation League, International Affairs Department, Jan. 26, 2024.

28 *Washington Post*, Feb. 13, 2024; *Times of Israel*, Feb. 13, 2024; JNS, Feb. 13, 2024. UNRWA chief Philippe Lazzarini said that his organization did not know Hamas tunnels ran under its Gaza headquarters, sparking an IDF spokesman to retort: "You have to be very naive to think that the UNRWA personnel did not know what was happening under their feet." Israel National News, Feb. 13, 2024.
29 *Jerusalem Post*, Feb. 13, 2024; *Wall St. Journal*, Feb. 13, 2024.
30 *Haaretz*, Feb. 13, 2024; Israel National News, Feb. 13, 2024.
31 Israel National News, Feb. 13, 2024; *Le Monde*, Feb. 13, 2024; *Haaretz*, Feb. 12, 2024. Albanese was responding to French President Emanuel Macron, who said that Hamas's October 7 terror attack was the "greatest antisemitic massacre of our century." The German and French foreign ministries and Washington's envoy to the UN Human Rights Council, which appointed Albanese to her role, condemned her statement. "Francesca Albanese Has a History of Using Antisemitic Tropes," JNS, Feb. 13, 2024.
32 Israel National News, Feb. 14, 2024; *Times of Israel*, Feb. 14, 2024; *Jerusalem Post*, Feb. 14, 2024.
33 *Times of Israel*, Feb. 14, 2024.
34 *Jerusalem Post*, Feb. 14, 2024. Pahlavi's downfall marked the end of the 2,500-year-old Persian Empire and monarchy.
35 JNS, Feb. 14, 2024; Israel National News, Feb. 14, 2024. *Tzav* (Order) 8 is the emergency call-up to return to IDF service.
36 Israel National News, Feb. 15, 2024.
37 *Wall St. Journal*, Feb. 15. 2024.
38 *Washington Post*, Feb. 15, 2024; Israel National News, Feb. 15, 2024; World Israel News, Feb. 15, 2024.
39 *Jerusalem Post*, Feb. 15, 2024; *Israel Hayom*, Feb. 8, 2024.
40 Israel National News, Feb. 15, 2024; *Times of Israel*, Nov. 23, 2023. While failing to condemn Hamas's atrocities and sexual violence perpetrated against Israelis on October 7, Tlaib spoke against the resolution thus: "I am disturbed that it completely ignores and erases any sexual violence and abuse committed by the Israeli forces against Palestinians, especially children."
41 JNS, Feb. 15, 2024.
42 *Jerusalem Post*, Feb. 15–16, 2024; *Haaretz*, Feb. 15, 2024; World Israel News, Feb. 15, 2024; United with Israel, Feb. 15, 2024. After three years, Bari Weiss resigned from the *New York Times*, citing "bullying by colleagues" and an "illiberal environment." *New York Times*, July 14, 2020.
43 *Jerusalem Post*, Feb. 15, 2024; *Haaretz*, Feb. 15, 2024. President Harry S. Truman signed the Marshall Plan on April 3, 1948, whereby aid was distributed to sixteen European nations. The plan, named after US Secretary of State George C. Marshall, provided much needed capital and materials that enabled Western European nations to rebuild the Continent's economy and prevent them from falling into the Soviet bloc after World War II.
44 Israel National News, Feb. 16, 2024; *Jerusalem Post*, Feb. 15–16, 2024
45 *Haaretz*, Feb. 15, 2024; *Hindustan Times*, Feb. 16, 2024; Seth J. Frantzman, "Will Incrementalism Work in Lebanon?," *Jerusalem Post*, Feb. 16, 2024.
46 Israel National News, Feb. 17, 2024.
47 *Haaretz*, Feb. 17, 2024; *Jerusalem Post*, Feb. 17, 2024.
48 Israel National News, Feb. 17, 2024; *Haaretz*, Feb. 17, 2024; IDF News, Feb. 17, 2024. The IDF declared that "As was proven with the Shifa Hospital, Rantisi Hospital, Al-Amal Hospital, and many other hospitals across Gaza, Hamas systematically uses hospitals as terror hubs. According to intelligence assessments and information we gathered on the ground, over 85 percent of major medical facilities in Gaza have been used by Hamas for terror operations." United with Israel, Feb. 15, 2024. Na'ami was later killed in an IAF strike targeting his house in Nuseirat, along with five of his children and one of his wives. Israel National News, Feb. 19, 2024.

49 Ramadan, the ninth month of the Muslim calendar, is one of the most sacred times for Muslims. It is the month in which it is believed that the Qur'an was sent down from heaven "as a guidance for men and women, a declaration of direction, and a means of salvation." During this month, the Qur'an is recited, prayers are offered five times a day, and fasting is done between dawn and dusk.

50 *Times of Israel*, Feb. 17, 2024; *Jerusalem Post*, Feb. 17, 2024; *Haaretz*, Feb. 17, 2024. The latest national poll by Israeli TV Channel 12 news indicated that the current opposition, along with Benny Gantz's National Unity Party (previously in the opposition but now he a member of the emergency government), could secure 75 of the Knesset's 120 seats if elections were held today, with the bloc loyal to Netanyahu far behind at 45. The poll projected Gantz's party with 37 seats, while Netanyahu's Likud party at 18 seats—unchanged from the results of a previous Channel 12 poll. Opposition leader Yair Lapid's Yesh Atid party received 15 seats in the Channel 12 poll. *Times of Israel*, Feb. 12, 2024.

51 *Times of Israel*, Feb. 17, 2024.

52 *Wall St. Journal*, Feb. 18, 2024; JNS, Feb. 18, 2024.

53 *Haaretz*, Feb. 18, 2024; *Jerusalem Post*, Feb. 18, 2024; World Israel News, Feb. 18, 2024.

54 Israel National News, Feb. 18, 2024; JNS, Feb. 18, 2024.

55 *Times of Israel*, Feb. 21, 2024; Reuters, Feb. 22, 2024. A few days later, tens of thousands, including opposition leader and former Brazilian President Jair Bolsonaro carrying an Israeli flag, marched in São Paulo demanding Lula's impeachment. Times of Israel, Feb. 25, 2024. Also see Rafael Medoff, "Brazil Abandons the Jews—Again," *Jewish Journal of Los Angeles*, Feb. 20, 2024.

56 JNS, Feb. 19, 2024; IDF News, Feb. 18, 2024; Israel National News, Feb. 19, 2024. The IDF also claimed that about 900 drone strikes had been launched against Israel since the war began, but only 11 succeeded to harm effectively. Most came from the Lebanon area, but also some from Yemen, Syria, and Iraq. IDF News, Feb. 19, 2024.

57 JNS, Feb. 19, 2024; Israel National News, Feb. 19, 2024: *New York Times*, Feb. 19, 2024. *Yesha* is the Hebrew acrostic for Yehuda, Shomon, and Aza (Judea, Samaria, and Gaza). For Neeman, see Tova Lazaroff, "A Land of His Own: How a Soviet Childhood Links to West Bank Annexation," *Jerusalem Post*, Aug. 19, 2023.

58 *Haaretz*, Feb. 19, 2024; World Israel News, Feb. 19, 2024.

59 JNS, Feb. 20, 2024; Israel National News, Feb. 20, 2024; *New York Times*, Feb. 20, 2024.

60 *Haaretz*, Feb. 20, 2024; JNS, Feb. 20, 2024; *Jerusalem Post*, Feb. 20, 2024.

61 *Haaretz*, Feb. 21, 2024; *Jerusalem Post*, Feb. 21, 2024.

62 ABC News, Feb. 21, 2024; *New York Times*, Feb. 21, 2024; Israel National News, Feb. 21, 2024; *Jerusalem Post*, Feb. 21, 2024.

63 *New York Times*, Feb. 21, 2024; *Times of Israel*, Feb. 21, 2024. A smaller portion of the aid bill was earmarked to help Taiwan deter Chinese aggression and another portion would fund humanitarian aid for Palestinians in Gaza, but the Israel portion of the aid was significant. That figure was more than three times the $3.8 billion the United States sent to Israel in a normal year, and it would be a clear signal that Washington continued to stand behind the Israeli war effort as it continued deeper into its fifth month.

64 *Times of Israel*, Feb. 22, 2024; *Haaretz*, Feb. 22, 2024; World Israel News, Feb. 22, 2024.

65 *Washington Post*, Feb. 22, 2024; *Jerusalem Post*, Feb. 22, 2024; *Haaretz*, Feb. 23, 2024. As for Jordan, its rejection of Jerusalem's urging Amman not to join the war of other Arab armies in June 1967 (the Six-Day War) led to the West Bank and East Jerusalem coming under Israel's control. In addition, the army of Abdullah's father, King Hussein bin Talal, killed between 3,000–4,000 Palestinians in what his adversaries called Black September (also the Jordanian Civil War) in his 1970 war against the PLO. Bruce Reidel, "Fifty Years after 'Black September' in Jordan," *Studies in Intelligence* 64, no. 2 (June 2020): 35–37.

66 *Haaretz*, Feb. 22, 2024; Israel National News, Feb. 22–23, 2024. Black September, a terrorist group linked to the Palestinian Liberation Organization, took 11 members of the Israeli

Olympic team hostage and demanded the release of 234 Palestinians imprisoned by Israel. Negotiations with the German authorities, who took command, were botched, and the result was the massacre of all the hostages, and the deaths of five terrorists and a German policeman. Also see chapter 4, note 5.

67 Israel National News, Feb. 23, 2024.
68 Israel National News, Feb. 23–24, 2024; World Israel News, Feb. 24, 2024; JNS, Feb. 23, 2024.
69 *Jerusalem Post*, Feb. 24, 2024. Pompeo quickly took to X to voice his disapproval of the reversal of his policy. He wrote, "Judea and Samaria are rightful parts of the Jewish homeland, and Israelis have a right to live there." "President Biden's decision to overturn our policy and call Israeli 'settlements' illegal will not further the cause of peace." "It rewards Hamas for its brutal attacks on October 7th and punishes Israel instead. These Israeli communities are not standing in the way of peace; militant Palestinian terrorism is," Pompeo concluded. World Israel News, Feb. 25, 2024. The preceding US ambassador to Israel, Trump appointee David Friedman, wrote on X: "Blinken is 100% wrong. I researched this for over a year with many State Department lawyers. There is nothing illegal about Jews living in their biblical homeland. Indeed, Undersecretary of State Eugene Rostow, also the Dean of the Yale Law School (who negotiated UNSCR 242), stated that Israel has the best legal claim to Judea and Samaria." "For Blinken to announce this in the middle of a war and when the Jewish Sabbath already has begun in Israel is unconscionable," added Friedman. Israel National News, Feb. 25, 2024.
70 *Haaretz*, Feb. 22, 24, 2024; *New York Times*, Feb. 24, 2024; Israel National News, Feb, 23, 2024;
71 Israel National News, Feb. 25, 2024; *Haaretz*, Feb. 25, 2024. The same Abu Marzouk had claimed in October that Hamas's labyrinth of tunnels had been constructed to protect its fighters, and that it was Israel's and the United Nation's responsibility to protect Palestinian civilian lives.
72 *Jerusalem Post*, Feb. 25, 2024; JNS, Feb. 25, 2024.
73 *Wall St. Journal*, Feb. 26, 2024; *Times of Israel*, Feb. 26, 2024.
74 *Haaretz*, Feb. 26, 2024; Israel National News, Feb. 26, 2024; Al-Jazeera, Feb. 26, 2024; i24 News, Feb. 26, 2024.
75 *New York Times*, Feb. 27, 2024; *Times of Israel*, Feb. 27, 2024; i24 News, Feb. 27, 2024; CNN News 18, Feb. 27, 2024.
76 *Jerusalem Post*, Feb. 27, 2024; *Haaretz*, Feb. 27, 2024; JNS, Feb. 27, 2024.
77 *Jerusalem Post*, Feb. 28, 2024; *New York Times*, Feb. 28, 2024; *Times of Israel*, Feb. 28, 2024; *Haaretz*, Feb. 28, 2024.
78 Israel National News, Feb. 28, 2024; JNS, Feb. 25, 2024; *Haaretz*, Feb. 28, 2024.
79 Editorial, *Jerusalem Post*, Feb. 29, 2024; World Israel News, Feb. 29, 2024; *New York Times*, Feb. 28, 2024; Israel National News, Feb. 29, 2024; *Haaretz*, Feb. 29, 2024.
80 *Wall St. Journal*, Feb. 29, 2024; Israel National News, Feb. 29, 2024; ABC News, Feb.29, 2024.
81 *New York Times*, Feb. 27, 2024; *Jerusalem Post*, Feb. 29, 2024.

CHAPTER 7

Resolution Awaits

Obscurity clouded the first day of March, as Hamas and Israel offered sharply different accounts of a thirty-truck aid convoy to three sections in northern Gaza two days earlier, coordinated and operated by Israel in partnership with local Palestinian businessmen, that ended with the deaths of 115 Palestinians. In the Hamas-Palestinian Authority (PA) narrative, this was "a massacre" and a "heinous crime" by Israeli forces; the IDF claimed that most of the victims were killed in a stampede by several thousands to grab food supplies and by trucks running over them.

In the third stage of delivery, once a large group of Palestinians converged on a few dozen meters away from Israeli soldiers, the military forces fired in the air and issued warnings to stay away. When the same Palestinians continued to come closer to a point where the soldiers felt threatened, they were directed to fire at the Palestinians' legs. During this incident, an estimated ten Palestinians were killed. It was unclear if they had aggressive intentions or were civilians caught up in a chaotic moment. France and the UN called for an immediate cease-fire. At first, the Associated Press and other Western outlets credulously (and falsely) reported the tragedy as an Israeli attack on civilians. Hours after Biden called the incident "tremendously alarming" and the White House called on Israel to investigate what occurred, the United States blocked a UN Security Council resolution blaming Israel for the deaths. The disaster reflected the desperation and spiraling lawlessness in the territory following Israel's ground invasion and threatened, as Biden acknowledged, to derail the ongoing cease-fire talks.[1]

On Saturday, the United States carried out its first airdrop of aid using three C-130 planes, sixty-six aid packages including 38,000 meals, in an operation carried out with the Jordanian air force, while White House spokesperson John Kirby announced that Washington was also discussing a maritime aid route into Gaza with Cyprus, the UN, and commercial firms. A senior Biden administration official said the path to a cease-fire was straightforward, and that the Israelis had "more or less" accepted the deal, which could start today if Hamas released the sick, wounded, elderly, and women hostages. About 1,500 protesters in Kafr Kanna, an Arab town in Israel's northern Galilee, called to end the war in Gaza in a demonstration organized by Israel's Higher Arab Monitoring Committee. The UN agency for gender equality, UN Women, urged an immediate humanitarian cease-fire, calling the war in Gaza "a war on women."

Three Israeli soldiers were killed and fourteen wounded, six in serious condition, in a booby-trapped building in Khan Younis. Two days earlier, three terrorists, including a PA policeman, had murdered two Israelis near the Eli settlement on Route 60 before being killed. The IDF claimed responsibility for eliminating with a drone strike three travelers in southern Lebanon, adding that the men were part of the Imam Hossein Division, affiliated with Iran and operating on behalf of Hezbollah. The *MV Rubymar*, a UK-owned ship attacked by Yemen's Houthi rebels in February, sank after days of taking on water, the first to be sunk by the Houthis since the start of their assaults on shipping in the Red Sea.[2]

The IDF carried out an extensive wave of airstrikes on Sunday in the Rafah area, including near the Philadelphi Corridor. The negotiations for a Gaza hostage and cease-fire deal were near collapse, Israeli media reported, after Hamas refused to provide information on the status of the remaining hostages in the Strip. Defense Minister Gallant declared to troops of the 98th Division at the Gaza border "We will not end this war until we eliminate Hamas." US Vice President Kamala Harris sharply rebuked Israel for not doing enough—"no excuses"—to ease a "humanitarian catastrophe" in Gaza, and she urged Hamas to accept the release of all hostages in return for a six-week cessation of hostilities just when the Biden administration faced increasing pressure in a presidential election year from left-leaning voters to rein in Israel while the IDF waged war with Hamas.

Israel began taking steps to test the rule of local Gazan clans in the Gaza Strip after Hamas would be destroyed, according to a report by London-based Arabic newspaper *Asharq Al-Awsat*, COGAT's Major General Ghassan Alian seeking to organize the protection of the humanitarian aid convoys by local armed groups. The sources further claimed that the Hamas leadership decided to take action against such groups and that they "will pay for their actions." Hamas officials also criticized the US parachuting aid into Gaza on Saturday, saying that it was a cover for continued US support for Israel's offensive.[3]

On March 4, day 150 of the war, while Israeli forces conducted one of its largest Ramallah operations in a six-hour overnight raid and the IDF arrested thirteen suspects throughout the West Bank, Hamas official in Beirut Osama

Hamdan called on Palestinians across the Middle East to "turn every day into a day of clashes" during Ramadan. A mission team led on a trip through Israel by the UN Special Representative of the Secretary-General on Sexual Violence in Conflict, Pramila Patten, found substantial evidence to conclude that both hostages and survivors of October 7 were sexually abused and raped by Hamas terrorists. She, therefore, called on Hamas to "immediately and unconditionally release all individuals held in captivity and to ensure their protection, including from sexual violence." A thirty-year-old Thai worker was killed and seven Indian nationals wounded by a Hezbollah anti-tank missile in Israel's Upper Galilee. Senior Biden Mideast adviser Amos Hochstein visited Beirut and warned that a Gaza truce would not automatically trigger calm in southern Lebanon, adding that the Middle East could not contain a "limited war" there.[4]

Biden told the *New Yorker* he was hoping to see a significant reduction in the use of force by Israel in Gaza. Biden declared he understood the rage sparked by October 7, "but you can't let the rage consume you to the point where you lose the moral high ground." He later said that the humanitarian aid "flowing into Gaza is nowhere near enough." In the interview, Biden stated that when he had asked members of the Israeli War Cabinet to be cautious on the battlefield, members of the cabinet answered him "America carpet-bombed Germany in the Second World War." Biden responded, "That's why we ended up with the United Nations and all these rules about not doing that again." Regarding the October 7 massacre, he commented: "Hamas and Putin represent different threats, but they share this in common—they both want to completely annihilate a neighboring democracy." Nine Republican Senators wrote to the US president calling on him to rescind Executive Order 14115 imposing sanctions on settlers and National Security Memorandum 20 "undermining Israeli operations against Hamas in Gaza," which "undercut our most valuable alliance in the Middle East. We call on you to sanction terrorists and their supporters instead of their victims."

Israel recognized 19,407 of the country's children as victims of terrorism since October 7 according to a report by the National Council for the Child. The figures recorded children, thirty-seven percent of them under the age of six, who suffered physical or psychological injuries. According to Israel's *Bituach Leumi* (social security) agency, the number of the country's civilian casualties since October 7 had risen to 806, and almost 62,000 people were now defined as victims of the hostilities, meaning that they had been impacted physically and/or mentally due to the war or terrorism. The IDF dead in the war to date reached 586, 246 of these in the Gaza campaign. The Hamas-controlled Health

Ministry in Gaza said that at least 30,534 Palestinians had been killed and 71,920 had been wounded since the start of the war.[5]

US Secretary of State Blinken, while declaring that the question of whether there would be a new six-week cease-fire in Gaza was "in the hands of Hamas right now," called on Israel on March 5 "to maximize every possible means, every possible method" to increase aid to Gaza, calling the situation for civilians "unacceptable and unsustainable." Vice-President Harris echoed the second part of this message in a talk with Israeli war cabinet minister Gantz. For his part, Netanyahu's political foe—his visit to Washington not sanctioned by the Israeli government—stressed in meetings with Biden administration officials the importance of removing the threat of Hamas, finding a way to distribute humanitarian aid to Gazans, and acting "today" to "establish an international administration" there, in coordination with regional states, as part of the normalization process. "Ending the war without clearing out Rafah," Gantz told National Security Council advisor Jake Sullivan, "is like sending a firefighter to extinguish 80 percent of the fire." As Meir Ben-Shabbat, Israel's former National Security Advisor, Chief of Staff for National Security, and past head of the Southern Region in the General Security Service, just pointed out in *Yisrael Hayom*, Hamas's Rafah brigade, with its four battalions, had yet to be dismantled; the combat-worthiness of Hamas's top brass and rank and file were intact; and the scale of damage to the tunneling infrastructure and weapons was hard to assess, but it was premature to declare them destroyed.[6]

At home, Netanyahu, overruling Minister of National Security Ben-Gvir, said Israel would do "everything to maintain freedom of worship" at the Al-Aqsa Mosque during Ramadan. Bassem Naim, a senior Hamas leader, told Agence France-Presse in Cairo that since "there are prisoners [sic] held by numerous groups in multiple places" across the Gaza Strip, "a ceasefire is necessary so that we can carry out [checks] on the fate of the prisoners . . . regarding the names, numbers and their status whether alive or dead." The IDF completed a two-week-long clearance operation in the southern Gaza City district of Zeitoun, including the capture of eighty terror suspects attempting to hide among the civilian evacuees from western Khan Younis. At night, twenty-one wanted suspects were arrested in the West Bank. Hezbollah's attacks on Israeli territory were pushing Jerusalem towards a "critical point" in its decision-making process regarding a possible operation against that terrorist group, Gallant told senior White House envoy Hochstein during a meeting in Tel Aviv on Tuesday. The Shin Bet announced that it had thwarted a plot by terrorists in the Hebron area to carry out a bombing attack inspired by ISIS against Israeli forces last month. Foreign Ministry spokesman Lior Haiat wrote on X that the European

Commission's move on Friday to pay fifty million euros to UNRWA prior to completion of a probe into its links with Hamas and the October 7 attack "legitimizes the involvement of UNRWA workers in terrorist activities and cooperation with Hamas."[7]

The next day, Israel National News reported that Brigadier General Amit Sa'ar, head of the investigations department in the IDF Intelligence Corps, wrote a serious warning that was supposed to have been sent to Netanyahu and the Political Security Cabinet after the holiday of Simchat Torah regarding a possible Hamas attack. These warnings were written on the eve of October 7 and made their way to the head of the Intelligence Corps and to the Chief of Staff. The two approved the delivery of the letter to the prime minister, but the October 7 massacre took place before the letter could be sent. Over the past year, the Intelligence Corps had sent four such letters, with the last one having been sent in July. The Intelligence Corps claimed that politicians either ignored the letters or viewed them with suspicion. Kan TV reported that Sa'ar warned in the letter that Iran, Hamas, and Hezbollah believed they had an opportunity to attack Israel, according to intelligence the IDF had collected. He stated that the opportunity in question stemmed from the internal conflicts in Israel and the IDF's preparedness at the time. He also added that senior officials in Iran believed that the time for attacking Israel and causing it critical damage had finally arrived.[8]

Washington condemned the Israeli cabinet's approval of approximately 3,500 new housing units in Ma'aleh Adumim, Efrat, and Kedar. "Settlements continue to be a barrier to peace. Settlements continue to be inconsistent with international law," the US State Department's Matthew Miller told reporters on March 6. "These settlements don't just harm the Palestinian people, but they ultimately weaken Israel's security and weaken the prospects for a lasting agreement that would provide real peace and real security for the Israeli people," he added. In response to a question about the vote in the Knesset on February 21 in which 99 MKs out of 120 voted to reject unilateral attempts to impose an Palestinian state on Israel by international actors, Miller replied, "We are focusing our diplomatic efforts on that, not just because we think it's in the interests of the Palestinian people, but because we think it is in Israel's short, medium, and long-term security interests as well."[9]

A six-week cease-fire was possible if Hamas agreed to release the "sick, wounded, elderly and women" hostages, the White House stated after NSC advisor Sullivan met with Qatari Prime Minister Mohammed Al-Thani. Yet Hamas sources said negotiations with Israel on a hostage release/cease-fire deal were on the verge of collapse because Israel had not agreed to meet its demands, including a total cease-fire, retreat from Gaza, and returning displaced Gazans to their homes in the north of the Strip. British Foreign Minister David Cameron told parliament that Israel's handling of aid for Gaza, "as the occupying power" (*sic*!), raised questions over its compliance with international law. At the same time, an Israeli N12 TV investigation disclosed that unlike most Gazans for whom the $6,000–$7,000 charge per person to enter Egypt past the Rafah Crossing was "an unattainable fantasy," Hamas relatives could easily do so. These included Sinwar's nieces and nephews, two children of the Hamas police spokesman Ayman Al-Batanji, and the four children of Sameh Elsraj, a member of Hamas's political bureau. Hamas denied a UN report finding Palestinian terrorists committed "sexual violence" during their attack on Israel on October 7, saying it was based on "false claims." All the while, IDF troops operating in the Khan Younis area arrested about 250 Hamas and PIJ fighters, and killed Nukhba forces and other terrorists who were involved in the Nir Yitzhak massacre on October 7. One Israeli soldier was killed in the southern Gaza Strip fighting and thirteen wounded, five seriously.[10]

Hamas leader Haniyeh, living a life of comfort in Qatar, accepted the proposed deal for a six-week cease-fire in exchange for the release of Israeli hostages, but Sinwar rejected it, the *Wall Street Journal* reported. Diplomatic sources in Israel said on March 7 that Sinwar "wants to bring Israel, on Ramadan, to bloodshed and worldwide condemnation, and prefers to ignite the field instead of ensuring humanitarian aid and allowances for Gazan citizens." According to deputy Khalil Al-Hayyan, Sinwar demanded a cessation of the war in Gaza for one week before the hostages were released, as well as Israel's complete withdrawal from Gaza and international guarantees that the Israeli forces would not return to the area. The terror group would also not provide the information on which hostages will be released or their conditions, and the Israeli hostages would be released in stages.[11]

In Gaza, the IDF destroyed Hamas infrastructure and weaponry in Khan Younis's Hamed neighborhood, including Hamas's headquarters. An Israeli airstrike in the central Strip eliminated Omar Atiya Daruish Aladdiny, a senior Hamas figure who had been involved with the terror group for decades. In addition to organizing preparations for the October 7 invasion, he also was responsible for embedding the organization's rocket operations in the central Gaza Strip since the 2008–2009 conflict between Israel and Hamas. Overnight, twenty-nine terrorist suspects were arrested in Judea and Samaria, while the IDF responded to rocket fire from Syria toward the Golan Heights by striking two Syrian Army sites in southern Syria, just six miles from the Israeli-Syrian border—a significant escalation in the region. The United States had quietly approved and delivered more than 100 separate foreign military sales to Israel since the Gaza war began October 7, the *Washington Post* reported the previous day, citing comments made by US officials to members of Congress in a recent classified briefing. The sales included thousands of precision-guided munitions, small diameter bombs, bunker busters, small arms and other lethal aid. At the same time, State Department spokesman Matthew Miller accused Israeli ministers of being an "obstacle" to Gaza aid.[12]

In his State of the Union address that evening, Biden turned to some family members, present in the chamber, of hostages who were still being held in Gaza, and pledged "to all the families that we will not rest until we bring all of your loved ones home." "Hamas could end this conflict today by releasing the hostages, laying down arms, and surrendering those responsible for October 7th," he went on, stressing that Israel had the right to go after Hamas but also "has an added burden" since Hamas hid behind civilians. Israel had a "fundamental responsibility" to protect civilians in Gaza, the president said, adding, "This war has taken a greater toll on innocent civilians than all previous wars in Gaza combined"; accepting the Hamas casualty figure of more than 30,000 dead, he called the situation "heartbreaking." In his harshest criticism to date of Netanyahu's government, Biden then declared: "To the leadership of Israel, I say this: Humanitarian assistance cannot be a secondary consideration or a bargaining chip. Protecting and saving innocent lives has to be a priority." He then announced that the US military would lead an emergency mission to establish a temporary pier in the Mediterranean on the coast of Gaza that could receive large shipments carrying food, water, medicine and temporary shelter. "No U.S. boots will be on the ground," he announced, and "Israel must allow more aid into Gaza and ensure humanitarian workers aren't caught in the crossfire."[13]

The European Commission, Germany, Greece, Italy, the Netherlands, the Republic of Cyprus, the United Arab Emirates, the United Kingdom, and the United States announced they were opening a maritime corridor to deliver aid by sea to Gaza. Israel's Foreign Ministry welcomed the decision, although sources in the defense echelon said in closed conversations that so long as the humanitarian convoys entering Gaza by truck or by sea were not secured by armed sources unaffiliated with Hamas, the looting would not end, *Yisrael Hayom* reported. A senior Israeli defense official asserted during a briefing that, contrary to Biden's charge of Jerusalem using aid as "a bargaining chip," most of the food that Israel had been sending into the Strip had "immediately been taken by Hamas terrorists, who then sold some of the supplies for ten times more than what it's worth." An IDF investigation reported to Chief of Staff Halevi that Israeli forces did not fire on Thursday at the humanitarian convoy itself, "but at a number of suspects who approached the nearby forces and who posed a threat to them." Relatives of Israelis held captive by Hamas blocked the main Jerusalem-Tel Aviv highway by locking themselves in cages placed on the road and torching tires. They said their actions were to remind the prime minister and the Israeli public that "the hostages have been rotting in hell for 154 days" and told Netanyahu: "Bring home those you abandoned." The UN Human Rights Office said that an Israeli offensive in Rafah could not be allowed to happen because it would cause a "massive loss of life."[14]

Early Saturday morning, after a half-hour warning to tenants of the Al-Masri residential twelve-floor building in Rafah, the Israeli Air Force struck the tower landmark, which the IDF claimed was a Hamas command center from which attacks were to be launched against Israel. In a statement summarizing its operations in Gaza over the past day, the Israeli military said that it had conducted arrests, located weapons, and killed over thirty fighters in Khan Younis, including in the Hamad area, in central Gaza, and in the area of Beit Hanoun in the north. The Mossad, Israel's national intelligence agency, charged that Hamas was seeking to escalate tensions ahead of Ramadan, rather than a hostage deal, at the expense of Palestinians in the Gaza Strip. The US Central Command (CENTCOM) carried out another humanitarian airdrop into Gaza, in which C-130s dropped over 41,400 US meal equivalents and 23,000 bottles of water into northern Gaza, even as its forces conducted a self-defense strike against two Houthi anti-ship missiles and shot down fifteen unmanned aerial vehicles fired by the Yemen-based group.[15]

Biden's growing frustration at this point with Netanyahu could not be mistaken. Twenty minutes after the US Chief Executive finished delivering the State of the Union address on Thursday night, he was caught on a hot mic telling Secretary Blinken, Senator Michael Bennett (D., Colorado), and Secretary of Transportation Pete Buttigieg that Netanyahu must have a "come to Jesus" experience.[16] Two days later, in a wide-ranging interview with MSNBC News, he said "you cannot have 30,000 more Palestinians dead as a consequence of going after Hamas—there's other ways." Warning in sharper criticism that Netanyahu was currently "hurting Israel more than helping" by not working hard enough to protect civilian lives in Gaza—"It's contrary to what Israel stands for and I think it's a big mistake"—Biden added this: a Rafah operation by the Israeli military would cross "a red line," although he would not abandon this ally or cut off weapons. Concomitantly, Vice President Harris said in an interview with CBS News that "It's important to distinguish between the Israeli government and the Israeli people. The Israeli people are entitled to security, as are the Palestinians."[17]

Netanyahu lost little time in responding to Biden's criticism, asserting in a Politico TV interview that his policies were supported by the overwhelming majority of Israelis. They supported the action the government was taking to destroy the remaining terrorist battalions of Hamas, he continued, and that once the IDF destroyed Hamas, the last thing we should do is put the Palestinian Authority in charge of Gaza, an entity that educated its children towards terrorism and paid for terrorism. Furthermore, the Israeli public also supported his position that "resoundingly" rejected "the attempt to ram a Palestinian state down our throats." It also was in the interest of Israel, he added, because the majority of Israelis understood that if the government did not do this, Israel would have a repetition of the October 7 massacre, which was bad for Israel, bad for the Palestinians, and bad for the future of peace in the Middle East. The vast majority of Israelis, he ended, was "united as never before." "They understand what's good for Israel. They understand what's important for Israel. And I think they're right."[18]

As for Netanyahu's claims, an Israel Democracy Institute poll, released the same day, indicated a division between Jewish and Arab Israelis regarding the conduct of the war. Approximately seventy-five percent of Jewish respondents supported expanding the operation in Rafah in order to pressure Hamas to agree to a more advantageous deal to release the hostages. Approximately sixty percent of Arab respondents favored refraining from this, so as not to endanger relations with Egypt or the emerging deal to release the hostages. The majority of Israelis opposed a prisoner exchange deal that would include ending the fighting and releasing all security prisoners in Israeli prisons.

According to the survey, 25 percent of the Jewish public suspected that such a deal would be incorrect, and 35.1 percent were sure that it would be incorrect. Additionally, 21.1 percent of the Jewish public responded that such a deal would be correct, and 10.4 percent said they were sure that such a deal would be correct. However, 57.8 percent of the Arab public were sure that such a deal would be correct, and 20.7 percent suspected that such a deal would be correct. Another 7.5 percent of the Arab public suspected that such a deal would be incorrect, and 3.8 percent were sure that such a deal would be incorrect. In total, 51.8 percent of Israelis were against such a deal, as opposed to 39.5 percent who supported it. On a related note, 730 Israeli academics called on their government to "take urgent measures to prevent starvation in the Gaza Strip" before "the humanitarian catastrophe gets out of control, causes mass death and becomes an indelible stain."[19]

As for Israel's mounting conflict with Hezbollah, with thirty-seven rockets in two barrages from Lebanon fired in one day at the Mt. Meron area in northern Israel, IDF Northern Command chief Maj. Gen. Ori Gordin, at a meeting with the regional councils Mateh Asher and Ma'ale Yosef security coordinators, declared "We are constantly preparing for an offensive in Lebanon." Three days earlier, according to a report from the Hezbollah-affiliated *Al Akhbar* newspaper, the Israeli government had given March 15 as the deadline for a diplomatic resolution having Hezbollah forces withdraw north of the Litani River or face military escalation.

The IDF's Home Front Command, Israel National News reported on March 10, undertook an operation over the last few weeks to install protective measures for tens of thousands of Israelis in the north who did not otherwise have access to a bomb shelter. As the IDF practiced delivering supplies in the area from the air and on the ground in the event of war, leaders of the northern communities demanded from Netanyahu that if any agreement were signed to prevent a war with Hezbollah, only Israel would be responsible for ensuring that Hezbollah could not come near the border. They also demanded that the government provide a clear timetable for getting schools open in the north in the coming school year and provide a five-year development and growth plan in the amount of NIS 3 billion per year.[20]

Nor did quiet reign in the West Bank. Palestinian gunmen set off an improvised explosive device near IDF troops in the town of Silat ad-Dhahr two days earlier, wounding seven soldiers. Following intelligence provided by the Shin Bet on a major suspect's whereabouts, troops of the Duvdevan commando unit and Border Police officers raided the northern village Silat al-Harithiya in the Jenin Governorate and killed him. According to defense authorities, Muhammad Shalabi had been involved in advancing "significant terror activity" on behalf of Palestinian Islamic Jihad, including shooting attacks, preparing explosive devices, and delivering funds for terrorism. Troops also detained nine more wanted Palestinians during overnight raids across the West Bank.

Since October 7, the IDF troops had arrested some 3,500 wanted Palestinians across the West Bank, including more than 1,500 affiliated with Hamas. The Haifa District Court indicted seven men, most of them residents of Sakhnin in northern Israel, for involvement in planning terror attacks in Israel. Members of the squad purchased weapons from a West Bank resident. The group's leader was in contact with Hamas in Gaza and was taught how to prepare explosives. Some of the suspects were also found to have participated in throwing Molotov cocktails at the town of Eshbal, near Sakhnin, during Operation Guardian of the Walls in May 2021.[21]

Uncertainty persisted on Monday. An IDF attack in Rafah would not happen anytime soon, Israeli officials told CNN, as the IDF was not yet prepared and had not completed plans to evacuate civilians, which was expected to take at least two weeks. They also said the Israeli cabinet had not yet approved plans for the attack. Nor was it clear who would distribute aid reaching Gaza by sea, Hamas sources and clan leaders in Gaza told *Haaretz*, adding that even after five months of fighting, only Hamas had the capability to oversee the process, and that no other organization, including UNRWA or the Red Cross, was currently capable of conducting such a large operation. A Hamas-linked website warned Palestinians against co-operating with Israel to secure aid convoys, saying those who did would be treated as collaborators and be handled with "an iron fist." Israel's government had not explained how it would find a replacement for UNRWA despite requests from the IDF, which suggested that the UN World Food Programme, that had taken about half of food deliveries in Gaza, could take on an even larger and decisive role as to food security in the future.[22]

The United States was trying to broker a six-week cease-fire deal in Gaza that would allow for the release of forty hostages as well as Palestinian Arab prisoners being held in Israel, CIA director William Burns testified to a Senate hearing on Monday. This was critical to addressing the "massive humanitarian crisis" in the enclave, he stated, with the reality that "there are children who are starving." Under questioning, Burns replied that he understood "Israel's need to respond" to the attack by Hamas, "but I think we all also have to be mindful of the enormous toll this has taken on innocent civilians in Gaza." "Israel's war against Hamas has shown the difficulty of using military force alone to eradicate a non-state actor imbedded in a civilian population, especially one that has been so adept at using underground tunnels," he said. "I worry," Burns concluded, "that Netanyahu's conduct in the war threatens to undermine support for Israel in the long-term including in the United States. This international support has been key to Israel's security." Netanyahu told Fox News that the war effort was served by "the extent that the world thinks that America and Israel are united." He also said that he appreciated the support which Biden had given Israel since the start of the war and hoped "it will continue until victory comes." Yet, when asked by reporters that day if he had scheduled a meeting with Netanyahu, Biden replied that he had not. When then asked if he planned to have one soon, he said, "We'll see what happens."[23]

Foreign Minister Israel Katz used a Monday emergency UN Security Council meeting on sexual violence perpetrated by Hamas on and after October 7 to urge that it "must be declared a terrorist organization and face the heaviest sanctions possible." "We are asking you to condemn the sexual violence crimes these barbarians committed in the name of the Muslim religion," Katz declared, while also urging the body "to put as much pressure as possible on the Hamas organization to release immediately and unconditionally all the kidnapped hostages." He also called out the UN for being "silent on Hamas's actions."

The report compiled by UN official Pramila Patten, the first speaker that day, had stated that there was "clear and convincing information" to indicate that hostages held captive in Gaza were subjected to "sexual violence including rape, sexualized torture, cruel, inhuman and degrading treatment," and there were "reasonable grounds" to believe that Hamas terrorists perpetrated rape and gang rape against victims in at least three main locations during their October 7 attack on Israel. At the same time, Patten said that "nothing can also justify the collective punishment of the people in Gaza, which has left tens of thousands of Palestinians killed and injured." Responding to the Russian envoy's blasting the United States and Israel, US Ambassador Linda Thomas-Greenfield, referring to the report's alleging that Palestinian men and women in Israeli prisons faced "increasing instances of various forms of sexual violence," cautioned members against "drawing a false equivalency between these actions and hostage-taking by a foreign terrorist organization. These two things are not the same."

Speaking prior to Katz, Palestinian Authority Ambassador to the UN Riyad Mansour repeatedly castigated Israel throughout his speech but did condemn sexual violence against civilians in general. "We once again reiterate that nothing can justify violence targeting civilians, including sexual violence—one of the most abhorrent forms of violence," Mansour said. He bemoaned the fact that the UN had never held a similar session on allegations of Israeli sexual violence against Palestinians. After the session, Mansour was confronted by Bedouin Ali Ziyadne, whose brother Yousef and nephew Hamza were among the hostages in Gaza. During the filmed exchange, Ziyadne asked Mansour why Hamas had kidnapped his relatives and why the terror group agreed to return Thai nationals while leaving fellow Muslims in the tunnels of Gaza for over five months. "Remember your Muslim brothers and sisters who died in Gaza—30,000 of them along with 75,000 who have been wounded along with the destruction caused [by Israel]," Mansour responded, before reiterating a general condemnation of harming civilians. He also told Ziyadne that he was being taken advantage of by Israeli authorities, who had brought him to the session along with other relatives of the hostages.[24]

Six thousand miles away, the Egoz Commando Unit continued its operations in Khan Younis's Hamad residential complex, where troops had killed several Hamas fighters in recent days. IDF Chief of Staff Halevi issued a disciplinary note to Brigadier General Barak Hiram, commander of Division 99, for ordering the demolition in January of the Israa University compound in southern Gaza City without proper authorization. Speaking with the IDF General

Staff Forum chaired by Halevi, Gallant said that while there had been successes in the last days and going in "the right direction," an apparent reference to the reported assassination in Nusirat by an airstrike of Marwan Issa, deputy to al-Qassam Brigades leader Mohammed Deif and Hamas's third highest-ranked leader in Gaza as the strategist who led Hamas's military directive, "we have to take into account that there may be additional challenges before us—the most pressing of which is in the north."[25]

Responding to incessant rocket attacks from Hezbollah, IAF fighter jets struck deep in Lebanon 100 kilometers from the Israeli border, as well as Hezbollah infrastructure and launching sites in the south of the country. Hezbollah then launched more than 100 rockets at the Golan Heights and the Galilee in response to the strikes in Lebanon's Bekaa Valley and "as a show of support for Palestinians in Gaza"; Israeli retaliatory strikes followed, including at Syrian Army infrastructure from which Hezbollah operated. A Hezbollah official told the Qatari newspaper *Al-Araby Al-Jadid* that the organization was prepared for any expansion of fighting, declaring "we will not be silent about the Israeli attacks in any area of Lebanon, and the response to them will be the stronger."[26]

The next day, Israel National News highlighted that in the annual report on the national security threats facing the United States, presented to Congress on March 11, the US intelligence community had assessed Netanyahu's "viability as a leader" to be "in jeopardy." "Distrust of Netanyahu's ability to rule has deepened and broadened across the public from its already high levels before the war, and we expect large protests demanding his resignation and new elections," according to the report. "A different, more moderate government is a possibility." While noting that the Israeli population broadly supported the destruction of Hamas, the assessment warned that Israel would probably face lingering armed resistance from Hamas for years to come, and its military would struggle to neutralize Hamas's underground infrastructure, "which allowed insurgents to hide, regain strength, and surprise Israeli forces." It also added that both Al-Qaeda and ISIS had been inspired by Hamas, and "have directed their supporters to conduct attacks against Israeli and U.S. interests."[27]

The stakes were getting exponentially higher with every passing minute as multitudes sought to enter Al-Aqsa during Ramadan. Two days earlier, marking the start of the Islamic holy month, Biden had issued the following statement: "As Muslims gather around the world over the coming days and weeks to break their fast, the suffering of the Palestinian people will be front of mind for many. It is front of mind for me." He then added; "This year, it comes at a moment of immense pain. The war in Gaza has inflicted terrible suffering on the Palestinian people. More than 30,000 Palestinians have been killed, most of them civilians, including thousands of children."[28]

Tensions were bound to run high during this fraught time. Even in quieter years, Al-Aqsa Mosque was a Ramadan tinderbox, clashes there a repeated flash point for war. In 2021, fighting between Border Police and Palestinians during Ramadan sparked a two-week escalation with Hamas fifty miles away in Gaza. An Israeli police raid last spring to clear protesters who had locked themselves inside ignited a second round of fighting. Last year, the Ramadan crowd totaled about 1.4 million. On one peak Friday, the compound had hosted more than 300,000 worshipers. Jordan's Foreign Minister Ayman Safadi warned that restrictions imposed now by Israel on Muslim worshippers was pushing the situation towards an "explosion."

Fully aware of Hamas's exhortation that East Jerusalem and West Bank Arabs converge there to protect the Mosque, Israeli police prevented hundreds of young Palestinians from entering the Al-Aqsa compound for the first prayer on Sunday evening. Jerusalem District commander Doron Turgeman, commenting on a situation assessment, announced: "We are entering a complex Ramadan, and I feel certain that along with you, it is clear to all of us that Hamas is trying as hard as possible to create significant escalation, especially in Jerusalem." Gantz declared that, as had been shown in the brutal attacks on October 7, "the Hamas murderers want to see the month of Ramadan turn from a month of prayers into a month of blood. But this is not our path. I know that they do not represent the absolute majority of the Arab citizens of Israel."[29]

Addressing the American Israel Public Affairs Committee (AIPAC) conference delegates in Washington, D.C., on March 12 via a video link, Netanyahu declared "Israel will win this war, no matter what," adding that "in order to win this war we must destroy Hamas's remaining terrorist brigades in Rafah." The international community must stop applying double standards when it comes to IDF actions during the Hamas-Israel war, he charged. "To our friends in the international community, I say: You cannot support Israel's right to defend itself, and then object to Israel's actions, when it exercises that right." Perhaps hinting at Biden, Netanyahu added, "You cannot say that you support Israel's goal of destroying Hamas, and then oppose Israel when it takes the necessary actions to achieve that goal." The prime minister continued, "You can't say you oppose Hamas's strategy of using civilians as human shields, and then blame Israel for the civilian casualties that are the result of Hamas's strategy." He concluded, "Our victory is within reach. I know that the vast majority of the American people stand with us."[30]

For the first time, a small barge carrying almost 200 tons of food to Gaza, enough for nearly half a million meals, left a port in Larnaca, Cyprus, that Tuesday, pulled across choppy waters by a tugboat. Separate from an initiative announced the past week by Biden, the shipment was funded and operated by José Andrés's World Central Kitchen, with a crew from Spanish NGO Open Arms in partnership with the United Arab Emirates (UAE), Cyprus, and Open Arms. Senior UN officials welcomed the opening by the United States and other nations of a maritime corridor from Cyprus to deliver additional aid to the Strip but said it could not replace the delivery of humanitarian assistance by land. "For aid delivery at scale, there is no meaningful substitute to the many land routes and entry points from Israel into Gaza. The land routes from Egypt, Rafah in particular, and Jordan also remain essential to the overall humanitarian effort," said UN Humanitarian and Reconstruction Coordinator for Gaza Sigrid Kaag and UN Office for Project Services (UNOPS) Executive Director Jorge Moreira da Silva. "The maritime corridor brings, however, much needed additionality and is part of a sustained humanitarian response to provide aid as effectively as possible through all possible routes," they added. The same afternoon, the Pentagon announced that three US Army vessels departed for the Gaza coast, beginning the process of building a floating dock there with the 7th Transportation Brigade and other units.[31]

The same day, Jerusalem permitted a convoy of six trucks carrying food to enter northern Gaza directly from an Israeli crossing for the first time since the war began, as global pressure intensified to let more desperately needed aid into the territory. This constituted part of a pilot program to test new ways to deliver aid without Hamas taking control of it, COGAT announced. The IDF had recently completed the division of Gaza into northern Gaza and southern Gaza, paving an east-west road which began near Kibbutz Be'eri and ended at Gaza's beach. It provided a direct path to northern Gaza, instead of the trucks driving through Gaza from south to north. According to Reuters, the aid was passed through the UN World Food Programme and would reach about 25,000 Gazans.[32]

As a *Wall Street Journal* report observed, the flight with aid supplies on a C-130 transport plane from Jordan to the Gaza Strip on Sunday had taken two hours, cost roughly $30,000, and needed nine experienced crew members. Its 3.2-ton payload was barely enough to feed 4,000 people in the besieged territory, where almost the entire population of 2.2 million was now in urgent need of lifesaving assistance according to the United Nations and nonprofit relief groups. Even the biggest airdrops rarely matched the 16.5 tons of aid that just one typical truck carried into Gaza from Egypt at less than one-tenth of the cost. Before the war, Gaza had relied on an average of 500 truck deliveries a day. Israel's promising offer of the new direct truck route to northern Gaza might have some tie to the IDF's evacuation, following the German Embassy's request, of sixty-eight Palestinian children, along with eleven caretakers, from an orphanage in Rafah to Bethlehem in the West Bank as part of a temporary humanitarian operation approved by Israel.[33]

And the war raged on. Officers from the Jerusalem District Police and Border Police, in a special operation overnight in the Shuafat neighborhood in east Jerusalem and Anata on the outskirts of the city, arrested twenty-three suspects for their alleged involvement in violent riots and attempts to harm security personnel. Twelve-year-old Rami Hamdan al-Halhuli was critically injured and later died of his injuries after being shot by a police officer during violent disturbances in that neighborhood on Tuesday evening. The police said the boy was fired upon because he shot fireworks directly at the officers who were operating at the scene. The disturbances in Shuafat lasted for many hours, with the rioters also hurling firebombs and explosives at the forces. Border Police officers shot five Palestinians who were planning to throw Molotov cocktails at a road near the West Bank urban settlement Givat Ze'ev. Wednesday morning, two people were slightly injured in a stabbing attack on Route 60 at the "Tunnel Checkpoint" at the entrance to Jerusalem; the terrorist was killed.

Early on Wednesday afternoon, the IDF said that an airstrike in the area of Tyre had eliminated Hadi Ali Mustafa, a significant operative in Hamas's department responsible for directing terrorist cells and activities in the field, and advancing terror attacks against Israeli and Jewish targets in various countries around the world. An IDF jet precisely targeted and eliminated in an UNRWA warehouse a terrorist in Hamas's Operations Unit in the area of Rafah, Muhammad Abu Hasna. A joint IDF and Shin Bet statement noted his involvement in "integrating extensive activity of the various Hamas units," and that he was also tasked with a Hamas intelligence war room that had collected information on IDF movements in the Strip.[34]

Israel had yet to launch a full-scale war on Hezbollah, Yonah Jeremy Bob explained in the *Jerusalem Post*, because the "mutual interests of both sides" were to avoid a general war at present. Furthermore, each of the adversaries consistently declared publicly that it wished to avoid a widespread conflict. Since October 7, escalation by one and retaliation by the other had been carried out in a measured way, leading to de-escalation. Even 100 rockets from Hezbollah did not compare to the 8,000 rockets per day that it could potentially fire on Israel, including hitting strategic areas of Tel Aviv, Haifa, and Ben-Gurion Airport. Even when hitting the higher-ranking Hezbollah officials and

Baalbek deep in Lebanon three times in the last month, the IDF had carefully avoided killing larger numbers of Hezbollah forces and key symbols of its rule in Beirut. The 330 Hezbollah terrorists Israel had killed were nothing compared to the likely 14,000 Hamas forces it had killed. And Israel had not tried to invade southern Lebanon with ground forces in any way.

In addition, the newspaper's senior military correspondent observed, both the IDF and Hezbollah had achieved much of their objectives. The IDF had moved around 90 percent of Hezbollah's elite Radwan forces north of the Litani River and destroyed around 100 percent of Hezbollah's lookout posts on the border. Hezbollah had said it would stop firing when Israel and Hamas agreed to a cease-fire, so, if a cease-fire occurred next week, Israel would have most of what it wanted. Likewise, Hezbollah wanted to show the region that it could bleed Israel. It did so. Over 80,000 Israelis had to evacuate the North, and over 50,000 were still evacuated five months later. The Iran-proxy group had managed to maintain rocket fire on Israel for five months without being forced to stop. Israel would like all the Radwan forces permanently expelled from southern Lebanon and Hezbollah would like to have lost fewer assets, but no one, Bob concluded, "expects to achieve everything they want in war."[35]

On March 14, day 160 of the war, Hamas called on the Palestinians in the West Bank and Jerusalem, as well as Arab citizens of Israel, "to be alert and ready to defend the Al-Aqsa Mosque" and "remain there days and nights." The White House said the United States "does not want to see [Israeli] operations in Rafah unless there is a credible, legitimate, executable plan to provide for the safety and security of the civilians that are there." It would be willing to support a limited Israeli offensive focused on eliminating Hamas's leadership as long as Israel did not launch a full-scale invasion, Politico reported, adding that senior Biden administration officials had relayed this message to their Israeli counterparts. The IDF said it planned to direct a significant portion of the 1.4 million displaced Gazans in Rafah toward "humanitarian islands" in the center of the territory, ahead of a planned ground operation in the southernmost Gazan city. As for the northern border threat, the International Fellowship of Christians and Jews announced a $1.5 million-plus initiative to place 123 shelters alongside bus stops serving 42 northern Israeli communities, amid Israel's ongoing conflict with Lebanon's Hezbollah.[36]

For its part, Hamas reportedly killed the leader of the powerful Doghmush clan in Gaza City because the group allegedly had been stealing humanitarian aid and was suspected of having contact with Israel. The murder was also seen as Hamas's wish to reassert its dominance in the northern part of the Strip. Doghmush, a large armed clan that clashed with Hamas in the past and had a history of engaging in organized crime as well as arms trading, led the Army of Islam terror group and was allied with Al-Qaeda. It had kidnapped and held British journalist Alan Johnston from March to July 2007, and was also reportedly involved in the kidnapping of IDF soldier Gilad Shalit in 2006. Despite the recent reports of cooperation with Israel, prominent clans put out a statement to international organizations and Israel saying they still supported Hamas and that their cooperation in distributing aid would only be allowed through the current Hamas channels.[37]

In a sign of growing US pressure on Israel over the war in Gaza, Senate Majority Leader Chuck Schumer, the highest-ranking Jew in American politics, said in a speech that day on the Senate floor "Netanyahu has lost his way by allowing his political survival to take precedence over the best interests of Israel." A "serious obstacle to peace," he had "bowed to the demands of extremists," and his government "no longer fits the needs of Israel after October 7." Warning that "Israel cannot survive if it becomes a pariah" and that it was "testing U.S. standards for assistance," he called for Israeli elections aimed at choosing a new government.[38]

Reacting to Schumer's speech, which made the front page of major US newspapers, Senate Minority Leader Mitch McConnell soon pushed back in strong criticism: "It is grotesque and hypocritical for Americans who hyperventilate about interference in our own democracy to call for the Israeli leader's removal." The primary "obstacles to peace" in Israel's region, he added, "are genocidal terrorists and corrupt Palestinian Authority leaders who repeatedly reject peace deals. Foreign observers who cannot keep this straight ought to refrain from interfering in the democracy of a sovereign ally." While Schumer's speech elicited expected stands from the progressive J Street (pro) and the rightist Zionist Organization of America (con), centrist American Jewish organizations, including the Anti-Defamation League, the American Jewish Committee, the Orthodox Union, Agudath Israel of America, and the Conference of Presidents of Major American Jewish Organizations, concurred with McConnell and other Republican senators, if in measured tones.[39]

Israeli representatives took a sharper tone. Not one to mince words, former Prime Minister Naftali Bennett posted this on X: "Regardless of our political opinion, we strongly oppose external political intervention in Israel's internal affairs. We are an independent nation, not a banana republic. With the threat of terrorism on its way to the West, it would be best if the international community would assist Israel in its just war, thereby also protecting their countries." In interviews on CNN and the "Fox & Friends" morning show, Netanyahu would deem Schumer's calls for his ouster "wholly inappropriate," emphasizing that the Israeli people would decide when elections in Israel were held, and it would not be "foisted on us." "It's wrong to try to replace the elected leaders of a sister democracy, a staunch American ally, at any time, but especially during a time of war," he declared. The Israeli ambassador to the United States, Michael Herzog, resorted to more diplomatic language. "Israel is a sovereign democracy," he asserted. "It is unhelpful, all the more so as Israel is at war against the genocidal terror organization Hamas, to comment on the domestic political scene of a democratic ally. It is counterproductive to our common goals." The same day, the Biden administration issued its second round of sanctions on Israeli settlers, including the first US sanctions on entire outposts in the West Bank.[40]

Brig. Gen. Dan Goldfus, who had been serving in Gaza since October 7 at the head of the IDF's elite 98th Division commandos and took down most of Hamas's toughest Khan Younis Brigade, offered in a press conference a rare officer's critique of the political echelon. He expressed the hope that Israel's political ranks would "one day be worthy" of the army's moral courage. Taking a swipe at "leaders on all sides," Goldfus said he hoped "they can find time to listen to the heart of a warrior." "We do not run away from responsibility," he declared of the October 7 fiasco, "we bow our heads in the face of our resounding failure, but you must be worthy of us." "You must be worthy of those soldiers who sacrificed their lives. Make sure that everyone takes part, that we will not return to October 6, that all the effort was not in vain."

At a time when, according to all polls, Israelis trusted the IDF far more than they trusted the government, domestic public reaction agreed with this high-ranking career officer. "It would be wise for leaders and citizens alike to take Goldfus's appeal to heart," stated a *Jerusalem Post* editorial on March 15: "We all must be worthy of the soldiers who are deep in Gaza, who risk their lives to defeat Hamas and bring our national family members back home. Until that is achieved, politics should be left on the side of the battle road." Meeting on Friday, Halevi told Goldfus that he "used the trust given to him in a way that harmed the dignity of the IDF, and the boundaries between the political and military echelons in a democratic country." Goldfus, according to the IDF, accepted that his remarks ran counter to military protocol and apologized for them.[41]

Hamas's latest proposal through Qatar for a deal to free hostages included several stages, Reuters reported that day, beginning with the release of women (including those Hamas defined as "soldiers"), children, the elderly, and male hostages who were ill, this in exchange for between 700–1,000 Arab terrorists. A discussion would then immediately be started on a permanent cease-fire in Gaza and setting a date for the withdrawal of IDF forces from the Strip, with all the hostages remaining in Gaza to be released in exchange for hundreds and possibly even thousands of terrorists. While the Israeli war cabinet, followed by the full cabinet, would convene on Sunday to discuss Hamas's terms. Netanyahu's office last night poured cold water on the proposal, stating, "Hamas continues making preposterous demands." The proposal came not long after Chief Warrant Officer Uri Moyal, fifty-one years old, died from wounds suffered from repeated stabbings by twenty-two-year-old Fadi Abu Latif, originally from Gaza, at a gas station in the Beit Kama Junction in southern Israel, having first killed his attacker and thus preventing further casualties. That same Thursday, dozens of Palestinians were killed and injured while waiting for humanitarian aid at Gaza's Kuwaiti roundabout, Hamas gunmen firing while they looted the trucks, which also ran over civilians at the scene.[42]

After Biden backed Schumer's call for Israel to replace its government, saying, "He made a good speech" and expressed "serious concerns, shared not only by him but by many Americans," White House advisor John Kirby rejected on Friday assertions that the president was calling for new elections in Israel and for Netanyahu to no longer be in power. "That's going to be up to the Israeli people to decide," he stated. A senior Israeli official told ABC News that the United States had begun slow walking some military aid to Israel, which was running out of 155-mm artillery shells and 120-mm tank shells and required sensitive guidance equipment, an assertion to which Kirby said Washington was continuing to "support Israel with their self-defense needs. That's not going to change, and we have been very, very direct about that." Two days earlier, the Biden administration had renewed a sanctions waiver that granted Iran access to $10 billion in previously escrowed funds. The waiver, which permitted the Islamic Republic to use electricity revenue from Iraq for budget support and debt repayment, came just six weeks after an Iran-backed drone attack by Iraqi militia killed three US soldiers and wounded dozens more on January 28 in Jordan.[43]

The NSC welcomed the appointment of Mohammad Mustafa as the Palestinian Authority's new prime minister, and urged him to form "a reform cabinet as soon as possible." However, Hamas, Palestinian Islamic Jihad, Popular Front for the Liberation of Palestine, and Palestinian National Initiative said they objected to the establishment of a new Palestinian government and to PA chairman Mahmoud Abbas's decision to appoint his economic advisor as its head. Their joint statement declared that "making individual decisions, and engaging in formal steps that are devoid of substance, like forming a new government without national consensus, is a reinforcement of a policy of exclusion and the deepening of division." Not long thereafter, Fatah lashed out at Hamas for "having caused the return of the Israeli occupation of Gaza" by "undertaking the October 7 adventure," which led to a "*Nakba*[44] even more horrible and cruel than the *Nakba* of 1948." "The real disconnection from reality and the Palestinian people is that of the Hamas leadership," Fatah concluded.[45]

Some 50,000 Muslims attended prayers on the first Friday of Ramadan at the Al-Aqsa Mosque under a heavy police presence, with no clashes reported. The next day, the IDF revealed that over the past two weeks in Gaza, the Nahal Brigade, other military units, and the IAF killed hundreds of Hamas operatives in battle, aerial attacks, and tank fire. Leading US senators from both parties lauded Qatar for facilitating hostage negotiations, but warned that "If Hamas refuses reasonable negotiations, there is no reason for Qatar to continue hosting Hamas's political office or any of its members." The first aid ship to Gaza, operated by World Central Kitchen, arrived in the Strip with almost 220 tons of food, just when a UNICEF report declared that about one in every three children under the age of two in northern Gaza suffered from acute malnutrition. According to satellite photos displayed by the *Wall Street Journal*, Israeli forces were carving through farmland and demolishing Palestinian homes and schools in the Strip to create a buffer zone alongside the enclave's border with Israel. a no man's land more than half a mile wide where Israeli troops would be able to see and stop anyone approaching the border. Israeli officials said the exclusion zone was a critical security measure in their plan to demilitarize Gaza and assure Israelis that they could return safely to the towns and communities near the border that were evacuated after the October 7 attack.[46]

On Sunday, Netanyahu reiterated that "no international pressure will stop us from realizing all the goals of the war: eliminating Hamas, freeing all our hostages, and ensuring that Gaza will no longer pose a threat against Israel." "In order to do this, we will also operate in Rafah; it will take a few weeks, and it will happen." "To our friends in the international community," he asked: "Is your memory so short? So quickly did you forget October 7, the most terrible massacre committed against Jews since the Holocaust? So quickly are you ready to deny Israel the right to defend itself against the monsters of Hamas? Did you lose your moral conscience so quickly?" He concluded: "Instead of putting pressure on Israel, which is fighting the most just war, against the cruelest of enemies, direct your pressure against Hamas and its patron—Iran. They are the ones who pose a danger to the region and the entire world." Ophir Falk, a foreign policy advisor to the prime minister, added in an op-ed for the *Wall Street Journal* that the IDF's having already defeated two-thirds of Hamas's battalions and killing or capturing 21,500 terrorists within six months of fighting. presaged that victory in Rafah "was not as far away as it seems." For validation, he quoted

John Spencer, chairman of urban warfare studies at West Point, who described Israel's achievements to date in Gaza as "unprecedented."[47]

Over the past week, the engineering forces of the 162nd Division, in cooperation with the special Yahalom Unit, had destroyed a section of Hamas's longest underground tunnel route located in the northern Gaza Strip. The length of the tunnel measured over two and a half kilometers, crossing battalions and brigades and connecting the northern and southern Strip. Givati Brigade units continued clearing out Hamas in Khan Younis, while the IAF struck a Hezbollah military compound in the area of Al-Khyam in response to missiles fired toward Acre overnight and a Hezbollah observation post in the area of Kafr Kila; IDF artillery struck a site to remove a threat in the area of Maisat. Seven suspects were arrested in West Bank overnight and thirteen during the week.[48]

The large number of civilian casualties that would be caused by an extensive Israeli operation in Rafah would make regional peace "very difficult," German Chancellor Olaf Scholz said after talks with Jordanian King Abdullah. In Israel, meeting with Netanyahu on Sunday, Scholz declared that Israel had the right to defend itself against Hamas, but the West Bank and Gaza belonged to the PA and a Palestinian state had to be acknowledged. Further, "We cannot stand by and watch Palestinians starve." In like vein, European Commission President Ursula von der Leyen stated that Gaza was facing famine and there must be a rapid cease-fire deal between Israel and Hamas. Trucks of flour reached areas of northern Gaza that had received no aid in four months, Palestinian media reported. The Hamas-linked Home Front media outlet announced that the aid was distributed by the "Popular Committees," a group that included powerful clan leaders in Gaza, with security from Hamas personnel.[49]

About 100 family members of abductees in Gaza protested that evening opposite Netanyahu's offices as members of the Israeli cabinet met in Jerusalem and meetings about a cease-fire/hostage exchange went on in Qatar, with another demonstration held near the IDF center in Tel Aviv, both calling for the release of those kidnapped by Hamas. No final decision was arrived at in this regard other than approving the return of the Israeli delegation, headed by Mossad chief David Barnea, to Doha on Monday to discuss a hostage/cease-fire plan—knowing full well that Hamas had broken the earlier four cease-fire agreements. The cabinet unanimously approved the observance of a national day of remembrance to commemorate the October 7 attack and subsequent war. This would be held every year on the 24th of the month of Tishrei in the Jewish calendar, two days after the savage Hamas assault on the country's southern communities near Gaza. The annual memorial would be marked by two state ceremonies on that day to honor the memory of the servicemen and servicewomen who fell in the ongoing war against Hamas and the civilians murdered during Hamas's initial attack.[50]

Early Monday morning, following IDF and ISA intelligence indicating the presence of senior Hamas terrorists in northern Gaza's Al-Shifa hospital, the IDF's Shayetet 13 naval commandos, 401st Armored Brigade, Infantry Division 162, and ISA forces began conducting a four-day "high precision operation" in the compound. More than 140 terrorists would be killed, including Faiq Mabhuoch, head of the Operations Directorate of Hamas's Internal Security and also responsible for the coordination of Hamas terrorist activities in the Gaza Strip, and some 650 Hamas and Palestinian Islamic Jihad members arrested. These included Mahmoud Kwasama, the senior Hamas official responsible for the kidnapping and murder of three Israeli teenagers in 2014, which sparked Operation Protective Edge. The two Israeli casualties were Jerusalem's twenty-year-old Staff Sgt. Matan Vinogradov of the Nahal Brigade's 932nd Battalion and Rosh HaAyin's fifty-one-year-old Sgt. Maj. (res.) Sebastian Haion of the 401st Arrmored Brigade, their deaths bringing the toll of slain troops in the ground offensive against Hamas to 251. In the West Bank, IDF, Shin Bet, and Border Police personnel arrested fourteen wanted individuals overnight, while the Jordan Valley region brigade interrogated many suspects during an operation in Dheisha in Etzion.[51]

Netanyahu had approved plans on Friday for an Israeli military operation in Rafah, where Hamas's final four battalions, comprising roughly 3,000 fighters, were concentrated and where the senior leadership and remaining Israeli hostages were believed to be. The Associated Press quoted IDF spokesman Hagari emphasizing that moving the Palestinian civilians before the expected offensive to designated "humanitarian islands" would be done in coordination with international actors, and with neighboring Egypt to ensure there was no influx of Gazans to the Sinai Peninsula. However, in a sign of the challenges of a Rafah operation to Israel's international standing, Egypt and European leaders agreed on Sunday to reject any military offensive. The Rafah operation "would double the humanitarian catastrophe that civilians in the Gaza Strip are suffering from, in addition to the effects of that operation on liquidating the Palestinian cause, which Egypt outright rejects," Egyptian President Abdel Fattah El-Sisi said at a press conference with European Commission President von der Leyen in Cairo. Washington had told Jerusalem that it could support a limited military operation against "high value" Hamas targets in Rafah. At the same time, American officials estimated that it would take weeks, at least, to complete the evacuation of more than 1,000,000 civilians from Rafah in southern Gaza once the green light was given to the IDF, *Kan News* reported on Monday.[52]

Across Gaza, the number of people facing "catastrophic hunger" had risen to 1.1 million, about half the population, reported the Integrated Food Security Phase Classification, which UN Secretary-General António Guterres declared "the highest number of people facing catastrophic hunger ever recorded" by the initiative in the decade of its operations, "anywhere, anytime." EU foreign policy chief Josep Borrell went far further, charging that Israel was "provoking famine" in Gaza and using starvation as a weapon of war. Israeli foreign minister Katz countered by noting that Jerusalem allowed extensive humanitarian aid into Gaza "despite Hamas violently disrupting aid convoys and UNRWA's collaboration with them," and adding this: "It's time for Borrell to stop attacking Israel and recognize our right to self-defense against Hamas's crimes." Israeli authorities denied permission for the head of UNRWA to enter Gaza, UNRWA and Egypt's foreign minister said, which they called an unprecedented move. The Australian government's decision to renew aid to UNRWA before any independent inquiry into the agency's terror links violated the country's domestic laws, a group of Australian lawmakers said. The parliamentary condemnation came just hours after Canberra announced that it was resuming funding for UNRWA, following similar moves by Sweden, the European Commission, and Canada even before the UN's own investigation of the agency was completed.[53]

In a telephone call on Monday, his first in more than a month, Biden told Netanyahu that Israel lacked a viable military strategy to eliminate Hamas in Rafah and secure the Egypt-Gaza border against arms smuggling, and he warned not to act without approval from Washington. "That strategy should not involve a major military operation that puts thousands and thousands of lives, civilian innocent lives, at risk in Rafah," Biden said. "I am for the defeat of Hamas. I believe that they are an evil terrorist group with not just Israeli, but American blood on their hands," but "there is a better way" than the strategy Israel had outlined. During the call, Netanyahu agreed to send a senior interagency team composed of military intelligence and humanitarian officials to Washington in the coming days to hear US concerns about Israel's current Rafah military plans, NSC advisor Sullivan briefed reporters. He added that Rafah remained a major entry point for goods into Gaza, where "anarchy reigns," and a military operation would complicate that delivery, deepening the "humanitarian crisis."[54]

In Gaza, Maglan and Egoz Unit soldiers continued to operate in the center of the Hamad area and raided dozens of terror targets located inside multi-story buildings. The Nuseirat camp police chief was killed in his car along with three other Hamas operatives in an Israeli airstrike on Tuesday evening. Qatar's foreign ministry said that the sides were not close to a cease-fire deal, but that Doha remained hopeful, and it warned that an Israeli operation in Rafah would set back negotiations and result in major destruction and "atrocities" that have not been seen in the conflict before. Israel filed a request to the International Court of Justice not to issue emergency orders for Jerusalem to step up humanitarian aid to Gaza to address a looming famine, dismissing South Africa's request to do so as "morally repugnant," in view of the "actions it has and is taking" to protect innocent lives in Gaza. Two people were wounded in a shooting attack between the Gush Etzion Junction and Migdal Oz; the terrorist was killed. Oxfam and Human Rights Watch sent a joint memorandum to the Biden administration detailing Israel's alleged violations of humanitarian law—including with US weapons and blocking US-funded humanitarian aid—which they said necessitated the immediate suspension of US arms transfers to Israel. Lebanese academic and political analyst Makram Rabah was detained by local security forces for five hours for criticizing Hezbollah's using the Baalbek region for their operations, which put civilians in danger.[55]

The IDF and Shin Bet announced on March 20 that an airstrike in Rafah earlier this week killed senior officers in Hamas's so-called emergency committee. Sayyid Qutb Hashash, Osama Hamad Dhahir, and Hadi Abu Al-Rous were eliminated, and Muhammad Awad al-Malalhi apparently wounded. The strikes came after the IDF targeted last week Nidal al-Eid, the head of the emergency committee in Rafah, the military added. The Biden administration was expected to suggest to the Israeli delegation heading next week to Washington that the IDF could secure the Philadelphi Corridor between Egypt and Gaza as an alternative to an invasion of Rafah, One of two officials who spoke to the Times of Israel on conditions of anonymity said that the ability to work with Cairo to terminate once and for all the weapons-smuggling routes into Gaza, whether above or below ground, would be more important than a military incursion in achieving Israel's goal of destroying Hamas. Israeli Foreign Minister Katz slammed his Canadian counterpart's decision to stop sending weapons to Israel, saying, "History will judge Canada's current action harshly." Canada's statement underscored the growing criticism of Israel's actions in Gaza. Thus, UK Deputy Prime Minister Oliver Dowden defended Israel's right to protect itself but called for an "immediate cease-fire" in Gaza on humanitarian grounds, while nineteen Senate Democrats urged Biden to "outline a path for the United States to recognize a non-militarized Palestinian state" that would recognize Israel and renounce Hamas.[56]

Dr. Khalil Shikaki, director of Ramallah's Palestinian Center for Policy and Survey Research, published a new survey on Thursday which showed that over 90 percent of "Palestinian" Arabs believed that Hamas did not commit any atrocities against Israel civilians during the October 7 massacre; just one in five had seen videos showing Hamas's atrocities. Those who had viewed the videos were nearly ten times more likely to believe that Hamas committed atrocities on that day. A full 71 percent of respondents believed that the October 7 massacre was a correct action on the part of Hamas. The survey also showed that 38 percent of Gazans expected the war to continue, while over half of those in Judea and Samaria believed that there would be a cease-fire. At the same time, nearly 60 percent of Gazans believed that Hamas would retain control of the area after the war's end; over 50 percent of Gazans supported Hamas's continued rule—a fourteen-point rise from the previous poll. A full 80 percent opposed the idea of Arab countries ruling Gaza from abroad.

Additionally, 70 percent of respondents would support Hamas leader Haniyeh in an election pitting him against Palestinian Authority chief Abbas; if Haniyeh were pitted against the jailed Fatah arch terrorist Marwan Barghouti, a leader of the First and Second Intifadas, Barghouti would win over 60 percent of the vote. Barghouti would also garner a majority if pitted against both Abbas and Haniyeh. The data also showed a clear drop in support for armed resistance as the best means of achieving a Palestinian state from its peak in December. In December, support for armed resistance across the Palestinian Territories was 63 percent, 68 percent in the West Bank and 56 percent in the Gaza Strip. The latest polling showed support for armed resistance at 46 percent across the Palestinian Territories, 51 percent in the West Bank and 39 percent in the Gaza Strip. When asked whether they would support a two-state solution, 60 percent of Gazans responded in the affirmative, compared to 35 percent in the previous poll. Among Arabs in Judea and Samaria, 34 percent said they supported a two-state solution.[57]

Netanyahu told Senate Republicans via cable in a closed meeting on Capitol Hill that even if Israel would have to go into Rafah without US support, his position reflecting the Israeli consensus, "We won't stop." Netanyahu emphasized that Israel was not asking American ground troops "to fight its war," although he did ask for financial help to "finish the job," and urged senators to support whatever bill the House sent them that included billions of dollars in aid for Israel. Schumer denied him the opportunity to similarly speak to Senate Democrats, however, saying he thought "the partisan setting" inappropriate, thereby dramatizing the growing partisan split on Capitol Hill and in American politics over Netanyahu's leadership and Israel's offensive in Gaza. "The bipartisan support for Israel seems to be cracking," Senator McConnell said, making it clear he thought the Democrats were responsible. Subsequently, after Republican House Speaker Mike Johnson said he was ready to invite Netanyahu to address Congress, Schumer's office told JTA that the Democratic

Senate majority leader would support the move: "Israel has no stronger ally than the United States and our relationship transcends any one president or any one prime minister," declared Schumer in the statement. "I will always welcome the opportunity for the Prime Minister of Israel to speak to Congress in a bipartisan way."[58]

The State Department received Israel's required written assurances, ahead of a Sunday deadline, that its use of US-supplied defense equipment did not violate international humanitarian or US human rights law. The department now had until early May to formally assess whether those assurances were "credible and reliable" and report to Congress under a national security memorandum issued by Biden in February. If Israel's pledges were found wanting, the US president had the option at any point of suspending further US arms transfers. In the meantime, the United States, aside from continuing its ban on funding the UN Relief and Works Agency until at least March 2025, drafted a UN resolution to be presented Friday for "an immediate and sustained cease-fire to protect civilians on all sides" and in connection with "the release of all remaining hostages." Calling for "the delivery of essential humanitarian assistance" to Gaza, it also expressed "deep concern about the threat of conflict-induced famine and epidemics." The Biden administration used the resolution as well to state "concern that a ground offensive into Rafah would result in further harm to civilians and their further displacement including potentially into neighboring countries." While condemning Hamas's attack and hostage-taking on October 7, the strong language markedly ran counter to the US veto in February of a Security Council resolution demanding an immediate humanitarian cease-fire, signaling, as the *New York Times* put it, "an apparent shift for Israel's closest ally."[59]

Great Britain, which is considered an ally to Jerusalem, declared that it would no longer sell weapons to Israel unless Israel allowed Red Cross personnel to visit the Nukhba force terrorists being held prisoner for carrying out the October 7 massacre. The ultimatum came on the background of Hamas's continued refusal to allow Red Cross personnel to visit the Israeli hostages. Foreign Minister David Cameron told Israel that if the demand were not met, Britain would support an embargo on arms sales from all of Europe. He also said that a permanent cease-fire in the Gaza Strip was "essential," but stressed that before reaching a permanent cease-fire, we must "get Hamas leaders out of Gaza; we have to dismantle the terrorist infrastructure." "We must try to turn the pause into a permanent cease-fire, which will also allow the release of the hostages." Cameron's declaration appeared the same day that an *Haaretz* exclusive reported that a massive leak of documents revealed how Iran's Shahed-136 missile project, with each drone carrying a $200,000 price tag, had become a lethal weapon in Russia's arsenal for Moscow's war against Ukraine.[60]

On Friday morning, China and Russia, with whom the Houthis reached an agreement not to fire on their ships, vetoed a US-drafted resolution at the UN Security Council, saying the text did not go far enough in calling for a cease-fire in the war against Hamas. Arriving at Ben-Gurion Airport, Blinken, echoing a joint Australia-UK statement, warned Israel that a major IDF operation in Rafah "risks killing more civilians, risks wreaking greater havoc with the provision of humanitarian assistance, risks further isolating Israel around the world, and could jeopardize its long-term security and standing." The IDF, reporting that the second Friday prayers of Ramadan at Jerusalem's Al-Aqsa Mosque had passed without incident, said it opened a new entry point for aid to cross into Gaza and was allowing unlimited supplies. Foreign Minister Katz accused the United Nations of becoming "an antisemitic and terror-supporting entity" after UN Secretary-General António Guterres implied that Israel was guilty of a "moral outrage" over a line of aid trucks sitting at the Egypt-Gaza border that had not been able to enter the Gaza Strip, noting that Guterres did not condemn "the Hamas-ISIS terrorists who plunder humanitarian aid," or UNRWA that "cooperated with terrorists," and did not call for "the immediate, unconditional release of all Israeli hostages."[61]

The IDF's Southern Command Commanding Officer, Yaron Finkelman, announced that to date more than 800 suspects had been questioned and 170 terrorists in the Shifa Hospital and surrounding area eliminated, including Nablus terror leader Amad Atzida and Hamdala Hassan Ali, who had managed much of the terror in the Qalqilya area. The Palestinian Health Ministry reported that Muhammad Hawashin, the commander of Palestinian Islamic Jihad's Jenin Battalion, died of wounds sustained in an IAF strike, and four PIJ operatives were killed following an Israeli airstrike at the Nur al-Shams refugee camp. Some fifty left-wing and Arab-Jewish shared society groups coalesced to launch a campaign for a cease-fire. Named "Peace Partnership," the anti-war coalition made its first public appearance in January in Haifa, with a rally of Arabs and Jews that drew about 500 people. The following protest was held in February in Tira, a town in the majority-Arab "triangle area" in central Israel and drew about 250. On March 9, an International Women's Day event in Taybeh, also in the triangle, was followed by another peace rally in nearby Tira, and showed a similar attendance figure of about 300, twice what the organizers had expected.[62]

Seventeen Senate Democrats warned the Biden administration that Israel did not meet the "credible and reliable" test detailed by a national security memorandum requiring recipients of US weapons to assure unobstructed delivery of humanitarian aid in conflict zones. Relatives of eighty-one hostages held in Gaza wrote to Biden, urging him to "convince all parties, including the Israeli prime minister, to agree to the deal that you assess is reasonable." They cited their frustration over a "lack of ongoing communication and commitment" from Netanyahu and the war cabinet on the hostage release cause. At the same time, a bill passed by the House of Representatives, headed next to the Senate, with several pro-Israel measures, including $3.3 billion in foreign military financing to the Jewish State; $500 million for US-Israel missile-defense cooperation; and $87.5 million in US-Israel counter-drone and anti-tunneling cooperation.[63]

On March 24, day 170 of the war, the IDF's nearly week-long operation at Gaza City's Shifa Hospital continued, with the military saying that among some 800 suspects detained so far, discovered hiding in the medical facility, 480 of them had been confirmed to be members of the Hamas or Palestinian Islamic Jihad terror groups. These included Hasem Zarzur, the governor of Gaza's eastern precinct's emergency board, and Diab Tatar, a senior member of the emergency board of southern Gaza. The military announced the death the previous day of twenty-one-year-old Sgt. First Class Lior Raviv of the Nahal Brigade's 932nd Battalion, bringing the total of soldiers killed to 252 during the ground operation in Gaza. In central Gaza, troops of the Nahal Brigade killed several Hamas gunmen over the past twenty-four hours. Meanwhile, IAF fighter jets struck some sixty-five targets in northern and central Gaza over the previous day. In southern Gaza, the 7th Armored Brigade killed several gunmen with sniper fire, combat engineers destroyed a rocket launcher, and an aircraft struck infrastructure belonging to a terror group. Hezbollah launched fifty missiles into northern Israel following an IDF strike on a terrorist weapons plant in Lebanon.[64]

US-Israeli ties were further strained on Monday, when Security Council Resolution 2728, calling for an immediate cease-fire in Gaza during the remaining two weeks of Ramadan, passed by fourteen votes. Secretary Blinken explained that the United States cast the one abstention—rather than veto—because, while it did not condemn Hamas for the October 7 massacre, the resolution did pair a cease-fire with the release of the Israeli hostages yet in Gaza. The chamber broke into applause after the vote, Palestinian Authority representative Riyad Mansour saying "it has taken over 100,000 Palestinians killed and maimed, two million displaced, and famine for this council to finally demand a ceasefire." Welcoming the resolution by all "working to stop the Zionist aggression and war of annihilation," Hamas called on the Council to pressure Israel to implement a cease-fire. The terrorist movement also said it was ready to engage in "an immediate prisoner exchange process that leads to the release of prisoners on both sides," despite the resolution's requirement that the release of the hostages held by Hamas be conducted "immediately and unconditionally."

In response, Netanyahu called off a trip to Washington by senior Israeli officials to discuss plans for safeguarding Gazan civilians in Rafah ahead of an Israeli ground offensive, his office declaring: "The U.S. has backed down from its consistent stance in the Security Council since the beginning of the war." NSC advisor Kirby said that the abstention did not represent "a change in policy" for the Biden administration, to be viewed "as some sort of escalation." The United States also described the UN resolution as "non-binding," State Department spokesperson Matthew Miller declared. Further, Washington deemed Israel in compliance with the National Security Memorandum stipulating that recipients of US weapons must be in compliance with international law, nor may they block the provision of humanitarian assistance. Israel's UN ambassador retorted, however, that the Council had immediately condemned the ISIS attack at a concert outside of Moscow that killed at least 137 people and wounded more than 180 on Friday night, but still refused to condemn the massacre that Hamas carried out at the Nova music festival in Israel. "This is a disgrace—you discriminate between blood and blood," said Gilad Erdan.[65]

On Monday night, Hamas announced that it had decided to reject the new proposal for a deal to release hostages. Its official statement announced that "a short time ago we informed the mediators that the organization sticks to its position that was conveyed on March 14. Israel's response did not meet any of our basic demands—a comprehensive cease-fire, withdrawal from the Gaza Strip, the return of the displaced and an exchange of prisoners." "Netanyahu and his extremist government bear full responsibility for the failure of the negotiation efforts," Hamas charged. An Israeli official disclosed the previous evening that Israel had agreed to release 700 terrorists jailed in Israel in exchange for the release of 40 hostages held by Hamas in Gaza. Analyst Barak Ravid reported that of the 700 terrorists, about 100 were serving life sentences for serious acts of terror which they had carried out. Israel had rejected a similar offer proposed by the Qatari brokers several weeks ago, but Hamas at the time was demanding a significantly higher number of terrorists serving life sentences in Israel.[66]

That same night, a series of Israeli airstrikes targeted sites belonging to Iran's Islamic Revolutionary Guard Corps in the Deir Ezzor region of eastern Syria, with several deaths and injuries reported, according to the Hezbollah-affiliated Al-Mayadeen TV. The IDF said that it had ended its operation in the Hamad neighborhood of Khan Younis, during which it claimed 300 terrorists were arrested. Israeli forces foiled an attempt by Iran to smuggle weapons into the West Bank in order to carry out terrorist acts against Israelis. The *New York Times* featured an interview with the first Israeli woman to testify publicly about her horrific ordeal after being kidnapped by Hamas to Gaza, forty-year-old Amit Soussana speaking frankly about torture and sexual assault at gunpoint before her release after fifty-five days in captivity. In Amman, riot police fired teargas to push back hundreds of demonstrators marching on the Israeli embassy. With the United States, which had alone given UNRWA $422 million last year, pausing along with other governments their subsidies to that relief organization, the *Wall Street Journal* reported that UNRWA could continue its activities only until May. Arab monarchies did not want UNRWA to collapse, but also saw benefits in reforming it, such as by improving the way it screened staff to prevent Hamas from infiltrating that body. According to people familiar with Persian Gulf governments' thinking, they also did not see it as their job to step in fully to replace Western funding.[67]

Israel recalled its negotiators from Doha after deeming mediation talks on a Gaza truce "at a dead end" due to Hamas demands, a senior Israeli official said on Tuesday. A twenty-five-year-old Israeli Druze was killed and a second person lightly injured in a Wednesday morning missile barrage by Hezbollah of around thirty rockets towards Kiryat Shmona. He was the eighteenth Israeli to be killed on the Lebanon-Israel border since October 7. Sixty-nine percent of Israelis strongly believed that a war would soon break out between Israel and Hezbollah, according to a new poll by the Israel Democracy Institute. Another of its polls revealed that a majority of Israelis in total opposed a hostage/prisoner exchange deal that would include ending the fighting and releasing all security prisoners in Israeli prisons. In addition, a full 82 percent of left-wing respondents stated that Israel should coordinate itself with the United States instead of acting only in its own interests. Another 64.5 percent of centrist voters said the same, while 64 percent of right-wing voters stated that Israel must act only in its own interests.[68]

On Wednesday, Netanyahu said that he canceled an Israeli delegation set to go to Washington because he wanted to "send a message to Hamas." Defense Minister Gallant, in D.C. for meetings with top US officials, said that neither Israel nor Hamas would rule Gaza after the war, thus a local alternative must be built. Hamas published an alleged recording of its military chief Mohammad Deif calling on the "Arab and Muslim world to start marching to Palestine." The IDF announced that hundreds of terrorists were arrested by Division 162 and about 200 killed in the military's Shifa Hospital operation; scores were killed by Division 98 in Khan Younis's Al-Amal neighborhood. Fifty-five percent of

Americans disapproved of Israeli military action in Gaza, according to a new Gallup poll. This marked the first time the survey found a majority disapproval, a rise of ten percent since November 2023.[69]

At a record-breaking campaign fund event in New York City's Radio City Music Hall on Thursday evening, in which Biden, accompanied by past Democratic White House occupants Bill Clinton and Barak Obama, raised $25 million for the November presidential election, he declared the following: "It's understandable Israel has such a profound anger and Hamas is still there. But we must, in fact, stop the war effort that is resulting in significant deaths of innocent civilians, particularly children." In a related statement, the International Court of Justice unanimously ordered Israel to take "all necessary and effective action" to ensure basic food supplies get into Gaza unhindered "in view of the worsening conditions of life faced by Palestinians in Gaza, in particular the spread of famine and starvation," and to increase "the capacity and number of land crossing points" and keep them "open for as long as necessary." The ICJ, while calling for the immediate release of the hostages held in Gaza by Hamas, also ordered Israel to ensure its military "does not commit acts which constitute a violation of any of the rights of the Palestinians in Gaza" under the Genocide Convention "including by preventing, through any action, the delivery of urgently needed humanitarian assistance" and ordered Israel to report on its compliance in a month.[70]

In the last twenty-four hours, IDF killed sixteen terrorists in Lebanon and arrested eighteen in the West Bank. Three Israelis were wounded in a shooting attack against school buses and other cars on Route 90, the main north-south artery in the Jordan Valley, which passes through the Palestinian town of Al-Auja. The IDF began isolating Rafah in southern Gaza and taking steps to evacuate the city's civilian population, *Channel 12* reported. The final four Hamas battalions, comprising some 3,000 terrorists, were holed up there, according to the Israeli military. As part of the preparations for the military operation, Netanyahu ordered the purchase from China of 40,000 tents for Rafah evacuees, who would be moved to Khan Younis and elsewhere in the central Gaza Strip, according to the report. In addition, in response to the alarming surge of antisemitism and a near 800 percent spike in US college campuses, six survivors of the October 7 massacre at the Nova music festival launched the "Survived to Tell" tour, to commence on March 26 and run until April 19. It would span seven states and reach a dozen campuses.[71]

A training program on readiness for Israel's northern arena was held the same week at the Northern Command headquarters, led by Maj. Genl. Ori Gordin. "We have been at war for almost half a year now, and it doesn't end with

Hezbollah," he stated. Gordin added that "tonight, we are operating against al-Jama'a al-Islamiyya, and this morning Hezbollah itself decided to respond against Kiryat Shmona." The IDF confirmed on Friday that an IAF aircraft eliminated Ali Abed Akhsan Naim, the Deputy Commander of Hezbollah's Rocket and Missile Unit, in the town of Zuria in central Lebanon. He was one of the leaders of heavy-warhead rocket fire and was responsible for conducting and planning attacks against Israeli civilians. In Syria, state media accused Israel of launching airstrikes on the Aleppo area in conjunction with a drone attack launched by rebel groups based in Idlib and areas near Aleppo early Friday morning. According to Reuters, thirty-three civilians and military personnel and five Hezbollah terrorists were killed in the strikes. Afternoon prayers on the third Friday of Ramadan were held without incident; police arrested eleven suspects in the Old City of Jerusalem.[72]

The Biden administration signaled to Israel that it understood Jerusalem's demand to remain in the humanitarian corridor which divides between the northern and southern Gaza Strip in the event of a hostage deal, as well as the demand to only allow Gazans to return to the north gradually, Kan Reshet Bet reported on Friday. In the meantime, Hamas demanded that the passage of Gazans from south to north not be limited at all and that Israel withdraw completely from the humanitarian corridor. Al-Mayadeen, the Hezbollah-affiliated network, reported on Saturday that "Palestinian factions" in Syria rejected the proposal to establish a multi-national military force of Arab countries with the backing of the United States to control law and order in Gaza and escort humanitarian aid convoys. "Arab countries, together with the U.S., are trying to rescue the IDF from the situation it has found itself in Gaza. The Palestinian people are capable of choosing their leaders and institutions that will manage the Strip," the report stated.

An Israeli delegation would leave for Egypt on Sunday as part of hostage negotiations, where a new framework will be presented, KAN reported. Israel agreed to a proposal forwarded to Hamas that included returning the bodies of Oron Shaul and Hadar Goldin, two IDF soldiers who were killed in Operation Protective Edge a decade ago, according to a Saturday report by KAN. The proposal was forwarded to Hamas, but they had not yet responded. The proposal also included the release of prisoners who were formerly released in the Gilad Shalit deal but were then arrested again.[73]

Forces from the elite Shayetet 13, Duvdevan, and Nahal Brigade Reconnaissance Units conducted a targeted raid where intelligence officials determined that terrorists were in Gaza's Al-Shifa Hospital. Armed terrorists came out of the emergency room to fire on the soldiers. Several terrorists were eliminated in the raid, including senior Hamas leader Ra'ad Thabat, as well as Mahmoud Khalil Ziqzouq, who was the deputy head of the rocket unit in Gaza City. Thabat had served as the head of Hamas's Production Unit and was responsible for Research and Development. In addition, Fadi Dewik and Zakariya Najeeb were eliminated in an encounter in the maternity ward. Dewik, who carried out a shooting attack on the Adora settlement in 2002 in which four people were murdered, was released in the Gilad Shalit deal of 2011. Najeeb, a senior operative in Hamas's West Bank headquarters who also was released in the Shalit exchange, was responsible for linking the West Bank and Gaza Strip in directing terror attacks, including involvement in the 1994 abduction and killing of Nachshon Wachsman.

Over the last twenty-four hours, Israeli police arrested twenty-three residents of the West Bank, Kafr Qasem, and northern Israel on charges of terrorist incitement targeting the Temple Mount/Al-Aqsa Mosque. The *Washington Post* reported that, despite a deepening gap between the countries over the conduct of the Gaza war, the Biden administration quietly approved the transfer of twenty-five F-35 fighter jets and over 2,000 bombs to Israel over the past few days.[74]

Since entering the Shifa Hospital compound on March 18, the IDF declared that its soldiers had killed over 200 terrorists and detained 800 terror suspects, of whom at least 500 were confirmed as members of the Hamas or Palestinian Islamic Jihad terror groups. As part of the operation, patients and staff were moved to a designated area inside the Shifa compound for their safety. The IDF opened several Gaza border areas to the public, including the Supernova music festival site, a closed military zone since October 7. Some twenty relatives of Israeli hostages being held in Gaza called on Saturday evening for the first time to immediately replace Netanyahu, while thousands protested in Tel Aviv, Jerusalem, Haifa, Be'er Sheva, Caesarea, and other cities in support of releasing the hostages and called for early elections. A second shipment of aid carrying almost 400 tons of food for Gaza left Cyprus's Larnaca port on Saturday.

Thousands of Palestinians and Arab-Israelis took part in a march that ended with a rally in the town of Deir Hanna in the Galilee, to commemorate the forty-eighth anniversary of Land Day. That date had become an annual event commemorating protests which broke out on March 30, 1976, against government land seizures in which six Arabs were killed by Israeli security. Violent clashes between Jordanian forces and protesters erupted as well in the past couple of days, including instances of stone-throwing and arson aimed at the country's security forces against the backdrop of the nation's large anti-Israel protests, some directed by the Muslim Brotherhood.[75]

On day 177 of the war, while a four-day rally opposite the Knesset began in protest against the government, an Israeli delegation landed in Cairo for negotiations with Hamas on a hostage release/cease-fire deal, Pope Francis made renewed calls on Easter Sunday for an immediate cease-fire in Gaza and the release of all Israeli abductees. In a press conference that evening, Netanyahu stressed that he was making the utmost effort to retrieve all the remaining hostages in Gaza, but "Hamas is hardening its stance in the negotiations. It demands that we abolish the humanitarian corridor and allow Hamas terrorists back into northern Gaza." He further commented on recent calls by hostages' families for him to step down as prime minister, saying that holding elections will take Israel "months back." "The elections will paralyze Israel, and Hamas will be the first to congratulate [the new prime minister]," he asserted. He added that, besides the necessity to root out Hamas in Rafah for victory, whose strategy the war cabinet had approved, Israel needed "much more independent production capacity" of the weapons it required: "we need to be immune from external pressures because we need to make our own decisions."[76]

The IDF said it had struck a Palestinian Islamic Jihad command center in the courtyard of the Al-Aqsa Hospital in the central Gazan city of Deir al-Balah and killed Radwan anti-tank missile commander Ismail Al-Zin, who was also responsible for Hezbollah's communications and computer operations. The several terrorists who hid there were eliminated in a manner to reduce civilian casualties in the area. Meanwhile, the operation by the Nahal Patrol and other units in Shifa Hospital continued, killing many Hamas operatives and uncovering much weaponry. IAF fighter jets bombed Hezbollah rocket launching sites and lookout posts, along with buildings where terrorists were located. A young off-duty IDF officer was lightly wounded that morning in a stabbing attack by a Bedouin from Rahat at Be'er Sheva's Central Bus Station; another soldier nearby shot and killed the assailant. Defense Minister Galant, meeting with Division 98 command, declared that in the last two weeks hundreds of terrorists were arrested, who acknowledged in interrogation that Hamas was "crumbling from within, bearing heavy consequences."[77]

The IDF announced that twenty-year-old Sgt. First Class Sivan Weil from Ra'anana, a member of the Egoz guerrilla warfare commando unit, had succumbed to his wounds from an RPG attack on Friday in southern Gaza. His death brought the total number of Israeli military fallen since October 7, 2023, to 599, 255 of these since the invasion of the Gaza Strip. The number of wounded Israeli soldiers came to 3,180, 1,544 of these since the ground op began. As to the 134 captives tragically still held in Gaza, their fate remained a mystery. The Hamas-controlled Health Ministry in Gaza said that at least

32,782 Palestinians had been killed and 75,298 wounded since the start of the war 177 days ago. Thus did the twenty-four hours of March 31, 2024, draw to a close. With the end of the war which Hamas had launched on the State of Israel unknown at that moment in time, one wishing to steer clear of predictions could say no more than this: resolution awaits.[78]

Endnotes

1. World Israel News, Feb. 29, 2024; *New York Times*, Feb. 29, 2024; Mar. 1–2, 2024; *Jerusalem Post*, Feb. 29, 2024; Mar. 1, 2024; JTA, Mar. 1, 2024. The *New York Times*'s coverage of the tragedy implied that "many were killed" because "Israelis opened fire." IDF said that over 450 packages of food and medical aid were distributed through twenty-one airdrops to the Gaza Strip in recent weeks in coordination with Jordan, France, the UAE, and Egypt. *Times of Israel*, Mar. 4, 2024.
2. *Haaretz*, Mar. 2, 2024; *Jerusalem Post*, Feb. 29, 2024.
3. *Haaretz*, Mar. 3, 2024; Israel National News, Mar. 3, 2024; *Jerusalem Post*, Mar. 3, 2024.
4. *Jerusalem Post*, Mar. 4, 2024; *Haaretz*, Mar. 4, 2024.
5. *Jerusalem Post*, Mar. 4, 2024; JINSA report, Mar. 4, 2024; *Haaretz*, Mar. 4, 2024.
6. *Haaretz*, Mar. 5, 2024; Israel National News, Mar. 5, 2024; World Israel News, Mar. 4–5, 2024; *Yisrael Hayom*, Mar. 1, 2024.
7. *Jerusalem Post*, Mar. 5, 2024; IDF News, Mar. 5, 2024; JNS, Mar. 5, 2024. MK Mansour Abbas, chairman of the Islamist Ra'am Party, thanked Netanyahu for the "responsible decision" regarding attendance at the Al-Aqsa Mosque on Ramadan, while calling in his X account on the "Arab public to exercise their right to pray and observe the commandments during the holy month, while maintaining the law and public order." Times of Israel, Mar. 6, 2024.
8. Israel National News, Mar. 6, 2024.
9. *Times of Israel*, Mar. 6, 2024.
10. *Haaretz*, Mar. 6, 2024; *Jerusalem Post*, Mar. 6, 2024; *Times of Israel*, Mar. 5, 2024; IDF News, Mar. 6, 2024.
11. Israel National News, Mar. 7, 2024; *Jerusalem Post*, Mar. 7, 2024.
12. *Haaretz*, Mar. 7, 2024; IDF News, Mar. 7, 2024; *Washington Post*, Mar. 6, 2024; JNS, Mar. 5, 2024.
13. Israel National News, Mar. 8, 2024.
14. *Haaretz*, Mar. 8, 2024; Israel National News, Mar. 8, 2024; *Jerusalem Post*, Mar. 8, 2024.
15. *Jerusalem Post*, Mar. 9, 2024; IDF News, Mar. 9, 2024; *Haaretz*, Mar. 9, 2024.
16. *Haaretz*, May 9–10, 2024; JNS, May 9, 2024; Reuters, May 9, 2024. The Oxford English Dictionary defines the phrase "come to Jesus" as "designating a person or group of people who encourage others to accept Christianity. In secular usage, it means a moment of sudden realization, comprehension, or recognition that often precipitates a major change." Another reported version had Biden using the phrase in his latest talk with Netanyahu. *Haaretz*, May 9–10, 2024; JNS, May 9, 2024. When pressed by MSNBC as to what he meant by that comment, Biden said, it was a euphemism for a "serious meeting." He added, "I have known Bibi for fifty years and he knew what I meant by it." *Jerusalem Post*, Mar. 10, 2024. Netanyahu confirmed that assumption, telling Fox News that he took the idiom to mean a "heart-to-heart conversation," which he said they had had "plenty of times." JTA, Mar. 11, 2024.
17. *Haaretz*, Mar. 9, 202; Israel National News, Mar. 10, 2024.
18. Israel National News, Mar. 10, 2024.
19. Israel National News, Mar. 10, 2024; *Haaretz*, Mar. 10, 2024.

20 Israel National News, Mar. 9–10, 2024; Ynet, Mar. 10, 2024; i24 News, Mar. 7, 2024; *Jerusalem Post*, Mar. 10, 2024.
21 *Haaretz*. Mar. 10, 2024; *Jerusalem Post*, Mar. 10, 2024.
22 *Haaretz*, Mar. 11, 2024; *Jerusalem Post*, Mar. 11, 2024.
23 Israel National News, Mar. 11–12, 2024; *Jerusalem Post*, Mar. 12, 2024. As if to confirm Burns's concern, Australian Foreign Minister Penny Wong remarked that Netanyahu was undermining Israel with his approach to the war in Gaza, adding that she urged Israel to change course or lose even more international support. *Haaretz*, Mar. 12, 2024.
24 Times of Israel, Mar. 12, 2024. In far sharper language than Monsour, Queen Rania of Jordan once again criticized Israel in an interview that night with CNN. "As devastating and as traumatic as October 7th was, it doesn't give Israel license to commit atrocity after atrocity. Israel experienced one October 7th. Since then, the Palestinians have experienced 156 October 7ths," she accused. "This has been a slow-motion mass murder of children five months in the making. It is absolutely shameful, outrageous, and entirely predictable what's happening in Gaza today because it was deliberate," she claimed. Times of Israel, Mar. 12, 2024.
25 *Haaretz*, Mar. 11, 2024; Israel National News, Mar. 11, 2024; IDF News, Mar. 12, 2024; Times of Israel, Mar. 11, 2024. One week later, Hamas confirmed Issa's death, his body buried under a building's rubble, According to Palestinian Arab sources, Razi Abu Tuama, the commander of the Hamas Central Camps Brigade, was with him in the tunnel and was also killed. Israel National News, Mar. 17, 2024.
26 *Haaretz*, Mar. 12, 2024. National Security Minister Ben-Gvir slammed Defense Minister Gallant after Hezbollah's firing this huge barrage of rockets at Israel's North, calling for a "war now" against the Lebanese terror organization. *New York Times*, Mar. 12, 2024.
27 Israel National News, Mar. 12, 2024.
28 CNN, Mar.12, 2024.
29 *Washington Post*, Mar. 10, 2024; *Haaretz*, Mar. 11, 2024; Israel National News, Mar. 11, 2024. In the last day alone, a bag with six pipe bombs was seized in the eastern part of Jerusalem. The police also acted against instigators of violence before Ramadan and arrested twenty-one suspects on suspicion of this offense in the last two weeks. Charges were filed against six of them at the end of their investigation. Israel National News, Mar. 12, 2024.
30 Israel National News, Mar. 12, 2024.
31 *Wall St. Journal*, Mar. 12, 2024; *Haaretz*, Mar. 12, 2024. The pier, expected to be operational in approximately sixty days, would facilitate up to two million meals daily for the people of Gaza, according to the Pentagon. *Haaretz*, Mar. 13, 2024.
32 *New York Times*, Mar. 13, 2024; *Jerusalem Post*, Mar. 13, 2024; Israel National News, Mar. 13, 2024; *New York Times*, Mar. 13, 2024; *Jerusalem Post*, Mar. 13, 2024; Haaretz, Mar. 12, 2024.
33 *Wall St. Journal*, Mar. 13, 2024; *Haaretz*, Mar. 13, 2024.
34 *Haaretz*, Mar. 13, 2024; *Jerusalem Post*, Mar. 13, 2024; Israel National News, Mar. 13, 2024; i24 News, Mar. 13, 2024; *Times of Israel*, Mar. 13, 2024.
35 Yonah Jeremy Bob, "Why Has Israel Yet to Launch a Full-Blown War on Hezbollah—Analysis," *Jerusalem Post*, Mar. 13, 2024.
36 *Haaretz*, Mar. 14, 2024; JNS, Mar. 14, 2024.
37 Times of Israel, Mar. 14, 2024. The clans' response gave credence to a special analysis conducted by the business intelligence company Buzzilla for *Maariv, which* showed that in the last three weeks, the general discourse on Arabic-language social media in Gaza had been mainly positive towards Hamas in general and towards its leader in the Gaza Strip, Yahya Sinwar, in particular. The latter was surprising, since discourse on social media tended to be critical. The company's experts pointed out that it was possible to detect an increase in the positive discourse towards Sinwar personally when threats against him from the Israeli side came up in the media. *Jerusalem Post*, Mar. 14, 2024.
38 *New York Times*, Mar. 14, 2024.

39 *Wall St. Journal*, Mar. 14, 2024; JNS, Mar. 15, 2024; Israel National News, Mar. 20, 2024.
40 *Jerusalem Post*, Mar. 14, 2024; *Times of Israel*, Mar. 17, 2024; *Haaretz*, Mar. 14, 2024. On the other hand, Israeli political opposition leader Yair Lapid reacted thus: "Senator Schumer's speech is proof that Netanyahu is losing our best supporters in the U.S. Even worse is that he is doing it on purpose. Netanyahu is causing serious damage to the national effort to win the war and preserving Israel's security." Israel National News, Mar. 14, 2024.
41 *Haaretz*, Mar. 13, 2024; *Jerusalem Post*, Mar. 15, 2024; *Times of Israel*, Mar. 15, 2024.
42 Israel National News, Mar. 15, 2024; *Jerusalem Post*, Mar.15, 2024; JNS, Mar. 15, 2024.
43 Israel National News, Mar. 15, 2024; *Times of Israel*, Mar. 17, 2024. The Foundation for the Defense of Democracies (FDD) pointed out that while the Biden administration claimed that the waiver was just for Iraq to physically import electricity, the waiver unlocked billions of dollars for Iran to use as budget support. The new policy also allowed Iran to convert the money from Iraqi dinars to euros. Iran could then process euro-based transactions for imports and debt payments out of Iranian bank accounts in Oman. Accessing $10 billion or more out of Oman frees up to $10 billion or more in Iran that Tehran could use for other purposes, including terrorism, missiles, and nuclear capabilities. FDD, Mar. 14, 2024.
44 The usage by Palestinians around the world of the noun *Nakba* (the Arabic term for "catastrophe") refers to the mass displacement and dispossession of Palestinians during the 1948 Arab-Israeli war. Nakba Day was instituted on May 15 (one day after Israeli Independence Day) by Palestinian Authority leader Yasser Arafat in 1998, although the date had been unofficially used for protests from 1949 onward. See Hussein Aboubakr, "The Perennial Power of the Nakba," *Mosaic*, Sept. 10, 2023. The *Nakba* represents the creation of the modern State of Israel in 1948, but this narrative of colonialist Jews from abroad consciously uprooting an indigenous population neglects a Jewish presence in the Land of Israel for millennia, the responsibility of the Palestinian and outside Arab leadership for the events of 1948, and that the collapse and dispersion of Palestinian Arab society was not described at the time as a systematic dispossession of Arabs by Jews. See Efraim Karsh, *Palestine Betrayed* (New Haven: Yale University Press, 2010).
  In 2022, the United Nations General Assembly requested that this anniversary be officially commemorated on May 15, 2023, for the first time in the history of the UN. The United States, Canada, and the United Kingdom were among thirty countries that voted against the UN resolution to adopt that year's commemoration. Israeli officials, meanwhile, urged UN member states to boycott the event. "Attending this despicable event means destroying any chance of peace by adopting the Palestinian narrative calling the establishment of the state of Israel a disaster," Israeli UN Ambassador Gilad Erdan declared. Israel said that tens of countries had agreed not to attend, including the United States, United Kingdom, Czech Republic, and Ukraine. A State Department spokesman told NPR that the United States would not be represented at the event, and Ukraine's ambassador to Israel, Yevgen Korniychuk, told NPR that Ukraine was declining in order "not to harm [the] Israeli interest." NPR, May 15, 2023.
45 The White House, Mar. 14, 2024, https://www.whitehouse.gov; *Haaretz*, Mar. 15, 2024; *Times of Israel*, Mar. 16. 2024.
46 *Jerusalem Post*, Mar.16, 2024; *Wall St. Journal*, Mar. 16, 2024; *Haaretz*, Mar. 16, 2024.
47 Israel National News, Mar. 17, 2024.
48 Israel National News, Mar. 17, 2024; IDF News, Mar. 17, 2024; *Jerusalem Post*, Mar. 17, 2024.
49 *Haaretz*, Mar. 17, 2024; IDF News, Mar. 17, 2024.
50 IDF News, Mar. 17, 2024; *Haaretz*, Mar. 17, 2024; *Times of Israel*, Mar. 17, 2024.
51 *Jerusalem Post*, Mar. 22, 2024; *Times of Israel*, Mar. 18, 2024; IDF News, Mar. 19, 2024; Israel National News, Mar. 20, 2024.
52 France 24, Mar. 15, 2024; *Times of Israel*, Mar. 17, 2024; JNS, Mar. 18, 2024.
53 *Haaretz*, Mar. 18–19, 2024; JNS, Mar. 16, 2024.
54 *Jerusalem Post*, Mar. 19, 2024.

55 Israel National News, Mar. 19, 2024; *Haaretz*, Mar. 19, 2024; *Jerusalem Post*, Mar. 19, 2024.
56 *Times of Israel*, Mar. 20–21, 2024; World Israel News, Mar. 20, 2024. Canada's statement was declaratory in essence since that country does not provide meaningful weaponry to Israel.
57 Israel National News, Mar. 21, 2024; *Jerusalem Post*, Mar. 21, 2024. Israel accused Barghouti of having founded the Al-Aqsa Martyrs' Brigades in the early 2000s and indicted him on twenty-six charges of murder and attempted murder attributed to the Brigades. He was sentenced by an Israeli court to five cumulative life sentences, plus forty years for attempted murder and membership in a terrorist organization. Barghouti offered no defense, refusing to recognize the authority of the Israeli court and saying only that he supported the armed resistance but opposed the targeting of civilians. Supporters call him the Palestinian Mandela, recalling the South African leader who was imprisoned by the apartheid regime for twenty-eight years. Barghouti has been in jail for twenty-two years. Al-Jazeera, Feb. 25, 2024.
58 *New York Times*, Mar. 21, 2024; JTA, Mar. 21, 2024. Further confirmation of the growing political divide came from a new survey, taken in the days before and after Schumer called for new Israeli leadership. The Grinnell College National Poll showed that 57 percent of Democrats viewed Netanyahu critically and 53 percent of Republicans viewed him favorably. Among respondents who said they planned to vote for Biden in November, 69 percent expressed unfavorable views of Netanyahu. Among those who planned to vote for former President Trump, 61 percent expressed a positive view of Netanyahu. *Forward*, Mar. 20, 2024.
59 *Washington Post*, Mar. 21, 2024; *Haaretz*, Mar. 21, 2024. The United States is UNRWA's largest donor, contributing $300 million to $400 million annually. JNS, Mar. 20, 2024; *New York Times*, Mar. 22, 2024.
60 VIN news, Mar. 21, 2024; Israel National News, Mar. 21, 2024; *Haaretz*, Mar. 21, 2024.
61 JNS, Mar. 22, 2024; Israel National News, Mar. 22–23, 2024; *Haaretz*, Mar. 22, 2024.
62 *Jerusalem Post*, Mar. 23, 2024; Times of Israel, Mar. 21 and 23, 2024; *Haaretz*, Mar. 23, 2024.
63 *Haaretz*, Mar. 23, 2024; JTA, Mar. 21, 2024; JNS, Mar. 21, 2024.
64 Times of Israel, Mar. 24, 2024; Israel National News, Mar. 24, 2024.
65 *New York Times*, Mar. 25, 2024; *Jerusalem Post*, Mar. 25, 2024; *Washington Post*, Mar. 25, 2024; *Haaretz*, Mar. 25, 2024.
66 *Jerusalem Post*, Mar. 26, 2024; *Haaretz*, Mar. 25, 2024.
67 *Jerusalem Post*, Mar.26, 2024; *Haaretz*, Marr. 26, 2024; *New York Times*, Mar. 26, 2024; *Wall St. Journal*, Mar. 26, 2024.
68 *Jerusalem Post*, Mar. 27, 2024; IDF News, Mar. 27, 2024; *Wall St. Journal*, Mar. 27, 2024; *Haaretz*, Mar. 27, 2024; Israel National News, Mar. 27, 2024. At the same time, 57.8 percent of the Arab public in this poll were sure that such a hostage/prisoner deal would be correct, and 20.7 percent suspected that it would be correct.
69 *Haaretz*, Mar. 27, 2024; IDF News, Mar. 27, 2024.
70 Axios, Mar. 28, 2024; *Haaretz*, Mar. 28, 2024. The Israeli Foreign Ministry announced that Jerusalem was operating in conjunction with international law, and that Hamas was guilty in this regard, contemptuous of civilian life and purposely harming humanitarian efforts. IDF News, Mar. 29, 2024.
71 i24 News, Mar. 28, 2024; IDF News, Mar. 28, 2024; *Times of Israel*, Mar. 28, 2024; World Israel News, Mar. 28, 2024; *Jerusalem Post*, Mar. 28, 2024.
72 Israel National News, Mar. 29, 2024; *Jerusalem Post*, Mar. 29, 2024. A Sunni Islamist political party, al-Jama'a al-Islamiyya, referred to by Gordin, was founded in 1964 as the Lebanese branch of the Muslim Brotherhood.
73 Israel National News, Mar. 29, 2024; *Jerusalem Post*, Mar. 29–30, 2024.
74 *Jerusalem Post*, Mar. 30, 2024; *Haaretz*, Mar. 30, 2024; Reuters, Mar. 30, 2024.
75 United with Israel, Mar. 28, 2024; *Haaretz*, Mar. 30–31, 2024; Times of Israel, Mar. 31, 2024; JNS, Mar. 30, 2024; *Jerusalem Post*, Mar. 39, 2024.
76 *Haaretz*, Mar. 31, 2024; *Jerusalem Post*, Mar. 31, 2024.

77 Israel National News, Mar. 31, 2024; IDF News, Mar. 31, 2024; GlobalSecurity.org, Mar. 31, 2024.
78 Times of Israel, Mar. 31, 2024; *Yisrael Hayom*, Mar. 31, 2024; *Haaretz*, Mar. 31, 2024.

Conclusion

After October 7, 2023, the landscape of life in the State of Israel would never be the same. In a date that has etched itself into the annals of Israeli history, the Palestinian Arab terrorist organization Hamas's singular religious ideology, including a jihadist hatred of Jews, exploded into premeditated, methodical murder. Rape, mutilation, and pillage, intended by design as weapons of war to sow humiliation and terror, held sway. The country's southern communities near the Gaza Strip fell victim to death and destruction, the blackest day in the history of the Third Jewish Commonwealth, when radical evil reigned supreme and more Jews fell victim to the enemy's onslaught than on any other day since the Holocaust. Coupled with the grisly, uncompromising slaughter of more than 1,200 innocent human beings, 253 residents were kidnapped to Gaza, their families to occupy henceforth a planet of incessant tears, haunted memories, and indescribable agony.

On that Sabbath morning, as Jews were celebrating the joyous holiday of Simchat Torah, an Israeli strategic security concept that had been established over the past thirty years ever since the 1993 Oslo Accords, deflating the combative ethos of the Israel Defense Forces (IDF), collapsed. Ever since Hamas was elected by local Palestinian Arabs in 2006 to rule Gaza, the army had adopted a short-term strategy dubbed "mowing the lawn," dealing periodically with outbreaks of violence as isolated incidents, keeping them down to what was considered a reasonable number per year rather than addressing the greater picture. Hamas's military capabilities were consistently dismissed by the high command of the IDF, which also ignored earlier warnings of an impending assault, while the different coalition governments under Prime Minister Binyamin Netanyahu assumed that economic incentives and playing Hamas off the Palestinian Authority (PA) would bring satisfactory quiet to the Jewish State. Eerily, a similar situation characterized the beginning of the October 1973 Arab-Israeli war exactly fifty years and one day earlier, when the Egyptian and Syrian surprise attacks were launched on Yom Kippur, the holiest day in the Jewish calendar. Across the globe, the common perception of a militarily invincible Israel came rudely into question now, while Israel's citizens felt abandoned by their army and political echelon that were meant to secure for them protection and peace.

Throughout the first nine months of 2023, the Israeli public had been consumed by one domestic issue that seemed to pose a foundational challenge to the country's existence, a fight over judicial reform so fierce that, by that summer, the nation's leaders openly warned of civil war. Tens of thousands had rallied in the streets against what they saw as the attack by an ultranationalist, religious government threatening a national identity rooted in liberal, secular traditions. Many wondered if the rift could ever heal, so wide that the pressing problem of Israel's conflict with the Palestinian Arabs barely got mentioned despite a recent surge in violence.

The polarizing Netanyahu, indicted on corruption charges in 2019, had eked out an election victory three years later and promptly moved to overturn court decisions and appoint judges on the grounds that the liberally inclined Supreme Court should not block laws passed by the democratically elected Knesset or government decisions that the judges deemed "unreasonable." Critics viewed this, however, as a transparent power grab. In light of the unprecedented protests across Israel, Netanyahu temporarily suspended this plan, but the deep fissures created in society remained. Hamas's pitiless butchery, carefully orchestrated, abruptly put this internal political divide on hold, an unprovoked, shocking earthquake forcing adversaries to unite in defeating the external threat from a foe whose founding charter called for their very annihilation.

The systematic, venomous assault on October 7, 2023, under the leadership of Hamas's elite Nukhba force, joined by members of the Palestinian Islamic Jihad, of the Al-Aqsa Martyrs' Brigades associated with the PA's ruling Fatah party, and some Gazan civilians of all ages, made the noun "pogrom" (a Russian word that means "wreaking havoc") insufficient to characterize the methodical barbarism that unfolded. The first pogrom of the twentieth century, breaking out in Kishinev on Easter Sunday of April 1903, remains the classic prototype of such brutal attacks on Jewish communities, before and afterwards. Yet, as I have shown elsewhere, that was a chaotic attack of emotional frenzy ending fewer than two days later after the Russian interior minister dispatched a telegram to disperse the Christian mobs, leaving a toll of 49 dead and 495 wounded.[1]

Nazi Germany's "Final Solution of the Jewish Question," unprecedented in Jewish history, led some to employ "Holocaust" as a referential point. In this vein, Israel's UN ambassador chose to don a yellow star with the words "Never again," recalling the star which Jews under the yoke of the Third Reich were ordered to sew on their clothing in the years of the *Shoah*. Eight decades later, however, the restored Jewish nation-state possessed a powerful army to combat those bent on mass murder and effectively go on the offensive. A previous "Black Sabbath" had stunned the Palestinian yishuv (Jewish community) on June 29, 1946, when the mandatory British military sought to disarm its underground forces and arrest its political leadership. Twenty-seven settlements were searched, more than 2,700 Jews were arrested, four killed, and scores wounded. By contrast, what Israelis called the "Black Sabbath" of October 2023, Hamas's meticulously thought out and implemented operation of what can accurately be termed "genocide" against Jews, would spark a firm, sovereign response.[2]

Heroes quickly emerged in the war forced upon Israel that bloodbath day. Before IDF units could reach the embattled kibbutzim, moshavim, and cities near the Gaza border, there were Israelis like retired Generals Noam Tibon and Yair Golan, farmer Rami Davidian from Moshav Patish who drove many Nova music festival participants to safety. Col. Roi Yosef Levy, the head of the IDF Multidomain Unit, also known as the Ghost Unit, killed as his forces battled Hamas terrorists in the southern community of Re'im on October 7. Magen David Adom senior medic Aharon Haimov, killed as he drove an ambulance to his hometown of Ofakim to help treat victims on October 7. Inbal Rabin-Lieberman who warned her Kibbutz Nir-Am of the impending attack, and Rachel Edri of Ofakim who offered attackers home-made cookies and coffee until her police officer sons could join an operation of rescue. Kfar Aza's Netta Epstein, to be married in April to Irene Shavit, threw himself on a grenade tossed into their shelter by Hamas in order to protect his fiancée; he died, she survived. Holit's Deborah and Shlomi Matias were murdered while successfully shielding their sixteen-year-old son Rotem. Otniel's Menachem Kalmanson, his brother Elhanan, and their nephew Itiel Zohar saved many residents in Kibbutz Be'eri where a terrorist killed Elhanan. His gravestone is the first in Israel's many cemeteries to bear the symbols of both the IDF and the Mossad, the country's national security agency.

Other heroes: 2nd Lt. Avichail Reuven, an Israeli paratrooper of Ethiopian descent, who put on his uniform and *ran* eight miles from his parents' home in Kiryat Malachi to the Gaza border to defend his people, where he displayed exceptional valor. Nasreen Yousef, the Arabic-speaking Druze mother of four, who on the morning of October 7 boldly emerged from her shelter, outsmarted the terrorists around her, and extracted information from them that would later save the entire community of Moshav Yated. Bedouin Muslim police officer Raymond (Remo) Al-Husayl and drivers Youssef El-Zaidneh and Hamed Alkarnawi rescued hundreds caught at the Nova festival. Paramedic

Awad Darawshe was killed there while refusing to abandon his wounded Jewish patients. Hamid Abu Arar, although a Hamas shooting on October 7 killed his wife and injured him, saved dozens of IDF soldiers the same day by leaving a hideout with his infant baby to warn them of an impending attack. Among the first respondents, ZAKA volunteers who collected parts from often charred bodies and even blood for a proper burial according to Jewish law, deserve special mention.[3]

Among the 600 IDF soldiers who died in the war's first six months, nineteen-year-old Matan Abergil jumped without hesitation on a terrorist's grenade thrown into his armored vehicle in Kibbutz Nir Am on October 7, saving the lives of six comrades. His last words before dying: "I tried to do everything to protect the people of Israel." Twenty-two-year-old Aner Shapiro, standing at the entrance to what became known as "the Death Shelter" at the Nova festival, calmed down the thirty people inside, saying the army was only half an hour away and he was sure everything was going to be okay. The off-duty soldier then threw back seven grenades flung in by Hamas attackers, but the eighth exploded in his hand and he died. Hamas operatives entered and took a few hostages before opening fire on those who remained. It took hours before help arrived, meaning only those who had suffered relatively minor injuries survived.

Twenty-two-year-old Eden Nimri found herself on October 7 fighting for her own life, as well as the lives of other female soldiers at the Nahal Oz military post. This professional swimmer's quick-witted response helped to save at least eleven of them, while she herself was killed. Thirty-two-year-old Dvir David Fima, who said on Israeli TV after returning home from fifty days of combat in Gaza to his wife Ofek and their six-month-year-old son Harel that "when it comes to the lives of those who are fighting with you . . . you know what you need to do," was killed in battle on December 27, not long after he gave that interview. Fima had seen a trapped shaft that would injure his troops and jumped onto it, using his body as a shield between the detonated weapon and three other soldiers in the unit. These and many other ultimate sacrifices reflected a society strained but resilient, determined to press forward with two primary objectives: the return of hostages and the elimination of Hamas.[4]

The Hamas terror group's mass invasion of southern Israel on October 7 was actually intended to be even larger, according to journalist Ilan Kafir of Israel's *Channel 12 News*. Mastermind Yahya Sinwar had planned for terror squads to travel to Tel Aviv, where they would murder civilians in a number of crowded, high-profile locations selected in advance. Operatives were also meant to infiltrate the southern city of Dimona, the location of Israel's nuclear reactor, although it is unclear whether they had the knowledge or technical ability to harm or disable it. Terror cells also intended to reach Shikma Prison near Ashdod and free hundreds of jailed terrorists affiliated with Hamas. That plan was thwarted by an apparent technical error from the group's GPS devices, as well as the squad's navigator becoming disoriented. The plan to storm the prison was "carefully developed, in great detail," a source in the Gaza Strip told the Arabic-language news outlet *Asharq Al-Awsat*.

The squad bound for Shikma Prison deviated from its intended route and retreated southward, to the Nativ HaAsara moshav, where the cell murdered at least twenty residents of the community. Sinwar believed that, if the terrorists from the Strip reached Tel Aviv and Dimona, other Iranian regional proxies would join the attack against Israel. However, despite a slow response from the IDF, local security forces had blocked off northbound roads near a major intersection in southern Israel. This barrier prevented additional terror squads, who left Gaza hours after the original invasion wave, from reaching the rest of the country.[5]

Regrettably, as the IDF began relentlessly pummeling Gaza in retaliation, world media and public opinion shifted from near unanimous support for Israel in light of October 7 to strident condemnation. Demands for boycott of Israel, under the acronym BDS—boycott, divestment, and sanctions—had become a staple of American university agendas. Now a massive wave of toxic antisemitism, not seen in close to a century, erupted across world capitals and university campuses, which stage annual "Israel Apartheid Week" hate fests and rip down posters of hostages in Gaza, making little distinction between Jews and Israel. "Globalize the Intifada!" appears regularly on demonstration placards. On three successive days last summer, the Boston police had to protect a student rally for Israel from pro-Palestinian mobs shouting "Jews back to Birkenau!" When the walls of Sydney's opera house lit up with the Israeli flag, protestors yelled "Gas the Jew!"

Such incredibly virulent calls in other major cities brought to mind the warning of Nobel Prize laureate Imre Kertész: "The antisemite of our age no longer loathes Jews; he wants Auschwitz." Years earlier, Rev. Martin Luther King had warned of this, responding to a student who attacked Zionism: "When people criticize Zionists, they mean Jews. You're talking anti-Semitism." "One of the world's most complicated moral and political dilemmas," observed Yossi Klein Halevi but two weeks after the attack on Israel's southern communities, "has been turned into a proverbial passion play, in which The Israeli plays the role of Judas (in place of The Jew), betraying his destiny as noble victim and becoming the victimizer."[6]

Hamas's unalloyed evil was portrayed in these circles as justified against occupation, even though Israel unilaterally had left Gaza in the summer of 2005, uprooting over 9,000 Israeli citizens who were living in twenty-five settlements scattered through Gaza and northern Samaria, and Hamas would establish its authoritarian rule there. That charge was more than hinted at in assertions by UN Secretary-General António Guterres and former US President Barack Obama that a broader "context" was needed to understand Hamas's vicious assault on the Jewish State, thereby dismissing the history of Israeli peace offers and Palestinian rejection. After the "9/11" jihadist attack on the United States, elected officials regularly declared that Islam had nothing to do with terrorism, and that accusing Muslims of supporting Islamic terrorism was a dangerous bigotry which they dubbed "Islamophobia."[7]

Israel was also accused of "ethnic cleansing," despite the fact that since 1967 the Palestinian Arab population in the West Bank and Gaza had at least quintupled from just over 1 million to nearly 5.5 million people. Furthermore, while critics point to the estimated 700,000 Palestinian Arabs who fled or were expelled from the country during Israel's War of Independence in 1948, it was rarely noted that over half of Israeli Jews today have their roots in their families' departure from Arab countries of the Middle East and North Africa. Some 650,000 were forced to leave their homes after the State of Israel's rebirth on May 14, 1948, and became fully absorbed as Israeli citizens. Another 200,000 moved to the United States and the West. Although US House Resolution 185, passed unanimously on February 16, 2007, acknowledged the facts, these are forgotten refugees. Very few Jews live in Arab countries today. By contrast, the United Nations Relief and Works Agency (UNRWA), which remains the only UN body created to deal with a specific refugee problem, continues to bestow refugee status on the descendants of the Palestinian refugees from seventy-five years ago. As for the chants by Hamas champions of "from the river to the sea Palestine shall be free," this hollered cry meant, in bold fact, a radical Islamist state free of Jews, much as Hitler's Third Reich had crusaded for a *Judenrein* world.

Advocacy for Hamas meant that its atrocities on October 7 were either outrightly denied, although the assailants had gleefully posted for world consumption photographs of the attack, or condoned as legitimate resistance by what protesters unabashedly trumpeted as "any means necessary." The use by Hamas of its own people, including children, in Gaza as human shields (even the Nazis, who kept their Holocaust killings secret, did not engage so, nor in beheading Jewish victims); the spending of more than 100 million dollars on underground tunnels for warfare against Israel rather than for local hospitals, housing, and schools; the seizing of humanitarian aid to Gaza for their own operatives; embedding rocket launchers in civilian locations—all received little or no notice by demonstrators avidly pillorying Israel as the enemy. The massive tunnel network alone made it clear just how much of the Palestinians' future Hamas had stolen. One had to look long and hard at his/her moral compass if thinking otherwise. None could be oblivious to the terrible devastation that befell Gaza after October 7, yet, as British political commentator Douglas Murray regularly had to remind critics of Israel, it was Hamas who consciously turned Gaza into a war zone, a military fortress, rather than an enclave for peace. Consequences had to follow.[8]

US Supreme Court Justice Louis Dembitz Brandeis, in his famous 1913 article "What Publicity Can Do," had reflected on the wickedness of people shielding wrongdoers. In so doing, he astutely commented that "sunlight is said to be the best of disinfectants." Alas, darkness had descended with Hamas's crimes against humanity, threatening world civilization. Rachel Goldberg-Polin, whose twenty-three-year-old son Hersh was kidnapped to Gaza, declared at the UN on October 27 that "the pro-Palestine camp has succeeded in doing what neo-Nazis have failed to do, and that is to popularize the killing of Jews under the excuse of justice and liberation." This "grotesque" phenomenon, she rightly added, should serve as "a wake-up call" to all of those who consider themselves civilized. She concluded thus: "We cannot allow Hamas's murder of Jews and crimes against humanity to be whitewashed with assertions of human rights. When Hamas comes for your children next, ask yourself: 'Why did I stay silent and overlook what happened on October 7th, 2023?'"[9]

Despite Israel, as the metaphorical canary in the coal mine, providing an early warning of radical Islam's threat to the world, it was also accused of acting "disproportionally" against Hamas in replying to October 7. Yet the IDF, risking the lives of its own soldiers, regularly warned civilians to leave their dwellings before airstrikes, and provided land corridors for Gazans to reach safety. Unforeseen, unintended tragedies do occur in war, as witnessed by an Israeli drone strike that killed seven World Food Programme workers delivering food to Gaza, for which the IDF immediately admitted responsibility and sacked the two senior officers involved. Declared John Spencer, chair of urban warfare studies at West Point, on X at the end of January 2024: "Israel has done more to prevent civilian casualties in Gaza than any other army in the world." In addition, former British head of forces in Afghanistan Col. Richard Kemp pointed out that the UN says that global civilian to combatant death ratio in urban conflict is 9:1. In Gaza, even when accepting the casualty figures of the Hamas-controlled Health Ministry—not verified and not distinguishing between terrorists and civilians, the IDF seems to have achieved an extremely low ratio of 1.5:1. Notwithstanding strident champions of Hamas (which embeds itself within homes, hospitals, mosques, and schools, civilians used as human shields), Israeli forces in Gaza are not committing genocide, currently defined by the Encyclopedia Britannica as "the deliberate systematic destruction of a group of people because of their ethnicity, nationality, religion, or race."[10]

Vociferous opponents of Israel's battle against Hamas "hardly flinch," observed the French philosopher, author, and documentary filmmaker Bernard Henri-Lévy, when China commits genocide against its Uyghur Muslims, Iran its Kurds, and Russian President Vladimir Putin the Chechens or the Ukrainians. They find no complaints with the fact that Turkey resumes, in the Azerbaijan's Nagorno-Karabakh region, its endless war against the Armenian people. No mobilizations on campus can be seen when an Arab state, Syria, kills hundreds of thousands of its own civilians, backed by Iran, which promises even greater massacres against Jews and anyone in the region who dares to oppose it. Never mind that a fifth of the Israeli population, charged by critics with being "under apartheid," is made up of Arabs, Muslims, and Palestinians, who (without mentioning the Christian, Druze, or Bedouin minorities) enjoy the same civil rights as their fellow Jewish citizens. Israel responded after October 7 like any other democracy would have in its place. Yet, instead of supporting Israel in its legitimate self-defense, the world accused the Jewish commonwealth of poisoning wells and starving the civilian population. "It is no longer opinion, it's demonization," Henri-Lévy declared. He concluded: The only way this war can end is "with the defeat of Hamas."[11]

Even those who acknowledged Israel's inherent right to self-defense continue to speak about the importance, echoing the phrase of US Secretary of State Anthony Blinken, of creating an "irrevocable" path to a Palestinian state. They choose to overlook the widespread support in all polls for Hamas in Gaza and across the West Bank, even though from that latter region the lives of more than 500,000 Israeli Jews, who prefer to call the area *Yehuda v'Shomron* (Judea and Samaria), the biblical heartland, are threatened daily. Those living in Gaza and the West Bank concur with Hamas's Sinwar, who sent a message to Egyptian officials soon after October 7 that "We brought the Palestinian cause to the forefront. We have changed the status quo." (In like vein, Iranian Chief of Staff Mohammed Bagheri praised the attack as "unique," stating it had shattered Israel's invincible image.) Champions of a Palestinian state also ignore the Palestinian Authority's "pay for slay" program honoring terrorists, its educational system encouraging children to kill Jews, and its refusal to condemn the October 7 attack. Such a state at this point in time would be another jihadist entity, what author Salman Rushdie calls a "Taliban-like state—a satellite state of Iran." Not surprisingly, most Israeli residents whom Hamas's single-minded assault targeted that day have dramatically shifted from their former left-wing politics endorsing a two-state solution. The same is now true for the majority of their fellow citizens after Hamas's vicious incursion on "Black Sabbath" 2023.[12]

True to the slogan soon adopted by Israelis for the wanton war unleashed by Hamas's sadistic frenzy to kill as many Jews as possible—*b'yachad n'natzeiach* ("united, we will win"), they banded as one family to do battle. The government formally declared a state of war the very next day under Article 40A, the first such declaration since the 1973 Yom Kippur War, and the IDF called up over 300,000 reservists. Responding to the largest mobilization in Israel's history, an overwhelming, unexpected number quickly showed up at their units. Another 300,000 Israeli young men and women, then traveling abroad, scrambled onto planes to join the ranks. While the IDF's regular troops completed the initial phase of regaining control over the devastated southern communities on Monday afternoon, these soldiers were fed, clothed, and equipped by the people. Individuals of all political camps spontaneously joined groups like *Achim LaNeshek* (Brothers in Arms), reservists who had marched for months against Netanyahu over judicial reform and now put aside protest for rescue work. Civilian volunteers brought food every day, provided clothes and toiletries, prepared *tzitziyot* (religious fringed garments), and even showed up with washing machines on pickup trucks to do the laundry. Israeli housewives formed the Baking Battalion to make cookies, a cooking school produced meals for the troops, restaurants operated free food trucks. Others stepped in to harvest crops and run the shops of the reservists called up to serve in Gaza.

October 7, 2023, gave world Jewry a sense of outrage and purpose as well. The title of Bret Stephens's op ed essay in the *New York Times* one month later, "For America's Jews, Every Day Must Be Oct. 8," rang true for Jewish communities worldwide.[13] Shocked at overt, rampant manifestations of primal Jew-hatred that quickly surfaced across the planet, understanding that anti-Zionism was the new antisemitism, they banded together in support of the one Jewish State. 60,000 volunteers streamed to the embattled commonwealth; families even came on *aliya*, choosing to cast their future lot with Israel. More than $1 billion was raised by American Jewry alone in the first month of the war to aid the war effort. Israeli Finance Ministry Director-General Yali Rothenberg completed a public issuance of US bonds in the international markets totaling $8 billion; demands reached approximately $38 billion, the highest in Israel's history. Duffels filled with clothing, medicines, and energy bars were collected and shipped to Ben-Gurion Airport. Ceramic armor vests, rifle scopes, night vision goggles, and headlamps made their way directly to soldiers' bases. Rallies sprang up with the defiant, clarion assertion "*Am Yisrael chai!*" ("The People of Israel lives!"), most impressively at the National Mall in Washington, D.C. on November 14, 2023, the largest pro-Israel demonstration in US history that saw some 300,000 present and another 250,000 tuning in online. They were determined to contribute towards ensuring that the fight would be won.

The almost indescribable devotion of Israelis to their nation, and particularly the commitment, courage, and passion of a younger generation to rival their grandparents' belief in "something greater than themselves," surfaced with an intensity to stand steadfast against the forces of radical evil and religious animosity aimed at one distinctive sovereign state. Having shown their mettle, they embraced a newly adopted slogan, *lo noflim mi'dor tashach!* ("Not Falling Short of the '48 Generation!"), in demanding, along with 130 senior reserve officers' open letter to the Israeli war cabinet, perseverance until victory. Soldiers Save Lives, started by twenty-five-year-old Gidon Hazony after his childhood friend David Newman was murdered at the Nova music festival, raised millions of dollars from abroad for the war effort before shifting to aid displaced civilians and survivors of the Hamas attack.[14] Poetry and soldiers' letters (see the Appendices), along with new songs like Ehud Banai's "Something Dormant is Beginning to Wake Up" and the HaTikva Shesh's "Superheroes," reflect a dramatic change in mood, a sense that the struggle to keep and renew their nation was far from over. Allies, led by the United States, played a crucial part in opposing Iran and its Middle East proxies.[15] Yet the decisive role in determining Israel's destiny, as former IDF chief of staff Moshe Dayan had warned early on when viewing his country's embattled existence (see the Appendices), had to rest in the Jewish State's hands.

The right of the Jewish people to live in their own ancestral homeland remains an open question in many quarters. Antisemitism in the political far right and far left, wherever on the globe, must be challenged forthrightly. The world has yet to fully appreciate the late Rabbi Lord Jonathan Sacks's admonition: "No soul was ever saved by hate. No truth was ever proved by violence. No redemption was ever brought by holy war."[16] Hamas, Hezbollah, Houthi rebels, and other groups in that volatile region are resolved in their genocidal campaign against Jerusalem. Tehran's Shi'ite mullahs, implacable antagonists of Israel's very being, continue to seek an alliance with Russia, China, and North Korea—all totalitarian governments.

Hard questions about Israel's long-term sustainability must be confronted. Its political and military echelons face the daunting task of taking responsibility for past failures of magnitude in conjunction with October 7 and of learning the appropriate lessons. From the prime minister, no longer trusted by a clear majority of the country, to the IDF's chief of staff and the commanders of military intelligence, resignations will be called for. Israelis will not forget that nine years earlier, on the TV satire program *Matzav HaUma*, Netanyahu made the following declaration to interviewer Lior Schlein: "The Jewish nation never excelled in foreseeing danger. We were surprised time after time, and the last time was the most awful. It won't happen under my leadership." IDF strategy, too, beginning with border settlement defense, many more divisions and armaments, and new approaches to deterrence, is undoubtedly due for major changes.[17]

Additional challenges abound. Better treatment of Arab citizens, as well as Druze and Bedouin, should not be delayed. Mohammad Darawshe, a faculty member at Jerusalem's Shalom Hartman Institute and an administrator at the Givat Haviva Educational Center, noted that, while prior to the October 7 attack trust between Jewish and Arab Israelis typically hovered between 65–75 percent, his most recent survey found that now 34 percent of the Israeli-Jewish population said they trust Arab citizens and 50 percent of Arab citizens say they trust Israeli-Jews. At the same time, there are what he calls "islands of success." For example, some 83 percent of Arabs surveyed said they were willing to share a workplace with a person who is Jewish or study with them at university, either now or perhaps in the future. Among the Jewish community, 71 percent and 67 percent said they were willing to work together or study together at a university, respectively, with a person who is Arab either now or maybe in the future.[18]

Nor should the need be deferred to ease the religious conversion process for non-Jews who eagerly protect their new homeland. The war, with the IDF declaring an urgent need for more soldiers in the near future, also sparked overwhelming support for more equitable service by the ultra-Orthodox (*hareidim*), long exempt through Torah studies, in the army and other vital sectors of society's welfare, as well as by thousands of secular Israeli youth who avoid the IDF draft. Professional help to the traumatized and wounded in this war, as well as to bereaved families, will be essential. Equally imperative, the rehabilitation of the many thousands forced to abandon their homes in the south and north. Above all, the current leadership must acknowledge that a new generation, born in the heat of battle, is determined to create a vibrant Jewish and democratic country worthy of their fallen comrades' devotion and sacrifice, as well as of the children who witnessed the atrocities committed on October 7.

What offers hope, in the first instance, is the unfathomable resilience shown by Israelis under fire. A few examples: Ariel Zohar of Kibbutz Nir Oz, whose parents, two older sisters, and maternal grandfather were murdered in the Hamas slaughter of October 7 while he had gone for a run one week before his Bar-Mitzva. At Ariel's request, a ZAKA volunteer retrieved at personal risk his father's *tefillin* (phylacteries), given by his father, a Holocaust survivor at the age of fourteen, to "celebrate" the historic occasion. Antonia Meorer-Levi of Netanya, an eighty-five-year-old who was orphaned at the age of two in France during the *Shoah* and twice had to struggle with cancer, decided to knit dolls for children who suffered through the Hamas attack. Iris Haim, whose twenty-eight-year-old son Yotam of Kfar Aza, along with Alon Shamriz and Samer Fouad Talalka, had escaped from a Gaza building where they were being held captive by Hamas terrorists. They were shot and accidentally killed by Israeli forces who thought them Hamas operatives despite the fact that they were not wearing shirts, spoke Hebrew, and one of them was waving a white flag, symbol in war of cease-fire or surrender. Hearing that the brigade's morale was low, she sent a message to its soldiers: "I wanted to tell you that I love you very much and I know that what happened is not your fault, it is the fault of no one except Hamas, may their names and memory be erased from the earth."

The 8103th Battalion of the Etzioni Brigade, engaged in the armed conflict since October 7, understandably took great delight on day 100 of the war in announcing that twenty-six babies had been born to its soldiers during that fraught time. Another hero is Corporal Ori Megidish, rescued from captivity in Gaza on October 29, who joined the ranks of the IDF's Military Intelligence Directorate in February. Jeweler Alon Mesika of Even Yehuda, whose twenty-three-year-old son Adir died in the Nova music festival when charging terrorists in an attempt to protect his girlfriend, Yuli, who ultimately survived. To date, Mesika has handed out gratis eighty-one diamond rings to soldiers about to propose marriage to their betrothed. Young adults returning to Kibbutz Be'eri, twenty-seven-year-old Dafna, a female IDF officer, explaining: "It's my generation's turn to guard our homeland. We have no other country." The family of Shlomit village's forty-one-year-old Sgt. Maj. (res.) Aviad Gad Cohen of the Etzioni Brigade, who was killed in battle on October 7. Visitors to their home on the recent festive holiday read a sign posted on the front door: "Happy Purim! We request that you enter this house with your head held high and back straight up! Then fill yourself with courage and joy. And only then, knock on the door. Here lives the family of a hero who in his life and death spread life and hope!! Proud of you!!"[19]

Hope also rests in the palpable sense of togetherness, of a nation with a sense of mission. Thirty-three-year-old Salman Habaka, the first Druze Arab tank commander in the IDF, personified this with personal calls from the battlefield for unity. Leaving immediately his wife Arin and their two-year-old son Imad in the village of Yanu-Jat near the Lebanon border when ordered to mobilize his 53rd Battalion of the 188th Armored Corps for heading south on the morning of October 7, some of his tanks joined the Paratrooper Corps in Kibbutz Be'eri. Killing dozens of Hamas terrorists there and turning the tide, he declared "We have no choice but victory," and then moved up to the front in northern Gaza. Just prior to entering, this devoted fan of the Maccabi Haifa soccer team posted a short video for the Israeli public with one message: "Our strength is in our unity. This is the time to be together. This is the time to unite and to be there for each other." On the night of November 2, leading his troops, Lt. Col. Salman Habaka was ambushed by Hamas fighters emerging from a tunnel as his tank was covering a Golani Brigade advance. A true hero who saved countless lives, he died in defense of his country.[20]

After six months of war, considerable uncertainty remained. How and when would it end? What of the fate of the remaining hostages abducted to Gaza, an open wound that will never totally heal, leaving a terrible abyss behind and endless heartbreak? What would "the day after" and beyond look like for a devastated Gaza, now moonscapes of leveled buildings and dust, each destroyed structure another jagged tomb for those still buried within? What of its residents, including the hundreds of Gazan children who are now amputees? How would the conflict affect the region and the international arena in years to come? What leaders might emerge in Israel and the Arab world to contend with change? Could the Abraham Accords be the harbinger of a yet brighter dawn and further meaningful compromise in that dangerous neighborhood, the cusp of a new era, or would rancor and mistrust hold the field? What of final judgment on the International Red Cross and on UNRWA regarding their activities during the war? What of Qatar, charged with acting both as arsonist (funding Hamas, ISIS, and the Muslim Brotherhood besides hosting Hamas's political leadership) and as firefighter (taking active part in hostage/ceasefire negotiations)?

On Israel's domestic scene, would contending political and social forces hold onto the remarkable unity that pervaded its citizenry during the war's half year? Would the months before October 7 of heated disagreement between factions over judicial review subside, allowing for respectful future dialogue? Might the noticeable shift during the war towards a strengthened religious faith and a greater connection to the people of Israel, particularly among the young, aid in better understanding and mutual appreciation? Many took note that close to half of the fallen had come from the religious Zionist ranks, including leading left-wing activist Uri Zaki, the executive committee chairman of the Meretz Party, who declared that "we should salute" that community which "gives its life for the defense of Israel." Perhaps the time had come to harken to a message found on the clothes of twenty-year-old Sgt. Reef Harush from Kibbutz Ramat David, a member of the elite Egoz Commandos, who fell in Khan Younis on April 6, 2024. The IDF reported that he carried a piece of paper with the words of the early Hasidic master Reb Elimelech of Lizhensk, to be recited before prayer: "Make our hearts such that we see only the good in our friends and not their faults. May we speak to one another in a way that is upstanding and desirable before You, and let not any hatred arise between one person and the next, Heaven forbid."[21]

Could the separate prayer of a legendary Israeli songwriter find its way into hearts scarred by acrimony and by the horrors of war? In the refrain to her *"HaChagiga Nigmeret"* ("The celebration ends"), the late Naomi Shemer, whose *"Yerushalayim Shel Zahav"* ("Jerusalem of Gold") became the anthem of the 1967 Six-Day War, had hoped for this: "To wake up tomorrow morning with a new song in our hearts / To sing it with strength, to sing it with pain / to hear flutes in the open breeze / and to start from the beginning." Tikun 2024, a new nonpartisan organization led by IDF reservists intent on preserving the spirit of cooperation brought on by the war, thinks so. Its members say they want civilian Israel to reflect the comradeship of its military, where units and tank crews are made up of right-wingers and left-wingers, religious and secular Jews, Bedouin and Druze, settlers from the West Bank and high-tech entrepreneurs from Tel Aviv. "We all learned a lesson," said forty-eight-year-old Eyal Naveh, a leader of the organization. "We don't want to go back to the polarizing discourse of trampling on one another." He said his group was also talking to Israelis across the social and political spectrum, including the ultra-Orthodox community. "In the end," he said, "we all say it's time to act in consensus."[22]

As the Preface to this volume began with Ofir Leibstein, the first Jew to be murdered in Hamas's attack on October 7, 2023, it is fitting to conclude with the thoughts of his widow, Vered. Founder with Ofir of the *Darom Adom* (Scarlet South) festival nineteen years earlier, when brilliant red anemones bursting forth as spring approaches brought hundreds of thousands to southern Israel, she feels that everything now is different. With the festival canceled and the dramatic red blooms returning after so much loss, the sight pierces her heart. "On one side it's hard," she said while walking through a field, "but on the other side it just proves to us that life is stronger than everything, and it renews itself, and we'll need to find the strength to renew ourselves as well."

Today, Vered Leibstein visits the south sporadically, living with much of the Kfar Aza community in a hotel north of Tel Aviv. She is helping oversee their move into mobile homes on a kibbutz about twelve miles east of Kfar

Aza, while their houses, many of which were badly damaged, are rebuilt. Even though nature is marking the passage of time, it is impossible to move on while members of her community are still held captive in Gaza. "It's a symbol to us about the importance of blooming again, but it will take a long time," she said.[23]

Israelis will need to find the strength to renew themselves after October 7, 2023, when they woke into a nightmare and unimaginable vulnerability struck. Returning to his grandmother's home in Kfar Aza for the first time since the Hamas massacre, Omer Ronen found a letter the terrorists wrote in her planner, which remained in the living room after she was murdered. This handwritten note read, "The Izz ad-Din al-Qassam Brigades passed through here and stamped out the occupying Zionists. You will die and you will not remain here." The majority of the residents of fence-adjacent towns that bore the brunt of the terrorist onslaught still live in temporary accommodations farther away from Gaza, awaiting the reconstruction of their homes. Of the nearly 80,000 people living near the Lebanese border who were evacuated or fled during the war, a recent survey showed that only sixty percent of them are sure they want to return.[24] Israel is at a fateful crossroads. How to move on?

Jewish traditions offer the possibility, like the red anemones in the deeply scarred Kfar Aza, of renewal and redemption. A first-of-its-kind edible forest and community garden was recently unveiled in the Negev to pay homage to Bedouin war victims and to Vivian Silver, the Canadian-Israeli peace activist of Kibbutz Be'eri whose burnt remains were identified by DNA on October 7. The new name for that stricken southern area near Gaza is *Chevel HaTekuma* ("the Region of Revival"), expressing not geography but rebuilding and rebirth. The restoration of the State of Israel after centuries of one people's exclusion, banishment, and persecution, culminating in the Holocaust, confirms this long-held faith, reflecting as it does the greatest collective Jewish affirmation of life in two millennia. An uprooted people, having inhabited Eretz Israel thousands of years before European colonialism, had returned home with full international backing. In a remarkable process of self-transformation, having dreamed for one hundred generations of the return to Zion and Jerusalem, they shed the yoke of victimhood for the grace of national independence.

The National Library of Israel, occupying its magnificent new quarters in Jerusalem, is taking the lead in collecting diverse material to document October 7, ensuring that the testimony of those who lived through these moments resonates for generations to come. An anonymous group of Israeli high-tech developers launched a geo-visualization project, "Mapping the Massacres," to preserve the history of that brutal carnage. The bereft southern communities of what was called *Otef Aza*, bearing the weight of the country's grief, are sealed into memories which, with the blameless martyrs, live on. To borrow from Puerto Rico's Holocaust memorial, let candles glow against the darkness of their unfinished lives. Adjacent to that memorial is another dedicated to the memory of seventeen Christian pilgrims from Puerto Rico who arrived for a pilgrimage to the Holy Land on May 30, 1972, when three Japanese Red Army terrorists, recruited by the Popular Front for the Liberation of Palestine, gunned down twenty-six people at Israel's major airport and wounded seventy-eight others.

Tales of bravery, fortitude, resilience, and unity, surfacing ever since the war erupted, live on as well. *Acheinu*, the prayer uttered for the welfare of "the whole house of Israel who are in distress or captivity," beseeching "the Omnipresent" to lead them speedily "from darkness to light, and from oppression to freedom," became the anthem of October 7.

One of many stories encapsulates this: In the immediate aftermath of the Russian invasion of Ukraine, ninety-four children, aged six months to seventeen years, fled their home in Zhytomyr, traveling through the Carpathian Mountains and across the border to Romania. Days later, the children boarded a plane for Israel. Initially, the orphanage was hosted at the Nes Harim Field School in the Jerusalem hills. A few months later, more permanent accommodation was arranged in the city of Ashkelon, on the shores of the Mediterranean Sea, in the Chabad educational center. On October 7, 2023, the children once again found themselves in the midst of a war, as shrapnel rained down around them, landing in the front yard of their home. The Alumim Orphanage residents of Zhytomyr were forced to seek safety again; they traveled to Kfar Chabad, about eight kilometers southeast of Tel Aviv near Lod. After a short stay, they returned to Ashkelon where they resumed their regular routine as much as possible, despite frequent sirens and other emergency alarms.[25]

Perhaps these tales should not be cause for surprise. Notwithstanding several months of war with Hamas, Israel ranked fifth of 143 countries in the annual World Happiness Report, released in March 2024. "Despite domestic division and war," explained historian Gil Troy in an op ed for the *Wall Street Journal*, "our families and community give us a sense of purpose." Israelis, he added, "live in an intimate society that runs on trust and generates hope."[26]

A common sight over the past six months. In their cars on the way to the cemetery for IDF burials, families are surrounded by neighbors, friends, and people they did not know, all around the nation's white and blue banner with the Star of David in the center held aloft, so they do not leave their homes alone to accompany a loved one during his/her last journey on earth. As seriously wounded soldiers leave hospital care for rehabilitation centers, the halls are also lined with people, Israeli flags in hand. Most Israelis in a population of over 9.5

million are one person removed from someone who was kidnapped, someone who was recalled to serve in the military, someone who was killed. What of the future? **The final narrative has yet to be told.**

Endnotes

1. Monty Noam Penkower, *Twentieth-Century Jews: Forging Identity in the Land of Promise and in the Promised Land* (Boston: Academic Studies Press, 2010), chap. 1.
2. Monty Noam Penkower, *Palestine to Israel: Mandate to State, 1945–1948*, vol. 1: *Rebellion Launched* (New York: Touro University Press, 2019), chap. 4; *On October 7* (Jerusalem: Sela Meir, 2014); Alon Penzel, *Testimonies without Boundaries, Israel: October 7th, 2023* (Jerusalem: Spines, 2024).
   Two earlier events during the Holocaust became known as "Black Sabbath." On July 11, 1942, 9,000 Jewish men between the ages of 18–45 were gathered at Liberty Square (Plateia Eleftheria) in central Thessaloniki and were forced that Saturday to do calisthenics all day in the blazing sun. If they slowed down, they were beaten. Some 2,000 of them were sent to forced labor for the German Army. By October, 250 had died; the community ransomed its young men. In February 1943, the Jews of Thessaloniki were confined in a ghetto. Deportations started in March, and, by August, almost all of the Jews of Thessaloniki had been deported and murdered in Auschwitz and Treblinka. 54,000 out of 56,000 Jews living in Thessaloniki before the war were murdered in the Holocaust.
   At 5:30 a.m. on October 16, 1943, 300 German soldiers began their hunt and brutal roundup (*Razzia*) of Jews in Rome. By 2 p.m., the anti-Jewish operation led by the SS's Theodor Dannecker and local Gestapo chief Herbert Klapper was complete. After being held for thirty hours, at least 1,035 Jews who were arrested in the raid were sent from the city's Tiburtina train station to Auschwitz-Birkenau. Just sixteen of the victims—fifteen men and one woman—returned home two years later. Subsequent raids in early 1944 at the hands of the Germans and their Italian accomplices resulted in the arrest of another 1,084 Roman Jews.
3. One reporter wrote this of his meeting with a ZAKA volunteer: "I'd seen a video in which a volunteer poured cold water on one of the burned corpses. I asked why. To cool it off, I was told, so that when it is placed in a plastic collection bag the bag doesn't melt." David Remnick, In the Cities of Killing," *New Yorker*, Nov. 6, 2023. The Chevra Kaddisha Women's Unit, working under the Chief Rabbinate of the IDF, also had the heartbreaking task of helping to identify and prepare bodies of women soldiers for burial. Also see Yair Agmon and Oriya Mevorach, *One Day in October: Forty Heroes, Forty Stories* (Jerusalem: Koren, 2024); Nachum Avniel, *We're on Our Way: The Civilians Who Saved Lives on October 7* (Jerusalem: Sela Meir, 2024).
4. *Jerusalem Post*, Oct. 29, 2023; *Times of Israel*, Oct. 18, 2023; *Haaretz*, Dec. 11, 2023. Fima's last words from that interview, words that he asked to add, even when the interviewer had thought that they had finished, were these: "You asked if we miss our families. We all miss our families, but it is also important for me say that we will stay here for as long as we need to, and however long they say so that in another forty years, fifty years, the residents of the south and the State of Israel will actualize its sovereignty. So that every farmer who is close to the border can pick his orange, his lemon, and his tangerine safely. And that is our mission here, to ensure this, I hope for generations to come." Daniel Gordis, *Israel from the Inside*, podcast, Jan. 10, 2024.
5. World Israel News, Feb. 20, 2024, and Mar. 24, 2024. The *Washington Post* reported that Hamas terrorists also managed to infiltrate Israel all the way to the outskirts of Unit 8200's Urim SIGINT base, situated about twenty-two kilometers from the Gaza Strip, essentially

reaching halfway between Gaza and the West Bank. According to the article, intelligence documents and maps found on terrorists hint at their intention in a second attack phase to reach the West Bank. Ynet News.com, Nov. 13, 2023.

6   Alvin Rosenfeld, "Longing for Auschwitz," *Tablet*, Mar. 4, 2024; Seymour Martin Lipset, "The Socialism of Fools—The Left, the Jews and Israel," *Encounter*, December 1969, 24; Yossi Klein Halevi, "Why Is Israel Being Blamed for the Hamas Massacre?," Times of Israel, Oct. 25, 2023. Jean Améry (Austrian-born Hanns Chaim Mayer), a fighter in the anti-Nazi resistance, a survivor of Auschwitz and Buchenwald, and the author of a classic book on the Holocaust, *At the Mind's Limits*, was also quite prescient in this regard. In the late 1960s, he identified the anti-Zionism then already developing among European elites as an "honorable [form of] anti-Semitism." In Améry's memorable phrase, this type of anti-Zionism contained Jew-hatred "as a cloud contains a storm." Susan Garment, "Is Anti-Zionism on Campus a Passing Nuisance, or a Fundamental Threat?," *Mosaic*, June 6, 2016. Also see Abe Greenwald, "The Woke Jihad," *Commentary*, June 2024; "The Campus Crisis: Essays," *Mosaic*, May 2024; James Kirchick, "A Chill has Fallen over Jews in Publishing," *New York Times*, May 27, 2024.

7   If "occupation" is meant to include the West Bank, it should be noted that, in defending itself legitimately against attack from the Jordanian army in June 1967, Israel seized that territory from a hostile neighbor. Moreover, the UN never recognized Jordanian sovereignty there, making the territories disputed, not occupied. For Hamas, all of Israel is "occupied" territory. The rhetorical inversions by Hamas's defenders of charged nouns like "occupation," "ethnic cleansing," "genocide," "racist," "apartheid," "colonialist," "imperialist," "atrocity," and "resistance," all words weaponized to spread bigotry, are a mark of what the twentieth-century Russian literary theorist Mikhail Bakhtin called "the carnival sense of the world." Also see Ben-Dror Yemini, The Industry of Lies: *Media, Academia, and the Arab-Israeli Conflict* (New York: ISGAP, 2017), the Hebrew original published three years earlier.

8   Palestinian sources claimed that 4,000 homes were destroyed and 100,000 people left homeless in Gaza. That was a tragedy which must also be seen in context. Michael Oren, a former Israeli ambassador to the United States, notes that a single battle in Fallujah during the second US war in Iraq displaced 300,000. And many of the Gazan homes were devastated not by Israel but by Hamas booby traps. Michael Oren, "How Gaza Became Israel's Unsolvable Problem," *Mosaic*, June 7, 2021. Further, Barry Posen, a professor at the security studies program at MIT, has written that Hamas's strategy could be "described as 'human camouflage' and more ruthlessly as 'human ammunition.'" Hamas's goal, he concluded, is to maximize the number of Palestinians who die and in that way build international pressure until Israel is forced to end the war before Hamas is wiped out. David Brooks, "What Would You Do to have Israel Defend Itself?," *New York Times*, Mar. 24, 2024.

9   Randy Lee, "Louis Brandeis's Vision of Light and Justice as Articulated on the Side of a Coffee Mug," *Touro Law Review* 33, no. 1 (2017): article 16; Israel Ministry of Foreign Affairs, Facebook, Oct. 27, 2023. Also see Jodi Rudoren, "'Everybody Needs to be Uncomfortable': Rachel Goldberg-Polin's Tireless Campaign to Bring Her Son Home," *Forward*, Dec. 23, 2303.

10 *Jerusalem Post*, Jan. 30, 2024; Kemp statement, *X*, Jan. 17, 2024; Eugene Korn, "The Death of Genocide," *Jerusalem Post*, Apr. 26, 2024.

11 Bernard Henri-Lévy, "Stop the War in Gaza," *Tablet*, Mar. 13, 2024. He could have added that no world protests occurred over the Pakistan decision to push more than 1.5 million Muslim refugees back to Afghanistan. Al-Jazeera, Nov. 7, 2023. Nor has there been a world outcry against attacks by Boko Haram Islamist militants, a jihadist organization based in northeastern Nigeria, also active in Chad, Niger, northern Cameroon, and Mali, in which Muslims have massacred thousands of Christians and driven hundreds of thousands more from their homes. *Mosaic Daily*, Mar. 17, 2024. Turkey's atrocities against Kurds, including military operations against civilians, restrictions on freedom of speech, jailing politicians, attacks on

the press, and forced displacement of civilian populations, also go on without world protest. The same is true of the current massacring, raping, and mutilating of non-Arab ethnic groups in Sudan's Darfur region by the same Arab forces responsible for the genocide two decades earlier in that area. Nicholas Kristof, "From the Embers of an Old Genocide, A New One May be Emerging," *New York Times*, May 15, 2024. Nor were there outcries when Saudi Arabian guards killed several hundreds of Ethiopian migrants and asylum seekers who tried to cross the Yemen-Saudi border between March 2022 and June 2023. Human Rights Watch, Aug. 21, 2023, https://www.hrw.org.

12 *Wall St. Journal*, Feb. 29, 2024; *Jerusalem Post*, Mar. 29, 2024; "No Biden, Most Palestinians Support Hamas," Editorial, *Jerusalem Post*, Feb. 25, 2024; Israel National News, May 20, 2024. Also see Gadi Taub, "Sorry, but There Is No Two State Solution," *Tablet*, Feb. 13. 2024; Douglas Murray, "Don't Reward Hamas with a Palestinian State," *Mosaic*, Feb. 19, 2024.

13 Bret Stephens, "For America's Jews, Every Day Must Be Oct. 8," *New York Times*, Nov. 7, 2023.

14 The slogan referenced the many youngsters who had died fighting in Israel's 1948 War of Independence. Gadi Taub, "Israelis Won't Stand for Anything Short of Victory in Gaza," Tablet, Feb. 5, 2024. For Soldiers Save Lives, see Times of Israel, Apr. 21, 2024.

15 In so doing, these Israeli allies were carrying out a UN mandate. On September 28, 2001, after the deadly attacks by Al-Qaeda on US soil, the Security Council adopted Resolution 1373 under chapter VII of the United Nations Charter. It obligated member states to implement more effective counter-terrorism measures at the national level and to increase international cooperation in the struggle against terrorism. Chapter VII of the UN Charter sets out the Security Council's powers to maintain peace. It allows the Council to "determine the existence of any threat to the peace, breach of the peace, or act of aggression" and to take military and nonmilitary action to "restore international peace and security." A fine analysis of the role of the United States in this regard can be found in "America's Test," *The Economist*, Oct. 28, 2023. For more on the US military's "expanding footprint in the Middle East," see *Washington Post*, Mar. 17, 2024.

16 Jonathan Sacks, *Not in God's Name: Confronting Religious Violence* (New York: Schocken, 2015), 265.

17 For a strong critique of the present political leadership, see Ari Shavit, "The Israeli Spirit Will Not Forgive Those Who Turn Their Backs on It Again" (in Hebrew), *Makor Rishon*, Feb. 26, 2024. Four suggested evaluations for mandatory alterations in strategy are Yair Ansbacher, *And Rises like a Lion* [*U'ch'ari yitnasa*] (Jerusalem: self-published, 2023); and Yoav Gelber, "Israel's Revised National Security Doctrine Must Include Border Defense," *Jerusalem Strategic Tribune*, Feb. 11, 2024, reprinted by JNS, Feb. 11, 2024; Meir Finkel, "Preventive War: Its Disappearance from Israel's Security Toolbox and the Need for Its Return," *BESA Center Perspectives*, Apr. 21, 2024; David Weinberg, "Long Wars Ahead for the IDF," *Jerusalem Post*, Apr. 26, 2024.

18 *Stanford Report*, Feb. 7, 2024. A survey of Israel's Arab minority (20 percent of the population), conducted by the Israel Democracy Institute (IDI) at the end of December 2023, found that 56 percent overall of Arab Israelis said that the Hamas attack on October 7 did not reflect Arab society and Islamic values, and that a significant majority (86.5 percent) supported civilian efforts during the war, such as aiding evacuees or assisting the medical system. A large majority of Arab Israelis, across religious groups, said they felt a part of the State of Israel, including its problems. 80 percent of Druze respondents indicated this, as did 73 percent of Christians and 62 percent of Muslims. *Jerusalem Post*, Dec. 26, 2023. Also see William F. S. Miles, "After Israel's Nationality Law of 2018: Is the 'Blood Covenant' Broken for the Druze?," *The Journal of the Middle East and Africa* 14, no. 4 (Oct.-Dec. 2023): 415–433; Y. Yahel and A. Galili, eds., *Bedouin in the Negev: Tribalism, Politics, and Criticism* [*Beduim baNegev: Shivtiyut, politika, u'vikoret*] (Be'er-Sheva: Ben-Gurion University of the Negev, 2023).

19 Israel21c, Oct. 30, 2023; "Title," Tapinto, Oct. 20, 2023, https://www.tapinto.net/towns/coral-springs/articles/ariel-s-bar-mitzvah; *Makor Rishon*, Oct. 30, 2023; Israel National News, Dec. 26, 2023; *Jerusalem Post*, Feb. 26, 2024; Tablet, Apr. 9, 2024; Hillel Kuttler, "Arise and Build," Tablet, Dec. 18, 2023; Daniel Gordis, *Israel from the Inside*, Mar. 27, 2024.
20 Times of Israel, Nov. 2, 2023; *Guardian*, Nov. 2, 2023; *Yisrael Hayom*, Jan. 8, 2024; "Braving Battle Twice: Lt. Col. Salman Habaka," https://www.israel21c.org.
21 *Jerusalem Post,* Dec. 23, 2023, and Feb. 9, 2024; IDF News, Apr. 12, 2024. Israel's economy also faces unprecedented challenges, echoing the struggles of the Yom Kippur War era. With the nation embroiled in war, recent developments have seen Israel's GDP plummet by an alarming 19.4 percent in the last quarter of 2023, starkly contrasting the growth witnessed in previous years. The economic impact of the conflict also reaches deep into Israel's workforce, with the business sector's GDP plummeting by 32 percent in the last quarter of 2023 due to the massive reserve draft. Times of Israel, Feb. 19, 2024; INSS, Tel Aviv University, Dec. 27, 2023; *Globes,* Jan. 11, 2024.
22 *New York Times,* Feb. 28, 2024. Also see Micah Goodman's recent *The Eighth Day [HaYom HaShmini] (Tel Aviv: HaKipod v'HaShual, 2024),* which views the end of this war as an opportunity for restructuring and revitalizing Israelis, as long as they embrace a new paradigm—the reservists, who join individualist Western values with nationalist Jewish identity.
23 Vered Leibstein interview, Associated Press, Feb. 16, 2024.
24 *Israel National News,* Feb. 3, 2024; *Haaretz,* Jan. 23, 2024.
25 *Tablet,* Mar. 7, 2024.
26 Gil Troy, "Why Israelis Are So Happy," *Wall St. Journal,* Apr. 7, 2024. Also see Dan Senor and Saul Singer, *The Genius of Israel: The Surprising Resilience of a Divided Nation in a Turbulent World* (New York: Simon and Schuster, 2023). The newly elected president of Argentina acknowledged this when visiting Yad Vashem, Israel's official memorial to the Holocaust, soon after the war erupted. Opening the visitors' book, Javier Milei wrote: "In this symbolic and transcendent place, where darkness reaches unimaginable extremes of cruelty, it is precisely here that we can see the greatness of a people. The greatness of going through the pain and rising up again even stronger than before. We all bear the duty not to remain silent. Never again is now." Meir Y. Soloveichik, "Do Cry for Me, Argentina," *Commentary,* March 2024.

Appendices

I. Moshe Dayan's Eulogy for Roi Rotenberg, April 19, 1956, Jewish Virtual Library

On April 18, 1956, twenty-one-year-old Roi Rotberg was patrolling the fields of Nahal Oz, just outside Gaza, where he lived, on horseback. He had left Tel Aviv to live there. This eulogy is as poignant and as true as it was then.

Early yesterday morning Roi was murdered. The quiet of the spring morning dazzled him and he did not see those waiting in ambush for him, at the edge of the furrow.

Let us not cast the blame on the murderers today. Why should we declare their burning hatred for us? For eight years they have been sitting in the refugee camps in Gaza, and before their eyes we have been transforming the lands and the villages, where they and their fathers dwelt, into our estate.

It is not among the Arabs in Gaza, but in our own midst that we must seek Roi's blood. How did we shut our eyes and refuse to look squarely at our fate, and see, in all its brutality, the destiny of our generation? Have we forgotten that this group of young people dwelling at Nahal Oz is bearing the heavy gates of Gaza on its shoulders?

Beyond the furrow of the border, a sea of hatred and desire for revenge is swelling, awaiting the day when serenity will dull our path, for the day when we will heed the ambassadors of malevolent hypocrisy who call upon us to lay down our arms.

Roi's blood is crying out to us and only to us from his torn body. Although we have sworn a thousandfold that our blood shall not flow in vain, yesterday again we were tempted, we listened, we believed.

We will make our reckoning with ourselves today; we are a generation that settles the land and without the steel helmet and the canon's maw, we will not be able to plant a tree and build a home. Let us not be deterred from seeing the loathing that is inflaming and filling the lives of the hundreds of thousands of Arabs who live around us. Let us not avert our eyes lest our arms weaken.

This is the fate of our generation. This is our life's choice—to be prepared and armed, strong and determined, lest the sword be stricken from our fist and our lives cut down.

The young Roi who left Tel Aviv to build his home at the gates of Gaza to be a wall for us was blinded by the light in his heart and he did not see the flash of the sword. The yearning for peace deafened his ears and he did not hear the voice of murder waiting in ambush. The gates of Gaza weighed too heavily on his shoulders and overcame him.

II. Professor Monty Noam Penkower's Remarks on Receiving a 2023 ASMEA Bernard Lewis book award, Washington, D.C., November 5, 2023

Greetings to all from Jerusalem, the capital of the State of Israel and my home for the past twenty-one years.

I am delighted at having been selected as a recipient of the Bernard Lewis book prize this year for my volume *After the Holocaust*. Aware of the pioneering scholarly contribution made by the late Professor Lewis in alerting our world to the dangers of radical Islamism, I am particularly moved to accept this award. At a time when Israel continues its war with Hamas, a terrorist adversary guilty of unprecedented atrocities against civilians and one that is committed, along with Hezbollah (another Iranian proxy), to a genocidal campaign aimed at destroying the one Jewish State, I had to stand with my fellow citizens and forego the ASMEA annual conference.

The chapters of *After the Holocaust* examine facets in the drama of how the survivors of the *Shoah* contended with life after the darkest night in Jewish history. They include the Earl Harrison mission and its significant report, the effort to keep Europe's borders open to refugee passage, the murder of the first Jew in Germany after V-E Day and its aftermath, and the iconic sculptures of Nathan Rapoport and Poland's landscape of Holocaust memory up to the present day.

After a third of world Jewry had been obliterated by Nazi Germany and collaborator nations into anonymity and ash, most survivors had few doubts about the pressing, vital need for sovereignty in their ancestral homeland, Eretz Yisrael. From then onwards, that tiny sliver of land hugging the Mediterranean continues to serve the Jewish people and their allies in the ongoing struggle for decency and truth as a bridge against apocalyptic despair, providing some solace and even joy in the wake of hitherto unimaginable horror.

Alas, the Holocaust is still at times trivialized, universalized, even brazenly denied outright. Furthermore, senseless hatred of Jews and the depersonalization of the powerless are not alien to our age. Anti-Zionism is the new antisemitism. All who cherish freedom must champion Israel's right to exist and to thrive as a beacon of light in a very troubled planet. Forty years ago, I concluded my volume *The Jews Were Expendable* with these words: "The cancer of bestiality is the concern of us all, and the infinite preciousness of life requires daily affirmation." Embracing that same credo tonight, I thank Michael Lewis and the ASMEA prize committee for this great, prestigious honor. It is one that I shall long cherish. *Shalom!*

III. IDF Soldiers' Letters

1. A Letter by Sgt. First Class Ben Zussman, Broadcast by Kan TV on December 11, 2024

Sgt. First Class Ben Zussman, 22, from Jerusalem, of the Combat Engineering Corps' 601st Battalion, was killed fighting in Gaza on December 3, 2023.

I am writing this message to you on my way to the base. If you are reading this, something has probably happened to me. As you know me, there's probably no one happier than me right now. I was just about to fulfill my dream soon. I am grateful for the privilege to defend our beautiful land and the people of Israel.

Even if something happens to me, I don't allow you to sink into sadness. I had the privilege to fulfill my dream and my destiny, and you can be sure that I am looking down on you with a big smile. Perhaps I'll sit next to Grandfather and bridge some gaps. Each one will share their experiences and what has changed between wars, and we'll talk a bit about politics, and I'll ask him for his opinion.

If, God forbid, you are sitting *shiva* [in mourning], turn it into a week of friends, family, and joy. Have food, definitely meat, beer, sweet drinks, seeds, tea, and of course, Mom's cookies. Laugh, listen to stories, meet all my friends you haven't seen yet. Seriously, I envy you. I would like to be there to see everyone.

Another very, very important point. If, God forbid, I fall captive, alive or dead, I am not willing for a soldier or civilian to be harmed because of any deal for my release. I do not allow you not to conduct a campaign or protest or anything like that. I am not willing for terrorists to be released in exchange for me. In no way, shape, or form. Please do not twist my words.

I'll say it again. I left home without even being called up to reserve duty. I am filled with pride and a sense of duty, and I always said that if I have to die, I hope it will be in defense of others and the country. "'Jerusalem, I have set watchmen' (Isaiah 62:6), that the day will come when I will be one of them" [from the 1967 poem "Guardian of the Walls" by Dan Almagor].

2. A Letter by Sgt. First Class (Res.) Joseph Yosef Gitarts, 25, from Tel Aviv, of the 179th Reserve Armored Brigade's 7029th Battalion who was Killed Fighting in Gaza on December 26, 2023.

Dear Mom and Dad,

I love you so much.

Everything is as it should be. I chose this. I lived a good and interesting life, yet, at the same time, I was never afraid of death. I could have chosen to hide and not to come here. But that would go against everything that I believe in and value, and who I consider myself to be.

So, I had no alternative, and I would make the same choice all over again. I would do the same again and again. I made this choice myself and pursued it to the end. I died honorably for my people. I have no regrets. I love you very much and I am proud that you are my parents. You gave me a great deal. I had a very interesting, full, happy, unique life. My death only emphasizes that.

I'm certain that you're feeling a great deal of pain. But you will overcome it. That's what I very much want. That's the main thing that I want. You both have many people close to you who will support you.

Please find something positive in all of this. Be with the grandchildren. Help Israel. I'm fine.

When this horrible war—which may or may not be winnable according to the definition that Israel initially set (destroying Hamas and getting all the hostages back) and which may or may not be just at its beginning—first broke out, a dear friend (an Orthodox rabbi) wrote me a note from the States which concluded with his prayer that "we would find redemption" in this war. He quite understandably prayed for a world described in the books of prophets like Isaiah, Hosea, and Micah. Images of a universal world, a world moving towards peace. A world in which swords were beaten into plowshares, in which the fox and the sheep could lie down next to each other.

That was, I told him, not the redemption we needed. The redemption we needed was not the pastoral vision of those latter prophets. The redemption we needed was to be had in slaughtering and then eradicating Hamas. It would come not from Amos or Hosea, but from the vision of the Israelites as portrayed in the Books of Joshua and Judges, books that I struggled with when I was young. Redemption would come from the Israelites being warriors. If the hatred of the Jew is eternal, which it obviously is, then the survival of the Jewish people demands that our willingness to go to battle be no less everlasting.

There are still parts of the worldview of Joshua and Judges that are challenging for me, but I've come to understand them better, I think. Part of their message is that, if the Jewish people wants to have a hope of surviving, it is going to have to be a nation of warriors, a nation of young people who care about their companions more than they care about their own lives. It will have to be a nation of young people like those reflected in the letters above.

The tragedies of this war are too numerous to name. There is suffering everywhere one turns, and things are likely to get much worse for everyone, likely including for countries not yet involved. But here is what we have learned that we might have doubted in "the world that was," in the world that ended in the early hours of the morning of October 7.

We have learned that our enemies underestimated the Jews' determination to survive. They underestimated the degree to which "never again" resonates to a young Israeli generation in a way that it no longer does to many young Jews outside of Israel—first and foremost, about Jews.

Our enemies underestimated the degree to which Israeli young people are entirely comfortable with particularism—no matter how alluring the universalist vision that has their many of their Diaspora cousins in its grip. They underestimated the degree to which a generation of Israelis that sometimes quotes Isaiah and Hosea (when it quotes from the Bible, which is not all that often) is actually a generation descended not from Micah, but from Joshua.

The outpouring of support for Israel among American Jews has been nothing less than extraordinary since October 7. But if I had to bet, I'd bet that it's support that will soon begin to wane. Because the images coming from Gaza are going to get more painful. Because this war may well drag on and on and on, and spread . . . and as it does, American Jewish passion, I suspect, is going to be difficult to sustain; October 7, instead of healing the gap that so many of us have bemoaned, may ultimately be seen as the day that marked the beginning of its permanence.

3. *A Letter Written by Master Sergeant (Res.) Rabbi Elkana Vizel, 35, of Neveh Dekalim.*

Vizel, a married father of four, who was previously called up to fight in Gaza as a reservist in Operation Protective Edge in 2014, where he was injured in battle, spoke of his experience in a YouTube video recorded two years ago. In it, he said that he made sure he had his tefillin *with him before he was evacuated to safety. He also said how thankful he was to God for saving him and giving him a new lease of life. Vizel, commander in the Brigade 261's 8208th Battalion, wrote this letter before he left to battle. It was found by his family after he fell in the building collapse tragedy in the Gaza Strip on January 22, 2024.*

If you are reading these words, something probably happened to me. First of all, if I was taken prisoner by Hamas, I demand that you do not make any deal to free me from any terrorist. Our crushing victory is more important than anything else, so please, just keep on working with all your might so our victory will be as crushing as possible.

Maybe I fell in battle. When a soldier falls in battle, it's sad. But I ask of you, be happy. Don't be sad when you part from me. Sing a lot, hold each other's hands, and support each other. We have so much to be happy about and proud of. We are the generation of redemption! We are writing the most significant moments in the history of our nation and the entire world. So please be optimistic. Continue choosing life constantly. Lives of love, hope, purity, and optimism. Look at those dear to you in the white of their eyes and remind them that everything they go through in life is worth it and they have a lot to live for.

Live! Don't stop the power of life for a moment! During Operation Protective Edge I was injured. I had the option to stay behind, but I don't regret for a moment that I returned to combat. On the contrary, that was the best decision I made.

IV. President Isaac Herzog's Speech on the First Hundred Days of the War, Israel National News, January 14, 2024.

A hundred days have passed since life was halted, the skies darkened, and we, all of us, were exposed to a boiling and horrifying cauldron of terror and deep-seated hatred unleashed upon us. One hundred days of a war forced upon us, a test for the entire nation. A test of our collective heart, courage, determination, righteousness, strength, mutual support, unity, and the values and principles that define us as a nation.

In these challenging times, we cannot help but reflect on the sacrifices of our daughters and sons, who fall as civilians and soldiers alike. Their bravery, their commitment, their love for life, and their dedication to ideals dear to us are a testament to the strength within all our hearts. We must not nor cannot forget, not for a moment, the hostages and the missing. It is difficult to fathom an ordeal more arduous and painful than that of the families whose loved ones are in the hands of Hamas murderers. We all carry a prayer, echoing the words of the prophet: "And your sons and daughters shall return to their borders."

We mourn the loss of the fallen heroes, their courage, sanctity of will, and self-sacrifice that permeated in the fierceness of battle. We weep for the many lives, far too many, snuffed out brutally—victims of monstrous and antisemitic violence. Yet, we remember that even in the darkest hours, we witnessed the strength, courage, resilience, and compassion that define us as a people. We made a grave and painful mistake by not being ready. But the greatest mistake is that of the enemy.

The enemy, whose 'great heroes' indiscriminately murdered, massacred, violated, and slaughtered infants, the elderly, girls, boys, burned homes with people inside, and committed the worst crimes against humanity. An enemy for whom Hitler's playbook, *Mein Kampf*, has pride of place in their homes, whose children's summer camps were centers of murderous brainwashing and blind hatred. An enemy who thinks he knows us and belittles the bravery of our sons and daughters until he sees with his own eyes how "a people rise like a lioness and lift itself like a lion."

The forces of courage within our midst have erupted in an inspirational manner. We saw how the "TikTok generation" emerged as a generation of historic strength, whose bravery will be etched in the annals of Israeli history. I met with the fighters and commanders, the leaders on the front—made of steel, eager to engage the enemy, with the oath of "never again." We all witness the strength of communities and displaced families, the bravery of our wounded in hospitals, the unwavering faith and pride of the bereaved families, the volunteerism and mutual responsibility in Israeli society—Jews and Arabs alike—the determination of our allies standing by our side, headed by the United States, and the Jewish communities around the world standing with us as one, sometimes at personal risk. No one can defeat such a people, such a united and determined nation.

Even though this war broke out in one of the most challenging periods in our history, and while the enemy hoped that the terror attack would deepen the rifts and weaken the internal Israeli alliance—we chose life, we chose our shared commitment. We chose to unite immediately and fight together, shoulder to shoulder, for the present and the future of our shared home. Unfortunately, it is hard not to see that there are those who choose, even now, to return to the discourse of hatred and division that prevailed here until October 6. Any retreat to those dark places directly threatens us—our security, our lives. Criticism is always permitted, it is sometimes necessary to argue—it's a clear part of our democracy, but it is time to conduct our debates and discussions responsibly, to preserve our unity, to remember that we are one people and one country. We must not let Hamas win the battle for Israeli resilience. This is true for all of us, especially for public officials and leaders. Leadership in times of war implies responsibility for Israeli resilience, which is the foundation of any victory. When our brothers and sisters are risking their lives on the front, we must rise above the campaigns, above petty politics, and divisive rhetoric—both regarding the day before and the day after—and listen to the cries of our children who wish to return home safely to a peaceful home. Peaceful from within and without.

Despite the challenges ahead, I have no doubt that we will emerge from the shadows of this conflict stronger and more determined than ever. Together, as one nation, we will overcome the darkness, rise from the ashes, rebuild, replant, sow, affix mezuzahs on homes, turn each and every hell into a paradise—as we have always done, and create a future of hope and abundance for us, our state, and the entire region—one that is worthy of the fallen, one that honors the memories of the victims, and reflects our commitment to being a beacon of hope for ourselves and for all of humanity. Our enemy made a mistake. The spirit of the people of Israel will always overcome. Even this time, our spirit will prevail.

V. Poems for Our Days

1. My Daughter

My daughter
You will not walk alone
Daddy and his friends
Are fighting for you.

Indeed, there is a bit of belly
And the back hurts some
But we the elderly
Are fighting from the heart.

And we see Zionism
And we breathe a state
But between us,
We are here for you
My young child.

Because we promised way back then
That in this land
You will walk safely
In the gilded field
For that—the sweat
For that—the battle.

And together with you my child
Thousands more children
This night will go safely to sleep
For this daddy is here
With the rest of his brothers.

                Netanel Ellinson
                Translation by Avi Penkower

The father's fervent wish for his daughter before he turns to battle in Khan Younis recalls the famed Israeli poet Lea Goldberg's "You will walk in the field." In that work, written in 1943 as perhaps Goldberg's response to the Holocaust in her native eastern Europe, the narrator describes a woman walking barefoot through a freshly plowed field, and wonders if one day she will again be able to walk there peacefully rather than be stabbed by the sharp undergrowth. The relevance of the poem to the country's post-October 7 feelings of being devastated and yet surviving to yearn for peace is clear.

2. Do Not Lay Your Hand[1]

Do not lay your hand on the door
Do not do anything
They are there
Lying in wait for you
The shattered fragments of your life
Scattered in the center of the living room
On the old couch
On the stained floor
The wounds, the scratches, the pain
They are waiting to sacrifice you
On the altar
Do not lay your hand

Esther Maharat Freedman
Translation by Heather Silverman, Michael Bohnen,
Rachel Korazim, and Esther Maharat Freedman

This poem, referencing the biblical story of the patriarch Abraham's raising his hand in a sacrifice of son Isaac, recalls Israelis trying to hold the doors of safe rooms secure against the slaughter by Hamas invaders from the Gaza Strip on October 7.

3. One Tiny Seed

There is a lullaby that says your mother will cry a thousand tears before you grow to be a man.
I have cried a million tears in the last sixty-seven days.
We all have.
And I know that way over there
there's another woman
who looks just like me
because we are all so very similar
and she has also been crying.
All those tears, a sea of tears
they all taste the same.
Can we take them
gather them up,
remove the salt
and pour them over our desert of despair
and plant one tiny seed.
A seed wrapped in fear,
trauma, pain,
war and hope
and see what grows?
Could it be
that this woman
so very like me
that she and I could be sitting together in fifty years
laughing without teeth
because we have drunk so much sweet tea together
and now we are so very old
and our faces are creased
like worn-out brown paper bags.

And our sons
have their own grandchildren
and our sons have long lives;
One of them without an arm
But who needs two arms anyway?
Is it all a dream?

>   Rachel Goldberg-Polin
>   Translation by Rachel Korazim

The author, whose American-born son Hersh lost his arm during the October 7 attack and was kidnapped to the Gaza Strip (he was subsequently killed by Hamas), became the eloquent voice of those families pressing for the quick return of their abducted sons and daughters Note the very last line's reference to the iconic poem "V'Ulai" by the early Palestinian pioneer Rachel Bluwstein, which ends with these words. It was written in 1923, while Rachel was living a lonely life in a small, one-room apartment in Tel-Aviv. She was dying of tuberculosis, and the poem recalls her love for the Land of Israel and a nostalgia for her youthful days at Kibbutz Degania, on the south shores of Lake Kinneret (the Sea of Galilee), between 1909 and 1913.

4. And These Are the Names[2]

And these are the names of the children of Israel
Eighty and another six nights
And these are the names of those covered by darkness.
And these are the names of those descending to the abyss of grief
Whose lives were abducted and cut off from their life".
And these are names of the children of Israel whose cry
Rises from the depth of the tunnels of darkness
And there is no angel nor seraph[3] to save them
Not even a single expression[4] of deliverance.
But there is hope
With trembling wings
With the power to break out of the straits[5]
And call them by their names
And draw them out
To bring them back—to the land of the living.

>   Yael Lifshitz
>   Translation by Michael Bohnen, Heather Silverman, and Rachel Korazim

This poem focuses on the hostages kidnapped in the Hamas assault on October 7, who were brought to the labyrinth of tunnels in Gaza. Referencing the Jewish people redeemed by divine intervention from slavery in Egypt millennia ago, the ultimate hope is expressed that they, too, will be delivered to safety and home.

5. Hill of Heroes

Yonina Simon of Hashonaim penned this poem after the funeral on January 9, 2024, in Har Herzl of Sgt.-Maj. General (res.) Yakir Hexter, 26, from Jerusalem, a fighter in the 8291th Engineering Battalion, Hace Hash formation (551), who fell in battle one day earlier in the south of the Gaza Strip.

It was the rows of fresh graves
that did me in,
and the dates of their short lives.
It was the choke in the voices
of his parents and teacher.
It was the strangled cries and moans that could be heard in the hundreds of people who came.
And the gunshots
The honor shots.
The awful loud pronouncement of death.
In the Line of Duty.
No one wants their son to be a hero in death-
No one.
And yet the mountain is covered in them,
filled with them.
As if it's growing these 100 days.

Yonina Simon

6. Blood Touched Blood

In memory or Maoz Morell and Maoz Fenigstein
Maoz Fenigstein, Sgt. First Class (res.), 25, of the 551st Brigade's 7008th Battalion, from Susya, fell in battle in northern Gaza on December 19, 2023. Maoz Morell, Staff Sgt., 22, of the Paratroopers Brigade Patrol, from Talmon, injured while fighting in southern Gaza on February 15, 2004, succumbed to his wounds six days later.

The gates of heaven opened,
And Maoz stands at the entrance, in the light.
A smile spread across his lips,
To greet his good friend, the hero.

And they meet with a strong embrace,
From the Garden of Eden tears turn to rain.
And Maoz encourages Maoz forward,
In their youth the tie was bound.

And the two of them stand facing the Creator,
They seek no reckoning.
For with devotion and faith they gave their lives,
Only one request on their tongues:

That the heart of a mother be healed from breaking and pain,
That a father's pride serve him as an anchor.
That a young sister's smile brighten her face,
That no other friends join them in Heaven.

>Noya Amram
>Translation by Avi Penkower

7. *A Coat of Many Colors*

My son returned from the battle with a knapsack bulging
with everything I didn't pack for him.

Socks donated by a community in Argentina
A patchwork quilt with the scent of a different home
A blue towel from a moshav [small community] family
Tzizit [ritual fringes] from Jerusalem
A fleece gifted by a high-tech company
A scarf knitted by an old woman
Undershirts purchased by a Paybox group
A sheet given to him by a friend
Gloves bought by young girls
A coat from the closet of someone who came and wanted to give.

I spread out all these cloths
and knit a new coat of many colors,
Joseph—see! Your brothers have taken responsibility for you.

    Racheli Moshkovitz
    Translation by Avi Penkower

This poem, conscious of a war whose first day of genocidal, uncompromising bloodbath was unprovoked and unprecedented in Israeli history, hails the pervasive unity brought forth in the Jewish world after October 7. The author hopes that it may serve as a traditional *"tikun"* (repair) for the biblical Joseph's fate, as portrayed in Genesis, at the hands of his jealous brothers.

8. Could Someone

Could someone create more words?
Because I fear they've finished
and left only silence in their wake
Could someone create more words
that might heal
and give comfort?
Could someone?
Find words
great enough
for great people?
Words of prayer
from bleeding hearts?
Like those that may reach
his compassionate throne?
Anyone?

    Michal Avraham
    Translation by Yonina Simon

Endnotes

1. God's angel told Abraham not to sacrifice his son: "Do not raise your hand against the boy, or do anything to him" (Genesis 22:12).
2. These are the names of the children of Israel who came to Egypt (Exodus 1:1).
3. From the Passover *Haggadah*: "'And the Lord took us out': not through an angel, and not through a seraph."
4. As Rashi explains in his biblical commentary, there are four different terms used by God in describing the deliverance from Egypt, for the Scripture states (Exodus 6:6–7): "And I will bring forth," "and I shall deliver," "and I shall redeem," "and I shall take out."
5. The Hebrew word for "straits" is similar to the word for Egypt in the first line.

Index

'100 Days in Hell', 122–123
9/11 attacks, 11, 109n63, 224, 237n15 compared with Hamas October 7 attack, 11, 25n29, 25n30, 109n63, 224

A

A'ashur, Yakub, 62
Abbas, Mahmoud, 6, 11, 16, 24n13, 62, 68, 87, 103–104, 155, 168, 170, 198, 204 defends Hamas October 7 attack, 6, 11
does not condemn October 7 attack, 104
rejects Olmert peace offer, 16
seeks Palestinian unity, 103–104
unpopular and ineffective in Palestinian opinion, 170 urging Hamas to reach prisoner swap agreement, 155
Abbas, Mansour, 29, 214n7
Abd el-A'el, Majdi, 147
Abdallah, Bou Habib, 146
Abdelsalam, Mohammed, 91
Abdollahian, Amir Hossein, 15, 31, 42–43, 83
Abdullah, II, and Abdullah, King, 64, 115–116, 119, 121, 153, 177n65 200
Abergil, Matan, 222
Abraham Accords, 10–11, 15, 25n26, 101, 113, 231
Abraham, 175n21, 248, 253n1
Abraham, Yuval, 51
Abu Ajawa, Ali Salem, 114
Abu al-Rous, Hadi, 203
Abu Arar, Hamid, 222
Abu Baker, Essam, 84–85
Abu Baqir al-Saadi, Wissam Mohammed, 149
Abu Daoud (Mohammed Daoud Odeh), 106n5
Abu Hasna, Muhammad, 194
Abu Kabir Forensic Institute, 59
Abu Latif, Fadi, 198
Abu Madighem, Ata, 88
Abu Marzouk, Mousa Mohammed, 18, 125, 169, 178n71
Abu Obada (Muhammad Suwala), 80
Abu Omar, Ismail, 158
Abu Rashad, Amin, 80
Abu Rida, Musab Abdel, 117
Abu Rudeineh, Nabil, 168
Abu Sabila, Amer Odeh, 29
Abu Srour, Obada Saed, 117
Abu Tuama, Razi, 215n25
Abu Zina, Mohsen, 56
Abu Zuhri, Sami, 95, 97, 134
Abu-Fanounah, Wael, 127
Abu-Maghsib, Ibrahim, 56
Abusada, Mkhaimar, 96–97
Abu-Shalal, Amed Abdullah, 125
"Acheinu," 234
Achim LaNeshek, 227
"Across the Wall," 51
Adato, Orit, 5
Adora, 121, 212
Adraee, Avichay, 64, 96–97, 131
Afghanistan, 12, 25n29, 109n63, 120, 225, 236n11
Afghanistan war, 109n63
After the Holocaust, xii, 240
Agam Institute, 29
Agence France-Presse, 168–169, 182
Agudath Israel of America, 196
Ahmed, Qanta A., 2–3
AI attacks, 45
AIPAC, 192
Akre, Azzam, 138n3
Aladdiny, Omar Atiya Daruish, 184
Al-Ahli Anglican Hospital, Hamas propaganda, 14
Al Akhbar, 188
Al-Ali, Osama, 119
Al-Amal Hospital, 143, 152, 176n48
Al-Amal neighborhood, 133
Al Aqsa TV, 5, 52
"Al-Aqsa Flood", xii, 3
Al-Aqsa Hospital, 213
Al-Aqsa Intifada, 23n7
Al-Aqsa Martyrs Brigade, 73, 217n57, 220

Al-Aqsa Mosque, 4, 23n7, 41, 59, 62, 102, 164, 169, 172, 175n21, 182, 192, 195, 199, 206, 212, 214n7 past clashes on Ramadan, 206
Al-Arabiya, 17, 20, 119, 159
Al-Araby Al-Jadeed, 95
Al-Araby Al-Jadid, 191
al-Araja, Muhammad, 161
Al-Arouri, Saleh, 5, 42, 78, 104, 111–112, 114, 138n9
al-Assad, Bashar, 4
al-Atifi, Mohamed, 136
al-Auja, 210
Alayoubi, Zaid, 147
Al-Azhar University, 96–97
Albanese, Anthony, 157
Albanese, Francesca, 154, 176n31
al-Banna, Hassan, 3
Al-Baraa, Abu, 150
Al-Batanji, 184
Albright, David, 127–128
'Al-Buraq, 175n21
Al-Bureij refugee camp, 97, 116
Al-Dabas, Ali Muhammad, 158
al Dabs, Abbas Muhammad ("Hajj Abdullah"), 148
al-Eid, Nidal, 203
Aleppo, 105, 211
Alexandroni Brigade, 93
Al-Falih, Khalid, 56
Algeria, 106n5, 133, 164
Alghad TV, 169
al-Halhuli, Hamdan, 194
Alhandi, Amr, 59
al-Hayya, Khalil, 56, 153, 184
Al-Houthi, Abdul Malik, 66
Al-Houthi, Hussein, 75n54
Al-Husayl, Raymond, 221
al-Husseini, Haj Amin, 16, 23n7
Alian, Ghassan, 180
Ali Mustafa, Hadi, 194
Aliya, xivn2, 227
al-Jama'a al-Islamiyya, 211
Al-Jazeera, 4, 22n2, 26n55, 48n38, 71, 78, 83, 93, 100, 106n5, 128, 152, 158, 160, 162, 165, 168, 217n57, 236n11
Al-Kaddoumi, Aref Ali, 166
Al-Kaddoumi, Faruq, 24n13
Alkarnawi, Hamed, 29, 221
Al-Kharaz, Khalil, 138n3
al-Khasawneh, Bisher, 126
Al-Khyam, 200
"Allahu Akbar!," xii, 34, 44
Al-Ma'azi, 118
Al-Malalhi, Muhammad Awad, 203

al-Maliki, Riyad, 164
Al-Masira, 100
Al-Masri building, 186
Al Mawasi, 135, 153–154
Al-Mayadeen TV, 208, 211
al-Muasi, deadliest IDF loss, 129
al-Nahyan, Abdullah bin, 25n26
al-Nakhalah, Ziyad, 42
Alnaouq, Ahmed, 51
Al-Omar oil field, 149
Alon, Nitsan, 18
Aloni, Emilia, 126–127
"Al-Qadsia" compound, 144
Al-Qaeda, 11, 25n29, 30, 109n63, 191, 196, 237n15 founded, 25n29 inspired by Hamas, 11, 25n29, 30, 109n63, 191, 196, 237n15
Al-Qahoum, Ali, 89
al-Qassam Brigades, 3–6, 25n24, 25n25, 36, 71, 99–100, 137, 173, 191, 233
Al-Quds, 55, 59, 172
Al-Quds Day, 62
Al-Quds hospital, 55
al-Rahi, Bechara Boutros, 106
al-Rantisi, 18, 23n6, 111
al-Rantisi, Abdel Aziz, 18, 23n6
al-Raqab, Saleh, 41
al-Sayed, Abbas, 96
al-Sayed, Hisham, 7
Al-Shati refugee camp, 45, 55, 59–60, 67
Al-Shifa Hospital, 43, 45, 59–60, 65–66, 68, 112, 158, 176n48, 201, 206–207, 209, 211–213
Al-Sudani, Mohammed Shia', 69, 149
al-Tawil, Wissam (Jawad), 115
Al-Thani, Mohammed, 183
Al-Tufayli, Subhi, 121
Alumim orphanage, 234
Al Waqea, 145
Alwiyat al-Waad al-Haq, 38
al-Yaakobi, Ahmed, 150
al-Zayani, Abdullatif bid Rashid, 25n26
al-Zin, Ismail, 213
"*Am Yisrael chai!*" 65, 228
Amal neighborhood, 133, 209–210
American Jewish Committee, 196
American Muslims for Palestine, 79
Améry, Jean, 236n6
Amidror, Yaakov, 31–32
Amir-Abdollahian, Hossein, 42–43, 83
Amman, 177n65, 209
Amnesty International, 32
Amram, Noya, 251
"And These Are the Names," 249–250

Andrés, José, 193
anemone festival, ix–x, 232–233
Anti-Defamation League, 175n27, 196
antisemitism, 16–17, 54, 58, 64–65, 85–86, 102, 112, 134, 157, 210, 223, 227–228, 241 challenged, 58, 64–65 global outbreak, 85–86 spike in the United States, 210, 223
anti-Zionism, 61, 227, 236n6, 241
"any means necessary," 224
apartheid, 164, 166, 217n57, 223, 226, 236n7
Arab gangs in Israel, 171
Arab Gulf States Institute, 7
Arab heroes on October 7, 29
Arab League, 60, 97
Arab World for Research and Development, 63
Arabs, ix, 10, 12, 15, 28–29, 35, 78, 94–95, 99, 133, 148, 158, 171, 192, 203–204, 206, 212, 216n44, 219–220, 224, 226, 229, 239, 245
  against the Jewish State, 133
  in Middle East pro-Hamas, 133
  Israeli citizens, 29, 147, 187, 212, 229
  Israeli citizens' views, 237n18
Arafat, Yasser, 16–17, 23n7, 24n13, 25n24, 29, 103, 149, 216n44
  rejects Barak peace offer, 16
a-Rantisi, Iman, 150
Arazim Industrial Zone, ix
Arce, Luis, 163
Archbishop of Canterbury, 99
Ardakani, Hossein Hatefi, 130–131
Argentina, xivn2, 23n8, 148, 238n26
Argentina bombings, 23n8
Armed Conflict Location and Event Data Project, 98
Armenians, 226
Armored Corps Memorial Site and Museum, 146
armored troops, 50
Army of Islam, 196
Arrow defense system, 45
Article 40A, 227
Asa-El, Amos, 11
Asar, Muhammad, 49
Asefa, Wael, 53
Asharq Al-Awsat, 118, 180, 223
Ashdod, 132, 223
Ashkelon, 5, 85, 234
Ashtiani, Mohammad Reza, 89
Asira al-Qibliya, 167
Associated Press, 47n22, 62, 79, 88, 179, 201
Association for the Study of the Middle East and Africa (ASMEA), 240–241

At the Mind's Limits, 236n6|
Ateek, Naim, 99
Atrash, Hassan, 98
"atrocity," xii, 8, 20, 34, 37, 42, 64, 103–104, 128, 133, 148, 157–158, 176n40, 203–204, 215n24, 224, 229, 236n7, 236n11, 240
Atzida, Amad, 206
Auschwitz, 65, 140n60, 223, 235n2, 236n6
Auschwitz-Birkenau, 140n60, 235n2
Austin, Lloyd, 66, 89–91, 144
Australia, x, 79, 120, 129, 130, 134–135 139, 144, 157, 202, 206, 215n23
Australian National University, 93
Avigal, Ido, 73
Avraham, Michal, 252
Axios news website, 37, 48n33, 148, 153, 167, 172, 213n70, 217n70
Axios, 37, 48n33, 153, 172, 217n70
"axis of evil," 12
"Axis of Resistance," 15, 66
Ayalon Highway, 125–126
Ayalon, Barak, 122
Ayalon, Meirav, 122
Ayelet HaShahar, 44
Ayoub al-Ansari Mosque, 20
Ayta al-Sha'ab, 124
Ayyash Yahyah, 6
Azerbaijan, 226

B
b'yachad n'natzeiach, 138, 227
Ba'athist regime, 4
Baalbek, 171, 194–195, 203
Bab el-Mandeb strait, 7, 89
Babylonians, 175n21
Bagheri, Mohammad, 226
Bahrain, 25n26, 42, 56, 60, 91, 101, 120, 129, 144, 11
Bakhtin, Mikhail, 236n7
Baking Battalion, 227
Balata refugee camp, 125
Baluchistan, 126
Banai, Ehud, 228
Bani Suheila cemetery, 137
Bar, Ronen, 8, 78
Baradaar, Abdul Ghani, 109n63
Barak, Ehud, 16
Barak, Tamir, 33
Barakat, Khaled, 80
Barghouti, Marwan, 95, 204, 217n57
Barji, Ali Hussein, 116
Barkan, 94
Barnea, David, 112–113, 153, 200

Bar-Oz, Tzur, 80
Barud, Shadi, 42
Bates, Andrew, 81
Bayan-gate news, 149
Bayern Munich soccer game, 61
BBC, 9, 15, 24n13, 75n54
BDS (boycott, divestment, and sanctions), 223
Be'er Sheva, 45, 146, 212–213, 237n18
Be'eri Forest, 61
Be'eri, xii, 29, 34, 47n9, 61, 65–66, 84, 110, 114, 122, 161, 171, 193, 221, 230–231, 233
Bedouin, ix, 2, 29, 69, 88, 146, 190, 213, 221, 226, 229, 232–233
Begin-Sadat Center for Strategic Studies. see BESA Center
Beijing, 68, 122
Beirut, 7, 24n13, 34, 42–43, 51, 81, 111–112, 149, 168, 180–181, 195
Beit Hanoun, 56, 90, 186
   IDF attacks in, 56, 90, 186
Beit Jinn, 115
Beit Kama Junction, 198
Beit Lahiya, 124
Beitunia, 72
Bekaa Valley, 191
Ben Gvir, Itamar, 136, 156, 171, 215n26
   against prayer at Al-Aqsa Mosque during Ramadan, 182
   criticized by Biden, 171
   for reducing Arabs entry to Temple Mount on Ramadan, 171
   for war on Hezbollah, 215n26
   Itamar, on humanitarian aid, 156
Ben Haim, Paul, 30
Ben-Barak, Ram, 64
Ben-Gurion International Airport, 131
Benjo, Omer Sarah, 154
Bennett, Aharon, 80
Bennett, Michal, 186
Bennett, Naftali, 196
Ben-Shabbat, Meir, 182
Berlin, 58, 106n5, 122
Bernard Lewis book award, xii, 240–241
Bernstein, Leonard, 30
Berri, Nabih, 129
BESA Center, 8, 24n17
Beth Zion synagogue, 58
Bethlehem, 67, 167, 194
Bibas, Ariel, 123
Bibas, Kfir, 46, 77, 123, 125
Bibas, Shiri, 46, 77
Bibas, Yarden, 46
Biden, Joseph, 7, 14, 27, 38–42, 52–53, 58, 61, 65, 67–68, 71, 73, 82–83, 85–86, 88, 90–91, 95, 98–99, 103, 107n24, 113, 116, 118, 120–121, 123, 126–127, 129, 131, 133–136, 142–144, 146, 148–151, 153, 156-157, 159–160, 162, 166–167, 169, 171–173, 174n5, 178n69, 179–182, 185–187, 189, 191–193, 195, 197–198, 202–203, 205–208, 210–212, 214n16, 216n43, 217n58, 237n12
bin Al-Hussein, Abdullah II, 64
bin Laden, Osama, 25n29, 109n63
bin Mosaad, Abdul Rahman, 51
Bin Salman al-Saud, Mohammed, 115
Bin Talal, Hussein, 177n65
Binyenei HaUma, 135
Birzeit University, 63
Bislamach Brigade, 96
Bitton, Yuval, 5
Bituach Leumi, 181
Black Lives Matter, 79
"Black Sabbath," xivn1, 235n2
"Black Sabbath" (1946), 221
"Black Sabbath" (2023), 221, 227
"Black Sabbath," xi, xivn1, 29, 110, 235n2
Black September, 106n5, 177n65, 175n66
"Black Tuesday," 86
Blinken, Anthony, 36, 40–41, 46, 50, 53, 55, 64, 81–83, 95, 111, 114–115, 117–118, 120, 124, 147–149, 160, 163, 169, 178n69, 182, 186, 206-207, 226
blood libel, 134, 152–153, 175n27
"Blood Touched Blood," 250–251
Bloomberg New Economy Forum, 56
Blue Line, 93
Bnei Re'em, Arab shooting attack, 159
Bob, Yonah Jeremy, 130, 194
Bohnen, Michael, 248–250
Bok, Scott, 107n11
Boko Haram, Islamist attacks, 236n11
Bolivia, 50, 163
Bolsonaro, Jair, 177n55
Bondi Beach, 61
Border Police. see Israeli Border Police
Borrell, Josep, 35, 154, 202
Bosnia, 139n28
BP, 88–89
Brandeis, Louis Dembitz, 225, 236n9
Brandenburg Gate, 58
Brazil, 56, 163, 177n55
   Hezbollah cell in, 56
Brigade 401, 43, 124 46th Battalion, 43
"Bring them home now!" 122, 131
"Bring Them Home," 125, 152
Brooklyn Bridge, 44

Brothers in Arms, 111, 227
Buenos Aires bombings, 4, 23n8
Burns, Bill, 133
    Burns, William, 160, 189, 215n23
Bush, Cori, 141n68
Bush, George W., 17
Bushnell, Aaron, 174
Buttigieg, Pete, 186
Buzzilla, *Maariv* analysis, 215n37

C

Caesarea, 114, 212
Cairo University, 21–22, 24n13
Callamard, Agnès, 32
Cambodia, 139n28
Cameron, David, 132, 143, 184, 205–206
    questions Israel's aid for Gaza, 184
Cameroon, 236n11
Camp David Summit, 16
Camp Re'im, 1
Canada, 81, 91, 129, 134, 144, 157, 202–203, 216n44, 217n56
Cape Town, x
Captagon stimulant, 19–20
"car graveyard," 47n21
"carnival sense of the world, the," 236n7
CBS News, 4, 12, 77, 143, 153, 170, 186
cease-fire, 9–10, 22, 38–43, 45–46, 50, 53, 55, 60, 63, 67, 69–73, 77–78, 81–82, 91, 93–95, 97, 100, 111, 118, 131, 133–134, 137–138, 143, 146–147, 153, 156–157, 160, 162, 164–165, 167, 169, 171–172, 179–180, 182–184, 189, 195, 197, 200, 202–208, 213, 230
    calls, 35, 40, 97, 116, 164, 173, 182, 200, 206
    Hamas plan, 183–184
    possibilities of, 184
CEDAW. see UN Committee on the Elimination of Discrimination Against Women
CENTCOM. see US Central Command
Center for Peace Communications, 158
Central Camps Brigade, 53, 56, 126, 215n25
Central Intelligence Agency, 12, 75n27, 121, 133, 160, 189 view of the war, 189
CGM, 88
Chabad, 234
Chabahar, 99
Chad, 236n11
Channel 12 News, 3, 24n16, 60, 71, 82, 134, 136, 150, 166, 177n50, 210, 222
Chanuka, 84–85
Charity Association for Palestine Support, 80
Charleston, 116

Chechens, 226
Chevel HaTekuma, 233
Chevra Kaddisha Women's Unit, 235n3
Chikli, Amichai, 79–80
Chile, 50
China, 40–41, 68, 70, 115, 139n29, 163, 177n63, 206, 210, 226, 228
Christian Lebanese Forces, 106
Christians in Israel, 61, 99, 195, 237n18
Christians, attacked by Boko Haram, 236n11
CIA. see Central Intelligence Agency
civilian to combatant ratio, 225–226
Clinton, Bill, 16, 210
CMA, 88
CNN, 15, 24n11, 44, 61, 83, 106n5, 149–150, 173, 188–189, 196–197, 215n24
"A Coat of Many Colors," 251-252
COGAT. see Coordination of Government Activities in the Territories
Cohen, Aviad Gad, 230
Cohen, Eli, 36, 65, 81, 94, 106
Cohen, Yoram, 19
Cold War, 40
Colombia, 50, 163
"colonialism," 233
"colonialist," 236n7
Colonna, Catherine, 94
Combat Engineering Corps, 33, 65–66, 96, 130, 241–242
"come to Jesus", 186, 214n16
Commando Brigade, xi, 28, 149, 160
Conference of Presidents of the Major American Jewish Organizations, 162, 196
Conricus, Jonathan, 34
Cooper, Nurit, 33
Coordinator of Government Activities in the Territories, 84, 123, 180, 193
"Could Someone," 252
Council on American-Islamic Relations, 79
"Covenant of Victory and Renewal of Settlement," 136
"cult of death," 51–52
Cyprus, 65, 82, 106, 149, 179, 185, 193, 212
Czarny, Anat, 42
Czech Republic, 216n44

D

da Silva, Jorge Moreira, 193
da'wa, 3
Dababash, Mohammed Khamis, 62
Dagestan, 44
Dahab, 89
Daily Mail, 154
Damascus, 101, 106n5, 127, 136, 166

Dannecker, Theodor, 235n2
Danon, Danny, 64
Dar al-Harb (House of War), 23n4
Dar al-Islam (House of Islam), 23n4
Daraj district, 104
Daraj Tuffah Mosque, 111
Darawshe, Awad, 29, 222
Darawshe, Mohammad, 229
Darfur, 236n11
Darom Adom festival, ix, 232
Darshan-Leitner, Nitzana, 32, 123, 157
Davidian, Rami, 221
day 120 of the war, 144
Dayan, Moshe, xii, 228, 239–240
Dead Sea, 84
"Death Road, The," 47n21
Deif, Muhammad, 6, 52, 106, 118, 191, 209
 favors martyrdom, 52
Deir al-Balah Battalion, 53, 110, 131, 213
Deir ez-Zur, 149
Deir Hanna, 212
Delhi, 122
Democratic Socialists of America, 79
Denmark, 61, 87, 144
Dewik, Fadi, 212
DeYoung, Karen, 40
Dhahir, Osama Hamad, 203
Dhahiriya, 130
Dheisha, 201
Dilmoni, Yigal, 108n32
Dimona, 222–223
Division 162, 145, 171, 200–201, 209
Division 252, 90
Division 98, 137, 145, 180, 197, 209–210, 213
Division 99, 190
Djibouti, 60
"Do Not Lay Your Hand," 247–248
Doghmush clan, 195
Doha Forum, 83
Doha, 17, 133, 164, 173, 200, 202–203, 209
Dome of the Rock, 175n21
Dowden, Oliver, 203
Draft Law, 172
Dresden, fire-bombed by Allies, 32
Druze, 129, 209, 221, 226, 229–230, 232, 237n18 hero, 230
Duvdevan Units, xi, 188, 211

E
"Each Hostage Has a Story," 71
East Jerusalem, 35, 84, 103, 120, 153, 156–157, 159, 166, 177n65, 192, 194
Eastern Battalion, 137
Edri, Rachel, 221

Efrat, 167, 183
Egoz Commandos, 190, 202, 213, 232
Egypt, 3, 5, 7, 10, 13, 29, 33, 35, 37, 42, 46, 50–51, 56, 60, 68, 71–72, 74, 84, 89, 93, 100–101, 103–104, 111, 115, 119, 121, 125, 131–133, 135, 137–138, 145, 149, 151, 153, 159, 161–162, 164–165, 168–169, 172, 175n19, 184, 187, 193–194, 201–203, 206, 211, 214n1, 250, 253n2, 253n4, 253n5
Eichmann, Adolf, 75n32, 105
Eid, Bassem, 29
Eilat, 45
Eisin, Miri, 7–8
El Al, 33
El Arish, 125
El Reda, Samuel Salman, 23n8
El Zaidneh, Youssef, 29, 221–222
Elbit Hermes 450 drone, xi
"eleven points," 47n9
Eli settlement, 137, 180
Elimelech of Lizhensk, 232
Ellinson, Netanel, 247
El-Sisi, Abdel Fattah, 71-72, 121, 201
Elsraj, Sameh, 184
Elysee Palace, 148
Emad missiles, 156
EMDR Israel, 30
Epstein, Bilha, xi
Epstein, Netta, xi, 221
Erdan, Gilad, 35, 45, 81, 97, 208, 216n44
 criticizes UN, 208
 on UN resolution, 97
 opposes UN commemoration of *Nakba*, 216n44
Erdoğan, Recep Tayyip, 102–103
 against Israel, 44
 pro-Hamas, 39
 solution for war's end, 102–103
Erez Crossing, ix, 33, 56, 65, 89
Eroica symphony, 30
Esh Kodesh, 117
Eshbal, 188
Eshkol East Galilee, 128
Eshkol Regional Council, 9, 34, 101
Esther, xiv
Ethiopian Jews, 63
Ethiopian refugees, 236n11
ethnic cleansing, 63, 113, 224, 236n7
Etzioni Brigade, 230
EU. see European Union
European Commission, 185, 200–202
European Council, 42, 127
European Union, 16–17, 35, 61, 79, 81, 124, 127, 154, 164, 202 sanctions on Sinwar, 124

Even Yehuda, 230
Executive Order 14115, 181

F
Fadavi, Ali, 31
Fadlallah, Hassan, 154, 165
Falk, Ophir, 199
Fallujah, 86, 236n8
Families Forum, 59
Fanfare to Israel, 30
Farhat, Wessam Farhi, 78
Fatah, 6, 24n13, 64, 73, 88, 95–97, 103–104, 106n5, 166, 173, 198–199, 204, 220
    against Hamas, 198–199
    on October 7 massacre as a defensive war, 73
    participates in October 7 massacre, 73
    praises October 7 attack, 73
Fatahstan, 97
fatwa, 19, 48n45
    against Israel, 41
Fayed, Omar, 154
FBI, 45–46
FDD, See Foundation for the Defense of Democracies
Fenigstein, Maoz, xiii, 250–251
Ferwana, Subhi, 107n26
Filipino hostage, 71
Fima, Dvir David, 222, 235n4
Fima, Harel, 222
Fima, Ofek, 222
"Final Solution of the Jewish Question," 220–221
financial sanctions, 142
Finkelman, Yaron, 18–19, 45, 206
First Intifada, 50
First Lebanon War, 2, 55–56, 174n6
Fleischman, Yinon, 45
Fogel, Sahar, 100
Foundation for the Defense of Democracies, 216n43
"Fox and Friends," 196
Fox News, 24n12, 158, 189, 214n16
France, 18, 43, 61, 81, 91, 94, 101, 103, 106n5, 125, 134, 136, 148, 154, 164, 172, 175n16, 176n31, 179, 214n1, 230
Frankel, Lois, 158
Frankel, Naftali, 25n25
Frantzman, Seth J., xivn1, 160
"Free Palestine," 43–44, 174
Free Press, The, 158
Freedman, Esther Maharat, 248
"freedom tags," 131
Friedman, David, 178n69

"From the river to the sea Israel will forever be," 64
"From the river to the sea Palestine shall be free," 224
"From the river to the sea, Palestine will be free," 63

G
G20 gathering, 167
G7, 55, 81
Gal On, 47n9
Galant, Yoav, 12, 213
Galei Tzahal, 31
Galilee, 44, 70, 120, 122, 128, 180–181, 191, 212, 249
Gallant, Yoav, 28, 36, 43, 71, 85–86, 90–91, 101, 113, 116, 125, 129, 132, 136–137, 142–145, 149, 161, 166, 170–172, 180, 182, 191, 209, 215n26
    battle one of national determination, 132
    fight continues against Hezbollah, 143
    on "day after" status, 91
    on access to Temple Mount, 171
    on Hamas casualties, 142–143
    on Hezbollah threat, 113
    on war with Hezbollah, 143, 145, 172
    on West Bank threat, 101
    says IDF out to destroy Hamas, 137
    views on postwar Gaza, 209
    war to eliminate Hamas, 180
Gamliel, Gila, 69
Gantz, Benny, 8, 36, 57, 71, 74, 85, 88, 94, 131, 136, 161–162, 167, 169, 172, 177n50, 182, 192 on the war's prospects, 88
    need for the war, 57
    on distancing Hezbollah from the border, 94
    on duration of the war, 136
    on Hamas intent during Ramadan, 192
    on IDF losses, 131
    on invasion of Rafah, 161–162
    on ultra-Orthodox and army draft, 172
    polls favoring, 161
    visit to Washington, 182
Garmai, Shai, 114
Gay, Claudine, 112
Gaza City, 23n6, 43, 50, 53, 55, 59, 65, 81, 96, 104, 131, 153–154, 158, 162, 165, 172, 182, 190–191, 195, 207, 212
Gaza City Brigade, 104
Gaza elections, 5–6
Gaza Envelope, xii, 2, 168. *see also Otef Aza*
Gaza Freedom Flotilla, 21

Gaza Health Ministry, 40, 46, 51, 56–57, 81, 87, 93, 96, 99, 101, 102, 112–114, 123, 130, 132–133, 135, 143, 147, 173
"Gaza Metro, The," 35
Gaza Strip, ix, xii, 1, 6, 11–12, 16–19, 21–22, 31, 37, 39, 42–43, 47n9, 55–56, 59–60, 62–63, 66–67, 71, 73, 77–78, 82, 84–85, 88, 97–98, 100–101, 103, 105, 107n26, 110, 112, 114, 116, 118–125, 130, 132, 135–137, 144, 148–149, 154, 156, 159–163, 165, 168, 170–171, 175n24, 180, 182, 184, 186–187, 193, 200–201, 204–206, 208, 210–213, 214n1, 215n37, 219, 223, 235n5, 244, 248-250
Gaza, 1–2, 4–13, 15–23, 26
   2014 war, 6–7, 10, 13, 21–22, 25n25, 34, 92, 111, 118, 201, 243–244
   aid airdrops limitation, 193–194
   airdrops of aid received, 179, 186, 193
   casualties, 13, 21–22, 30, 55, 68–69, 90–91, 100, 133, 135, 137–138, 138n3, 142–149, 152, 154, 158–159, 162, 166–167, 171, 173, 175n27, 177n65, 179–181, 184, 186, 190, 192, 194–195, 198–203, 206–207, 209–214, 214n1, 221–222, 225, 230, 241–242
   ceasefire, 35, 40, 97, 116, 164, 173, 182, 200, 206–207, 231
   child indoctrination, 112
   children, 112, 147 clans, 180, 189, 195–196, 200, 215n37
   clans support Hamas, 196
   delay in IDF invasion, xii, 31, 33
   destruction, 236n8
   favors Hamas, 204, 215n37
   favors Sinwar, 215n37
   food from Cyprus, 193
   governments opening a maritime corridor for aid to Gazans, 193
   Health Ministry report on casualties, 213–214
   hospitals condition, 147
   hospitals used by Hamas, 176n48
   humanitarian aid convoys, 31, 35, 39, 42, 45, 50–51, 81, 83–86, 88, 91, 96, 101–102, 115, 121, 123, 125, 132, 137, 140n59, 146–147, 156, 160–161, 164, 166, 170–172, 177n63, 180–182, 184, 195, 198, 202–203, 206–207, 211, 224–225
   humanitarian aid delivered, 35, 156, 164
   hunger in, 123, 131, 160, 165, 202
   Israeli unilateral withdrawal, 6, 9, 21, 47n9, 57, 64, 224
   Jewish resettlement in, 135
   naval blockade of, 21
   Palestinian casualties, 95, 173, 175n27, 177n65, 179, 182, 190, 192, 198, 207, 213–214
   Palestinians took part in October 7 attack, 27, 32
   pier created for food deliveries, 215n31
   poverty in, 4
   protests against Hamas, 135
   reasons for IDF ground invasion delay, 6–10, 12–15, 18–22, 24–26
   residents against Hamas, 162
   residents flee towards Rafah, 135
   residents move southward, 59
   residents react to October 7 assault, 43
   truck convoy attack, 185, 193, 202, 211
   tunnels, 6, 12, 22, 34, 45–46, 50, 78, 90, 96, 104, 115, 120, 123–124, 128, 130, 137, 145, 165, 176n28, 178n71, 189–190, 224–225, 250
   war's economic impact, 92–93
   worsening health conditions, 92, 96
Gazans, ix, 1, 15, 34, 91, 99, 119, 123, 125, 128, 151, 161, 182, 184, 193, 201, 204, 211, 225
   against Hamas, 96, 162
   leave for the south, 8, 13, 21, 55, 64, 147, 157, 195
Geagea, Samir, 106
Geneva Conventions, 32
Geneva, 73, 81, 116
Genocide Convention, 122, 139n28, 140n59, 210
genocide, xii, xiv, 2–3, 36–37, 44, 59, 81, 103, 105, 112–113, 120–122, 126, 134, 139n28, 140n39, 140n59, 164–165, 174, 210, 221, 226, 236n7, 236n11
Gerhartz, Ingo, 54
Germany, 18, 32, 43, 45, 50, 75n32, 81, 101, 106n5, 134, 150–151, 176n31, 181, 185, 194, 200, 220, 240
Gheit, Ahmed Aboul, 97
Gitarts, Joseph, 242–243
Givat Haviva Educational Center, 229
Givat Ze'ev, 194
Givati Brigade, 41, 46, 112, 116, 144–145, 147, 149, 165, 200
Golan Heights, 111, 184, 191
Golan, Yair, 221
Golani Brigade, 19, 50, 86, 96, 115–116, 231
Goldberg-Polin, Hersh, 225
Goldberg-Polin, Rachel, 225, 236n9, 249
Goldfus, Dan, 197
Goldin, Hadar, 6–7, 211

Goodman, Michah, 238n22
Goodman, Vasfije Krasniqi, 157
Gordin, Ori, 188, 210–211
Gordis, Daniel, 89, 108n32, 235n4
Graham, Philip L., xii
"Great Satan, The," 144
Greece, 117, 185
Green Line, 70
Green Party, 61
Greenfield, Linda Thomas, 164
Griffiths, Martin, 57, 114, 159, 161
Grossi, Rafael, 127
Grossman, David, 2, 22n1
Guardian, The, xivn1, 119
"Guards Day," 155
Gul, Ahmed, 158
Gulf Arab states, 7, 24n13, 38
Gush Etzion Regional Council, 163
Gush Katif, 21, 136
    Conference favors return to, 136
    governments' opposition to return there, 136
Guterres, Antonio, 35–36, 122, 161, 202, 206, 224
    accuses Israel, 35
    urges cease-fire, 81

H

Haaretz, 9, 22n2, 24n16, 26n40, 26n51, 47n21, 47n22, 51, 86, 100, 107n26, 108n31, 108n59, 123, 133, 139n28, 140n39, 140n59, 176n16–17, 175n21, 176n31, 176n42–43, 176n48, 177n50, 177n65–66, 178n71, 189, 205, 214n16, 215n23, 215n25–26, 215n29, 215n31, 216n40, 217n70, 235n4
Haas Promenade, 63, 122
Habaka, Salman, 230–231, 238n20
Habeck, Robert, 61
Habonim Dror movement, x
HaChagiga Nigmeret, 232
Hadera, 6
Hagari, Daniel, 14, 35, 45, 50, 53, 59, 97, 114, 118, 153, 171, 201 on UN resolution, 97
Haggadah, 253n3
Hague, The, 120–121, 126, 134, 152, 164
Haiat, Lior, 182
Haifa, 2, 31, 114, 136, 188, 194, 206, 212, 231
Haim, Iris, 230
Haim, Yotam, 230
Haion, Sebastian, 201
Hakashah, Hassan, 115–116
Halabi, Mohand, 80
"*Halev shelanu shavui b'Aza,*" 131

Halevi, Herzi, 12, 57, 72, 102, 104, 115, 169, 185–186
    critical of IDF commander, 190–191
    IDF achievements against Hezbollah, 154–155
    on Israel's war goals, 37
    on Khan Yunis operation, 150
    on northern border residents' security, 165
    on northern campaign, 142–143
    on October 7 attack, 12
    on war's length, 102
    reprehends Goldfus, 197
Halevi, Yossi Klein, 15, 26n40, 223, 236n6
    on war aims, 60-61
Hamad neighborhood, 186, 190, 202, 210
    IDF attacks in, 208–209
Hamad, Ghazi, 34, 49, 77
    on hostages, 77
Hamas, ix–xii, xiv, 1–22, 22n2, 23n6, 24n16, 25n24, 25n25, 26n32, 27-46, 47n21, 47n22, 48n38, 49–74, 77–106, 107n26, 108n33, 110-138, 138n3, 142–174, 175n27, 176n28, 176n31, 176n40, 176n48, 178n69, 178n71, 179–214, 215n25, 215n37, 217n70, 219–234, 235n5, 236n6, 236n7, 236n8, 237n18, 240, 242, 244–246, 248–250
Hamastan, 97
Hamdan, Osama, 104, 168, 180–181
Hand, Emily, 72
Hanegbi, Tzahi, 82
Haniyeh, Ismail, 4, 15, 31, 80–81, 95, 111, 146, 165, 172, 184, 204
    on Al Arouri's death, 111
    favors cease-fire, 81, 95, 111
    favors martyrdom, 52
    calls on Palestinians to protest on Ramadan, 172
    on hostage release, 95, 111
Hanon, Mohammed Ahmed, 80
Hapag-Lloyd, 88
Har HaBayit, 175n21
Har Herzl, 45, 54, 250
Har, Louis Noberto, 152
Harakat al-Muqawama al-Islamiya, 3
Haram al-Sharif. *see* Noble Sanctuary
Hareidim
    and army draft, 172, 229
    and army exemption, 229
Harris poll, 171
Harris, Kamala, 180, 182, 186
Harrison, Earl, 240
Harush, Reef, 232
Harvard University, 112

president's response on genocide of Jews, 81
Hashash, Sayyid Qutb, 203
Hasid, Israel, 70
Hassan Ali, Hamdala, 206
Hassan, Tirana, 27
HaTikva Shesh, 228
Hatikva, xiv, 30, 54, 122
Hatzalah, 125
Hatzalah Judea and Samaria, 85
Hatzerim, 47n9
Hatzor HaGlilit, 44
"Have You Seen the Horizon Lately?," 29
Hawashin, Muhammad, 206
HaYom HaShmini, 238n22
Hazony, Gidon, 228
Hebrew University, 71
Hecht, Eado, 8, 24n17
Hecht, Richard, 6
Hegyi, Yaniv, 34
Heichal HaTarbut, 30
Helicopter 669 Unit, 50
Henri-Lévy, Bernard, 226, 236n11
Heroism Forum, 170–171
Herzog, Michael, 197
Herzog, Yitzhak (Isaac), xiii, 12, 30–31, 65, 88, 106, 122, 126, 129, 131, 134, 152, 160, 244–246
  on deadliest IDF loss, 129, 131
  on ICJ ruling, 134
  on Israel's security and Hamas's eradication, 160
  loss of trust in the peace process, 126
  on need for unity, 131
  on October 7 attack, 12
Hexter, Yakir, xiii, 250
Hezbollah, 4, 7–10, 13–14, 20, 21, 23n8, 38–40, 42–45, 51–52, 55–56, 59–60, 67, 70, 75n27 80–81, 85, 93–94, 96, 98–106, 112–117, 119–124, 126–130, 133, 135, 137, 143, 146–149, 154–155, 158–160, 165, 167, 169–174, 180–183, 187–188, 191, 194–195, 200, 203, 207–209, 211, 213, 215n26, 215n35, 228, 240
Higher Arab Monitoring Committee, 180
"Hill of Heroes, "250
"hilltop youth," 117
Hiram, Barak, 190
Hitler, Adolf, xi, 16–17, 63, 102–103, 163, 224, 245
  IDF compared to, 102–103
Hochstein, Amos, 113, 126, 181–182
Hochul, Kathy, 122
Hoffman, Maayan, 60, 75n36

Holocaust, xi, 2, 22, 32, 36, 54, 58, 65, 85, 105, 122, 130, 134, 140n60, 163, 199, 219–220, 224, 230, 233–234, 235n2, 236n6, 238n26, 240–241, 247. *see also Shoah*
  followed by Israel's restoration, 233
  references to, 32, 36
  trivialization of, 163
Holy Temples, 23n7
  destroyed, 175n21
"holy war" of Al-Qaeda, 25n29
Home Front Command, 143, 188
hostages, xi, xiii, 2, 6, 12–14, 18, 22n2, 27, 29–31, 33–37, 39, 41–43, 45–46, 49, 52–55, 58–59, 61–62, 64–74, 77–79, 81–83, 85–88, 90, 92, 95, 97, 99–100, 105–106, 110–113, 116–119, 121–125, 127–128, 130–138, 143–173, 175n16, 177n66, 180–181, 183–187, 189–190, 197–201, 205–213, 217n68, 222–223, 231, 242, 244, 250
Hostages and Missing Persons Families Forum, 119, 152
Hostages Square, 52, 88, 121, 125
House Education Committee, 81
  hearing, 107n11
House of Islam, 23n4
House of War, 23n4
Houthis, 38, 45, 66, 75n54, 81, 88–91, 98–100, 103, 106, 118, 120–121, 124, 126–127, 129, 136, 144–145, 169, 180, 186, 206, 228
  attacks, 45, 88–89, 99, 103, 106, 118, 120, 124, 126, 129, 131, 144, 180, 186
  help from Iran and Hezbollah, 118
  militia, 38, 71, 129, 169
  movement, 66, 75n54
Human Rights Watch, 27, 203, 236n11
human shields, 22, 32, 42, 52, 61, 65, 95, 116, 130, 157, 192, 224, 226
humanitarian aid, 31, 35, 39, 42, 45, 50–51, 81, 83–86, 88, 91, 96, 101–102, 115, 121, 123, 125, 132, 137, 140n59, 146–147, 156, 160–161, 164, 166, 170–172, 177n63, 180–182, 184, 195, 198, 202–203, 206–207, 211, 224–225
  Israeli citizens against, 84
  protests against, 125
Hungary, 164

I

IAF. see Israel Air Force
Ibish, Hussein, 7
ibn al-Jarrah, Abu Obaidah, 71
Ibn Sina Hospital, 138

ICC. see International Criminal Court
ICEJ. see International Christian Embassy Jerusalem
Idan, Avigail, 72
IDF. see Israel Defense Forces
Idlib, 211
Idna, 121
IDP. see "internally displaced persons"
IfNotNow, 64, 79
Imam Hossein Division, 180
Independent Women's Forum, 2–3
India, 129
Indian Ocean, 99
indiscriminate bombing, 86, 90–91, 107n24
Indonesia, 43, 68
Industry of Lies, The, 236n7
Infantry Division 162, 201
Institute for Forensic Medicine, 152
Institute for National Security Studies, 146
Integrated Food Security Phase Classification, 202
internally displaced persons, 35, 44–45, 92–93, 106, 151, 159–160, 169–170, 183–184, 195, 207–208, 228, 236n8, 245
International Atomic Energy Agency, 102, 127
International Christian Embassy Jerusalem (ICEF), 61
International Court of Justice, 50, 105, 113, 134, 164, 166–167, 202–203, 210
 ruling, 121–122, 133–134, 140n59, 166, 210
 on Israel's obligations in Gaza, 210
International Criminal Court, 22, 32, 60, 152
International Fellowship of Christians and Jews, 195
International Holocaust Remembrance Day, 134, 140n60
International Labor Organization, 92
International Red Cross, 52, 70, 123, 231
International Union of Muslim Scholars, 19
International Women's Day, 206
intifada, 3, 10, 16–17, 23n7, 50, 95–96, 123, 163, 204, 223
invasion of Gaza, 13, 33, 35, 37, 43–44, 62, 102
Iqtait, Anas, 93
Iran Nuclear Agreement Review Act, 62
Iran, ix, 4–7, 9, 11, 14–17, 20, 31, 36, 38–40, 42–43, 48n41, 52, 58, 61–63, 66–72, 75n54, 80–83, 86, 90–91, 93, 99, 101–103, 108n59, 111, 113–115, 119–120, 124, 126–127, 129–131, 133–134, 143–144, 146, 149, 154–156, 160, 163, 166, 169, 171–172, 174, 174n5, 180, 183, 195, 198–199, 205–206, 208–209, 216n43, 223, 226–228, 240

Iranian Revolution, 155
Iranian/Islamic Revolutionary Guard Corps, 4, 7, 17, 31, 39, 42, 68, 101, 120, 127, 129, 131, 136, 143–144, 155–156, 172, 208
Iraq, 3, 12, 15, 20, 38–39, 42, 61–62, 66, 69, 86, 101, 124, 133, 136, 143–144, 149, 174, 174n5, 175n19, 177n56, 198, 216n43, 236n8
Iraq War, 86
 casualties, 236n8
Iravani, Amir Saeid, 36
IRC. see International Red Cross
Ireland, 72, 164
IRGC. see Iranian/Islamic Revolutionary Guard Corps
Iron Dome system, 21–22, 31, 33, 38, 101, 160
Iron Sting mortar, 20
ISA. see Israeli Intelligence Security Agency
Isaac, 175n21
ISIS. see Islamic State of Iraq and Syria
Islamic caliphate, 175n19
Islamic Emirate of Afghanistan, 109n63
Islamic Jihad, 4, 7, 14, 18, 22, 27, 32, 38–39, 42–43, 49, 58, 72–73, 98, 100, 104, 127, 136–137, 154, 168, 188, 198, 201, 206–207, 212–213, 220
Islamic Resistance Movement, 3
Islamic Revolution, 58
Islamic Revolutionary Guard Corps. see Iranian/Islamic Revolutionary Guard Corps)
Islamic State of Iraq and Syria, 20, 30, 46, 103, 120, 126, 149, 175n19, 182, 191, 206, 208, 231
Islamic University, 5, 41, 116
Islamophobia, 79, 224
Israa University, 190
Israel, xi, 2–4, 7–8, 10, 12–15, 18, 20–21, 23–24, 29–31, 40, 43–46, 49–51, 54–57, 61, 63–64, 67–69, 78–79, 82, 84–86, 88, 91–93, 104, 106, 110–111, 116–117, 119, 121–122, 126, 128, 133, 144, 146–147, 149, 151–152, 156, 159–160, 163, 166–167, 170–171, 174n6, 180–181, 184, 187–188, 192, 194–196, 199–201, 205, 207–211, 213, 217n70, 218n68, 219, 224–225, 227–234, 235n3, 236n7, 237n17, 237n18, 238n21, 244–245
Israel Air Force, 13, 56, 68, 80, 99, 111, 115, 121, 186
 amount of sorties, 163
 strikes Hezbollah sites, 191
"Israel Apartheid Week," 223
Israel Defense Forces, xi–xiii, 1–2, 6–10, 23n3, 24n16, 12–15, 18–22, 22n2, 23n7, 24n17,

25n23, 27, 29–31, 33–35, 37–46, 47n22, 48n38, 49–57, 59–60, 62, 64–73, 77–94, 96–106, 107n24, 108n32, 108n33, 110–138, 140n59, 142–143, 145–155, 157–159, 161–169, 171–174, 175n21, 175n24, 175n27, 176n28, 176n35, 176n48, 177n56, 180–181, 179–190, 192–197, 199–201, 203, 206–213, 214n1, 214n7, 215n25, 217n68, 217n70, 219, 221–223, 225–230, 232, 234, 235n3, 238n21, 241–242
Israel Democracy Institute, 28–29, 113, 132, 146, 187, 209, 237n18
Israel-Gaza Economic Development Unit, x
Israel Victory Project, 28
Israeli Arabs, 28–29, 78, 158, 171
  on war's priority, 158
  oppose Hamas October 7 attack, 78
Israeli Association for Early Childhood, 68
Israeli Border Police, 35, 52–53, 85, 87, 112, 114, 117, 131, 145, 154, 188, 192, 194, 201
Israeli Intelligence Security Agency (Shin Bet), 6, 8, 19, 34–35, 49, 54, 69, 78, 87, 98, 104, 110, 112, 120, 124–125, 131, 145, 150, 154, 171, 182, 188, 194, 201, 203
  foil Hebron attack, 182
  intelligence errors, 8–9, 12, 40, 197, 228
Israeli Jews, 44, 71, 113, 132, 146–147, 224
  on war's priority, 158
  polled, 28–29
Israeli Opera, 42
Israeli Philharmonic Orchestra, 30
Israeli police, 56, 110, 192, 212
Israeli settlements legal, 22, 71, 136, 178n69
Israeli Society Index, 158
Israeli Supreme Court, Netanyahu against, 11
Israelis
  against a two-state solution, 227
  evacuees today, 233
  now oppose Arab coexistence, 151
  proud identity, 233
  resilience in war, 229–230
  volunteerism, 230
  younger generation's commitment, 227
Israel-US plan for ceasefire, 116
Issa, Hassan Ibrahim, 159
Issa, Marwan, 191, 215n25
Issawiya, 53
Italy, 39, 43, 80–81, 91, 134, 185
Izz ad-Din al-Qassam Brigades, 3–6, 25n24, 71, 99–100, 233

J

J Street, 196
Jabaliya refugee camp, 3, 49, 56, 81, 89, 93, 165
Jabarin, Zaher, 114
Jalamneh, Mohammad, 137
Japan, on October 7 attack, 81
Japanese Red Army, 234
Jazan province, 66
Jenin Battalion, 206
Jenin, 20, 37–38, 52, 57, 67, 72–73, 87, 114, 136–138, 154, 163, 166, 188, 206
"Jericho Wall," 77
Jerusalem Center for Public Affairs, 17
Jerusalem Central Bus Station, 6, 213
Jerusalem Institute for Strategy and Security, 86
"Jerusalem of Gold," 232
Jerusalem Post, xivn1, 22n2, 23n7, 24n17, 25n23, 25n24, 31–32, 47n21, 47n22, 49, 60, 69, 75n27, 90, 106n5, 107n11, 108n31, 108n59, 138, 138n3, 175n17, 175n19, 175n24, 176n34, 176n42, 176n43, 177n50, 177n57, 177n65, 178n69, 194, 197, 214n1, 214n7, 214n16, 215n23, 215n37, 216n40, 217n57, 217n68, 217n72, 235n4, 237n18, 238n21
Jerusalem, Old City, 16, 53–54, 63, 122, 211
Jerusalem, x, 4, 6, 8, 11, 16–17, 21–22, 29, 42, 45, 50, 52–54, 56, 59–60, 63, 65–66, 71, 74, 77, 80, 84, 91, 94, 99, 103, 113, 117, 121–122, 135–136, 140n59, 145–146, 148, 150, 153, 156–160, 163, 165–166, 168, 170, 172, 177n65, 182, 185–186, 192–195, 200–203, 205–206, 211–212, 228–229, 233–234, 240, 242, 250–251
Jewish National Fund Australia, x
Jewish People Policy Institute, 158
Jewish Voice for Peace, 64, 79
Jews, xii, xiv, xivn2, 2, 16–17, 23n7, 29, 32, 41, 44, 45–46, 58, 61, 63–65, 71, 75n32, 75n54, 79–81, 87–89, 99, 112, 120, 140n39, 154, 158, 163, 175n21, 175n27, 177n55, 178n69, 195, 199, 206, 216n44, 219–221, 223–227, 229, 232, 235n2, 236n6, 241, 243, 245
  1948 refugees from Arab lands, 224
  living in West Bank, 226
  worldwide response to the war, 227
Jibaliya, 80
jihad, 3–4, 6–8, 12, 14, 18, 20, 22, 23n4, 27, 32, 38–39, 41–43, 46, 49, 58, 65, 72–73, 79, 98, 100, 104, 127, 136–137, 154, 168–169, 175n19, 188, 198, 201, 206–207, 212–213, 219–220, 224, 226–227, 236n11
JNS (Jewish News Syndicate), 22n1, 22n2, 24n16, 28, 75n27, 109n63, 140n59, 176n28, 176n31, 176n35, 177n56, 214n7, 214n16, 237n17
Joffe, Alex, 79, 107n8

Johnson, Mike, 204
Johnston, Alan, 196
Jordan River, 63, 168, 175n24
Jordan Valley, 87, 101, 125, 152, 163, 201, 210
Jordan, 7, 23n6, 36, 39, 42–43, 50, 56, 60, 63–64, 68, 84–85, 115–117, 119 , 121, 126, 133, 135, 143–144, 149, 153, 172, 177n65, 179, 192–193, 198, 212, 214n1, 215n24, 236n7
Jordanian Civil War, 177n65
Joseph, 252
JPPI. see Jewish People Policy Institute
Judas, 223
Judea, 4, 45, 67, 70, 85, 87, 94–95, 101, 103, 115, 117, 125, 130–131, 133, 136, 143, 148, 152-154, 157, 163–164, 167–168, 177n57, 178n69, 184, 204, 226
  increase in population, 163
  rising attacks on, 163
  seeking restrictions on Palestinian Arab workers, 125
Judea-Samaria settlement leadership against hilltop youth, 117
Judenrein, 63, 224
Judicial reform, 111, 220, 227
Jumblatt, Walid, 129
Just Stop Oil, 79
Justice and Development Party (AKP), 102

K

Kabul, 109n63
Kafir, Ilan, 222
Kafr Kanna, 180
Kafr Kila, 200
Kafr Qasem, 212
Kahlout, Muhammed, 59
Kahn, A. A. Karim, 32
Kalmanson, Elchanan, 46, 221
Kalmanson, Shlomit, 171
  Kalmanson, Menachem, 221
Kan 11 TV, 66
Kan News, 19, 81, 146, 201. see also Channel 12 News
Kan Reshet Bet, 94, 211
Kan TV, 183, 241–242
Kanaani, Nasser, 63, 112
Karine A, 17
Karmi, Meir, xivn1
Karni Crossing, 165
Kastina Communications, 157
Kata'ib Hezbollah, 149
Kataib Hezbollah militia, 38
Katz, Israel, 111, 160–161, 169–170, 189–190, 202-203, 206
  accuses UN, 206
  criticizes Canada, 203
  on UNRWA-Gaza collaboration, 202
Kedar, 167, 183
Kedma, 47n9
Kemp, Richard, 225
Kennedy, John F., 30
Kepel, Gilles, 23n4
Kerem Shalom Crossing, 65, 84, 88, 117, 123, 125, 132, 140n59, 156, 166
Kfar Aza, ix–xii, xivn1, 3, 47n21, 122, 221, 230, 232–233
  today, 232–233
Kfar Darom, 47n9
Kfarkela, 105
Kfir Brigade, 114
Khairbat al-Luz, 130
Khamenei, Ali, 68, 133, 174
  denies Iran involvement in October7 attack, 36
  meets Yassin, 58
  pro-Hamas, 119
Khan Younis Brigade, 62, 135, 137, 144–145, 158, 197
Khan Younis, 5, 62, 78, 80–81, 100, 104–106, 112–113, 115–116, 118, 121, 126–130, 132–133, 135–138, 142–148, 150, 152–153, 158, 160, 165, 172, 180, 182, 184, 186, 190, 197, 200, 208–210, 232, 247
  Palestinians against the war, 133
Khirbat Ikhza'a, 104, 119
Khirbet Khuza, 112
Khirbet Selm, 115
Khomeini, Ayatollah, 144, 174
  Khomeini, Ruhollah, 155
Khuwajari, Haitham, 78
Kibbutz Alumim, xivn1
Kibbutz Be'eri, xii, 29, 34, 61, 66, 84, 110, 114, 122, 161, 171, 193, 221, 230–231, 233
Kibbutz Ein HaShlosha, xii, 119
Kibbutz Erez, 56
Kibbutz Kfar Aza, ix–xii, xivn1, 3, 47n21, 122, 221, 230, 232–233
Kibbutz Kisufim, xii, 22n2, 31, 33, 110
Kibbutz Magen, 117
Kibbutz Movement, 34
Kibbutz Nahal Oz, xii, 1, 22n2, 27, 65, 78, 222, 239
Kibbutz Nir Eliyahu, 33
Kibbutz Nir Oz, xii, 33, 46, 69, 104, 119, 151, 229
Kibbutz Nir Yitzhak, 152
Kibbutz Nir-Am, 221
Kibbutz Nirim, 34, 47n9, 110, 119
Kibbutz Ofakim, xii, 45, 65, 221
Kibbutz Re'im, xii, 110, 128, 172, 221

Kibbutz Sa'ad, 53
Kibbutz Sufa, xii
Kibbutz Zikim, 37, 59
"Kidnapped," xi, 18, 22n2, 25n25, 30, 37, 42, 46, 49, 52–53, 61, 64, 72–73, 77, 79, 113, 169–172, 190, 196, 200, 209, 219, 225, 235, 249–250
Kilat Jaber, 133
King, Martin Luther, 223
Kirby, John, 38, 54, 58, 68–70, 78, 113, 118, 136, 161, 165, 169, 179, 198, 208
    John, says Israel not committing genocide, 113
    on continued US support for Israel, 113, 118
    on Hamas, 161
    on US abstention at UN vote, 208
    praises Israel's "more targeted" strikes in Gaza, 136
Kirya military base, 89
Kiryat Gat, 45
Kiryat Shmona, 14, 33, 44, 104, 102, 143, 154, 160, 209, 211
    residents evacuated, 104
Kishinev pogrom, 220
Kisufim, xii, 22n2, 31, 33, 110
Klapper, Herbert, 235n2
Knesset, 11, 14, 29, 54–55, 64, 71, 110, 124–125, 128, 130–131, 136, 165, 170, 172, 177n50, 180, 213, 220 against unilateral declaration of a Palestinian state, 165
Kohavi, Aviv, 12
Kontorovich, Eugene, 73
Korazim, Rachel, 248–249
Korniychuk, Yevgen, 216n 44
Kosovo, 157
Kristallnacht, 58, 75n32
Kuperwasser, Yossi, 16–17
Kurdistan, 124, 126
Kurds, 103, 226, 236n11
Kuwait, 17–18, 38–39, 42, 133, 198
Kwasama, Mahmoud, 201

L
Land Day, 212
Lapid, Yair, 88, 151, 177n50, 216n40
    on Schumer speech, 216n 40
Latin Patriarch of Jerusalem, 99
Latrun, 146
Lau, David, 99
Lavi, Nehemia, 80
Lazar Research, 104–105
Lazzarini, Philippe, 57, 135, 176n28
LBCI, 49
LCBI television, 34

Le Figaro, 103–104
LeanIn.org, 157
Lebanese Taif Agreement, 93
Lebanon, 2–4, 7, 10–15, 21, 23n8, 28, 44, 49, 55–56, 60, 62, 67–68, 80–81, 84–85, 93-94, 98–101, 103–106, 112–117, 122–124, 128–129, 130, 133, 138n3, 143, 149, 154–155, 159–160, 163–165, 167, 171, 173–174, 174n6, 177n56, 180–181, 187–188, 191, 195, 207, 209–211, 231
Leibstein, Nitzan, xi, 32, 157
Leibstein, Ofir, ix–xi, 73, 232
Leibstein, Vered, 232–233
Leiter, Moshe, 67
Leiter, Yechiel, 67
Lemkin, Raphael, 122, 139n28
Lenderking, Tim, 89
Les Misérables, 42
"Let our people go," 64
Levin, Yariv, 111
Lewis, Bernard, 23n4, 240–241
"liberation theology," 99
Liberman, Avigdor, 9
Libya, 20, 133
Lifschitz, Yocheved, 33
Lifshitz, Yael, 249–250
Likud Party, 111, 145, 177n50
Lipshitz, Lavi, 46
Lipstadt, Deborah, 65
Litani River, 93–94, 103, 146, 188, 195
lo noflim mi'dor tashach!, 228
Lobby 1701, 103
London, pro-Palestinian marchers, 43, 59
Lone Soldier, 53
"lonely people of history, the," 61
lookouts (*tatzpaniyot*), warnings about Hamas, 1, 9, 22n2
Louk, Shani, 34, 47n22
LTF Danish gang, 138n3
Lubin, Ross Elisheva, 53
Lula da Silva, Luis Ignácio, 163
Luxon, Christopher, 157

M
Ma'aleh Adumin, 167, 169, 183
    terrorists attack Jews, 167
Ma'ale Yosef, 188
Ma'alot, 14
Maariv analysis, 215n 37
Mabhuoch, Faiq, 201
Maccabi Haifa soccer team, 231
Macron, Emmanuel, 35, 41, 93, 113, 148, 155, 176n31
    against Rafah invasion, 155

on October 7, 176n31
Maersk, 88
Maghazi, 103, 121
Magill, Elizabeth, 107n11
Maglan Unit, 28, 147, 202
Mahler, Gustav, 30
Maisat, 200
Majdal, 5
Makhachkala, 44
Mali, 236n11
mamad, 152
Mandela, Nelson, 120, 217n57
    statue in Ramallah, 120
Mansour, Riyad, 97, 190, 207
"Mapping the Massacres," 233–234
March of Mothers of Combat Soldiers, 102
Marciano, Noa, 66, 158
Marcus, Itamar, 73
Mark, Pedaya, 46
Marman, Fernando, 152
Maronite Patriarch, 106
Marshall Plan for Gaza, 159, 176n43
Marshall, George C., 176n43
Martin, Micheál, 164
Meshal, Khaled, 17–18, 20, 23n6, 36, 103, 128
    rejects two-state solution, 128
    seeks PA connection, 103
Massoud, Ahmad Shah, 109n63
Mateh Asher, 188
Matias, Deborah, 221
Matias, Rotem, 221
Matias, Shlomi, 221
Matzav HaUma, 229
Mauritania, 60, 133
Mavi Marmara, 21
Mazra'a, 130
McConnell, Mitch, 196, 204
McGurk, Brett, 66–68, 166
Mecca, 48n45, 59, 175n21
Medan, Elisha, 142
Medan, Yaakov, 142
Medina, 175n21
Mediterranean Shipping Co. (MSC), 88
Mefalsim, xivn2, 34
Megiddo Junction, 158–159
Megidish, Ori, 45, 230
Meidan, Aya, 29
Mein Kampf, 245
Meir, Golda, 14, 106n5
MEMRI. see Middle East Media Research Institute
Mengistu, Avera, 7
Meorer-Levi, Antonia, 230
Meretz Party, 231–232
Merkava IV tanks, 43

Meshal, on October 7 attack, 36
Mesika, Adir, 230
Mesika, Alon, 230
Meta, 157
#MeToo movement, 158
Metula, 14, 143
Middle East Media Research Institute, 155
Milei, Javier, 148, 238n26
Miller, Matthew, 9, 173, 183, 185, 208
miluimnikim, 129
Misgav Institute for National Security and Zionist Strategy, 8
Mishmar HaGvul. see Israeli Border Police
Mishmar HaNegev, 47n9
Mishor Adumim, 94
Mismah, Adil, 110
MIT, president's response on genocide of Jews, 81
Mivtza Amud Anan. see Operation Pillar of Defense
Mivtza Charavot Barzel. see Operation Swords of Iron
Mivtza Oferet Yetzuka. see Operation Cast Lead
Mivtza Shomer HaChomot. see Operation Guardian of the Walls
Mivtza Tzuk Eitan. see Operation Protective Edge
Moody credit rating agency, 150–151
Morell, Maoz, xiii, 250–251
Morocco, 25n26, 42, 60, 101, 133
Morrison-Grady plan, 47n9
Moscow, hosts Hamas and Fatah, 173
Moshav Beit Hillel, 122
Moshav Ge'a, 154
Moshav Netiv HaAsara, 56
Moshav Patish, 221
Moshav Yuval, 122
moshavim, xii, 221
Moshkovitz, Racheli, 252
Mossad, 23n6, 56, 64, 69, 71, 75n27, 82, 86–87, 106n5, 112–113, 124, 133, 153, 186, 200, 221
"most moral army in the world, the," 103
Mother Emanuel AME Church, 116
Mothers of Combat Soldiers Foundation, 102, 118
Mount Meron, 115
Mount Moriah, 175n21
Mousavi, Sayyed Reza, 101
Mouttaki, Hichem, 112
"mowing the lawn," 219
Moyal, Uri, 198
"Mr. Security", 11
Mtenga, Felix, 69

Mughniyah, Imad, 75n27
Muhammad, Prophet, 48n45, 175n21
Munich Security Conference, 160, 162
Munich, attack on Israeli Olympic athletes 1972), 106n5
Murray, Douglas, 225
Musa, Ahmed, 59
Muslim Brotherhood, 212, 217n72, 231
Muslim immigration, effect of, 79
Muslim Students Association, 79
Muslims, attacks on Christians in Africa, 236n11
Mussa, Jamal, 52
Mustafa, Mohammad, 198
MV Rubymar, 180
"My Daughter," 246–247

N

N12 TV station, 165, 184
Naami, Faisal Ali Musalam, 161, 176n48
Nabatieh, 148
Nabil, Rasha, 20
Nablus, 52, 72, 125, 206
Nagorno-Karabakh, 226
Nahal Brigade, 145, 171, 199, 201, 207, 211
Nahal Oz, xii, 1, 22n2, 27, 65, 78, 222, 239–240
Nahal Patrol, 213
Nahariya, 44
Naim, Ali Abed Akhsan, 211
Naim, Bassem, 182
Najeeb, Zakariya, 212
Nakba, 199, 216n44
Nasrallah, Hassan, 129, 172
 and ethnic cleansing of Jews, 113
 committed to fight Israel, 154
 on Al-Arouri's death, 114
 on the war, 123
 praises October 7 attack, 42–43, 51, 104, 112–114, 123, 154
 speech hailing October 7 attack, 51
Nasser Hospital, 158, 160
Natal center, 30
National Council for the Child, 181
National Library of Israel, 71, 233
National Security Council, 31, 38, 54, 68, 70, 83, 86, 113, 182
National Security Memorandum 20, 181
National Unity Party, 36, 169, 177n50
Nativ HaAsara, 223
Nazis, 16, 35, 45, 58, 75n32, 102, 105, 122, 152, 220, 224–225, 240
 IDF compared to, 102
NBC News, 25n25, 38, 135, 149, 171
Ne'eman, Shlomo, 163

Nebenzya, Vasily, 50
Negev, ix–x, 2, 47n9, 69, 82, 124, 146, 233
neo-Nazis, 225
Netanyahu, Benjamin/Binyamin, 5, 8–11, 19–20, 24n10, 25n26, 28, 36, 40, 43, 45–46, 52, 55, 58, 63, 67, 69, 71–74, 77, 81, 88–89, 97–99, 101–103, 105–106, 110–111, 113–115, 125–128, 133–137, 142–143, 145–148, 150–153, 155–157, 159–164, 167–168, 170–173, 175n17, 175n24, 177n50, 182–183, 185–192, 196–202, 204, 207–210, 212–213, 214n7, 214n16, 215n23, 216n40, 217n58, 219–220, 227, 229
Netherlands, The, 91, 129, 134, 144, 151, 185
Netivot, xii
Nevatim, 47n9
"Never again is now!" 58, 65, 238n26
"Never again," 45, 58, 65, 220, 243, 245
New York City, xivn2, 122–123, 210
New York Philharmonic Orchestra, 30
New York Times, 7, 15, 22n2, 47n9, 52, 55–56, 61, 77, 105, 106n5, 118, 121, 124, 126, 140n39, 146, 158, 173, 174n5, 176n42, 177n57, 177n63, 205, 209, 214n1, 215n26, 217n58, 227, 236n6, 236n8, 236n11, 238n22
New Zealand, 134, 144, 157, 173
Newman, David, 228
"Nie wieder ist jetzt!," 58, 65
Niger, 236n11
Nigeria, 236n11
Nimri, Eden, 222
Nir Yitzhak, 152, 184
Nirim, 34, 47n9, 110, 119
Nitzana Crossing, 123, 156, 164
Noble Sanctuary, 175n21
Nofal, Bilal, 125
North Korea, 34–35, 70, 115, 228
Northern Alliance, 109n63
Northern Brigade, 132
Northern Gaza Brigade, 111
Norwich, 175n27
Nova music festival, xii, 1–2, 29, 34, 47n21, 100, 110, 125, 128, 130, 172, 208, 210, 221–222, 228, 230
NSC. see National Security Council
Nukhba elite troops, 119
Nukhba, 2, 9, 33, 53, 59, 78, 110, 119, 121, 127, 150, 157, 184, 205, 220
Nur al-Shams refugee camp, 206
Nur Shams refugee camp, 106, 112–114
Nuseirat Battalion, 114
Nuseirat, 114, 176n48, 202
Nusirat, 191

O

Obama, Barack, 21, 210, 224
Obeida, Abu, 18, 27, 83
"occupation," 236n7
October 7, 2023, attack on Israel, x, xii, xivn1, 1–2, 5–7, 9–11, 15, 19–20, 22, 22n2, 24n16-17, 27, 29–30, 32, 34–36, 39–44, 46, 47n22, 49–54, 56–57, 59–70, 72–74, 77–78, 80–81, 83–88, 90, 92–100, 102–106, 110–115, 117–119, 121–128, 130–131, 133–135, 137–138, 142–148, 151–152, 154, 157–162, 164, 166, 169–171, 173, 174n5, 175n27, 176n31, 176n40, 178n69, 181, 183–185, 187–190, 192, 194, 196–197, 199–200, 203–205, 207, 209–210, 212–213, 215n24, 219–234, 237n18, 243, 248–250
   buried cars of Jews killed, 70
   Israeli heroes, 221
   victims identified, 49, 54, 56
Odeh, Abdel-Basset, 25n24
Odeh, Ayman, 29
Odeh, Muath Raed, 117
Ofakim, xii, 45, 65, 221
Ofir settlement, 73
oil company shipments through Red Sea, 108n31
Olmert, Ehud, 16
Oman, 42, 62, 133, 216n43
Omar, Mullah, 109n63
ON television channel, 103–104
"One Tiny Seed," 248–249
Open Arms, 193
Operation Al-Aqsa Flood, 3–4
Operation Cast Lead, 21
Operation Defensive Shield, 10, 25n24, 138
Operation Guardian of the Walls, 22, 118, 188
Operation Oz and Nir, 104
Operation Pillar of Defense, 21–22
Operation Protective Edge, 21, 118, 201, 211, 243–244
Operation Swords of Iron, 27–28
Operation Wrath of God, 106n5
Order 8, 132, 176n35
Order 9, 132, 156
Oren, Michael, 21, 107n24, 236n8
Organization of Islamic Cooperation, 60
Orthodox Union, 196
Oslo Accords, 6, 219
Oster, Amichai Yisrael Yehoshua, 110
Otef Aza, xii, 2, 233–234. *see also* Gaza Envelope
Otniel, 104, 221
Otzma Yehudit, 69, 136

Oxfam, 203
Oz Commando Brigade, 28

P

PA. see Palestinian Authority
Pahlavi, Mohammad Reza, 155, 176n34
Pakistan, 3, 25n29, 43, 99, 126, 236n11
Palestine Economic Policy Research Institute, 92–93
Palestine/Palestinian Islamic Jihad, 4, 7, 10, 14, 18, 20, 22, 27, 32, 38–39, 42–43, 49, 58, 72–73, 98, 100, 104, 127, 136–137, 154, 168, 184, 188, 198, 201, 206–207, 212–213, 220
Palestine Liberation Organization, 3, 24n13, 103, 149, 177n65
   creation of, 3
Palestine Media Watch, 52
Palestine Scholars Association in the Diaspora, 41
Palestine Square, 96
Palestine to Israel, 235n2
Palestine, From Jerusalem to Munich, 105n5
Palestine, supporter protests, 123
Palestinian Arab leaders, oppose peace agreement with Israel, 16
Palestinian Arabs, 1948 refugees, 224
Palestinian Authority, 6, 11, 15–17, 23n7, 24n13, 27–29, 55, 57, 62, 64, 67–68, 70–73, 83, 86–88, 94–95, 97, 103–104, 119, 125, 132–133, 146, 155, 162, 164, 168–170, 179–180, 187, 190, 196, 198, 200, 204, 207, 216n44, 219, 226
Palestinian Center for Policy and Survey Research (PCPSR), 87, 96, 128, 203–204
Palestinian National Initiative, 198
Palestinian National Liberation Movement, 24n13
Palestinian state, 11, 22, 63, 72, 87, 115, 117, 120, 124, 128, 143, 146, 156, 159–160, 162, 165–166, 168, 183, 187, 200, 203–204, 226, 237n12
Palestinian Youth Movement, 79
Palestinian Jesus, 99
Palestinians
   active in October 7 attack, 151
   and blood libel, 177n27 arrested, 49, 72
   favor Hamas, 226
   in Israeli prisons, 5, 17, 49–50, 133, 137, 147, 150, 159, 177n66
   in West Bank and East Jerusalem support Hamas, 84–85
   leaving Gaza Strip, 135
   protests in support, 29, 32

view of October 7 atrocities, 128
views of Hamas and two-state solution, 204
work permits in Israel, 11
working in Israel, 94
Palmachim Air Base, 155–156
Paratrooper Corps, 231
Paratroopers Brigade, 96, 147, 250–251
Paratroopers, Battalion, 116, 149
Paris talks, 150
Paris, 57, 137, 148, 169, 175n16
   march against antisemitism, 61
Park Hotel massacre, 25n24, 96
Parolin, Peitro, 155
Parsons, David, 61
Partition, 16
Pascal, Blaise, 174
Passover Seder, 96
Passover, 25n24, 175n27
Patten, Pramila, 148, 181, 190
"pay for slay" program, 17, 64, 88, 226
Peace Partnership, 206
Pearl Harbor, 11
Peel Commission, 16
Penkower, Avi, 247, 251–252
Penkower, Monty Noam, 47n9, 235n1, 235n2, 240–241
Pensées, 174
Pentagon, 38–39, 53, 61, 82–83, 89–90, 131, 193
Persian Empire, xiv, 176n34
Petach Tikva, 42
Peters, Winston, 173
Petraeus, David, 12–13
Petro, Gustavo, 163
PFLP. see Popular Front for the Liberation of Palestine
Philadelphi Corridor, 115, 132, 138, 145, 148–149, 180, 203
Phillips, Melanie, 99
Phoenix Unit, 132
Physicians for Human Rights Israel, 105
PIJ. see Palestinian Islamic Jihad
Pizzaballa, Pierbattista, 99
PLO. see Palestine Liberation Organization
pogrom, 3, 58, 75n32, 220
Pol Pot regime, 139n28
Poland, and the Holocaust, 240
Politico, 83, 187, 195
polls, 28–29, 63, 71, 78, 87, 103–105, 113, 128, 133, 146–147, 161, 171, 177n50, 187, 197, 204, 209–210, 217n58, 217n68, 226
polygon, 101
Pompeo Doctrine, 169
Pompeo, Mike, 178n69

Pope Francis, 99, 155, 213
Popular Front for the Liberation of Palestine, 13–14, 79–80, 198, 234
Posen, Barry, 236n8
Press TV, 42–43
price tag attacks, 117
Prophet Muhammad, 175n21
Psagot, 130
Psyduck Music Festival, 100–101
PTSD, 92, 123
Puerto Rico, 234
Purim, xiv, 230
Putin, Vladimir, 41, 69–70, 73, 181, 226
   stance on October7 attack, 69–70

Q

Qaani, Esmail, 7, 39, 172
Qalqilya, 80, 112, 206
Qaradawi, Yusuf, 19
Qarfa, 37
Qasam rockets, 21
Qassem, Naim, 106, 116
Qatar, 4, 9, 11, 15, 33, 37, 41–42, 71–72, 83, 86, 111, 117, 119, 124–125, 127, 133, 153, 156, 162–164, 184, 197, 199–200, 202–203, 231
Qatmash, Mohammed, 33
qibla, 59
Qibya, 15
Qubbat as-Sakhra, 175n21
Quds Force, 7, 39, 136, 144, 172
Qur'an, 3, 41, 48n45, 109n63, 177n49
Qusra, 117
Qutb, Sayyid, 175n19

R

Ra'am Party, 29, 214n7
Ra'anan, Judith, 27
Ra'anan, Natalie, 27
Ra'anana, Hamas attack in, 124–125
Rabah, Makram, 203
Rabin, Yitzhak, 3
Rabin-Lieberman, Inbal, 221
racist, 236n7
Radwan force, 115, 158–159, 195
Rafah, 27, 35, 39, 43, 50, 83–84, 93, 97, 107n26, 127, 131, 135, 138, 143, 145, 147–148, 150–155, 157–165, 167–173, 180, 182, 184, 186–188, 192–195, 199–206, 208, 210, 213
   difficulties with projected invasion, 127
   Hamas battalions there, 210
   invasion delayed, 188–189
   invasion, opposition to, 157

need for IDF operation there, 195
Netanyahu says IDF must invade, 192
tunnels, 145
UN against Israeli operation, 186
Rahat, 2, 29, 88, 213
Raisi, Ebrahim, 44, 62, 101, 123, 144
Rajoub, Jibril, 73, 104
Ramadan, 150, 156, 161–162, 164, 167, 169, 171–173, 177n49, 181–182, 184, 186, 191–192, 199, 206–207, 211, 214n7, 215n29
    security threats, 215n29
Ramallah, 25n24, 63, 72, 83–84, 96, 120, 162, 180, 203
Ramirez, Delia, 141n68
Rania, Queen, 215n24
Rantisi Children's Hospital, 59, 65, 104, 176n48
Rapoport, Nathan, 240
Ravid, Barak, 208
Raviv, Lior, 207
Re'im, xii, 1, 110, 128, 172, 221
Reasonableness Standard Law, 110
Red Cross, 18, 52, 70, 72, 123, 125, 189, 205, 231
Red Sea, 7, 17, 38, 45, 66, 71, 88–91, 98, 103, 106, 108n31, 112, 118, 120–121, 123–124, 126–127, 129, 144–145, 169, 180
red siren warnings, 42, 45, 93
Red South, ix
Regavim organization, 70
Reich, Oded, 42
Reichel, Idan, 122
Religious Zionism Party, 136
Religious Zionist rabbis, against hilltop youth, 117
Relocating Gazans to Africa, 116
Remnick, David, 235n3
Rescuers Without Borders, 85, 125
reservists, 13, 33, 90, 113, 116–117, 129, 143, 227, 232, 238n22
Resolution 1373, 237n15
Resolution 185, 224
Resurrection, The, 30
Reuters, 17, 22n1, 37, 75n27, 79, 89, 91, 108n59, 127, 129, 132, 140n39, 154, 163, 177n55, 193, 197, 211, 214n16
revitalized Palestinian Authority, 64, 67, 169
Rewards for Justice program, 130–131
Rimal neighborhood, 65, 99, 150
Rio de Janeiro, 167
Riyadh, 56, 60, 64, 66
Road 232, 47n21
Rocket-Propelled Grenade, xi, 1, 31, 66, 129, 213

Romans, 175n21
Rome Statute, 32
Rome, 235n2
Romirowsky, Asaf, 79
Ronen, Omer, 233
Roosevelt, Franklin D., 11
Rosh Pina, 44
Rostow, Eugene, 178n69
Rotberg, Roi, 239–240
Rothenberg, Yali, 227
Route 60, 46, 180, 194
RPG. see Rocket-Propelled Grenade
Ruback, Ariella, 22n2
Russia, 32, 40–42, 44, 60, 69–70, 97, 108n31, 119, 166, 206, 220, 226, 228, 234
Rwanda, 139n28
Ryder, Pat, 38

S

Sa'ar, Amit, 9, 183
Saadat, Ahmad, 96
Saadon, Ilan, 6
Sabeel Ecumenical Liberation Theology Center, 99
Sacks, Jonathan, 228
Safadi, Ayman, 36, 162, 192
Safed (Tzfat), 116, 154
Saftawi, Jehad, 157
Sakhnin, 188
Salafi, 20, 175n19
Salah al-Din Road, 45, 51–53, 64, 126
Salami, Hassan Hossein, 156, 171
Samaria Regional Council, 20
Samaria, 4, 21, 45, 67, 70, 85, 87, 94–95, 101, 103, 115, 117, 125, 130–131, 133, 136–137, 143, 148, 152–154, 157, 163, 167–168, 177n57, 178n69, 184, 204, 224, 226
    increase in population, 163
    rising attacks on, 163
    seeking restrictions on Palestinian Arab workers, 125
Samidoun Palestinian Prisoner Solidarity Network, 80
Sammy Ofer Hospital, 2
San Diego, x
Sana'a, 75n54
Sandberg, Sheryl, 157
Sanders, Bernie, 126, 140n39
São Paulo, 177n55
Sapir College, x
Sasportas, Avi, 6
Saudi Arabia, 7, 11, 28, 38–39, 42, 56, 60, 66, 68, 101, 117, 133, 146, 157, 175n21, 236n11

Schlein, Lior, 229
Scholz, Olaf, 58, 61, 119, 200
Schumer, Chuck, 196–198, 204–205, 217n58
  criticizes Netanyahu, 196–197
  praised by Lapid, 216n40
"Screams before silence," 157
Sderot, ix, xii, 1, 29, 56, 65, 73
Sebutinde, Julia, 134
Second Battle of Fallujah, 86
Second Intifada, 10, 17, 23n7, 95–96, 163, 204
Second Lebanon War, 2, 10, 13, 28, 93, 103, 174n6
Security Council Resolution 242, 178n69
Security Council Resolution 2728, 207
Seibert, Steffen, 16
Seroka Medical Center, 146
"settler violence," 153
Sha'ar HaNegev, ix–x, 73–74
Shaar, Gilad, 25n25
Shabura Battalion, 152
Shahed-107 drone, 119
Shahed-131 drone, 119
Shahed-136 drone, 119, 205–206
shaheeden, 17
Shalabi, Muhammad, 188
Shaldag Unit, 96
Shalit deal, 21, 171, 211–212
Shalit, Gilad, 5, 10, 24n10, 196, 211–212
Shalom Hartman Institute, 229
Shamir, Eitan, 8, 24n17
Shamriz, Alon, 230
Shani, Lahav, 30, 34, 47n22
Shapiro, Aner, 222
Shapps, Grant, 40, 89, 145
Sharansky, Natan, 64–65
Sharon, Ariel, 21, 23n7, 25n24
Shas Party, 172
Shatat, Ibrahim, 150
Shati Battalion, 78
Shaul, Oron, 7, 211
Shavit, Irene, 221
Shayetet 13, 17, 160, 201, 211
Sheba Tel HaShomer Medical Center, 54
Shejaiya Battalion, 78, 86, 96
Shell oil company, 126
Shemer, Naomi, 232
Shi'ite, 4, 12, 15, 136, 228
Shifa Hospital. see Al-Shifa Hospital
Shikaki, Khalil, 96, 128, 203
Shikma Prison, 223
Shin Bet. see Israeli Intelligence Security Agency (Shin Bet)
Shlomi, 44
Shlomit village, 230
Shoah, xii, 58, 134, 220–221, 230, 240. *see also* Holocaust
Shoshani, Hila Rotem, 122
Shoukry, Sameh Hassan, 57
  against Hamas and Rafah invasion, 162
Shoval, 47n9
Shtayyeh, Mohammad Ibrahim, 57, 83, 162, 170
  on October 7 assault, 162
  PA wants all of Palestine, 170
Shuafat, arrests, 52, 159, 194
Shuja'iya, 80
Shura military base, 2
Shurat HaDin Law Center, 32, 157
Siam, Ahmed, 59
Siam, Ayman, 118
Sigd, 63
Silat ad-Dhahr, 188
Silat al-Harithiya, 188
Silver, Vivian, 233
Silverman, Heather, 248–249
Siman Tov, Amit, 152
Simchat Torah, x, 183, 219
Simon, Yonina, 250
Sims, Douglas, 121
Sinai Campaign, 2, 174n6
Sinai Peninsula, 145, 201
Sinwar, Muhammad, 118
Sinwar, Yahya, 4–7, 9, 21, 42, 62, 69, 86, 99–100, 106, 116, 118, 124, 133, 146, 149, 153, 165, 171, 173, 184, 215n37, 222–223, 226
Siraj, Ismail, 114
Six Day War, 2–3, 70, 174n6, 177n65, 232
Sky News, 36, 119, 147
Smotrich, Bezalel, 136, 142, 153, 161
  cancels UNRWA tax benefits, 161
  holding up humanitarian aid, 153
  on US sanctions, 142
Sochman, Ben, 84
Sochman, Tamar, 84
Soldiers Save Lives, 228
Soleimani, Qassem, 102, 120
"Something Dormant is Beginning to Wake Up," 228
Soussana, Amit, 209
South Africa, 105, 113, 120, 122, 126, 152–153, 166, 203
South Korea, 62
"southern closure," 168
Soviet Red Army, 140n60
Soviet Union, fight in Afghanistan, 25n29, 109n63
Spain, 61, 91, 164
Spencer, John, 200, 225

Spielman, Doron, 51
Srebrenica massacre, 139n28
State Hall of Remembrance, 54
Steinmeier, Frank-Walter, 106n5
Stephens, Bret, 61, 126, 140n39, 227
Strait of Hormuz, 7
Students for Justice in Palestine, 79
Sudan, 25n26, 60, 101, 133, 236n11
Suez Canal, 7, 44, 53
Suicide bombings, 6, 23n6
"suicide drones," 38, 119, 149, 205–206
"Sukkot Massacre," 32
Sullivan, Jake, 61, 86, 90, 144–145, 182–183, 202
Sunni, 3, 109n63, 175n19
"Superheroes," 228
Supernova music festival, 68, 212
Sur Baher, 74
"Survived to Tell" tour in the United States, 210
Suwala, Muhammad (Abu Obada), 80
Sweden, 134, 138n3, 202
Swisa family, 29
Sydney, 61, 223
Syria, 9, 20, 37–39, 42, 46, 61–62, 66, 101, 105, 115–116, 124, 126–127, 135–137, 143–144, 149, 166, 169, 174, 174n5, 175n19, 177n56, 184–185, 208, 211, 226
Syrian Civil War, 4

T
Ta'al party, 29
Taha, Jihad, 169
Taiwan, 177n63
Tajani, Antonio, against Erdoğan, 39
Talalka, Samer Fouad, 230
Taliban, 103, 109n63, 227
Tanzania, 25n29
Tapper, Jake, 83
Tasnim News, 31
Tatar, Diab, 207
tatzpaniyot. see lookouts, warnings about Hamas
Taybeh, 206
Tayelet, 63
Tekoa, 136
Tekuma, 47n9
Tekuma Authority, 69
Tel Aviv Expo, 130
Tel Aviv, x, 6, 30, 33, 37, 42, 50, 52, 57, 59, 67, 70–71, 78, 88–89, 92, 103, 105, 110, 114, 121–122, 126, 130, 146, 148, 182, 186, 194, 200, 212, 222–223, 232, 234, 239–240, 242, 249

Tel Nof Airbase, 24n10, 144
Tel Sheva, 146
Telegram channel, 118
Tel-Hai Academic College, 128
Temple Mount, 23n7, 150, 171, 173, 175n21, 212
   access to Arabs on Ramadan, 171
teuza, 8
Thabat, Ra'ad, 212
Thai hostages, 71–73
Thessaloniki, 235n2
Third Reich, 63, 220–221, 224
Thomas-Greenfield, Linda, 164, 190
Tibi, Ahmed, 29
Tibon, Noam, 221
"TikTok generation,"122, 139n29, 245
Tikun 2024, 232
Times of Israel, xivn1, 5, 22n2, 24n10, 47n9, 48n45, 75n32, 75n54, 88, 107n24, 107n26, 108n33, 139n28, 141n68, 175n27, 176n28, 176n40, 177n50, 177n55, 177n63, 203, 214n1, 214n7, 215n24–25, 215n37, 216n40, 216n43, 217n56, 235n4, 236n6, 238n21
Times Square, protests, 123
Tira, 206
Tlaib, Rashida, 141n68, 158, 176n40
Tobin, Andrew, 34
Toledano, Eliezer, 99
Torat Lechima organization, 102
"torch of life," 54
"total victory," 89, 146, 148, 163, 170, 175n17
Treblinka, 235n2
Troy, Gil, 234, 238n26
Trudeau, Justin, 157
Truman, Harry S., 176n43
Trump, Donald, 25n26, 41, 157, 169, 178n69, 217n58
   pro-Israel legislation, 157
Tu B'Shvat, 128
Tuba-Zangariyye, 44
Tufan Al-Aqsa. see Operation Al-Aqsa Flood
Tuffah district, 104
Tulkarm, 25n24, 52–53, 72, 106, 113, 126–127, 131
Tunis, 149
Tunisia, 133
"Tunnel Checkpoint", 194
Turgeman, Doron, 192
Turk, Volker, 173
Turkey, 19–20, 25n25, 72, 117, 124, 226, 236n11
Twentieth-Century Jews, 235n1
Twitter, xivn2, 44, 84. See also X (formerly the Twitter)

two-state solution, 5, 17, 39, 41, 64, 67, 88, 91, 126, 151, 153, 167, 204, 227 Israeli leaders oppose, 88
Tyre, 194
Tzahal, xiii, 31
Tzav 8, see Order 8
Tzav 9, see Order 9
Tzfat. see Safed

U
UAE. see United Arab Emirates
UAV drones, 69, 114, 116, 119
Uganda, 134
UK, hit drones, 118
Ukraine, 40, 70, 119, 166, 206, 216n44, 234
Ukrainians, 32, 226
UN. see United Nations
UN's Dag Hammarskjöld Plaza, 122
UNICEF, 147, 199
Unit 504, 98, 115
Unit 669, 82
Unit 71, xi
United Arab Emirates, 11, 38–39, 42, 50, 56, 60, 95, 101, 113, 117, 172, 185, 193, 214n1
United HaTzalah, 29
United Kingdom (and see Great Britain), 32, 43, 47n9, 51, 80–81, 89, 91, 118, 120, 122–123, 134, 136, 143–144, 151, 154, 164, 166, 169, 180, 185, 205–206, 216n44
United Nations, 4, 10–11, 16, 21–22, 31, 35–36, 38, 40–41, 43, 45, 50, 54, 57, 64, 68, 70, 73, 81–85, 92–95, 97, 102–103, 113–114, 118, 122, 127, 139n28, 140n59, 140n60, 146, 151, 158–159, 161, 164–165, 167, 169–170, 173, 176n31, 178n69, 179–182, 186, 189–190, 193, 202, 205–208, 210, 216n44, 220, 224–225, 236n7, 237n15
United Nations Relief and Works Agency, 57, 81, 161, 205, 224
complicit with Hamas, 114
employees took part in October 7 massacre, 136
funding suspended, 134–135
Gaza teachers pro-Hamas, 114, 118
gets funds from G7, 81
and Hamas tunnels, 176n28
funds paused, 161, 209
tie to Hamas, 150
US bans funding, 205
United States, 4, 7, 11–13, 16, 22, 25n29, 31, 37–44, 46, 52–55, 61–62, 64–66, 68–71, 83, 85–86, 88–89, 97, 101, 103, 106, 109n63, 111–113, 117–118, 120–121, 123–124, 126–127, 129–130, 135–137, 142, 144, 149–151, 158, 162, 164, 166–167, 169, 172, 174, 177n63, 179, 181–182, 185, 190–191, 193, 196–199, 201–210, 216n44, 217n59, 217n58, 227–228, 237n15, 238n8
United Torah Judaism Party, 172
"unity of the battlefields, the," 20
university campuses, 223
University of Pennsylvania, president's response on genocide of Jews, 81
UNRWA. see United Nations Relief and Works Agency
Upper Galilee, 120, 122, 181
Urim SIGINT Base, 235n5
Urim, 47n9
US Central Command (CENTCOM), 38, 127, 144, 186
US Defense Intelligence Agency, 115
US embassies attacked by Al-Qaeda, 25n29
US House of Representatives, 41, 54, 64–65, 137, 158, 166, 207
aid to Israel, 126, 166, 180, 185–186, 203–205, 207
anti-Hamas resolution, 158
pro-Israel, 41, 64–65, 207, 228
vote against Hamas October 7 massacre, 137
US Marine Expeditionary Unit, 44
US military forces in the Middle East, 25n29, 31, 38, 40, 44, 47n9, 149, 174n5
US military losses, 86
US Sixth Fleet, 111–112
US State Department, 4, 23n8, 79, 83, 95, 105, 120, 126, 130, 142, 150–151, 166, 173, 183, 185, 205, 208, 216n44. See also Blinken, Anthony
against South African petition to the ICJ, 122
against Rafah invasion, 150–151
weapons to Israel, 105, 172
USS Bataan, 44
USS Carney, 38, 88
USS Cole, 25n29
USS Eisenhower, 43
USS Gerald Ford, 111–112
USS Thomas Hudner, 70–71
US-UK air strikes against Houthis, 144, 169
Uyghurs, 226

V
Varadkar, Leo, 72
Vatican, on the war, 155
Vieira, Mauro, 167

Vinogradov, Matan, 201
Visek, Richard C., 166
Vizel, Elkana, 243–244
"Voices from Gaza," 158
von der Leyen, Ursula, 200–201

W

Wadi Saluki, 124
Wafa, 16
Wagner Group, 70
Wahdat al-Saha'at, 15
Wailing Wall, see Western Wall
"Waiting," 122
Wall Street Journal, 3, 7, 39, 47n21, 55, 64, 67, 73, 91, 96, 98, 101, 105, 114, 116, 127, 130, 136, 143, 147, 151–153, 157, 159, 162, 173, 175n19, 184, 193, 199, 209, 215n31, 234, 238n26
  criticizes Biden demands on Israel, 98
Wang Yi, 41, 68
War Crimes and Crimes against Humanity, 32, 60, 133, 173
War for Independence, Israel (1948), 2, 5, 87, 144, 216n44, 224, 237n14
war, future uncertainties, xii–xiii, 74, 125, 174, 188–189, 231
Waraqi, Jamal, 3
Washah, Mohamed, 152
Washington Free Beacon, 34, 47n22
Washington Post, xii, 22n2, 24n10, 24n16, 40, 48n38, 48n44, 75n27, 79, 108n37, 115, 117, 129, 136–137, 139n29, 140n59, 141n68, 151, 156, 161, 174n5, 175n19, 175n24, 176n28, 177n65, 185, 212, 215n29, 217n59, 235n5, 237n15,
Washington, D.C., rally, 64–65
"We are going to bring them back," 67
"We Will Dance Again," 130
Wehbe, Ahmed, 114
Weil, Sivan, 213
Weinberg, David M., 8, 24n17
Weiss, Bari, 158, 176n42
Weiss, Shmulik, 66
Weiss, Yehudit, 66
Welby, Justin, 99
West Bank, 3, 6, 10, 15–16, 20, 25n24, 27, 35, 42–43, 45, 49, 52–53, 55–57, 59, 63, 65, 67–68, 71–72, 80–85, 87, 98, 101–102, 106, 111–115, 117, 120–121, 124, 128, 131, 137–138, 142, 145, 147, 153–154, 156–158, 164, 166–167, 169, 171–172, 177n65, 180–182, 188, 192, 194–195, 197, 200–201, 204, 208–212, 224, 226, 232, 235n5, 236n7
West Point, 200, 225

Western Galilee, 44, 70
Western Sahara, 25n26
Western Wall, 54, 65, 121, 175n21"What Publicity Can Do," 225
White House, condemns new Israeli housing units, 183
"winter war," 56–57
Wisse, Ruth, xivn2
Wolf, Ro'I, 46
Wong, Penny, 215n23
Wood, Robert, 169
World Central Kitchen, 193, 199
World Children's Day, 68
World Day against Antisemitism, 112
World Food Program, 96, 165–166, 189, 193, 225
World Happiness Report, 234
"World Has to Know, The," 30
World Health Organization, 116
World Israel News, 22n2, 23n8, 116, 138n3, 140n39, 175n16, 176n42, 178n69, 214n1, 217n56, 235n5
Wray, Christopher A., 46

X

X (formerly Twitter), 44, 84, 96, 116, 119–120, 131, 152, 157, 167, 169, 174, 178n69, 182–183, 196, 214n7, 225

Y

Ya'ari, Ehud, 60
Yad Vashem, 81, 238n26
Yada'i, Tami, 19
Yahalom Unit, 31, 96, 130, 143, 175n24, 200
Yamam Unit, 131
Yanshuf Squadron, 82
Yanu-Jat village, 231
Yarkoni, Gadi, 9, 34
Yas'ur Squadron, 82
Yassin, Ahmed, 3, 5, 18, 23n6, 58, 111, 114
  meets Khamenei, 58
Yated, 221
Yediot Achronot, 154
Yehuda v'Shomron, 230
yellow star, 45, 220
Yemen, 25n29, 38, 66, 71, 75n54, 88–89, 91–92, 99, 101, 103, 120–121, 123–124, 126, 129, 129, 131, 133, 136, 144, 169, 177n56, 180, 186, 236n11
Yemini, Ben-Dror, 236n7
Yesh Atid, 177n50
Yesha, 163, 177n57
Yifrach, Eyal, 25n25
Yisrael Beyteinu, 9

Yisrael Hayom, 55, 182, 185
Yitzhar, 167
Yom Kippur War, 2–4, 7, 46, 47n9, 63, 161, 174n6, 219, 227, 238n21
Yossi Ambulances, 29
Yousef, Nasreen, 221

Z

ZAKA, xi, 3, 59–60, 65, 70, 222, 230, 235n3
Zaki, Uri, 231–232
Zarzur, Hasen, 207
Zeitoun area, 165–166
Zecharya, 65
Zeitoun, 89, 182
Zikim military base, 59
Zikim, 24n16, 37, 59
Zionist Organization of America, 196
Ziqzouq, Mahmoud Khalil, 212
Ziyadne, Ali, 190
Zohar, Ariel, 229
Zohar, Itiel, 221
Zubeidi, Mohammad, 73
Zuria, 211
Zussman, Ben, 241–242

www.ingramcontent.com/pod-product-compliance
Lightning Source LLC
Chambersburg PA
CBHW052057300426
44117CB00013B/2176